Indian Mounds of Wisconsin

Indian Mounds of Wisconsin

Robert A. Birmingham

and

Amy L. Rosebrough

Second edition

The University of Wisconsin Press

Publication of this book has been made possible, in part, through support from the Anonymous Fund of the College of Letters and Science at the University of Wisconsin–Madison.

The University of Wisconsin Press
1930 Monroe Street, 3rd Floor
Madison, Wisconsin 53711-2059
uwpress.wisc.edu

3 Henrietta Street, Covent Garden
London WC2E 8LU, United Kingdom
eurospanbookstore.com

Printed in the United States of America

This book may be available in a digital edition.

Library of Congress Cataloging-in-Publication Data

Names: Birmingham, Robert A., author. | Rosebrough, Amy, 1969– author.
Title: Indian mounds of Wisconsin / Robert A. Birmingham and Amy L. Rosebrough.
Description: Second edition. | Madison, Wisconsin: The University of Wisconsin Press, [2017] | Includes bibliographical references and index.
Identifiers: LCCN 2017010431 | ISBN 9780299313647 (pbk.: alk. paper)
Subjects: LCSH: Mounds—Wisconsin. | Indians of North America—Wisconsin—Antiquities. | Earthworks (Archaeology)—Wisconsin. | Wisconsin—Antiquities.
Classification: LCC E78.W8 B57 2017 | DDC 977.5/01—dc23
LC record available at https://lccn.loc.gov/2017010431

Contents

Illustrations vii
Preface to the Second Edition xi
Acknowledgments xv

1 The Mystery of the Mounds 3

2 In Search of the Mound Builders 15

3 Excavation, Chronology, and Meanings of the Mounds 34

4 Wisconsin before the Mound Builders 62

5 Early Burial Mound Builders: The Early and Middle Woodland Stages 79

6 From Middle Woodland to Late Woodland 102

7 The Effigy Mound Ceremonial Complex 109

8 Platform Mound Builders: The Mississippians 161

9 Burial Mound Construction and Use in Later Times 185

10 Indian Mounds in the Modern World 201

Appendix: Mound Sites Open to the Public 211
Notes 231
Bibliography 249
Illustration Credits 267
Index 271

Illustrations

1.1	Distribution of mounds in Wisconsin	2
1.2	Mounds along the Fox River	4
1.3	Map of effigy mounds and other earthworks	5
1.4	Compound mounds at Effigy Mounds National Monument	7
1.5	LiDAR image of an effigy group on the north shore of Lake Mendota	9
1.6	Soil shadow of a large eagle effigy	10
1.7	Earthen ridged enclosures	11
1.8	Platform mound at Aztalan State Park	13
2.1	Map of earthworks near Chillicothe, Ohio	21
2.2	Map of effigy mounds that once existed in modern-day Dane County	24
2.3	Increase A. Lapham and a map of effigy mounds in modern-day Waukesha	25
2.4	Bizarre mound pattern reportedly found in Wisconsin	28
2.5	Theodore H. Lewis and a map of the Boyer or Twin Lizard group	29
3.1	Charles Brown and Albert Yellow Thunder	42
3.2	William C. McKern and crew at the Schwert Mound	46
4.1	Location of sites mentioned in text	64
4.2	Reconstructed Kenosha County mammoth	64
4.3	Paleo-Indian spear points from the Skare site	65
4.4	Old Copper Complex weapons and tools	71
4.5	Distribution of Old Copper artifacts	72
4.6	Scaffold	75

4.7 Red Ochre Complex ceremonial blades 77
5.1 The Poverty Point site in Louisiana 80
5.2 Mound groups and other archaeological sites mentioned in text 82
5.3 The Henschel mound group on the Sheboygan Marsh 82
5.4 The Hopewell Newark earthworks site in Ohio 85
5.5 Early Woodland pot decorated with chevron and linear designs 89
5.6 Plan view and profile through the Nicholls Mound 91
5.7 Hopewell period artifacts found in the Nicholls Mound 93
5.8 Middle Woodland Hopewell–style pot 94
5.9 Kickapoo River enclosure; bird enclosure at the Newark earthworks 97
5.10 Excavation map of the North Benton Hopewell mound; sketch of stone effigy water-spirit-like creature from an Ohio Hopewell mound 98
5.11 Earthen effigy mounds in Ohio 99
5.12 Middle Woodland–style stone pipe with water spirit 101
6.1 Locations of site mentioned in text 105
6.2 LiDAR images of the Eagle Valley mound group overlooking the Mississippi River 106
6.3 Map of the Rehbein I site 107
7.1 Aerial photo of the Shadewald effigy mound group 110
7.2 Location of sites mentioned in text 111
7.3 Keyhole-shaped pithouses 113
7.4 Late Woodland pottery 114
7.5 Upper-world and lower-world symbolism on Late Woodland pottery 116
7.6 Thunderbirds at the Twin Bluffs rock-art site 117
7.7 Distribution of effigy mound sites 120
7.8 LiDAR images of Cranberry Creek mound landscape 121
7.9 LiDAR image of the Raisbeck mound group 123
7.10 LiDAR of the Marching Bear mound group at Effigy Mounds National Monument 126
7.11 LiDAR image of the Bloyer or Twin Lizard mound group; LiDAR image of the Nitschke mound group 127
7.12 Examples of effigy mounds shown in two perspectives 128
7.13 Common effigy mound forms in south-central Wisconsin 129
7.14 The Woodward Shores mound group on the north shore of Lake Mendota 131

7.15	Eagle Township mound group on the Wisconsin River; LiDAR image of the Kingsley Bend mound group on the Wisconsin River	133
7.16	Water-themed mounds at the Lizard effigy mound group	133
7.17	Subregions showing the most common forms of effigy mounds	134
7.18	Map of effigy mound group along the Milwaukee River; a water-spirit intaglio filled with water in Fort Atkinson	140
7.19	Lapham's Cross	141
7.20	Joined water-spirit mounds at the Ridge or Gasch mound group; examples of effigy mound pairings and crossed mounds	142
7.21	Human being and "bird-man" mounds	143
7.22	Winnebago (Ho-Chunk) and Fox medicine men	146
7.23	Large conical mound on Clam Lake in northern Wisconsin	158
8.1	Artist's conception of the Mississippian elite; Cahokia, around A.D. 1150	163
8.2	Mississippian-related sites mentioned in text	166
8.3	Platform mounds overlooking the town of Trempealeau; Trempealeau Mountain	168
8.4	Paintings and sandstone head from the Gottschall Rockshelter	169
8.5	Aztalan layout	172
8.6	Southwestern mound and mortuary structure on northwestern mound at Aztalan	174
8.7	Line of conical mounds at Aztalan	177
8.8	Plan of the Diamond Bluff site	183
9.1	Oneota village scene in Wisconsin, around A.D. 1450	188
9.2	The distribution of Oneota population centers in Wisconsin	189
9.3	Oneota pottery	191
9.4	Effigy mound with more recent grave house	199
10.1	State, local, and Native representatives at 2002 dedication of Monona mound group	207
10.2	Harry Whitehorse and family at mound dedication; sculpture by Harry Whitehorse	208
10.3	Bill Quackenbush at 2016 dedication of Devil's Lake bird mound	209

Preface to the Second Edition

The first edition of *Indian Mounds of Wisconsin*, published in 2000, was well received by both the general public and scholars because at that time much of the information about the numerous ancient Native burial mounds that spread over Wisconsin landscape could be found only scattered in academic journals and unpublished reports. As hard as it is to believe now, no websites on the topic even existed at the time. But interest in the mounds had been rapidly growing over the decades, leading to the original publication of the book. A major reason for this increase in interest was that mounds had drawn increasing public attention because of the passage, in 1985, of state law 157.70 of the Wisconsin Statutes, which seeks to protect all burial places on both public and private lands no matter the age and the ethnic association; this law eventually covered ancient earthen burial mounds. Consequently, what these mounds were about and why they are considered so important became topics that aroused great curiosity. Another reason for the growing interest was an increasing knowledge of and appreciation for the Indigenous cultures of America, which had been woefully lacking prior to the 1980s, fostering stereotypes and erroneous historical information as portrayed in the media of the time.

At the time of the first edition, the senior author, Robert Birmingham, was the Wisconsin State Archaeologist at the Wisconsin Historical Society, with responsibility for documenting and protecting the tens of thousands of archaeological sites in the state, many of which span the cultural evolution of Native cultures over a thirteen-thousand-year period, and for engaging in public education programs that promote the preservation of these important places. By the 1980s and the passage of the burial site preservation law, approximately 80 percent of the mounds had been destroyed by modern land use, and an inestimable number of other ancient places such as sites of people's camps and villages had also disappeared or been severely damaged, with the remainder largely unprotected and on private properties. During the 1970s, Birmingham fielded constant questions from the public about the ubiquitous mounds—why the mounds were built and when, along with questions about the tribal identities of the mound builders. Additionally, since so many of the Wisconsin mounds are unique and enigmatic effigy mounds—earthen representations, often huge, of birds, animals, and even humans—many people were curious about the meanings of these forms, not found in such numbers in other regions of the Americas.

The answers to these basic questions had been of great and long-standing interest to researchers and scholars going back 175 years. Research concerning the mounds had increased in the 1990s, stimulated by the state burial sites legislation and also by the National Historic Preservation Act of 1966 (amended in 1974), which requires identification of and protection efforts for significant archaeological sites and historical places when there is federal involvement in potentially destructive projects such as highway construction. The act also set up historic preservation offices in each state with federal funding, matched by state dollars, that passed federal grants to researchers to identify such culturally important places. Wisconsin's State Historic Preservation Office (SHPO) became part of the Wisconsin Historical Society. Throughout the 1990s the Office of the State Archaeologist (now the State Archaeology and Maritime Preservation Program), part of the State Historic Preservation Office in the Wisconsin Historical Society, administered a regional archaeology program in partnership with nine institutions to specifically record archaeological sites, including mounds in their area. All of this work greatly expanded knowledge of the ancient Native societies that once occupied the state, including those that used earthen mounds as burial and ceremonial places.

The first edition of *Indian Mounds of Wisconsin* was thus stimulated by both public interest and the amazing amount of new information that had come to light about the ancient Native societies in Wisconsin. It was the first book-length overview of ancient earthworks written for a general audience since Increase Lapham's *Antiquities of Wisconsin, as Surveyed and Described*, published in 1855. But, as with the nature of science in general, continuing research eventually replaces previous syntheses and models with new data and insights. Since the first edition, published nearly two decades ago, an enormous amount of new information has come to light regarding the history of mound building. A number of ancient habitation sites have been identified and excavated throughout Wisconsin and elsewhere in the Midwest that have refined the chronologies and explicated the lifeways of the societies that built the mounds, providing, for example, new and even more accurate dates based on refinements to radiocarbon dating. Further, while no new mounds have been excavated, new research questions have led major Wisconsin universities and other institutions to go back and reanalyze the data recovered from mounds excavated in earlier years using modern insights and techniques, and such studies have been the source of much new knowledge.

New technologies have emerged that allow close studies of some aspects of mound building without disturbing the actual sites. One series of technologies familiar to many readers is remote sensing, such as Ground Penetrating Radar, which can identify below-ground disturbances and features created long ago and not visible to the naked eye. More recently, the use of satellite- or aircraft-based LiDAR (Light Detection and Ranging) imaging has revolutionized archaeology throughout the world and is particularly suited for the three-dimensional study of landscapes of existing mound groups. In many cases LiDAR has led to the discovery of new mounds and whole groupings obscured by vegetation or otherwise not known to exist. This edition is illustrated by LiDAR imagery that replaces many of the drawings and maps used in the first edition and that clearly shows how Native people used the natural landscape to locate and orient mounds. With the proper software, discoveries of new archaeological sites that have above-ground features can be made in minutes on the computer, rather than requiring years of systematic searching of the ground. So rapidly have discoveries been made using LiDAR that it has been difficult to keep up on results. Ongoing discoveries of new sites in Wisconsin will keep archaeologists busy for decades as they go to the field to examine and further document the features observed on the LiDAR images.

Readers will also find other new and updated material throughout this second edition. New research and studies completed since the first edition are summarized in chapter 2 and the information incorporated in appropriate places throughout the book. Chapter 5 deals in great part with the remarkable effigy mounds, and this chapter has been rewritten by the effigy mound expert Amy Rosebrough, the new coauthor of the second edition, based on her comprehensive 2010 doctoral dissertation at the University of Wisconsin–Madison, as well as much other new research and publication.

Of special interest to readers will be the expanded list of Indian mounds that can be visited, which we have provided as an appendix. Since the publication of the first edition and in response to public interest, many more parks, preserves, and other public places have opened where a variety of the ancient mounds can be viewed.

We have used certain conventions in this new edition when referring to the Indigenous people of Wisconsin, variously called Indians or Native

Americans. Wherever possible, the specific names we have employed are those used by the Native nations themselves; an example is the Ho-Chunkgara or Ho-Chunk people, who have also been called Winnebago in the past. In most other cases, we simply used the words "Native" or "Indigenous" unless a different nomenclature is warranted by the context. In some cases we follow common usage, as the case of the mounds that are commonly called Indian mounds, as we call them in the title of the book.

Finally, the major goal of this book is to convince readers that the mounds should be valued as places that need continuing special protections from disturbances and destruction by competing land-use practices. As discussed in the final chapter of the book, proposals to lessen the legal protections for mounds have been discussed in the Wisconsin state legislature, but as of the writing of this book, none have been approved for legislation. The Indian mounds of Wisconsin are considered sacred places by Native people, whatever their age or specific cultural association. The rest of us should not only honor this view but also view the ancient earthworks as an especially important part of the history and identity of the state.

Acknowledgments

In addition to the many individuals and institutions that contributed to the first edition of *Indian Mounds of Wisconsin*, the authors would like to thank the following for their assistance in various ways in the preparation for the second edition: Robert Boszhardt, an expert on Wisconsin archaeology who read a draft of the manuscript and supplied many useful comments and corrections; Brad Lepper (Ohio Historical Connection); William Romain (Ohio State University Newark Earthworks Center); Douglas Norgord (Geographic Techniques LLC); Bill Quackenbush (Ho-Chunk Nation); Chip Brown (Wisconsin Historical Society); the Society of American Archaeology; the Wisconsin Archeological Society; the Milwaukee Public Museum; and the Wisconsin Historical Society.

Indian Mounds of Wisconsin

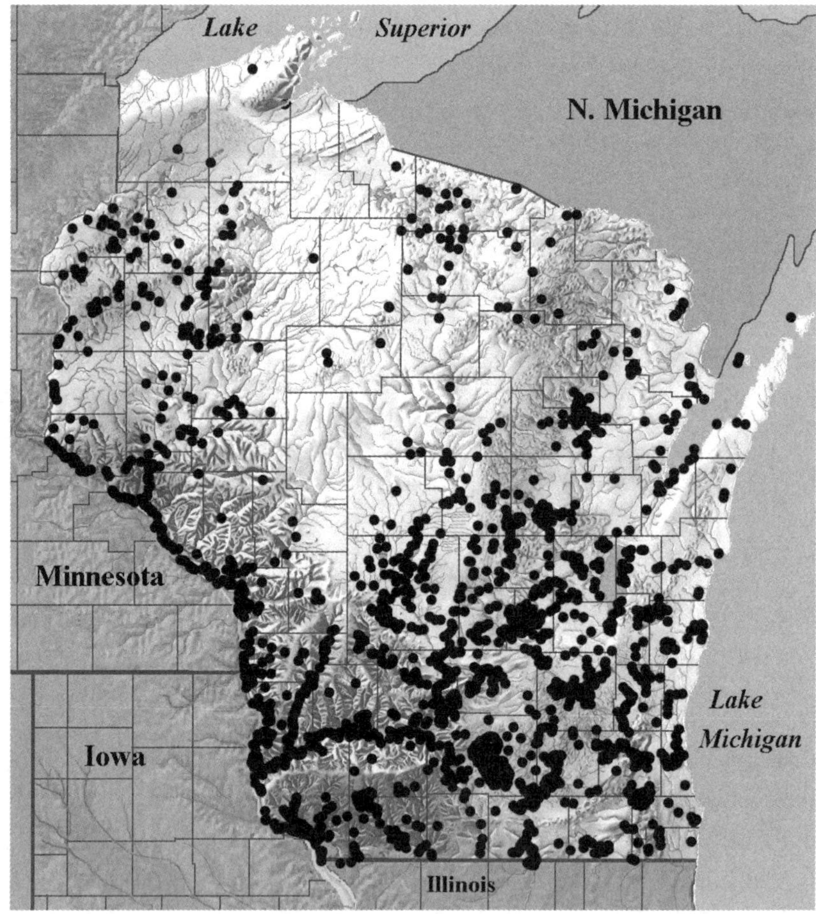

Figure 1.1. Distribution of mounds in Wisconsin. In most cases, the dots represent mound groups.

1

The Mystery of the Mounds

Indian mounds are a part of the Wisconsin landscape. When the first European and American explorers and settlers arrived in what would become the state of Wisconsin, between fifteen thousand and twenty thousand of these earthworks could be found clustered along lakes, beside rivers, and on hilltops, often arranged in complex patterns that harmoniously, even artfully, blended with the natural topography (figure 1.1). More Indian mounds were built in the territory now called Wisconsin than in any other equivalent area of land in North America. The ancient tumuli occurred almost everywhere in the state but were especially abundant in its southern region, where they actually presented a major obstacle to nineteenth-century farmers as they struggled to clear land to plant crops. Since that time, most mounds in this area have disappeared under the plow (figure 1.2).

The largest documented mound group in Wisconsin is located at the Diamond Bluff site in Pierce County, also known as the Mero Complex, where 390 small conical or round mounds as well as several effigies partially enclose a pair of one-thousand-year-old villages along the Mississippi River. Another huge grouping is along the swampy Cranberry Creek in a remote wilderness of Juneau County, where more than three hundred mounds, including conical or round mounds and effigy forms, have been thus far counted. The mound group is within a Wisconsin State Natural Area that can be visited by the public. The privately owned and virtually intact Raisbeck site in southwestern Wisconsin boasts 123 mounds spread across bluffs above a winding river. Many of these are effigy mounds, so called because they were made in the shapes of birds, other animals, supernatural beings, or, occasionally, human beings.

Figure 1.2. Indian mounds are still a familiar part of the Wisconsin landscape, although many, such as these near the Fox River being plowed in 1923, have been destroyed.

Mounds are still a common sight despite their destruction over the past 175 years by agricultural practices, urban expansion, and looting. Dozens of counties, towns, and villages have an "Indian Mound Park" or a similarly named green space. In Madison, for example, those living near the shores of the several lakes that surround the city are a short distance from at least one of the twenty-three mound locations preserved on public lands. Around the state, prominent mound clusters or groups can be viewed by visitors to High Cliff, Governor Nelson, Wyalusing, Nelson Dewey, Perrot, and Aztalan State Parks. Many more of these ancient earthworks survive in urban backyards, fields, and undeveloped woodlots in private hands. The records of the Wisconsin Historical Society indicate that more than four thousand mounds or fragments of mounds remain.

Even so, with many mounds now gone, it is difficult to appreciate the wonder that they evoked in early travelers and settlers. In 1817, Stephen H. Long, an army engineer and explorer, provided one of the earliest reactions (and an interesting interpretation) after visiting mound groups on the bluffs around Prairie du Chien:

[W]e had the occasion to be high[l]y gratified with a survey of curiosities that have baffled the ingenuity & penetration of the wisest to account for them. The curiosities alluded to are the remains of ancient works constructed probably for military purposes, which we found more numerous & extensive above the mouth of the Ouisconsin than any of which a description has been made public that have yet

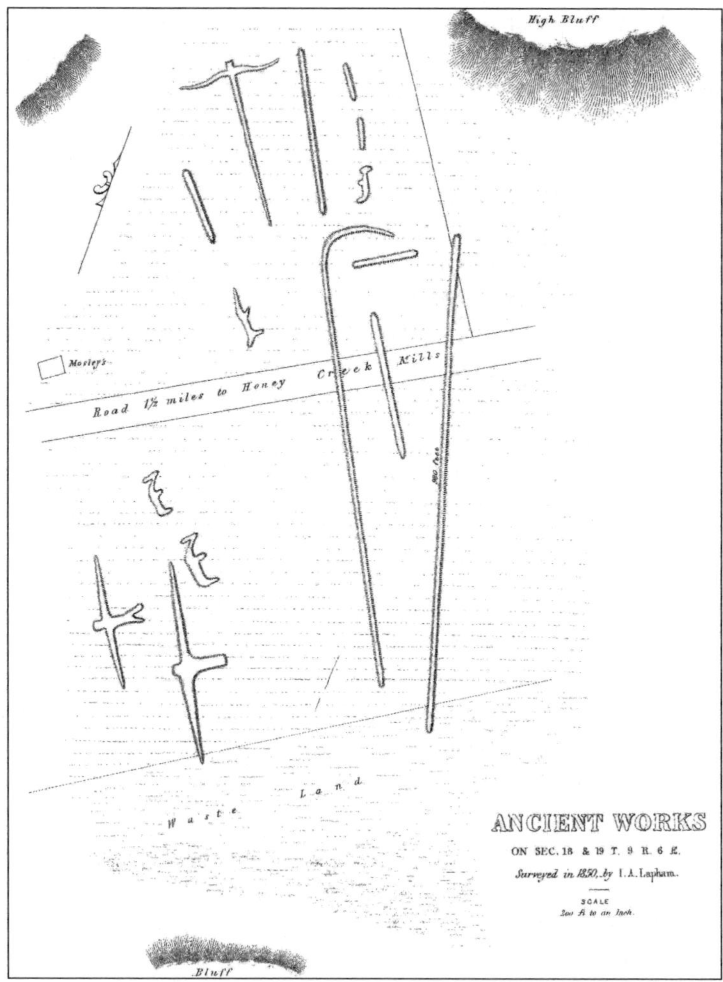

Figure 1.3. Huge effigy mounds and other earthworks, which awed early settlers and mound researchers, are depicted in this early map.

been discovered in the Western Country. They consist of ridges or parapets of earth and mounds variously disposed so as to conform to the nature of the ground they are intended to fortify. At what period they were constructed and by what race of people, must in all probability remain a desideratum.[1]

Observers were particularly impressed by spectacular and mysterious groupings of low effigy mounds (figure 1.3). Used as burial places, such "emblematic mounds" are not found elsewhere in the world in such concentrations and certainly constitute an archaeological world wonder. These mounds did not appear to some early observers to be the work of Indigenous peoples. These strange and often huge earthen sculptures easily conjured up images of mysterious gods that were worshiped during the course of long-forgotten rites and rituals.

In 1838, Richard C. Taylor drew public attention to the effigy mounds in Wisconsin with his maps and descriptions of the strange earthworks at Muscoda on the Wisconsin River, near small mountains called the Blue Mounds, along the shores of the Four Lakes (now the Madison area), and in other places. Familiar with the earthworks that settlers had discovered elsewhere in the Ohio and Mississippi River valleys, as well as with the great "barrows" of England and Europe, he nonetheless wrote of his astonishment at finding these "singularly formed Indian Mounds," which in some areas formed a "species of *alto relievo*, of gigantic proportions."[2] When he wrote the first book on the geography of Wisconsin, Increase Lapham found it necessary to refer to a class of earthworks "not found in any other country" that dominated much of the landscape. Lapham, a land surveyor, became interested in Indian mounds as he laid out streets along the bluffs and rivers of the new community of Milwaukee in 1836.[3] With support from the American Antiquarian Society, Lapham pursued his interest by researching and writing *The Antiquities of Wisconsin, as Surveyed and Described*, which was published by the Smithsonian Institution in 1855. This landmark book was the first attempt to systematically document the visible remnants of ancient civilizations in the state, mainly earthworks.

In the mid-nineteenth century, when Lapham was writing his book, the identity of the builders of the North American mounds was hotly debated, and he was among the first to assert that the ancestors of Indian people had made the mounds and that Indian people no longer made the monuments because customs had changed through time. It is now known that most mounds in Wisconsin were constructed by various Native societies during a relatively short period of time, between 800 B.C. and A.D. 1200, although conical mounds continued to be built occasionally along the rivers and lakes of northern Wisconsin into the historic period or time of European contact. Mound construction, which greatly expanded through time, reflected a long trend toward social complexity and population increases beginning when Native people first came to the Midwest at the end of the glacial period.

Those acquainted with Indian mounds are most familiar with round or conical and oval mounds as shown in figure 1.2. This class was the earliest burial mound form to be made by ancient Native people, and they continued to be made in great numbers throughout the mound-building era. The first such mounds appeared as early as five thousand years ago in the southeastern

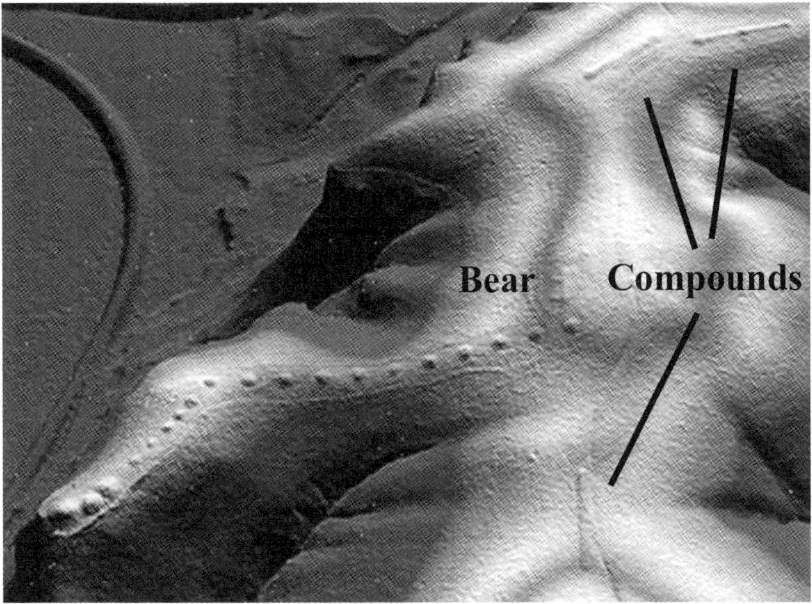

Figure 1.4. Compound mounds at Effigy Mounds National Monument in Iowa as shown by LiDAR.

United States, in areas now known as Arkansas, Louisiana, and Florida. Much later, people living in woodlands and parklands of the Midwest adopted the practice of building mounds. At some locations in northern Wisconsin, single conical mounds grew in size as additional mass burials were periodically added over the years. A few of these mounds attained diameters as great as sixty feet and heights of twenty feet.

A second class of mounds, often found in arrangements with other forms, consists of short linear mounds and occasionally compound or chain mounds, series of small conical mounds connected by short linear ridges (figure 1.4). The latter are largely but not exclusively found in the southwestern part of Wisconsin and in northeastern Iowa along the Mississippi River and the lower reaches of tributaries. As proposed later in this book, these appear to have been constructed during a wave of mound building that immediately preceded the explosion of effigy mound landscapes across the state after A.D. 700, although the meaning of the compounds is uncertain.

The third class of earthwork, and the one most commonly associated with Wisconsin, comprises effigy mounds. The effigy mound people carefully sculpted the terrain into more than one thousand groups of animals and supernatural beings, now recognized as ceremonial landscapes, in a broad band in the southern and west-central part of Wisconsin. The range of the effigy mound ceremonies spilled slightly into adjacent parts of what are now Illinois, Iowa, and Minnesota. Wisconsin, however, was clearly the heartland for this activity. The effigy mound people built their earthworks at the same locations where large conical mounds had been constructed hundreds of years earlier—a strong indication that the sacred character of a place continued to be recognized and shared over a long period of time, perhaps even by people from different cultural backgrounds.

Effigy mound groups frequently incorporated low conical burial mounds and short and long narrow embankments, or "linear" mounds. Many of the mounds commonly regarded as long, tapering linear mounds in the past are almost certainly the effigies of snakes that occupy the watery underworld. Effigy mound groups are arranged in complex and often obviously nonrandom patterns that have stimulated some interesting interpretations over the years but now are linked to differences in topography and geography, reflecting the supernatural meaning that people attributed to aspects of the natural landscape.

Some effigy mound forms are spectacular, such as the great human-shaped mounds concentrated in the rugged southwestern part of the state and the long-tailed "panther" or water-spirit mounds found throughout the state but especially in the east. Many effigies are gigantic, including a 700-foot-long snake-like mound along the shore of Lake Waubesa near Madison, Wisconsin; an enormous eagle effigy mound with an arrow-straight 624-foot wingspan that still "flies" with other large birds across the grounds of Mendota Mental Health Institute on Lake Mendota, also near Madison (figure 1.5); and a 656-foot-long panther-like water-spirit mound along the Baraboo River.

The largest effigy mound possibly ever built in Wisconsin was discovered in the early 1990s on an old aerial photograph by James Scherz, a mound researcher at the University of Wisconsin–Madison. A short distance from the Wisconsin River, across from a spot near modern-day Muscoda, ancient Native people built a phenomenal eagle-like effigy among other mounds with what appears to be a quarter-mile wingspan. Farming has obliterated the earthwork, but its soil shadow is still visible on the aerial photograph (figure 1.6).

The effigy mound groups are now considered reflections of an ancient belief and social system rooted in the more ancient past but expressed in monumental form during a relatively short period of time. They functioned as ceremonial centers that were periodically used for a range of social, religious, and political purposes but also as cemeteries. Excavations conducted

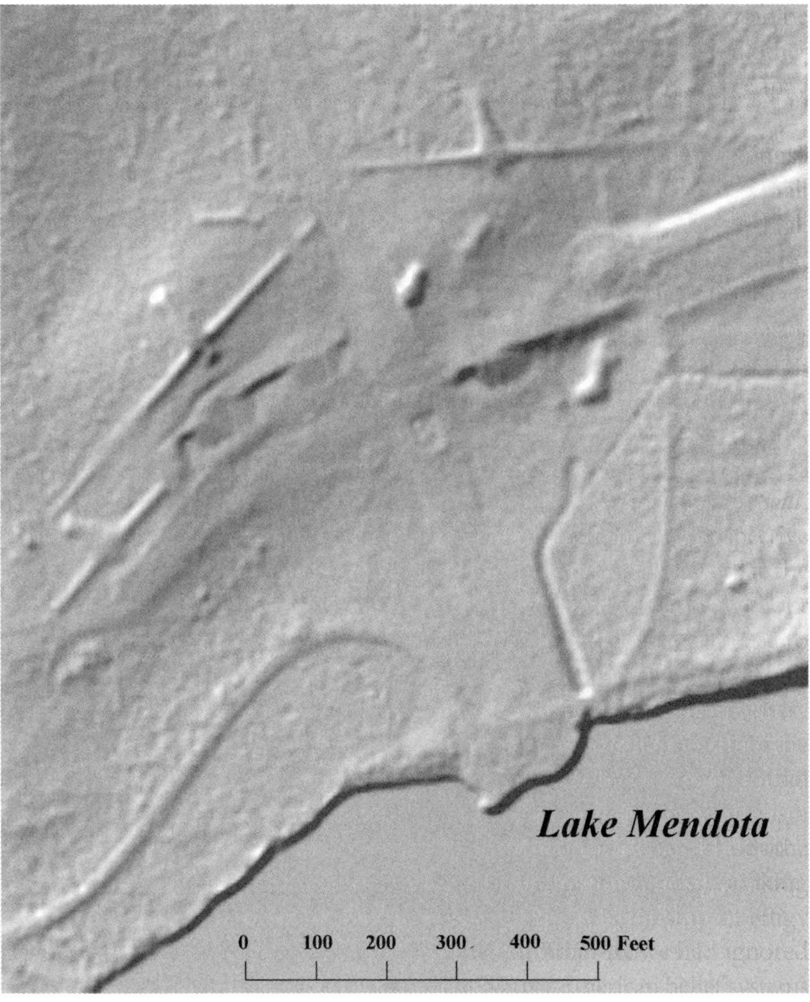

Figure 1.5. LiDAR image of an effigy group dominated by huge eagle effigies on the north shore of Lake Mendota. The one in the center has a wingspan of 624 feet. Darkened areas show mound areas that have been destroyed by former land use.

in the early twentieth century determined that most effigy mounds can be expected to contain human remains, indicating that burial of the dead was a necessary part of mound construction ceremonies. Effigy mounds are among the most interesting and mysterious of the Indian mounds in Wisconsin and the focus of continuing, albeit nondestructive, archaeological research.

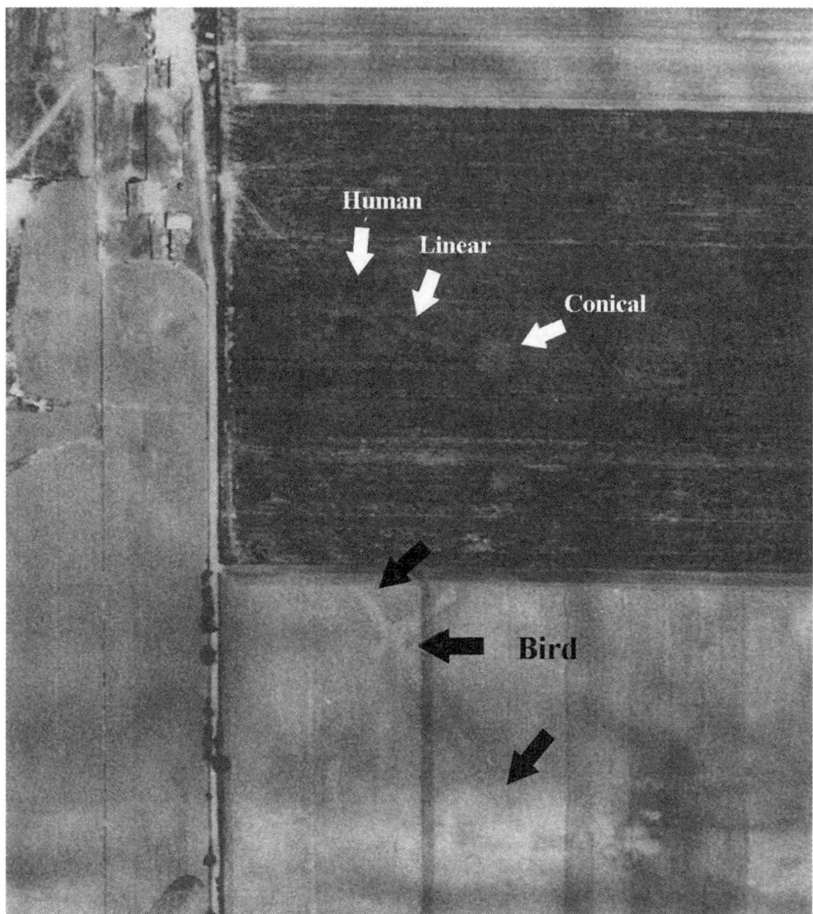

Figure 1.6. The soil shadow of a large eagle effigy is still evident on this 1968 aerial photograph. Also evident are the soil shadows of a 200-foot diameter conical mound, a linear mound, and an effigy of either a human being or a forked-tail bird.

Earthen enclosures, another class of ancient earthworks, consist of low, narrow ridges that form large circles, squares, and rectangles (figure 1.7). These earthworks sometimes occur alone but most often are found in mound groups, where they appear to have defined a sacred space. Some Wisconsin enclosures are smaller versions of spectacular two-thousand-year-old Hopewell enclosures and associated earthworks built in the Ohio River valley, although some types of enclosures in the Upper Midwest are known to have accompanied burial mounds hundreds of years before.[4]

Finally, very large flat-topped "temple" mounds once served as platforms for special ceremonial structures. These truncated earthen pyramids are

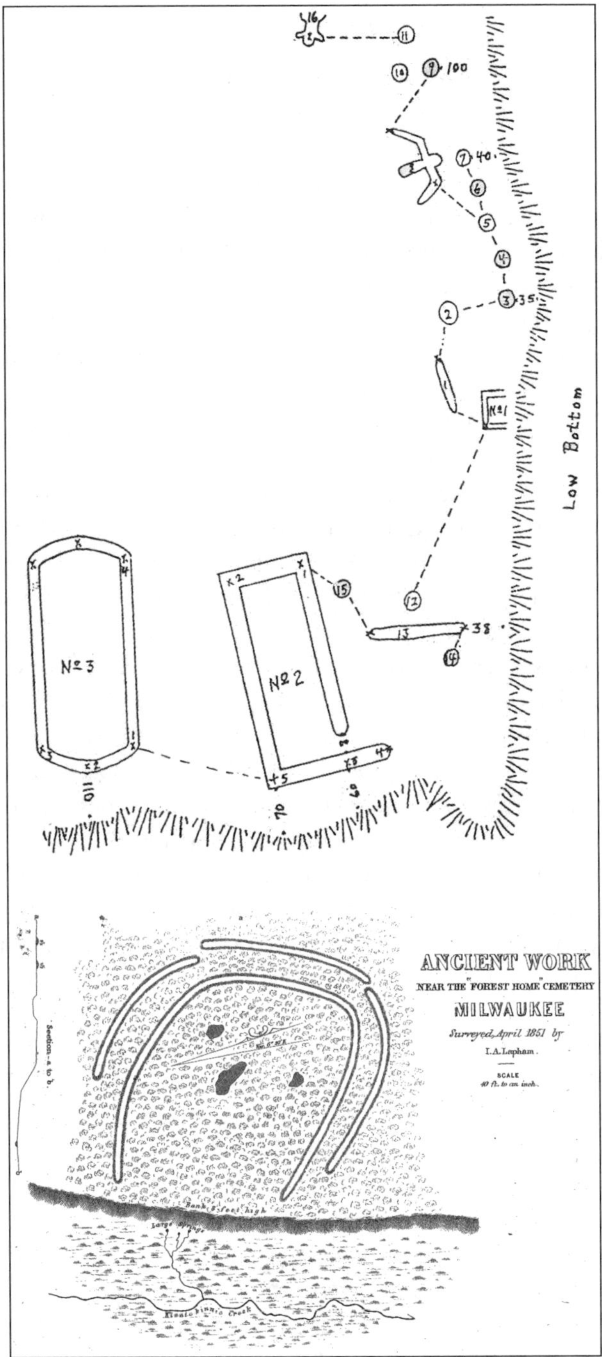

Figure 1.7. *Above*: earthen ridged enclosures mapped by Theodore Lewis in 1888 among effigy mounds overlooking the Black River, a tributary of the Mississippi River in Trempealeau County, Wisconsin. *Below*: enclosure in Milwaukee mapped by Increase Lapham in the mid-nineteenth century.

most at home far to the south of the present borders of Wisconsin, where they are associated with the spectacular Mississippian culture that arose after A.D. 1000. More is known about these huge earthworks than about the other kinds of mounds both because extensive archaeological excavations have been undertaken at Mississippian sites, such as the ancient city of Cahokia in southern Illinois, and because Native lords and their families still ruled from houses on the tops of such structures in present-day Arkansas and Georgia when Spanish conquistadors first explored these areas in the sixteenth century. The presence of these unique mounds at a few special locations in Wisconsin—the famous village site of Aztalan in Jefferson County (figure 1.8) and at modern-day Trempealeau along the Mississippi River—provide clues to the movements of ancient people and ideas.

Indian mounds have always been shrouded in mystery. Who were the mound builders? When did they build the mounds and for what purposes? What do the effigies represent? What is the relationship of the mound builders to modern Native nations? Lapham and his contemporaries asked these questions, and the search for the answers preoccupied subsequent generations of scholars and dilettantes. Several hundred articles and a half-dozen books have been written on the subject of the Indian mounds in Wisconsin. Graduate school theses and dissertations have examined aspects of mound construction, distribution, and history. Many aspects of the mound-building cultures have been clarified, but many more questions remain unanswered and new questions are constantly being raised.

Such mystery inspires modern myths and folklore, as is apparent even today in the proliferation of books, magazines, television programs, videos, and websites that present entertaining but highly dubious information on ancient peoples and cultures. The earliest myth to emerge attributed the origin of the many earthworks in North America to a fantastic "Lost Race" that was inexplicably replaced by modern Native American tribes in the distant past. For many, the "Ten Lost Tribes of Israel" or unrecorded colonizers from one or another Old World civilization made up this mysterious people. This explanation gained a popular following during the early years of the American republic, before the beginning of efforts to learn about Indigenous history and the cultures and traditions that were being swept aside by the flood of white settlement. This great "Mound Builder Myth" dominated the debate about Indian mounds throughout much of the nineteenth century, until the maturing fields of archaeology and ethnology put it to rest by demonstrating that the mound builders were none other than the ancestors of modern Native peoples, a fact always assumed by Indian people since, according to traditions, they have occupied the Americas since the beginning of time.

Figure 1.8. Platform mound at Aztalan State Park.

Some opinions are not easily dispelled. Variations of the myth of the Lost Race linger on and have a found place in a modern era in which mysticism, revisionism, mistrust of traditional science, and even blatant ethnocentrism persist. Alternate histories of the pre-Columbian Americas attribute influences to a variety of Old World cultures as diverse as the Vikings, the Britons, the Hindus, and various Asians and even to knowledge obtained from Old World "secret lodges," such as the Freemasons. The dubious premise of this "diffusionist" literature is that the Indigenous people of the Americas were frequently and routinely visited by people from the world over for thousands of years. Contacts between Native peoples of the Americas and other cultures of the world at various times have even been proposed by some professional archaeologists, but the evidence for such contacts (apart from a brief period of documented contact between the native peoples of eastern Canada and the Vikings) has been generally treated with skepticism by many others.

Perhaps the strongest argument against sustained outside contacts (at least with Europe) can be found in what happened right after Europeans arrived in the Americas. Within a short time, millions of Native people died of infectious diseases introduced from the Old World, because these diseases had not previously existed in the Americas and immunities to them had not built up. Had there been sustained contacts between the New and Old Worlds, diseases such as smallpox would have been introduced much earlier, resulting in disease resistance among the survivors, and the Native American population would not have been so decimated after the arrival of Europeans in the sixteenth century.

However, both the ubiquity of mounds in Wisconsin and the unanswered questions about them have guaranteed them a niche in popular Wisconsin folklore and legend. For example, one persistent story is that long-ago archaeological excavations into Wisconsin mounds discovered a mysterious race of giants, as reported by sensational articles in local newspapers.[5] The story has been incorporated into modern websites, and some who believe in a lost race of giants even accuse scientists of hiding this secret from the public. No giant skeletons have been discovered in Wisconsin (or elsewhere in the Americas) despite the tabloid-style accounts printed over the past two centuries, but the story is representative of the type of folklore that has been generated by modern people about Indian mounds.

Public interest in the Indian mounds in Wisconsin was also greatly stimulated by state legislation passed in 1985. Burial Sites Preservation Law 157.70 of the Wisconsin Statutes protects all human burial places from disturbance and destruction no matter how old they are, and this law was eventually applied to burial mounds. The publicity surrounding the effort to protect Indian mounds also encouraged many private landowners who have been conscientious stewards of mounds on their property, providing them with a renewed sense of pride.

The debate over the line between preservation and private property rights is by no means settled. For contemporary Native peoples, mounds are physical and spiritual links to their ancestors and to the land, and their existence represents an important symbol of cultural continuity and persistence in the face of change and competing cultural values. They consider mound sites to be sacred places. Wisconsin Indian Nations have become fiercely protective of the remaining mounds found throughout the state. The Ho-Chunk Nation closely identifies with the effigy mounds in particular because it sees its clan animals and important spirits in the effigy forms, and it has acquired several mound groups to ensure their permanent protection. When the possibility that the burial law would be changed was made public in the spring of 2016, hundreds of Native people from different Native nations, many dressed in traditional regalia, led a peaceful "Save the Mounds" demonstration at the state capitol in Madison, accompanied by the beating of ceremonial drums and supported by many non-Indian people.

As detailed in these pages, we have learned much about the ancient mounds in Wisconsin since the systematic surveys of Increase Lapham in the mid-nineteenth century and even since the first edition of the book in 2000. Even so, the answers to many questions continue to be elusive. The reason is that perceptions and interpretations of the Indian mounds and other aspects of the past continually change—molded and limited by the social and scientific climates of the times, as discussed in the next chapter.

2

In Search of the Mound Builders

Who built the mounds? This is the question still most frequently asked about Indian mounds. Today, the question most often concerns the identity of the specific Native peoples, among them the Ho-Chunk, Menominee, Potawatomi, Ojibwe (Chippewa), Dakota Sioux, and other modern tribes that live or have lived in the Wisconsin mound district. As ludicrous as it may now seem, when Euro-American settlers asked the question in the eighteenth and nineteenth centuries, most did not even believe that Native people were responsible.

Who Built the Mounds?

Immigrants to the New World found mounds and other mysterious earthworks just about everywhere they went in the eastern part of North America. In the South, they encountered abandoned communities dominated by large, flat-topped pyramids of earth, reminiscent of the massive stone structures described as having been built by the Aztecs of Mexico. In the Ohio River valley, they were astounded to come across colossal earthen embankments, ramparts, and ditches in complex geometric forms, as well as groups of massive conical mounds. Throughout the upper Mississippi River drainage in the Midwest, the new arrivals discovered other earthen mounds, including those sculpted into the shapes of giant birds and other animals.

But most Americans had never actually witnessed a Native community in the process of building a mound and, as a reflection of the prejudice of the day, seriously doubted that such "savages," in the midst of being displaced, starved, and killed, could organize the labor to achieve such a purpose.

Consequently, the colonial residents of the eastern seaboard and, later, settlers of midwestern lands hotly debated the origin of the mounds and elaborate earthen structures. They filled newspapers, books, magazines, and scholarly journals of the day with their theories, fueling the imagination of an American public hungry for information about their new home. On one side of the debate was a small cadre of scholars and scientifically inclined individuals—including the politician-philosopher Albert Gallatin, founder of the American Ethnological Society of New York, and Wisconsin's own Increase A. Lapham—who made the seemingly logical connection between the native inhabitants of North America and the ancient earthen structures. On the other, much larger, side were those people, many of them also well educated, who argued that the mounds were the products of a mysterious and distinctly non-Indian (that is, "civilized") "race" that had disappeared before both Native Americans and Euro-Americans came to occupy the North American continent. During the nineteenth century, interest in the question of the identity of the mysterious mound builders became so great that it precipitated investigations and publications by a new government agency, the Smithsonian Institution, and stimulated the growth of North American archaeology into a discrete and scientifically based field of inquiry.

The Myth of the "Lost Race"

Why was a "Lost Race" evoked to account for the mounds, and why was such wild speculation so universally accepted? The answers to these questions lie not only in the obvious lack of specific information concerning Native American cultural history but in the worldview of Europeans and their American descendants that limited all observations and interpretations to rigidly held religious and Euro-centric beliefs. The historian Robert Silverberg and the archaeologists Gordon R. Willey and Jeremy A. Sabloff cite a number of specific factors that contributed to the development of the myth of a Lost Race as the builders of the mounds.[1]

Before the mid-nineteenth century, there was an absence of not only reliable information about the cultural history of the New World but also a scientific framework in which to collect and evaluate such information. Much of what was known was derived from the accounts of explorers who were less interested in the history and culture of the natives they encountered than in gold, God, and glory and from the musings of "armchair explorers" who wrote books based on secondhand information and literary fantasy. Scientific reasoning, with its emphasis on the accumulation and analysis of objective and empirical data, had not yet fully emerged. Even basic concepts, such as that of an ancient and ever-changing natural world, would have to await the acceptance of the geology of Sir Charles Lyell and the evolutionary biology of Charles Darwin. Knowledge about the world and its history was not as much formed and tested by accumulated data as it was molded by Christian religious views. Conflicts that arose between observations and dogma were settled or rationalized in the context of church teachings and the Bible. Until the construction of a scientific and empirical foundation in the late nineteenth century, "theological explanations remained the accepted means of reconstructing events of the past."[2]

For a long time during the period of New World exploration, Europeans had trouble fitting their discoveries, especially the existence of other peoples, into this religiously based worldview. For example, it took a papal edict in 1537 to settle the issue of whether the inhabitants of the New World were even human.[3] With the humanity of Native Americans officially established, the question then necessarily turned to the origin of this exotic people. Since for Christian Europe all humans were descended from Adam and Eve through Noah and his family, the Native American genealogy, they believed, should be traceable through biblical writings. From this premise, one popular eighteenth- and nineteenth-century explanation for the existence of Native Americans was that they were none other than the descendants of the Ten Lost Tribes of Israel, a concept still adhered to by the Mormon Church, founded during the height of the debate about the Lost Race.

Intellectuals of the day applied reason to the problem. The eighteenth century was the time of the Enlightenment, a philosophical movement characterized by the belief in the power of human reason that facilitated enormous innovations in social, political, and even religious thought. Thomas Jefferson and many of his well-educated colonial contemporaries were men of this age who applied their prodigious intellectual skills to questions about the origins of North American Indians and the identity of the builders of the mysterious earthworks found throughout the eastern United States. As a young man, Jefferson even opened a burial mound and made the kind of meticulous observations that would not characterize archaeological investigations for another century. For this reason, some consider Jefferson the first American archaeologist. In true scientific fashion, he cautiously concluded that more data were needed to determine the origin of the mounds.[4]

A second factor that contributed to the speculation about a Lost Race was the need of the emerging American nation to create a heroic and romantic past for itself, one that could accommodate and justify the elimination of Native people. It is hardly a coincidence that, at the height of the popularity of the Lost Race explanation in the nineteenth century, Native Americans were being displaced and exterminated by the westward advance of American society. By denying these people an elaborate and colorful history, Euro-Americans found it easier to perceive them as interloping savages, undeserving of the land they occupied. The acceptance of Native Americans as the builders of the sometimes huge and wonderful earthworks would also make them an architectural people, a hallmark of civilization that Euro-Americans reserved for themselves.[5] Silverberg goes so far as to state that "the controversy over the origin of the mounds was not merely an abstract scholarly debate, but had its roots in the great nineteenth century campaign of extermination waged against the American Indian."[6]

This "campaign of extermination" obviously precluded the collection of information about mounds and other cultural customs and beliefs from Native Americans themselves. In large parts of the colonized East, there was nobody left to ask. There were some exceptions, but they did not settle matters. In 1819, for example, John Heckewelder, a Moravian missionary to a group of converted and transplanted Delaware, or Leni-Lenape, living in Ohio in the late eighteenth century, published an account of Leni-Lenape beliefs and traditions that gave one explanation for the existence of the monumental Ohio earthworks.[7] Heckewelder recounted a story of warfare between the Leni-Lenape and the Ohio mound builders, who, according to the account, were called the Tallegewi or Alligewi and were described as having been remarkably large in physical stature. Despite the construction of the fabulous earthen fortifications, the Tallegewi lost the war. They subsequently buried their dead warriors in earthen mounds and fled south. This story was used far into the nineteenth century to bolster arguments by both sides in the mound builder debate. Those who believed that mounds had been built by Indians identified the Cherokee as the Alligewi on the basis of traditions collected from the Cherokee that they had once lived along the Ohio River. However, believers in a mysterious Lost Race of mound builders, including the Reverend Stephen Peet, a Wisconsin antiquarian and mound researcher, pointed to the large size of the Tallegewi as evidence that the builders of the Ohio earthworks and other mounds had been a people different from the "Red Indians."[8]

A third factor that contributed to the popularity of the myth of the Lost Race was the prevailing view that Indigenous culture was simple and static: if Native Americans did not now construct earthworks, there was no reason to suppose they ever had. Significantly, eyewitness accounts of mound-building Native American cultures in the South, dating to the early years of New World exploration, were either not known or conveniently ignored. A Spanish *entrada* in the sixteenth century dutifully chronicled a mound-building civilization even as it destroyed it. In 1539, a lost and miserable expedition led by Hernando de Soto rampaged through what is now the southeastern United States, encountering a variety of people now known as the Natchez, Creek, and Choctaw, who built and lived on large earthen platform mounds.[9] Some years later, French explorers and colonists in the same area further described and even illustrated burial-mound-building ceremonies.[10]

These accounts describe a complex agricultural civilization referred to as the Mississippian, which maintained an elaborate social system of chiefs and commoners, buried its rulers in earthen mounds, and used huge earthen platform structures as bases for residences and civic and ceremonial buildings. By the time of major white settlement in the late eighteenth and the nineteenth centuries, however, the various Mississippian nations had been decimated by disease and warfare and the mound centers had been abandoned. This process had started even before de Soto's time: he described looting a town depopulated by disease.[11] In the early nineteenth century, the remnants of these populations were forced into western regions as part of the federal policy to remove Native Americans from lands needed for American settlement. The nature of their elaborate culture, including their architecture, was conveniently forgotten.

The Mound Builder Myth in the Nineteenth Century

Candidates for the mound builders were diverse and imaginative. Among them were such Old World peoples as the Phoenicians, Hebrews, Greeks, Romans, Persians, Hindus, Vikings, Welsh, and Danes and such colorful Mesoamerican civilizations as the Aztecs. Wherever there could be found a reference to heaping up dirt to make earthworks, there was also a group that, through migration, could have been the Lost Race mound builders of North America. Mythical civilizations, such as that of Atlantis, were also evoked. But what had happened to these wondrous people? "The answer was obvious," wrote Robert Silverberg in *Mound Builders of Ancient America*, "they had been exterminated at some past date by the despicable, treacherous, ignorant red-skinned savages who even now were causing so much trouble for the Christian settlers of the New World."[12]

The public interest in earthworks and these provocative explanations for their origin led to the proliferation of detailed surveys and crude excavations by a generation of "antiquarians"—self-trained archaeologists whose interest in antiquities went beyond the mere collection of ancient objets d'art. Among them were land surveyors, natural scientists, newspapermen, ministers, doctors, and other learned and curious people who especially took an interest in the spectacular earthworks district of the Ohio River valley. As accounts of these explorations were published throughout the nineteenth century, there steadily accumulated a body of empirical knowledge about mounds and Native American antiquities in general, even if the conclusions that accompanied the reports were fanciful and erroneous. Caleb Atwater, an Ohio postmaster, was one such antiquarian. He produced some of the earliest drawings and maps of the huge Ohio valley earthworks in 1820.[13] Like others, Atwater was nevertheless constrained in his interpretations by prevailing prejudices and stereotypes, so his conclusions did not follow from his observations. He thought it most likely that Hindus of India had been responsible for the construction of the earthworks of Ohio.

Another watershed study, the first real archaeology book published in the United States, derived from the work of Ephraim G. Squier, a newspaperman, and Edgar H. Davis, a physician, both of Chillicothe, Ohio. Chillicothe lies in the heart of the Ohio earthwork country and offered easy access for the men to study these monuments. Supported by the newly organized American Ethnological Society, Squier and Davis made detailed maps of earthworks and mounds (figure 2.1), excavated some, and brought together the work of other researchers, including the initial reports on the effigy mound district in what is now Wisconsin. The work, *Ancient Monuments of the Mississippi Valley*, became the first publication of the Smithsonian Institution, established in 1846 with a large amount of money willed to the United States by James Smithson, an Englishman, for the purpose of creating an institution that would increase and diffuse knowledge.[14]

This book contributed to the mound builder debate in two ways. First, it anticipated modern scientific methodology by both classifying the earthworks, albeit crudely (for example, Works of Defense, Mounds of Sacrifice, Mounds of Sepulcher), and forming testable hypotheses about the uses and purposes of the mounds.[15] Second, it engaged the Smithsonian, and thus the U.S. government, in the debate. Even though Squier and Davis quite clearly sought to be objective in their investigations, they could not intellectually extricate themselves from the power of the myth of the Lost Race and the negative stereotypes of Indians. They concluded that the native peoples of North America had been incapable of building the elaborate earthworks and speculated instead that mound builders from Mexico were the likely architects. But the Smithsonian continued to press the matter throughout the nineteenth century and in the last decade of that century finally settled the debate.

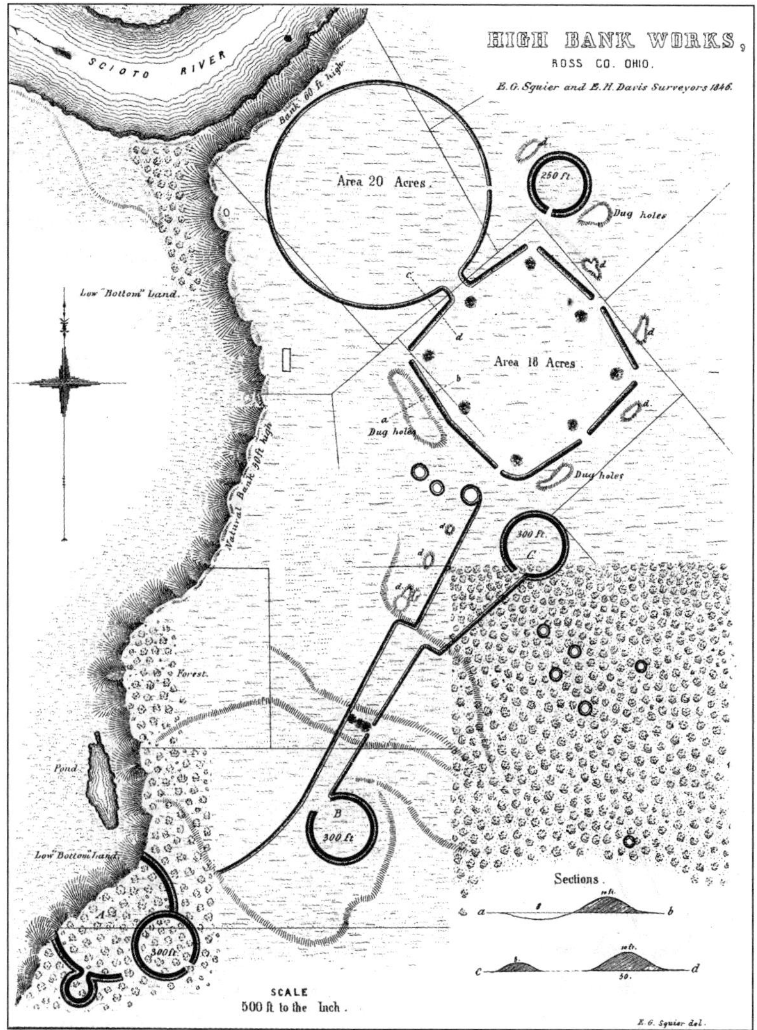

Figure 2.1. Map of earthworks near Chillicothe, Ohio.

Wisconsin and the Myth of the Mound Builders

The Lost Race hypothesis in its many versions had become the most popular explanation for the existence of mounds in North America just as the mounds in Wisconsin were brought to public attention in the late 1830s, during the first great wave of white settlement in the territory. The influx of settlers was made possible by the removal of much of the native population.

Until this time, the densest part of Wisconsin's mound district was occupied largely by the Ho-Chunk and the Potawatomi. The Ho-Chunk are a Siouan-speaking people, indigenous to Wisconsin, that in the nineteenth century maintained villages throughout southern Wisconsin from Green Bay to the Mississippi River. The Algonquian-speaking Potawatomi, a tribe related to the more northerly Menominee and Chippewa, apparently had migrated to Wisconsin from Michigan in the seventeenth century and in the early nineteenth century lived in villages throughout eastern Wisconsin.

Before the 1830s, the white population of Wisconsin was comparatively small. Several fur-trading communities had developed at such places as Green Bay, La Pointe, and Prairie du Chien. In the 1820s, lead miners had begun to trickle into the southwestern part of the territory, establishing a number of small mining communities, often in violation of treaties with the resident Native Americans. Following the infamous Black Hawk War of 1832 and other frontier conflicts, there began a popular call for the removal of the troublesome Native American population from Wisconsin's agriculturally rich southern region. Through treaties and coercion, most of the Ho-Chunk and the Potawatomi eventually moved to reservations in the "Indian Country" of Nebraska and Kansas. Two other Wisconsin Native communities, the Menominee and Ojibwe, lived in less desirable areas and retained reservations in the state by treaties with the United States.

By the 1840s, the white population had grown to more than thirty thousand people.[16] Small groups of refugee Ho-Chunk and Potawatomi continued to live on the fringes of white settlements, shifting residence as the frontier expanded.[17] These were people who defiantly refused to go to the western reservations or quietly walked back to Wisconsin from them. The existence of these "stray bands" and "lost tribes" was not formally recognized by the federal government until the twentieth century.

The first public reports of mounds in Wisconsin were made by settlers, surveyors partitioning lands for settlement, naturalists accessing the resources of the newly opened land, and various travelers who happened to notice, or deliberately went to see, the odd mounds situated along the Indian trails and waterways. In 1836, Increase A. Lapham, a young surveyor and engineer originally from Ohio, wrote to a Milwaukee newspaper about a large, long-tailed, "lizard"-shaped mound that he had encountered near Waukesha.[18] At about the same time, Judge Nathaniel Hyer published in several newspapers notes and a map of the ruins of an ancient town with huge flat-topped mounds along the Crawfish River in what is now Jefferson County.[19] As a reflection of the beliefs of the day, Hyer suggested that the town was of Aztec origin and called it Aztalan, a name still used for Wisconsin's premier archaeological site.

Richard C. Taylor first drew national attention to the now famous effigy mounds of Wisconsin. Traveling "in the society of some scientific friends," he examined effigy mounds in present-day Iowa and Dane Counties and obtained information from elsewhere in the territory. In 1838, he published his observations in an article in the *American Journal of Science and Art* (figure 2.2). Taylor, like many others who would follow him in Wisconsin, advanced a variation of the Lost Race idea that narrowed the argument: he accepted the notion that Native Americans had constructed the mounds but argued that these ancient mound builders could not be related to the modern tribes of the region, relying on both the familiar premise that these people were intellectually inferior to the ancient mound builders and his conviction that they, whom he called "degenerate" and "slothful," had only recently come to occupy the mound territory in what had been a long succession of tribal displacements in historic times: "But to a far different race, assuredly, and to a far distant period, must we look when seeking to trace the authors of these singular mounds, and the earthworks of such various forms, which are spread over the North American continent, from Lake Superior to Mexico. But who were they who left almost imperishable memorials on the soil, attesting to the superiority of their race?"[20]

Relying on their beliefs, he and others also continued to reject the possibility that local Native Americans could have any knowledge about or insight on the mounds, although many observers did report that various tribes, including those "disaffected" people, occasionally excavated new graves into previously existing mounds. The belief that Native Americans had no traditions that involved the mounds and the continuing stereotype of Native Americans as "savages" would continue to block potentially fruitful cross-cultural dialogues on this and other matters for a very long time.

At the same time, Taylor provided an insight that drew a powerful link between the social structure of contemporaneous Indians and the effigy mounds. Although he claimed no "positive evidence," he noted a correspondence between the different mound shapes, birds and animals, and the totems or clans described for many Native nations in some published ethnological accounts. Might not these shapes represent the "respective tribes or branches" of the people found buried in the mounds?[21]

In rapid succession, other travelers described and mapped mounds and offered their theories about their origin. But it was Increase Lapham, later to become Wisconsin's preeminent natural scientist, who was the first to comprehend and document the truly phenomenal nature of the Wisconsin mound district (figure 2.3). Intrigued by the mounds he had encountered in Milwaukee and sponsored by the American Antiquarian Society, he spent several years mapping and examining mound groups and other ancient

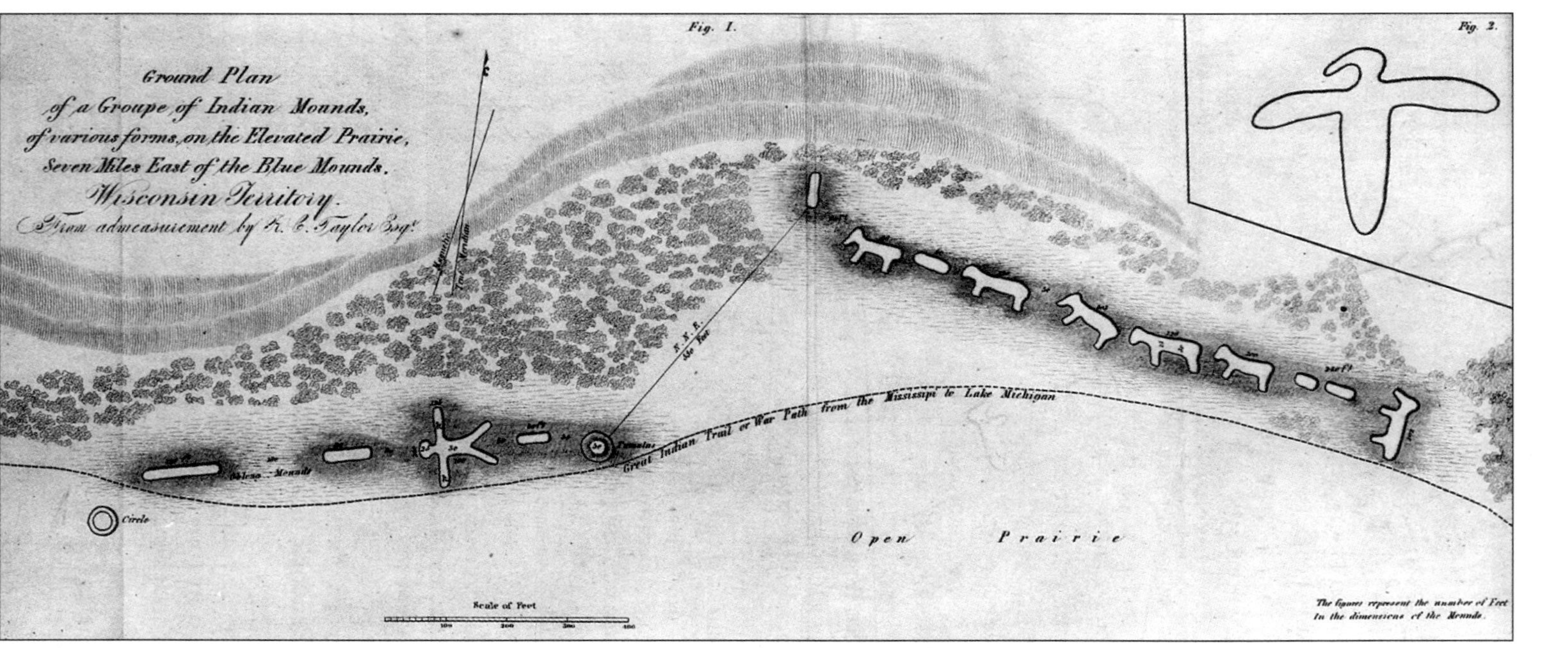

Figure 2.2. Group of effigy mounds that once existed in modern-day Dane County as mapped in the early nineteenth century.

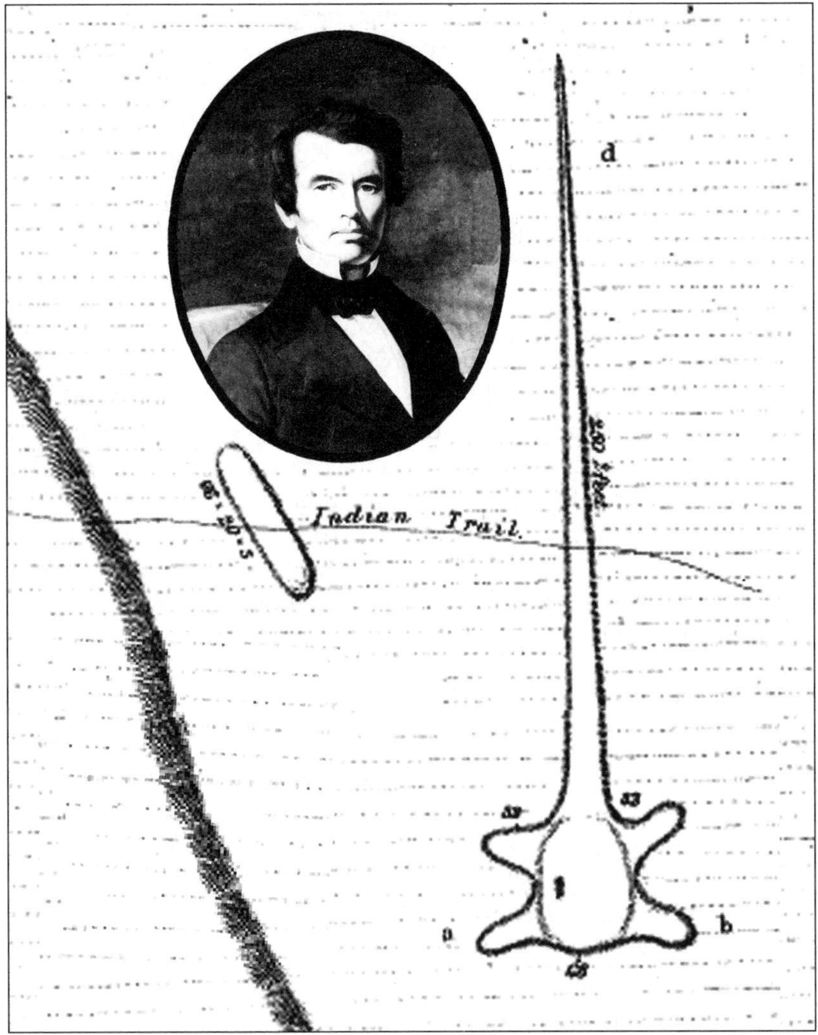

Figure 2.3. Increase A. Lapham and a map he made of effigy mounds in modern-day Waukesha.

places, such as Aztalan, throughout the southern part of the state. The Smithsonian Institution published the results of Lapham's research in 1855, seven years after Wisconsin became a state.[22] The book, *The Antiquities of Wisconsin, as Surveyed and Described*, is still a remarkable source of detailed maps of mounds that have long since disappeared and an important historical document of nineteenth-century mound research.

Lapham saw links between the mound builders and Native people in the types of artifacts recovered from the mounds, such as pipes and pottery.

In general, his research convinced him that the "mound builders of Wisconsin were none other than the ancestors of the present tribes of Indians."[23] He considered any other theories to be "far fetched." But Lapham also did not believe that the modern Indigenous peoples of the region, whom he considered "little advanced in civilization," were mound builders, although he left open that possibility. As to what had happened to the Native American mound builders of the past, Lapham was not certain. Perhaps they had been driven off or had migrated to another area and were living in some remote western region. Or perhaps they had simply been overrun by a stronger tribe with different customs. Lapham, however, anticipated the development of later theories of cultural evolution by pointing out that while dramatic changes in customs and institutions have occurred throughout history among the many cultures in the world, these changes were not necessarily accompanied by the replacement of Indigenous people with others. He pointed out that the Egyptians no longer built pyramids and the Greeks had ceased to erect temples but there was no doubt that the descendants of the ancient builders continue to occupy Egypt and Greece. So too with Native peoples: customs had simply changed over time, and the descendants of the mound builders were probably found in the "present red race of the same or adjacent regions."[24]

One of the most bizarre contributions to the Lost Race debate involving Wisconsin mounds was a popular book written by William Pidgeon, *Traditions of De-coo-dah and Antiquarian Researches*, subtitled, after the fashion of the day, *Comprising Extensive Explorations, Surveys, and Excavations of the Wonderful and Mysterious Earthen Remains of the Mound-Builders in America; the Traditions of the Last Prophet of the Elk Nation Relative to Their Origin and Use; and the Evidences of an Ancient Population More Numerous Than the Present Aborigines*.[25] The book is fantasy on an epic scale, but Pidgeon was a compelling writer and used a device known to modern writers of pseudoscientific literature: he wove just enough fact into his fiction to appear credible. The first part of the book is a collection of concocted evidence that purports to demonstrate pre-Columbian visits by just about all the usual Lost Race suspects, including Egyptians, Greeks, Romans, and Persians. Even Alexander the Great makes an appearance in the form of an alleged stone with his name on it found in Brazil. The greatest appeal is in the second part of the book, where Pidgeon claims to provide a perspective missing in most other discussions of mounds: the history and traditions of the mound builders *as told by themselves*.

Pidgeon acquired an interest in ancient monuments in his native Virginia. He claimed to have traveled to South America to examine mounds there. In 1829 he became a trader in Ohio, where he visited the spectacular tumuli and earthworks of that region. In the late 1830s he went to the upper Mississippi River valley, where he found "relics of many an ancient mound, varying much in size and form; some representing redoubts, or fortifications, others presenting forms of gigantic men, beasts, birds, and reptiles, among which may be the eagle, the otter, the serpent, the alligator, and others pertaining to the deer, elk, and buffalo species."[26]

Pidgeon ended up at Prairie du Chien, on the Mississippi River. There he engaged in some mound digging and made the acquaintance of local Native people who shared their language with him. According to his account, he had the extraordinary good fortune to be introduced to an old man named De-coo-dah, who was the very last member of the "Elk Nation," the ancient people who had built the mounds. As luck would also have it, De-coo-dah just happened to be descended from the very same family entrusted with the sacred traditions of the nation. The old man became Pidgeon's teacher, and for several years they lived together on an island in the Mississippi River where De-coo-dah revealed the secrets of the mounds and their builders.

From this rambling and frequently incoherent narrative, we learn that the Elk Nation, the mound builders, were descended from an indeterminate, non-Indian race that had intermarried with the Native Americans and then vanished before the appearance of Columbus. In giving us a history of the Elk Nation, Pidgeon crafted an epic story of ancient kingdoms, great wars and alliances, assassinations, and internal conflicts that reduced the great civilization to small bands that no longer built earthen monuments. On the last page of his book, Pidgeon brought in a flood of biblical proportions to hasten their extinction.

We also learn that effigy mounds, recorded in hieroglyph form, document this dramatic history. According to Pidgeon, in the guise of De-coo-dah, some mounds were built during national festivals of the Elk Nation, while others commemorate important events, such as the union, extinction, or migration of affiliated tribes. There were matrimonial mounds, sacrificial mounds, and mounds that told the stories of dynasties and battles. Accompanying the fanciful narrative are equally fanciful illustrations of mound groups in oddly geometric patterns (figure 2.4).

In a harsh modern critique, Silverberg characterized *Traditions of De-coo-dah* as a "crazy masterpiece of pseudoscience," the epitome of the grand era of humbug typified by Pidgeon's contemporary P. T. Barnum.[27] The Smithsonian Institution earlier came to the same conclusion and refused to publish Pidgeon's manuscript after he offered it. But as a commercial publication, the book became a big hit with the public and eventually gained some respectability even among a few uncritical scholars. A later mound

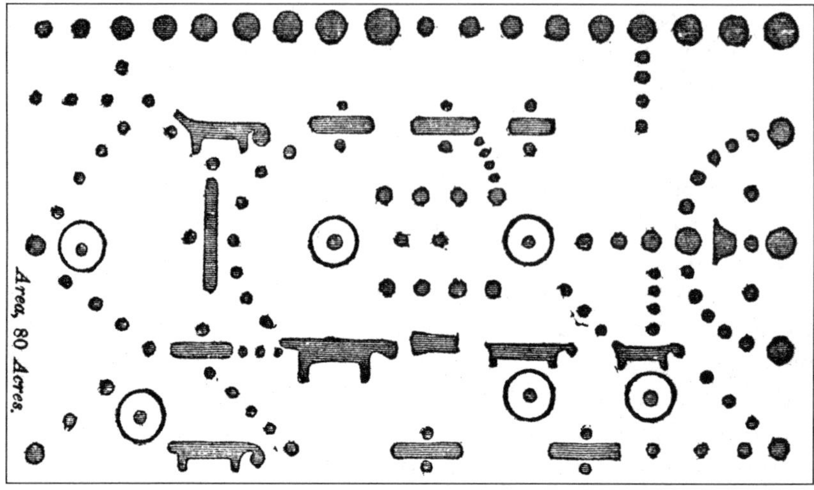

Figure 2.4. Bizarre mound pattern reportedly found in Wisconsin by William Pidgeon.

surveyor, Theodore H. Lewis, located some of the mounds that Pidgeon had discussed and illustrated and talked to some of the people who had known Pidgeon. He found little resemblance between Pidgeon's descriptions and reality and concluded: "The result of my research in this respect is to convince me that the Elk Nation and its last prophet De-coo-dah are modern myths, which have never had any objective existence."[28]

Mound researchers of a more serious vein continued to publish maps and discuss theories about the origin of the Wisconsin mounds throughout the late nineteenth century. Stephen Peet, a minister from the Beloit area, contributed to the effort by starting, in 1878, a periodical called the *American Antiquarian and Oriental Journal*, in which he published a number of studies of the mounds penned by people with antiquarian interests. A collection of these articles later appeared in *Prehistoric America*, a two-volume work by Peet.[29] Peet published maps and descriptions of a number of mound groups he had personally observed throughout the state, but, unlike Lapham and some of the other researchers, he was not a trained surveyor and seems to have had little patience for details. Consequently, his maps are quite imaginative and unreliable.

Of far greater value today are the maps made by Theodore H. Lewis of thousands of mounds. Lewis was a Minnesota land surveyor of remarkable skill and ability who worked in Wisconsin and adjacent areas of the upper Mississippi River drainage, from Canada to Missouri, during the years 1881 to 1894 (figure 2.5). Lewis's project, the Northwestern Archaeological

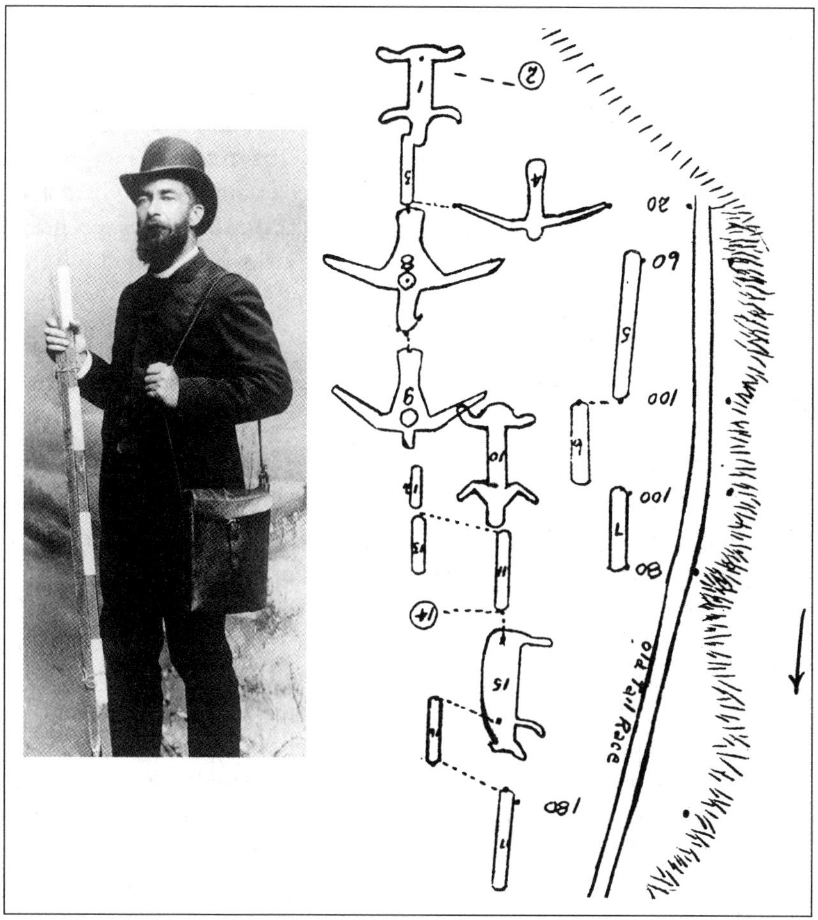

Figure 2.5. Theodore H. Lewis and a map he made of the Bloyer or Twin Lizard group on the Wisconsin River in 1886 as part of the Northwestern Archaeological Survey.

Survey, was organized and financed by Alfred J. Hill, a wealthy St. Paul businessman who shared with Lewis an intense interest in the ancient earthworks.[30] Lewis provided some of the most accurate surveys of mound groups ever made in the midwestern United States until modern times. So meticulous are they that some are being used as base maps to reconstruct, on paper, complex mound arrangements that once existed in several parts of the state.

The Northwestern Archaeological Survey was interrupted by Hill's death, but not before thirteen thousand mounds in eighteen states and one Canadian province had been recorded and meticulously mapped. Among them were more than nine hundred effigy mounds, most in Wisconsin.[31] The results of the survey were never published, but the many volumes of maps and notebooks generated by Lewis were diligently archived at the Minnesota Historical Society. Some of this information was used to help reconstruct the prehistory of Minnesota, but the excellent material on Wisconsin remained largely unknown or unused by most researchers until the 1990s. Today, the records are considered to be one of the best resources for maps and descriptions of mounds in Wisconsin, especially those that have been destroyed since Lewis's visits.

Mounds and the Development of American Archaeology

During the late nineteenth century, research on the histories and cultures of Native peoples became increasingly well organized on a national level. This was influenced in great part by a general trend begun in Europe toward a scientific formulation of human history brought about by discoveries of fossils of prehistoric humans, the publication of Charles Darwin's *On the Origin of Species by Means of Natural Selection*, and the emergence of the science of geology, all of which challenged prevailing theological dogma.

In the United States, attitudes toward Native Americans also began to shift. The perception, stimulated by the concept of Manifest Destiny, that Indians were simple savages was being gradually replaced in some scholarly quarters by the view that Native American cultures were sufficiently rich to deserve thorough documentation before they vanished. In 1878, John Wesley Powell, a Civil War hero and western explorer, wrote a report to the Department of the Interior arguing that the ignorance of Native cultures had "brought great trouble to our management of the Indians" and accounted for the "blunders we have made and the wrongs we have inflicted upon the Indians."[32]

Like many other people of the time, he assumed that Native cultures would one day become extinct, and so he advocated ethnological studies to record their customs and languages before they completely disappeared. Powell, like similar well-intended advocates during that period, sounds a bit condescending in that his concern seemed focused as much on the impending loss of the objects of study as on the plight of the people themselves. This attitude continued to characterize some American anthropological research well into the twentieth century—understandably creating resentment in Native communities. But this attitude helps explain a great nineteenth-century American paradox: at the height of the bitter fighting between the federal government and the western tribes, Congress appropriated money for the systematic study of the very cultures the government was systematically destroying. In 1879 it created the Bureau of Ethnology within the Smithsonian Institution, to be headed by Powell. Whatever the motivations for the creation of the bureau, the results of its ethnographic work, published as annual reports, are still used and cited widely by those engaged in Native cultural research. Furthermore, the formation of the Bureau of Ethnology gave voice to a number of critics (largely ignored at the time) of government efforts to force surviving Native people into the mainstream American culture. Finally, the bureau also gave encouragement and employment to a generation of formally trained anthropologists who at long last went to the Native Americans themselves to inquire about their beliefs and traditions about the mounds.

As the controversy about the identity of the mound builders continued to escalate, in 1881 Congress authorized the creation of the Division of Mound Exploration within the Bureau of Ethnology, and Cyrus Thomas, an entomologist and botanist from Illinois, was selected to head the division. His primary directive was finally to answer the question of who built the mounds. For the next ten years, division personnel systematically examined mounds and collected information from throughout the North American mound district seeking the answer to the question. Archaeologists today look at the project as the prototype for modern archaeological research: clearly stated research questions, a research program designed to collect data to answer the questions, an analysis of the data, and the preparation of a summary report.[33] Thomas's huge concluding work, simply called *Report on the Mound Explorations of the Bureau of Ethnology*, marks the formal birth of American archaeology.[34]

While the identity of the mound builders was the primary focus of the research, Thomas also sought to collect detailed information about the mounds and their construction. To accomplish this large task, he developed a sample that defined eight archaeological districts in the United States that contained mounds (Wisconsin was subsumed into what he called the Dakotan District) and then examined examples of the different mound types or classes found within the districts.

Most of the Smithsonian's work in Wisconsin took place in counties adjacent to the Mississippi River, although mounds in Dane, Barron, and Sheboygan Counties were also examined. Maps of selected mound groups were made, and measurements of individual mounds were taken. Dozens of the mounds in Wisconsin were opened and their contents and internal structures described and illustrated. Along the Mississippi River, Thomas excavated and studied large, round burial mounds as well as groups of effigies. In some of the conical mounds he found numerous burials, often represented as bundles of disarticulated bones in the mounds themselves or beneath the mounds in a central pit. Occasionally, burials were encased in stone vaults. Artifacts associated with the burials in a number of these mounds included copper ornaments, spears, knife blades made from obsidian from the western United States, and perforated bear-tooth pendants—distinctive items that one day would culturally link the ancient mound builders of the upper Mississippi River valley to the Hopewell builders of the spectacular Ohio earthworks.

While working in Grant County, Thomas's assistants took time to look into the problem of an alleged elephant-shaped mound, which had become embroiled in a side controversy that concerned the authenticity of artifacts reportedly recovered from some mounds and other sites near Davenport, Iowa. The artifacts were slate tablets elaborately inscribed with the characters of an unknown language and several stone effigy pipes carved in the form of elephants. All had been found by the same man. Taken at face value, these objects would support the case for Old World contacts in North America. A Smithsonian map of the mound, which had been heavily plowed, simply shows an animal with a large head, and the surveyors concluded that previous reports of a long trunk probably had been based on a shifting line of sand. The general shape of the mound is well within the variation of forms common to the Mississippi River bluff area called bear effigies. Furthermore, Thomas concluded that the tablets and pipes found near Davenport were badly conceived hoaxes, a view supported by modern research.[35]

For Thomas and the Bureau of Ethnology, there was no question about the real identity of the mound builders. Thomas presented several lines of evidence in a lengthy conclusion to his book to support his belief that the mound builders were none other than indigenous Native peoples. The conclusions came from historical accounts of mound building and from Native American oral traditions of mound building (although derived from second- and third-hand sources), as well as archaeological excavations that revealed the similarity between the types of burials found in many mounds and the observed burial customs of contemporary Native people. He also made the link between the mound-building people and more recent tribes by reporting the discovery, in some mounds, of objects introduced to Indians by Europeans after the time of Columbus.

Thomas's research and excavations were not precise by any means, and his report is far from perfect. Moreover, in his enthusiasm to embrace Indians as mound builders, he also uncritically accepted a number of uncorroborated historical accounts of mound building. For example, he reported as fact the legend that a great burial mound on the shore of Lake Butte des Morts in Wisconsin had been built by the Fox to bury victims of a war with the

French.[36] While the war actually occurred, the mound in question was almost certainly constructed about two thousand years earlier.[37] This and other similar errors led him to the generalization that the mounds had been built by modern and familiar tribes or at least by their immediate ancestors. He failed to recognize, and at the time could not have known, that most of the mounds he studied were very old. Nevertheless, he made the important observation, supported by compelling evidence in the form of differing customs, constructions, and artifacts, that the various earthworks could not have been constructed by a single "race" or group but were the work of various Native tribes and peoples. It would be up to later researchers to establish that some of these different tribes and peoples were also separated in time.

Cyrus Thomas's monumental work was well received, and the myth of the Lost Race was finally laid to rest. It can be argued, however, that the wide acceptance of the work by the Smithsonian's Division of Mound Exploration was due not just to the compelling nature of Thomas's evidence but also to the social climate of the late nineteenth century. As R. Clark Mallam pointed out, had Thomas presented the same evidence a little earlier—during the height of the Indian Wars, say—it might have been ignored.[38] But by the time of the publication of the report in 1894, the Indian Wars in the West had been concluded—unhappily for Native peoples—and the American conquest of North America had been completed. The idea that Native people were something other than simple savages no longer posed an uncomfortable challenge to American sensibilities and the promise of Manifest Destiny. They could now be accepted as historical and sophisticated peoples with ancient and visible links to the land because, to white America, it simply did not matter anymore.

But the resolution of the Lost Race debate had come at a high cost. Thousands of mounds had disappeared under the shovels and picks of mound diggers searching for artifacts and bones. It certainly can be argued that the westward expansion of the American frontier would have led to the destruction of many of these mounds in any case. Nevertheless, the remains of tens of thousands of Native American people had been disinterred as a direct result of the debate over the Lost Race. Only a fraction of the remains ended up neatly cataloged on the shelves of museums, such as the Smithsonian, allowing the descendants of those buried to claim their bones today. To these can be added the countless mounds and graves looted by curiosity seekers and relic hunters excited by the more scholarly debates and discoveries and destroyed during a wave of mound excavations conducted by the new profession of archaeology in the twentieth century in the continuing search of the mound builders.

3

Excavation, Chronology, and Meanings of the Mounds

During the first half of the twentieth century, mound research in Wisconsin took three different but occasionally intersecting paths. The first path, unfortunately short-lived, was ethnological. For practically the first time, both amateur and professional anthropologists seriously considered Native American beliefs, traditions, and opinions about the mounds and went directly to Native Americans for insights about mound origins and meaning. An archaeological and scientific path was taken by the Public Museum of the City of Milwaukee (the modern Milwaukee Public Museum) and similar institutions and led to the detailed and controlled archaeological excavation of mounds and other archaeological sites. This great period of mound excavation lasted until the 1950s and would help identify and define the several different cultures responsible for building mounds. The third path was wider, being both humanistic and anthropological. Drawing on a vast pool of amateurs and other interested members of the public, Charles E. Brown and the Wisconsin Archeological Society attempted to study, publish, and preserve all facets of Native culture and history—archaeological sites, antiquities, ritual practices and beliefs, customs, stories, and legends. This approach led to the first statewide inventory of mounds and other Native American sites in Wisconsin and to the first coordinated mound-preservation movement.

Ethnology: The Ho-Chunk as Mound Builders

Cyrus Thomas had demolished the Lost Race explanation for the erection of mounds in North America, but one of the "proofs" had directly linked mound building with more recent Native peoples. Since the antiquity of most mound types had been surmised but not firmly established, the next question in Wisconsin logically focused on which of the modern tribes were the mound builders. Of particular interest was the identity of the mysterious effigy mound people. Among the likely candidates were the three tribes that were believed to have ancient roots in Wisconsin: the Santee or Dakota, who had been driven from the state in early historic times by the westward movement of the Ojibwe; the Menominee; and the Ho-Chunk.

For many, the Dakota were most likely the builders of many of the large conical mounds found scattered throughout their former territory in northern Wisconsin. Working on the reservation in northwest Wisconsin that the Menominee had retained by treaty in 1852, the ethnologist Walter Hoffman reported in 1896 that the nearby Ojibwe believed that the mounds in the area had been built by the Dakota before they were pushed westward, a view apparently also held by some Menominee, as may be reflected in a story recorded by Samuel Barrett and Alanson Skinner of the Public Museum several decades later.[1] But, for the origin of the ubiquitous effigy mounds of southern Wisconsin, attention in the early twentieth century turned to the Ho-Chunk.

A connection between the Ho-Chunk and mounds had been made by researchers as early as the mid-nineteenth century, when the first annual report of the newly founded State Historical Society of Wisconsin reprinted a highly romanticized "legend," first published in 1829 by the *Buffalo* (New York) *Journal*. The legend, supposedly obtained from a Ho-Chunk chief, identified certain Wisconsin mounds as the graves of great Ho-Chunk chiefs who had died in battles with Sauk and Fox.[2] Thomas used this reference in establishing his proofs for the Native American authorship of mounds. In 1907, George A. West, a lawyer in Racine and later an officer of the Public Museum, published a lengthy review of the question of the identity of the mound builders in the newly established journal *Wisconsin Archeologist*. After delivering a literary coup de grâce to the Lost Race notion, which was still in its death throes, he reasserted an interpretation, first presented by Richard Taylor in 1838 and growing in popularity, that the effigy mounds represented clan symbols, in this case specifically of the Ho-Chunk.

As one piece of evidence that the Ho-Chunk had built mounds, West described a ceremony observed among the Ho-Chunk at a reservation in Nebraska during which miniature ritual mounds were made. West predicted that the hypothesis of the Ho-Chunk as builders of the effigy mounds "will be accepted as undisputed fact, within the next generation."[3]

In 1911, Arlow B. Stout wrote an assessment of the nature and distribution of mounds in Wisconsin based on surveys, including his own around Lake Koshkonong and in the Four Lakes region around Madison. He also stressed the probable relationship of effigies to Ho-Chunk clans.[4] In another article published about the same time, he told of his own surprise upon learning, firsthand, that, contrary to frequent earlier reports, Native people did have traditions and beliefs about the construction of the mounds.[5] Visiting a Ho-Chunk family camped in the Wisconsin Dells—the descendants of the Ho-Chunk who had stayed in Wisconsin—he inquired about their beliefs about mounds. A member of the band told him not only that the Ho-Chunk had constructed the mounds, both conical and effigies, but also that the elders had identified some long-tailed effigy forms, commonly called lizards or panthers, as representations of a prominent Ho-Chunk spirit being, a mysterious creature that lived in the water and came out at night. From this, Stout made the inference that unidentified effigy mounds, including linear mounds frequently associated with the effigies, might represent "spirit animals."

Charles E. Brown, the new director of the museum of the State Historical Society of Wisconsin, took up the argument for a connection between the Ho-Chunk and the effigy mounds in an article published in 1911.[6] He described his visit with two Ho-Chunk men, Oliver La Mere and John Rave, who were descended from the Ho-Chunk who had been removed from Wisconsin to Nebraska in the early nineteenth century and who had been working for Paul Radin, an anthropologist with the Bureau of Ethnology. La Mere, who served as Radin's interpreter, also traced his ancestry on his father's side to prominent Wisconsin fur traders. Brown reported that both men were well versed in Ho-Chunk traditions and beliefs.

Escorting the men to effigy mound groups in the Madison area, Brown elicited their views about the meaning of the various mound forms. La Mere and Rave told Brown, as they also had advised Radin, that the Ho-Chunk believed that the various animals represented both important spirit beings and clan symbols. Rave, for example, quickly identified a huge cross-shaped mound as the symbol of Earth-Maker, who is the creator of the world and human beings in Ho-Chunk cosmology and whose symbol appears on many types of ritual paraphernalia. Brown acknowledged that some of the information provided by the men appeared to be conjecture, but nevertheless he recognized the potential for Native beliefs and traditions to provide insights on effigy mounds in Wisconsin and advised researchers that "in this section of the country at least ethnological science may greatly assist in our archaeological history."[7]

More than anybody else, Paul Radin is identified with the theory that there is a connection between the Ho-Chunk and the builders of the effigy mounds. A trained ethnographer, Radin was employed by the Bureau of Ethnology to collect cultural information among the Ho-Chunk. From the data he gathered primarily from the Nebraska Ho-Chunk between 1908 and 1913, he wrote both an article addressing the relationship of the Ho-Chunk to the effigy mounds and a monumental work, *The Winnebago Tribe*.[8] In these studies, Radin "demonstrated beyond any doubt that the Effigy Mounds are the work of the Winnebago alone"—at least to his own satisfaction. To support his case, Radin offered four principal arguments. First, he contended that central Algonquian tribes (for example, the Ojibwe, Menominee, Potawatomi, Sauk, and Fox) had been intruders into Siouan territory and that ethnographic evidence on burial customs indicated that they had not built the mounds. By the process of elimination, that left the Siouan-speaking Ho-Chunk, since the other Siouan tribe, the Dakota, had left the area in the early years of the historic period. Second, he matched the known distribution of effigy mounds with the territory of the nineteenth-century Ho-Chunk. Third, he noted the close correspondence between types of effigy mounds and Ho-Chunk clan symbols and cited oral traditions to support this association. Finally, he rejected the notion, then becoming popular in archaeological circles, that the mounds were necessarily of great age, again citing information obtained from Ho-Chunk people that their ancestors had built mounds in relatively recent times.

Largely on the basis of Radin's work, the argument for the Ho-Chunk as the builders of the effigy mounds became widely accepted by both scholars and the public during the first quarter of the twentieth century. This conclusion was not seriously challenged until after the late 1920s, when archaeologists who used the archaeological evidence of the time began to argue that the mounds had been built in the far distant past and therefore could not be directly associated with the historic Ho-Chunk; they furthermore argued that the effigy mound builders were not even the ancient ancestors of the modern Ho-Chunk.

Radin's views and the uncritical use of ethnographic data to interpret the past in general came under harsh scrutiny as time went on. Radin was and still is criticized by scholars and Ho-Chunk people for accepting as fact the views of a few carefully selected people, especially since many of his sources had abandoned traditional belief systems.[9] In 1928, William C.

McKern even suggested that Radin's personal interpretations directly influenced Ho-Chunk oral tradition, convincing the Ho-Chunk that their forebears had made the mounds.[10]

As archaeology became more rigorously scientific during the twentieth century, it became cautious about accepting bodies of information that could not be objectively verified. This ultimately, and unfortunately, resulted in the dismissal of ancient ideologies as unknowable and the consideration of Native American traditions and belief systems as not useful except when they fit "archaeological facts." By the second half of the twentieth century, the use of the more subjective Native beliefs and traditions to form ideas about the past had again fallen into disfavor.

Preservation: Charles E. Brown and the Wisconsin Archeological Society

Excited by the research on mounds and the ever-growing literature generated by the emerging field of archaeology, popular interest in Native American antiquities was quite high in the late nineteenth century. Large collections of artifacts and information on archaeological sites grew in the hands of well-educated amateur archaeologists and antiquarians, among them doctors, lawyers, judges, professors, and farmers. Although the "opening of mounds" had become a popular Sunday-afternoon social activity, many of these enthusiasts sought to find a more productive outlet for their interests and hobby. In addition, many were becoming increasingly disturbed by the disappearance of Native American sites, especially the mounds, as a result of farming, road building, urban expansion, and looting.

This interest and concern gave birth to the Wisconsin Archeological Society as an organization of amateur archaeologists dedicated to "advancing the study and preservation of Wisconsin Indian Antiquities." It was established in 1899 as a special section of the Wisconsin Natural History Survey and then was reorganized as a separate society in 1903. A founding father and long-standing guiding force was Charles E. Brown, who also served for forty years as both organizational secretary and editor of *The Wisconsin Archeologist*, the society's publication.

A Milwaukee native, Brown began his archaeological career as an assistant at the Milwaukee Public Museum in 1900 and later in the decade moved to Madison, where he became the first director of the museum of the Wisconsin Historical Society, a post he held until his retirement in 1944.[11]

As secretary of and editor for the Wisconsin Archeological Society, Brown developed and maintained the "Records of Wisconsin Antiquities," an inventory of state archaeological sites that has since evolved into an ever-expanding computer database and map library kept by the Office of the State Archaeologist at the Wisconsin Historical Society. He communicated with thousands of individuals throughout the state to obtain information about the distribution of sites, especially mounds, and this correspondence fills fifty-three boxes in the archives of the Wisconsin Historical Society.

Alarmed by the destruction of mounds throughout Wisconsin, Brown urged the Wisconsin Archeological Society to make the preservation of mounds its first priority. He further helped the society formulate an elaborate strategy to preserve mounds and, in doing so, created Wisconsin's first historic-preservation movement. This strategy would be familiar to modern preservationists: systematic surveys to identify important sites, protective legislation, public acquisition and stewardship, partnerships with influential people and organizations, landmarking, fund-raising, and, above all, relentless promotion and public education.

One of the first projects undertaken by the Wisconsin Archeological Society was the preservation of three large conical mounds, now the centerpiece of Cutler Park in downtown Waukesha. In 1906 a special committee working with the Sauk County Historical Society raised money to purchase the famous Man Mound near Baraboo, thereby saving it from being turned into cropland.[12] A county park now preserves this unique monument, now a National Historic Landmark.

Collaborating with a variety of local historical societies and other public-service organizations, the Wisconsin Archeological Society placed historical markers and commemorative plaques on mound groups throughout the state as a means of calling public attention to the importance of these ancient structures. In 1912 it formed the Mounds Preservation Committee, a standing committee that actively worked to save mounds from destruction through acquisition by public agencies or the society. By the 1920s the committee was able to boast that five hundred mounds had been preserved largely by its efforts. Virtually all of them remain. In 1920 the society formed Save Aztalan, a movement that eventually led to the public ownership of the premier archaeological mound site in Wisconsin.

Throughout its early years, the Wisconsin Archeological Society encouraged and organized mapping expeditions undertaken by volunteers and published the results of these extensive studies in *The Wisconsin Archeologist*. Although written by amateurs, many of these reports stand as models of professional research reports. Like the information compiled by Increase A. Lapham and Theodore H. Lewis, these records are all the more valuable because of the subsequent loss of the mounds to agriculture and development.

In 1911 a delegation from the Wisconsin Archeological Society, headed by Brown, successfully lobbied the Wisconsin legislature to pass a law to protect antiquities on public lands—Wisconsin's first historic-preservation law. At the same time, the legislature made an annual appropriation of $1,500 to the Wisconsin Historical Society for the purpose of conducting a statewide inventory of archaeological sites, particularly mounds.[13] The work was carried out by volunteers under Brown's direction. The money provided by the state covered only their travel expenses. Funding for the project lasted for only two years, but during 1911 and 1912 as many as ten crews fanned out across the state to record the location of mounds and other sites, hundreds of which were inventoried and mapped. Public funding for such a worthy enterprise was not to become available again in Wisconsin until the 1970s.

Brown became personally committed to the preservation of the many mound groups found along the shores of the Four Lakes region surrounding Madison. Greatly concerned that the monuments in the Four Lakes area were doomed by rapid city and lakeshore development, Brown led a lifelong local campaign to save or at least document as many mounds as he personally could. From his base at the Wisconsin Historical Society and between his tasks as museum director, he launched a number of mound surveys that built on the work of Arlow B. Stout, then a student at the University of Wisconsin. Brown was assisted by a number of volunteers recruited from the vast academic and intellectual community in the Madison area.

Brown worked vigorously to gain public ownership of mound groups, the only way at the time to provide even the promise of preservation. He cajoled and badgered public officials into protecting mounds in their jurisdictions. Brown later worked closely with the University of Wisconsin when it acquired land for an arboretum on which he had identified three mound groups. He served on the arboretum's advisory committee and personally supervised the restoration of mounds that had been damaged by looting.

A large part of Brown's success was the result of his enthusiastic attention to public education. In addition to his many scholarly articles, he wrote a number of pamphlets, brochures, and feature articles for the general public. He was a popular speaker on the lecture circuit and, between 1923 and 1935, gave numerous lectures on WHA, the nation's first public-radio station. Each summer during the 1920s and 1930s, Brown offered the popular "Lake Mendota Historical Excursion" for university students and professors and for other interested residents of Madison. Using a motorized launch, he led "pilgrimages" to historical and archaeological sites along the lake, including a half-dozen mound groups.[14]

Brown was a tireless and innovative organizer who rarely missed an opportunity to promote mound preservation. In 1914 the Madison Board of Commerce asked him to arrange a reception and entertainment for the Society of American Indians, a national organization of "progressive and patriotic" Native people that had selected Madison for its annual congress. Brown seized the opportunity to draw public attention to his efforts to save a small effigy mound group overlooking Lake Wingra from urban expansion by arranging a well-publicized dedication ceremony at the mounds attended by representatives of thirteen tribes from throughout the United States.[15] During the 1930s, Brown took advantage of public-works programs by using laborers to repair and restore vandalized mounds on the University of Wisconsin campus.

The interests of both Brown and the Wisconsin Archeological Society went beyond the preservation of mounds as memorials to past civilizations. As an organization of archaeologists, amateur and professional, the society was driven by a quest to learn about Wisconsin's past. Mounds were preserved because they were important repositories of information that could and should be carefully excavated someday. Accordingly, Brown and members of the society excavated mounds when the situation presented itself, although usually when the mounds faced imminent destruction and could not be saved. In Brown's time, however, the knowledge that came from this work was limited to determining how the mounds had been constructed and learning what they contained. These were the days before radiocarbon dating and before the thirteen-thousand-year sequence of prehistoric Native American cultures had been ordered from stratigraphic layers in caves and rock shelters in southwestern Wisconsin. Therefore, the results of these digs were difficult to interpret. Nevertheless, valuable information, artifacts, and even the very bones of the mound builders themselves would have been lost in many cases had it not been for Brown and the Wisconsin Archeological Society.

Another direction in Brown's own mound research stemmed from his interest in Native traditions, stories, and folklore and from his firm conviction that the Ho-Chunk had constructed the effigy mounds in Wisconsin. He cultivated close ties with Wisconsin Native people from whom he gathered stories, beliefs, and oral history. He gained a profound respect for these people and, in return, became so highly regarded that he was reportedly adopted into several tribes. Brown's special relationship with Native Americans had begun shortly after he moved to Madison and while he was living in what was then the outskirts of town. One winter day, a Ho-Chunk man, Joseph White, came to his door and asked for food. His family was camped in the woods and had run short of supplies. Brown obliged and returned with White to the wigwam in the woods, striking up a friendship with the

Figure 3.1. Charles Brown and Albert Yellow Thunder (Ho-Chunk), who is wearing a Great Plains–style headdress.

family that lasted for many years. Brown returned frequently to the camps of the Ho-Chunk, which were seasonally maintained in the Madison area as late as 1925.[16]

Through the years, Brown expanded his friendships with and ties to Native Americans. Among the many Native American guests to his home were Oliver La Mere; John Blackhawk, from Black River Falls, a descendant of Chief Winneshiek; and Albert Yellow Thunder, from the Wisconsin Dells, a grandson of Yellow Thunder, a noted Ho-Chunk war chief (figure 3.1). From these and other friends, Brown collected Ho-Chunk stories and traditions, some of which pertained to effigy mounds. Although it still cannot be demonstrated with absolute certainty that the builders of the effigy mounds were ancestral to the Ho-Chunk, the perspectives that Brown obtained during this period add immeasurably to an understanding of the belief systems of ancient Native societies.

The mound-preservation effort spearheaded by Brown and the Wisconsin Archeological Society lasted into the 1940s, but the Great Depression and World War II had diminished public interest. The legacy of the effort is visible throughout the state. Just a few of the many mounds and mound groups that owe their existence to the activities of the Wisconsin Archeological Society can be found at Aztalan State Park near Lake Mills; Cutler Park in Waukesha; Indian Mound Park near Chetek; Lake Park in Milwaukee; Man Mound Park near Baraboo; Mound Cemetery in Racine; Myrick Park in La Crosse; and Wyalusing State Park near Prairie du Chien. As a tribute to Brown's own persistence, the Madison area alone has more than twenty-three different locations where mound groups can be visited by the public.

Excavation: The Development of Wisconsin Archaeology

In the nineteenth century, archaeology emerged in the United States as a branch of the broader field of anthropology devoted to the scientific study of the past. Through empirical observation, archaeologists established that mounds and other earthworks were the products of Native societies rather than some "Lost Race." Furthermore, they introduced the idea that variations in the archaeological record could be explained by the fact that ancient North America had been populated by differing Native cultures. But, at the time, no general or local sequence of Native cultures had been worked out, except in the most rudimentary fashion. Even the age of ancient cultures could only be guessed at, except in the southwestern United States, where they could occasionally be directly dated by examination of tree-ring sequences in preserved timbers.

The establishment of a chronology of ancient cultures in Wisconsin and elsewhere in North America became the primary goal of archaeological research in the first half of the twentieth century. Interestingly, the ultimate source of critical information would come not from the mounds but from the camps, villages, and rockshelters where the relationships among superimposed layers of the past could be more easily studied. But since the whole emphasis of preceding archaeological research had been on mounds, mounds remained the most visible and intriguing sources of information on ancient societies for researchers in the early decades of the twentieth century.

Samuel Barrett, one of the first professional American archaeologists, having been awarded one of the first doctorates in anthropology in the United States, joined the Public Museum of the City of Milwaukee in

1909. In 1917 he led excavations of a mound group at the Kratz Creek mound group at Lake Buffalo in Marquette County. The work at Kratz Creek was the initial step in a plan conceived by Barrett to investigate the history of Native people of Wisconsin by conducting a series of controlled excavations at "typical mound groups and other archaeological remains" throughout the state.

Barrett excavated thirty-six of fifty-one conical, linear, and effigy mounds, and the results of the investigation were published in the *Bulletin of the Public Museum of the City of Milwaukee* as part of a series that would publish the findings of mound researchers for the next several decades.[17] Barrett's work was different from previous mound explorations in that many mounds of a single group were examined, allowing for comparisons to be made among mounds. He also broke from nineteenth-century excavation methods by paying close attention to the internal structuring and layering of mound soils, concluding that two different cultures might have been involved. In addition, Barrett discovered that some effigy mounds had been made by first digging "intaglios," or negative images, of mound forms. The intaglios had been filled in and the mound constructed above. The dead had been buried in mounds as cremations, flexed "in the flesh," and as bundles of bones cleaned of flesh. Barrett also reported evidence that mounds were not simply cemeteries. The remains of ceremonial activities were found in the form of stone "altars," "sacrificial" items, evidence of fire, and, most interesting, what Barrett termed "sacred soils"—layers of different colored soils that had not originated on the site. On the floor of one mound, a circle of bright red sand neatly surrounded several bundles of human bones. Barrett speculated that these features and soils had ritual meaning.

Barrett moved the research on mounds conducted by the museum to the Menominee reservation in 1919 and then began an ambitious archaeological excavation at Aztalan, the famous site that contained large flat-topped "temple mounds" and remnants of a great clay-covered wall that enclosed the town. The results of this major work were published as "Ancient Aztalan."[18] On the basis of what he found, Barrett rejected the old notion that the site was somehow related to the Aztecs and instead compared it with similar but larger sites in southern Illinois and in the southeastern United States. The culture that had lived at Aztalan was called Middle Mississippian by archaeologists because of its location in the middle part of the Mississippi River drainage basin.

Also working at the Menominee reservation was Alanson Skinner, a trained ethnologist. He was assisted in the excavations by John Satterlee, a member of the Menominee tribe who also served as an interpreter for ethnological research. Skinner's research was enthusiastically supported by the superintendent of the reservation—his father-in-law—but the digging up of Native graves was not appreciated by other people on the reservation. Some years after the completion of the project, Charles Brown visited the reservation to inspect some Indian mounds and learned that Skinner's work had upset many who had warned that disturbing the dead was dangerous business. As if to confirm their fears, Skinner's wife had died between field seasons, and a short time after he finished the excavations Skinner himself was killed in an automobile accident. Some on the reservation interpreted these tragedies as punishment by angry spirits.[19]

Sadly, but with some notable exceptions, disregard for Native concerns about disturbing graves continued throughout much of the twentieth century in Wisconsin and elsewhere in the United States. For the archaeologists involved, it was a matter of the primacy of science over the religious sensibilities of a rather small group of people. For Native people, the disinterment of their ancestors was sacrilege and a continuing insult. Accordingly, tensions between archaeologists and Native Americans escalated during the heyday of mound excavation.

William C. McKern joined the staff of the Public Museum in 1925 and, in the words of one historian of Wisconsin archaeology, "moved Wisconsin to the forefront of scientific archaeology."[20] In order to gain a better understanding of the ancient cultures that had inhabited the state, McKern, along with Barrett, devised a strategy to sample archaeological sites along an imaginary east-west line that bisected the state, cutting across many river systems and ecological zones. Again, mounds tended to be the focus of attention, although some villages and campsites were also examined. During the 1920s and 1930s, McKern excavated more than a dozen mound groups throughout Wisconsin. Information resulting from this work led to a rudimentary classification of the different ancient cultures that once lived in the region.

During this time, McKern directly challenged Paul Radin's hypothesis about the relationship of the Ho-Chunk to the effigy mounds by establishing that the burials made in effigy mounds at the time of their construction contained no articles of European manufacture. This argued for dating prior to European contact. He went on to reject all of Radin's arguments for the Ho-Chunk as the builders of the mounds, contending that they did not fit the facts. What seems to have been at the center of the disagreement was the increasing conflict between ethnological and archaeological information as a means to reconstruct events. In 1930 McKern wrote: "When ethnological findings are in drastic conflict with known archaeological facts, I do not hesitate to insist that the ethnological data must give way."[21] He used the example of linear mounds that had been found to contain

Figure 3.2. Visitors look on as William C. McKern (*back to camera*) and his crew from the Public Museum of the City of Milwaukee excavate the Schwert Mound on the Mississippi River in Trempealeau County.

burials even though some Native people had earlier offered opinions that they had been built as defensive earthworks or for use in driving game.

But more than anything else, it was McKern's pioneering research on ancient Native pottery styles that led him to eliminate the Ho-Chunk from contention as the effigy mound builders. His inspection of pottery sherds from some habitation sites in areas that had been occupied historically by the Ho-Chunk, along with (ironically) some of Radin's ethnographic evidence on pottery making, convinced McKern that the Ho-Chunk had made a distinctive form of thin-walled pottery from clay mixed with crushed clamshell and decorated with incised geometric patterns, a type of pottery he called Upper Mississippian. In contrast, the mounds he excavated yielded a different type of pottery, tempered with crushed rock and decorated with cord impressions, that he believed was associated with Algonquian-speaking peoples, such as the Menominee and the Potawatomi. This type of pottery came to be referred to as Woodland pottery. Therefore, he thought the Siouan-speaking Ho-Chunk could not have been the builders of the effigy mounds.

McKern's viewpoints and classifications dominated archaeological thought in Wisconsin during the 1930s and 1940s, although research at the time was still hampered by the dearth of archaeological data from habitation sites. As the relationships between Woodland and Upper Mississippian peoples became clearer in the last quarter of the twentieth century, one popular hypothesis would emerge that would credit *both* McKern and Radin for having been right in some respects: the Upper Mississippian people did emerge as the Ho-Chunk (as well as several other related tribes) in the historic period, but the Woodland effigy mound people were, in turn, the ancestors of the Upper Mississippians.

By the early 1940s McKern had acquired sufficient information to develop the first classification of prehistoric cultures for Wisconsin.[22] This classification was defined on the basis of similarities and differences in artifact styles, as well as differing mortuary customs. What McKern termed the Mississippian Pattern was divided into the Middle Mississippian, as represented by Aztalan, and the Upper Mississippian or Oneota, which McKern believed to be ancestral to the Ho-Chunk and Ioway. The Woodland Pattern included the ancient effigy mound people and two other cultures that he linked to the Dakota and the Menominee. The classification included two other cultural phenomena in Wisconsin: Hopewellian, a variant of the famous Hopewell mound builders of Illinois and Ohio, and what McKern termed the Old Copper Industry (now known as the Old Copper Complex) because of the extensive use of copper tools and ornaments. Without proper dating techniques, McKern was unable to date these cultures or clarify their relationships to one another. Furthermore, because few villages and campsites had been explored, the lifestyles of these various peoples were unknown. Both of these topics occupied scholars for the next several decades, changing the course of archaeological research on the mound builders and shifting attention from tombs to the places where people had lived.

The Effigy Mound Tradition

The accumulated information collected by William McKern and his colleagues from their excavations of effigy mounds was summarized by Chandler Rowe in his book *The Effigy Mound Culture of Wisconsin*.[23] Rowe focused on the Raisbeck mound group in southwestern Wisconsin, presenting previously unpublished information that was derived from excavations conducted in 1932 by McKern, but he used for comparison more than four hundred mounds excavated to date, six of which he had dug himself. The purpose of his work was to define the effigy mound phenomenon by providing a comprehensive list of cultural characteristics, such as artifacts, methods of mound construction, basic effigy mound forms, and burial customs. Rowe did one other interesting thing: since the possible connection between effigy mounds and historic tribes, particularly the Ho-Chunk (Winnebago), was still being debated, he sought to put the matter to the test by comparing his list of identifiable effigy mound forms with lists of clans drawn from ethnographic accounts of the Menominee, Chippewa (Ojibwe), Sioux, Fox, Sauk, Winnebago (Ho-Chunk), and Prairie Potawatomi—all tribes that had, at one time or another, lived in Wisconsin. Assuming that the mounds represented clan totems, he reasoned that any tribe whose totem animals resembled the shapes of the mounds might be a candidate for the effigy mound builders. Rowe could not find a good match and, on this basis, confirmed McKern's earlier views that the Ho-Chunk (or any of the others, for that matter) could not have built the mounds. Somewhat illogically, Rowe went beyond this conclusion to suggest that even the clan-totem theory itself should be dismissed as an explanation for effigy mound forms.

Nonetheless, Rowe's study brought together an impressive amount of information on the customs and material culture of the effigy mound builders, even though he could not absolutely anchor it in time. This would await the general application of a technical advance that was in the making as Rowe completed his research—radiocarbon dating.

Dating Effigy Mounds

Until the 1950s, the dating of mounds and other ancient sites was a matter of educated guesswork. But in 1949, Willard Libby, a Chicago chemist, developed a process that revolutionized the field of archaeology. Aside from the basic recognition, in the nineteenth century, of stratigraphic relations of soil layers, there is probably no greater advance in the development of archaeology than radiocarbon dating, a technique for determining the time that has passed since a given organism, whether plant or animal, died. The principles of the technique are relatively simple. All organisms absorb radioactive carbon from the atmosphere. When an organism dies, absorption stops and the carbon decays at a rate that can be measured by special laboratory apparatus. Experience has shown that charcoal is the best substance for radiocarbon dating, but almost any organic material, including bone, can be used. Dates are given by radiocarbon labs in calendar years and are accompanied by a statistical standard deviation. Thus the radiocarbon date of 1200 ± 100 B.C. means that there is a high probability that an organism died between 1300 and 1100 B.C.

Among the first applications of radiocarbon dating in Wisconsin were samples from two mound groups: the Kolterman effigy mound site in Dodge County (A.D. 770 ± 250) and the Wakanda Park site in Menominee (A.D. 1200 ± 200). The dates supported the view that the mounds in Wisconsin are indeed very old.[24]

William Hurley wanted to determine the span of what was then viewed as an effigy mound "culture" when he began what might go down in history as the last major mound excavation in Wisconsin. In 1965 and 1966, while still a student, Hurley dug a total of fifty-six mounds and adjacent camps associated with the Sanders and Bigelow effigy mound sites near Stevens Point in central Wisconsin.[25] The sites are on the northern edge of the effigy mound region. Hurley combined radiocarbon dates taken from charcoal found in the mounds and living areas with data derived from other archaeological sites in Wisconsin to define the effigy mound culture as a tradition that persisted for 1,300 years—from about A.D. 300 to the historic period. He also defined a series of pottery styles characteristic of the effigy mound people that are commonly found in mounds and habitation areas. While he believed that the effigy mound people had continued to build effigy mounds into the time of European contact, he did not identify his candidates for the historical mound builders, although he made a broad nod in the direction of the Dakota Sioux.

Some of Hurley's conclusions were eventually superseded by the work of other archaeologists who argued that he had defined his effigy mound culture much too broadly and had included evidence from sites of other cultures that probably had little to do with effigy mounds. Furthermore, his argument that the effigy mound people persisted into the historic period could not be supported with evidence. Hurley's series of radiocarbon dates from the mounds at the Bigelow and Sanders sites are between A.D. 600 and 1200, a time range that most now agree brackets the effigy mound tradition.

The radiocarbon dates from the Bigelow and Sanders sites provided Hurley with a valuable observation with regard to the construction of effigy mound groups that set the stage for later interpretations: single mound groups had been constructed over a long period of time—perhaps even hundreds of years. The hypothesis that would emerge from this fact is that effigy groups functioned as long-lived ceremonial centers and cemeteries for specific bands or tribes.

From the Mounds to the Camps

By the late 1950s and well before William Hurley undertook his project, it was becoming increasingly clear that mound excavation alone, as a way to reconstruct the past, was approaching a dead end. Certainly there was, and still remains, a need to refine the dating of the various mound-building cultures, but little new information was being found about the people who had built the mounds. Archaeological research had revealed much about the way they had been treated in death but little about their day-to-day lives and the many social, technological, and economic changes that had taken place over millennia. These data could be valuable clues that could help explain the origins and context of mound building.

Aided by advances in technology and methods and fueled by the growth of anthropology departments at universities that provided eager student researchers, archaeology in Wisconsin during the 1950s and 1960s increasingly looked to the places where people had lived for information about the past. As it did, the era of mound digging slowly came to an end. A few mounds were excavated after the 1960s, but primarily to save the remains and other physical data from imminent destruction.

A great part of the new information about the ancient societies of Wisconsin came first from inside caves and beneath rocky overhangs in the deep valleys of southwestern Wisconsin. Generation after generation of Native people had used these rocky places as base camps from which to hunt deer that gathered in the valleys during the winter. The living debris cast aside by these seasonal occupants became sealed by sand, soil, and the disintegrating roofs of the shelters, encapsulating a cultural record. One cave excavated in the late twentieth century—the Gottschall Rockshelter—was found to have at least sixteen feet of alternating cultural and natural deposits. Such places are books on ancient Wisconsin that can be read by a careful archaeologist, layer by layer, ever deeper into the past. One such archaeologist was Warren Wittry, who, as a graduate student, carefully peeled back the layers of time in a number of rockshelter sites in southwestern Wisconsin.[26] Assisted by the judicious use of radiocarbon dating, Wittry was able to develop the first chronological sequence for the region.

Others of this generation of archaeologists explored village sites occupied by many different cultures, producing additional data on changing artifact styles and lifeways in the past. These sites also provided radiocarbon dates that helped place the different cultures in relation to one another. Combining all this information with discoveries made elsewhere in North America, archaeologists by the 1970s were able to construct the general succession of Wisconsin Native cultures extending back more than ten

Table 3.1. Wisconsin Archaeological Chronology

Tradition	Stage
Paleo-Indian	
Early	10,000–8000 B.C.
Late	8000–6000/5000 B.C.
Archaic	
Early	8000–4000 B.C.
Middle	6000–1200 B.C.
Late	1200–100 B.C.
Woodland	
Early	500 B.C.–A.D. 100
Middle	100 B.C.–A.D. 500
Late	Late A.D. 500–1200 (historic period in northern Wisconsin)
Middle Mississippian	A.D. 1000–1200
Upper Mississippian (Oneota)	A.D. 1000–historic period

Source: Robert A. Birmingham, Carol I. Mason, and James B. Stoltman, eds., "Wisconsin Archaeology" [special issue], *Wisconsin Archeologist* 78, no. 1–2 (1997).

Note: Some dates overlap because some traditions or stages lasted longer or started earlier in some areas. In addition, some traditions or stages are partially contemporaneous, such as Oneota, Late Woodland, and Middle Mississippian.

thousand years, expanding and filling in the frameworks and sequences developed by McKern and Wittry. The modern archaeological sequence, which is constantly being refined, now extends human occupation back to thirteen thousand years and is presented in Table 3.1. Advances in radiocarbon since it was first used have contributed heavily to the refinement of the sequence. Previous radiocarbon dates had statistical ranges that spanned hundreds of years; these ranges have been narrowed in many cases to a half century.

The Times They Are a-Changin': Cultural Ecology

During the 1960s, dramatic change not only swept across American society but also influenced the study of human culture itself. Broadly reflecting insights gained by ecology, the study of the relationships of organisms to their environment, the emphasis in anthropology turned to the relationship between culture and the environment. Using ecological and systems models, culture came to be regarded as a complex system of interconnected subsystems broadly adapted to specific natural and social environments. Culture was viewed as the *way* humans make such adaptations. This new view of culture was stimulated by the earlier writings of the anthropologist Julian Steward, who had noticed that societies living in similar environments in different parts of the world had developed many similar characteristics.[27] He and others reasoned that as the environment changed, so did cultural adaptations, leading to "cultural evolution." Thus, it is cultural evolution that accounts for similarities and differences among different societies, both past and present.

The concept of cultural evolution was introduced in the nineteenth century to explain cultural variation. At that time, cultural change was perceived as proceeding in one direction: all societies could be expected to go through similar stages of development. At the bottom level was "savagery." At the top was "civilization," a level that, not surprisingly, resembled the societies of Europe and North America. The nature of this model made it difficult for scholars to accept the mound builders as ancestral to the modern tribes. How could a society like that of the mound builders, obviously advanced well along the line of social evolution, have led to what were perceived as the much simpler Native American societies of the historic period? For obvious reasons, this ethnocentric approach to cultural evolution was soon abandoned. The new view of cultural evolution was multidirectional, acknowledging that societies could develop in any number of ways, depending on their adaptations.

In Wisconsin, as elsewhere, cultural ecology stimulated research into the ways that the different societies had adapted to their environments. Since the economic subsystem of culture is the one that directly interacts with the environment, research tended to emphasize economic issues, such as how the ancient peoples made a living (subsistence) and where they lived on the landscape in relation to a variety of critical natural resources (settlement patterns). Archaeologists also began to collaborate with such scientists as climatologists, palynologists (pollen analysts), and geologists, whose expertise helped reconstruct changes in prehistoric environments and landscapes.

This ecological approach also provided insights into the purpose of mound construction by ancient Native American cultures. In the late 1970s, R. Clark Mallam analyzed the location of effigy mounds in Iowa and showed that their distribution coincided with a biological province consisting of prairie, parkland, and forest that included the richest areas of seasonally recurring plant and animal resources for a people that lived off the land.[28] From this, he suggested that the mound groups were much more than simple cemeteries; rather, they were important ceremonial centers that drew together related families that shared proscribed territories, perhaps seasonally, for a variety of economic, social, and religious activities. The mound groups and the many rituals that were practiced at these sacred places, including burial ceremonies, served to bond people into bands or tribes.

The 1960s and 1970s witnessed other great advances in archaeological theory, methods, and technology. The field of archaeology became even more scientifically oriented, using "harder" sciences as models. It introduced new approaches, such as hypothesis testing, mathematical modeling, and statistical analysis. This trend added even more rigor to archaeological studies but continued the trend of distancing archaeology from the people it studied.

Archaeology also became more specialized. Beginning in the 1970s, archaeologists began to develop specialties, including the identification and analysis of animal- or plant-food remains and the study of certain artifact classes, such as stone tools. Among the specializations that gained prominence during this time was human osteology, the study of human bones. The analysis of human remains was only occasionally done in the past to describe the age and sex of an individual, to note pathologies and examples of violent death, or to make very broad generalizations about a population.

As people trained in osteology became available, however, discoveries of human remains at North American archaeological sites almost always led to study at one level or another. This, in turn, has resulted in new insights into ancient disease vectors, diet and nutrition, life expectancy, and genetic relationships among different cultures. Modern advances in DNA testing have the potential to help answer the question of the relationship of modern Native peoples to specific ancient ancestors, including the mound builders. DNA analysis was conducted on the famous and controversial Kennewick Man, eight-thousand-year-old skeletal remains found on the shores of a Washington State lake that had cranial features unlike those associated with later Native peoples and more like ancient populations of southeast Asia. When the skeleton's DNA was compared to that of modern Native peoples, the results confirmed that the Kennewick Man was indeed an ancestor of later Native populations, despite the biological differences.[29]

Many Native people, however, object to the scientific examination and testing of Native skeletons, and consequently such studies are not routinely undertaken. In the case of the Kennewick Man, archaeologists took DNA samples and did other lengthy but nondestructive analysis over the objections of local Indian nations that wanted the remains immediately reburied under federal law. The archaeologists believed that such an early representative of a Native population had to be studied because he provided critical information concerning the early immigration of humans from Asia to the Americas. The case went to a federal court, which decided in favor of the scientists. After study, the remains of the Kennewick Man were turned over to local Native nations for reburial.

Cultural Resource Management

A national ecology movement and deep public concern about environmental degradation led in the 1960s to important legislation to protect the environment. The landmark National Historic Preservation Act of 1966, for example, instructed federal agencies to help manage the nation's "cultural resources" by ensuring that their actions—such as funding, licensing, and building—did not destroy significant historic or archaeological sites. The measure of "significance" would be whether a property was eligible for listing on the National Register of Historic Places. The property could be a Victorian-era building, an archaeological site such as a Native burial mound, or even a "Traditional Cultural Property" or place that plays a major role in a living community's beliefs, customs, and practices, such as a Native ritual or ceremonial site.

The National Historic Preservation Act also set up State Historic Preservation Offices, which would be responsible for coordinating with federal agencies on matters of preservation and for conducting inventories of significant historic and archaeological sites. The primary way this was accomplished in Wisconsin was through grants given to communities, universities, and historic-preservation organizations. Some years later, the Wisconsin legislature also passed a series of measures designed to protect important historic and prehistoric sites during other publicly regulated projects that modified the landscape.

To help organize the collection of information for preservation purposes, the Wisconsin Historical Society, through the Wisconsin Office of the State Archaeologist, instituted a regional archaeology program that assigned cooperating institutions to research different areas of the state. A significant part of that research concerned mounds. In the late 1980s, for example, the Department of Anthropology at the University of Wisconsin–Milwaukee conducted the first modern inventory of mounds in a nine-county area of southeastern Wisconsin, while the Burnett County Historical Society compiled data on mounds in the northwestern part of the state.[30]

It is impossible to overestimate the impact of cultural research management on archaeologists' understanding of Wisconsin's past. Thousands of development projects, from the building of roads to the construction of sewer systems, have been first studied for their potential impacts on archaeological sites. If impacts could not be avoided, teams of archaeologists carefully excavated the sites in order to preserve the information they contained.

Thousands of ancient sites were found and documented. Spectacular archaeological discoveries were made that literally forced the rewriting of texts. Among them are a village of longhouses near La Crosse that provided a snapshot of life in Wisconsin as Columbus stepped ashore in the Caribbean and several villages in other areas where the effigy mound people may have lived. As a result of cultural resource management, more archaeological work has been conducted in the past few decades than in the preceding 150 years. More information has been collected than can presently be assimilated, guaranteeing dramatic changes in the interpretation of the archaeological record in the future.

Cultural resource management has also presented increasing opportunities for collaboration between Native people and archaeologists, especially in regard to the preservation of Indian mounds and other burial places. A number of federal historic-preservation grants administered by the Historic Preservation Division of the Wisconsin Historical Society went to Native nations such as the Ojibwe and the Ho-Chunk to locate cemeteries and mounds so that they could be preserved for the future.[31] The Dane County parks department used these federal grants to inventory and map mounds in Dane County, assisted by Larry Johns, a surveyor of Oneida nation ancestry.[32] Consequently, the Madison area has some of best mound data in the state. Federal law now requires consultation with Native nations on federally funded, permitted, or licensed projects such as road construction, but consultation is routinely done for other nonfederal projects as well.

Growing concern for Native cultural sensibilities has promoted "in place" preservation of mounds and other Native cemeteries rather than removal of graves to facilitate other land use. Exceptions to this policy have involved consultation with Wisconsin's Native nations. In 1977 road construction threatened six mounds in the Rehbein I mound group near the Kickapoo River in Richland County. Lacking alternative routes for the road, the Department of Transportation contracted with the Wisconsin Historical Society to excavate the mounds. In consultation with the Great Lakes Intertribal Council, the six mounds were later reconstructed nearby and all human remains reinterred.[33] Two mounds in the Bade mound group in Grant County were excavated under similar circumstances in 1980.[34] The mounds were rebuilt elsewhere on the site, and the human remains were reburied three years later under the guidance of Ho-Chunk religious leaders. Since then, however, there has been growing consensus among Native peoples, many archaeologists, and vocal sections of the general public that Wisconsin's surviving burial mounds are too special and sacred to be excavated for any reason other than unavoidable emergencies where human remains have to be saved from destruction.

Continuing dialogue on the matter of the unearthing and disposition of human remains has been mandated by the Native American Graves Protection and Repatriation Act, which requires consultation with appropriate Native nations on the removal of graves on federal land and, if requested, the return of human remains and other sacred items recovered in the past by federal projects.

While general federal and state historic-preservation legislation has helped preserve ancient Native sites, it was Wisconsin's Burial Sites Preservation Law, passed in 1985, that promoted the second great mound-preservation effort in the twentieth century. The law differs from other legislation in that it applies to all activities affecting burial places on both public and private land. The National Historic Preservation Act and equivalent state legislation can be brought into play only when governmental actions are involved. The Burial Sites Preservation Law was enacted when, in the early 1980s, Ojibwe people and archaeologists discovered that their objections alone could not block a housing project from being built on top of an eighteenth-century Ojibwe cemetery.[35] Preservation of burial places was later extended to burial mounds, and the first site to be formally cataloged as a burial place was an effigy mound on Lake Monona that had been a source of controversy since the landowner sought to have the mound removed to make way for a housing project. Since then, hundreds of burial places, both Native and Euro-American, have been saved from destruction, including a considerable number of Indian mounds. Though not everyone has been happy with the application of the law to mounds, the law has enjoyed broad support from citizens, tribal members, and legislators on both sides of the political aisle.

The Meaning of the Mounds: New Research

In growing frustration with the inability of archaeology to explain the meaning and purpose of the mounds, William Hurley concluded an essay on the effigy mounds in 1986 by suggesting that knowledge about why these unique forms were built had not progressed since the days of Increase A. Lapham.[36] But even as he expressed this view, changes in the way that mounds were being studied were again under way.

In reaction to archaeology's emphasis on statistics and objects rather than on people and ideas and to the use of models of cultural change that left out ideology as an important component, some anthropologically trained archaeologists began arguing in the 1970s that if archaeologists were ever really to understand ancient people and cultures, they had to try to view the world as the ancients did, not through the lens of modern culture. They also resurrected the perspective that clues to the ancient worldview can be readily found in the belief systems of more recent Native peoples. In other words, as Charles E. Brown observed in 1911, "ethnological science may greatly assist in our archaeological history."

The opening shot in this revolution focusing on "cultural meanings" was fired in 1976 by the prominent midwestern archaeologist Robert Hall in the pages of the national journal *American Antiquity*. In his article, Hall returned archaeology to the study of Native beliefs to help explain, in part, mysterious circular ditches and earthen enclosures found in the Ohio River valley and elsewhere, as well as ritual features found in mounds in Wisconsin. His point was that archaeologists have "to think in Native American categories and to proceed deductively in this frame of reference." The alternative, he feared, is that "prehistory may never be more than what it has become, the soulless artifact of a dehumanized science."[37]

In other articles and in a book provocatively called *Archaeology of the Soul*, Hall has explored other aspects of mound symbolism from the perspective of Native belief systems and traditions.[38] His premise is always that the dramatic period of mound building could not have come and gone without leaving clues in surviving Native traditions that archaeologists can use to reconstruct ancient ideologies. For example, he points out that things commonly found in mounds such as mucky soils and other offerings from watery environments are used as symbols for renewal of the earth and rebirth of the soul by many Native peoples and that these symbolic objects can be found in more modern rituals and ceremonies.

Using ethnographic information, Hall reopened the debate about the connection of the Ho-Chunk (Winnebago) to effigy mounds by taking Chandler Rowe to task for his faulty analysis of the relationship of effigy mound forms to clan symbols.[39] Hall pointed out that Rowe had ignored some vital pieces of information contained in Native American belief systems that had been presented by Arlow B. Stout, Charles Brown, and Paul Radin almost a half century earlier—notably, that one of the most common mound forms, that of the long-tailed panther, is equivalent to the "water spirits" found in the belief systems and clans of the Ho-Chunk and other native nations. Furthermore, Rowe had failed to see the rather commonsense connection between the thunder clans found in many tribes and the spirit beings called thunderbirds, who make the thunder and are easily recognized among common effigy mound forms. Although Hall did not argue that the Ho-Chunk built the effigy mounds, he did point out that Rowe had failed to eliminate them as candidates.

In perhaps the most dramatic example of the strength of oral traditions and their potential to illuminate the past, Hall used Ho-Chunk stories carefully recorded by Radin to "read" the famous Gottschall Rockshelter paintings.[40] The faded paintings were found by a child on the wall of a cave on the family farm in the 1980s and were documented by Robert Salzer. Among the paintings are opposing human beings, some much larger than others, as well as depictions of a turtle and a falcon or hawk. Hall was able to relate these figures to stories involving Red Horn, a legendary culture hero to the Ho-Chunk and to the closely related Ioway.[41] The Red Horn sagas are part of a cycle of traditions that are considered sacred and that must be passed down without modification. Members of the medicine society keep such sacred stories, but Radin obtained the stories from former medicine society members who had abandoned traditional ways, causing many Ho-Chunk to resent and mistrust Radin's information.

As a testament to the strength of oral traditions, the Gottschall paintings go back nearly one thousand years, while the story they tell comes from the Ho-Chunk in the early part of the twentieth century. Since then, archaeologists have connected Red Horn and related culture heroes and spirit beings to other ancient art and imagery, such as paintings in another ritual cave in Missouri.[42]

The use of Native traditions, worldview, and cosmology to interpret ancient cultural past cultural behavior has been called an "ideological approach" since these aspects of culture are central to ancient societies and are represented in artwork and many aspects of material culture, burial patterns, and monument building. With regard to the latter, the ideological approach adopts the position that one cannot understand what ancient people built without understanding what they believed.

This approach has been key to the study of the cultural meanings of mounds, beyond their role as places to put the dead. Analyzing the symbolism of pit features, ash and rock layers, earthen fills, scattered human bones, and other offerings found in effigy mound groups in Iowa, David Benn, Arthur Bettis, and R. Clark Mallam discerned major differences between the beliefs of the effigy mound peoples and those of the mound builders who preceded them.[43] From the physical remains of ancient ceremonial practices, they inferred that the ideological concerns of effigy mound builders reflected a need to maintain balance and harmony between human beings and the natural world by calling on the spirit world. In one study of effigy mounds in Iowa, Clark Mallam referred to the phenomena as "Ideology from the Earth."[44]

Archaeologists further suggested that dissimilarities in the mounds were clues to changing social arrangements and economic practices—an observation that is being further built upon as archaeologists come to understand that the mound-building peoples were not monolithic cultures but were composed of shifting coalitions of largely independent communities that shared religious traditions with one another to varying degrees.

More recent works by the authors of this book expand on these themes. The first edition of *Indian Mounds of Wisconsin* and a follow-up article on the meaning of effigy mounds furthered the case, first presented by Hall, that effigy mounds in particular reflected an underlying cosmology that divided the world into upper and lower realms and subdivided the lower into earth and watery underworld dimensions.[45] This worldview is reflected in clan organizations of the Ho-Chunk and other Native peoples who divide clans named for animal and spirit beings into upper or lower divisions, with thunderbird and other bird clans in the upper division and earth and water animals and supernatural beings in the lower. The mound builders sometimes used topographic features to model these relationships vertically and/or horizontally on the natural landscape, creating what may be maps of ancient cosmology and social systems. Bird mounds, for example, often occupy higher elevations, whereas water forms such as long-tailed water spirits are almost always directly associated with water bodies and, often, springs that are thought to be the abodes of these supernatural beings. One book-length case study by Birmingham examined the vast effigy mound landscape and found a clear relationship between types of effigy mounds and topographic and natural landscape features.[46]

The Birmingham study further proposed that the mounds were not simply spirit beings but ancestors reincarnated and reanimated at the places on the natural landscape where they were thought to continue on in spirit form, incorporating the dead in an ongoing cycle of rebirth and renewal of the earth and its people. In this view, the effigy mound ceremonial landscapes are living landscapes rather than static cemeteries marked only by symbolic earthen tombstone-like monuments.

Anthropologists have drawn the conclusion that a dualistic view of the world and the social structures derived from it were present in various forms throughout the Americas.[47] This view of the world, in fact, appears to be culturally universal. Opposite—yet necessarily complementary—upper and lower worlds and forces are a widespread concept across the globe. The concept of opposition, drawn from the contrasts in the natural world such as day/night, winter/summer, life/death, left/right, and male/female, are deeply embedded in human consciousness, our sensory perceptions, and the binary workings of the brain itself.[48] It is no accident that modern-day computers operate using binary codes. This new direction differs from older and more traditional archaeological approaches in that it focuses on cultural meanings as inferred from both archaeological evidence and Native traditions.

Elsewhere, an ideological approach has been widely used to explore the meanings of ancient art, ritual objects, the design of houses, and the layout of whole communities and ceremonial constructions and landscapes. But this view is not without its critics. Many researchers point out that it is impossible to crawl inside the heads of ancient people and that attempts to do so can lead to erroneous interpretations of the past. As William McKern and others argued many years ago, they assert that archaeology can ultimately describe only what people did; it is not within its capacity to attribute ideological motivations. Likewise, some archaeologists are deeply concerned about the uncritical use of oral traditions and "mythic history" as sources for credible information, citing such potential problems as alterations in the transmission of information from generation to generation, inaccurate translations, recorder bias, and reliance on only a few unrepresentative informants.[49]

Nevertheless, the serious consideration of such "distinct patterns of thought" and the reintegration of Native worldviews and traditions into archaeological studies have proved to be an interesting and exciting direction in the search for the mound builders. They give researchers much to think about regarding the meanings and purposes of the mounds and add a much-needed human dimension to the study of the mound builders.

Other New Research

With the aid of new tools, perspectives, comparative evidence, and research questions, mound research in Wisconsin has greatly accelerated over the past several decades, expanding in many other directions. New information and new perspectives have come not from opening more mounds, owing to both state law that protects mounds as burial places and sensitivity to concerns of Native nations, but in many cases from reanalysis of data acquired during the great wave of mound excavation in the early twentieth century century and occasionally thereafter.

State Archaeologist John Broihahn and Amy Rosebrough at the Wisconsin Historical Society, for example, reanalyzed data from Milwaukee Public Museum excavations at the Raisbeck mound group, the largest remaining cluster of effigy mounds in Wisconsin, and provided new and exciting insights into the effigy mound people. Appropriately, the lengthy study was funded by royalties received by Wisconsin Historical Society from the first edition of *Indian of Mounds of Wisconsin*. Faculty members at major universities encouraged graduate students with an interest in mounds to pore over other research, with the advantage of insights gained since the original investigations of early excavations and thus profiting from modern insights and tools that have provided new details and conclusions.[50]

Especially important with regard to the mysterious effigy mounds, the dominant and unique aspect of mound building in Wisconsin during the first millennium, has been the PhD dissertation of the coauthor of this book, Amy Rosebrough, the first comprehensive study to refer to the Effigy Mound Ceremonial Complex.[51] Among other things, this work provides descriptions and maps of every effigy mound and mound group for which information has been documented, and this will provide a basis for many new studies for a long time to come.

Among valuable recent studies are those derived from the field of osteology that have used nondestructive methods to examine human remains recovered from previous mound excavations.[52] Many of these were stimulated by the Native American Graves Protection and Repatriation Act, which requires federally funded institutions to inventory collections of human remains and to consult with appropriate Native nations regarding the return of the remains for reburial. Such studies have been invaluable in identifying patterns of disease, pathology, diet and health, biological relationships, and trauma from many periods of time.

Many new tools are now available for the study of mounds without the necessity of excavation. In their modern analysis of the Raisbeck site, for example, Broihahn and Rosebrough employed recently available LiDAR (Light Detection and Ranging) mapping to gain an accurate overview of the sprawling mound landscape and, in doing so, discovered mounds that had been overlooked or obscured during early twentieth-century fieldwork. LiDAR imagery is made by satellite or airborne lasers that map just the surface of the ground or other solid objects, ignoring reflections from higher obscuring vegetation.

All of this new and continuing research has added greatly to the story of mound builders. The overall picture keeps changing, but, as it does, it is becoming progressively clearer, steadily building on information acquired during 175 years of study.

4

Wisconsin before the Mound Builders

The story of the mound builders began when the first people came into what is the state of Wisconsin about thirteen thousand years ago. People first came to the Americas during the end of the great Ice Age as part of the spread of the modern human species that began in the Old World, tens of thousands of years in the past. How and exactly when people came to the Americas have been the great questions in American archaeology.

The Paleo-Indian Tradition in Wisconsin

The dates of the arrival of humans in Wisconsin are relatively easy to approximate because before twelve thousand to thirteen thousand years ago mountainous glaciers covered much of the land, except for the southwestern "driftless" area, preventing human settlement. As the Ice Age ended, the glaciers slowly melted, and people colonized the area. Over much of the state, these people, called Paleo-Indians by archaeologists, moved in an environment that had been shaped and influenced by glaciers.[1] Torrents of water and dirt from the melting ice fronts formed huge river channels, great and cold glacial lakes, and vast outwash plains of sand and gravel. In many areas, the landscape had been dramatically sculpted by glaciers, leaving behind hills—drumlins, moraines, and kames—and deep kettles, created by huge blocks of detached ice, that would later become the familiar lakes of the state. During this time of environmental change, the vegetation and wildlife were very different from the plants and animals in present-day Wisconsin. Nearer to the wasting glacial front was tundra, frozen and barren ground. Farther away were muskeg swamps and forests of spruce and fir. In some of these areas, large lumbering mammoth and mastodon browsed. Caribou herds undoubtedly migrated seasonally northward and southward over hundreds of miles. Now-extinct forms of bison, giant beaver, and other Ice Age animals could be found, as well as the more familiar elk and moose. Smaller animals, such as birds, rabbits, and aquatic life, also shared the Paleo-Indian world.

Paleo-Indians are known in Wisconsin from hundreds of scattered locations where their distinctive stone spear points and other stone tools have been found. The earliest of the spear tips or projectile points were fashioned with channels or flutes so they could be easily attached to wooden shafts. Later Paleo-Indian spear points are larger, in beautifully made lanceolate styles. Both of these Paleo-Indian styles found in Wisconsin are remarkably similar to those found throughout North America, indicating that the techniques for making tools were widely shared.

The Paleo-Indian population was very small, and these people's camp or habitation sites are rarely found. Further, because of the extreme age of Paleo-Indian sites, day-to-day items of a more perishable nature are rarely preserved. Thus there remain few clues from which to reconstruct Paleo-Indian lifestyles. A series of "bone beds" in Kenosha County near Lake Michigan offers evidence that Wisconsin's first people butchered mammoths for food (figures 4.1, 4.2).[2] Whether they systematically hunted these huge beasts or simply scavenged dead or dying mammoths is yet to be learned.

What physical evidence does exist suggests that the Paleo-Indians traveled great distances in small family groups in order to make a living off a comparatively sparse and barren landscape, probably erecting temporary shelters at many different locations. Every so often, perhaps annually, these small groups would gather to undertake communal hunts and to exchange goods and news. Such meetings also would have been important opportunities for people to find spouses outside the family. One gathering place was the Skare site on the Yahara River between Lakes Waubesa and Kegonsa in modern-day Wisconsin, occupied as early as 9000 B.C.[3] Through the years artifact collectors have reportedly found fluted points at the site dating as early as 11,000 B.C. and professional investigations as well as artifact collecting have yielded large numbers of later and smaller fluted points. Other artifacts include distinctive tools for working bone and scraping hides. Both the points and the tools suggest that the Skare site functioned as a communal base camp for hunting herd animals. Among the possibilities is that the ancient hunters followed the herds of caribou in small bands during the animals' annual lengthy north-to-south migrations, and the Skare site, located on a point in the vast glacial lake, may have been a particularly good place for communal hunters to intercept the migrating herds. Modern

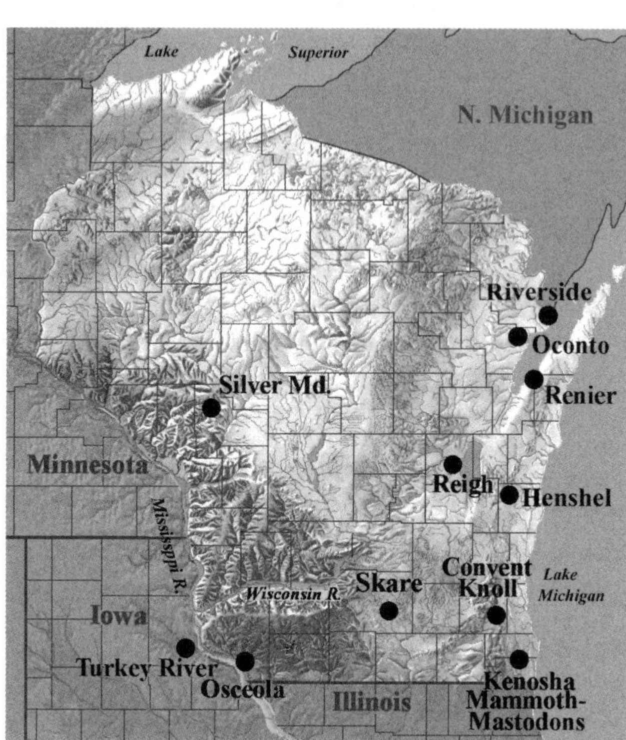
Lake
Superior
N. Michigan
Riverside
Oconto
Renier
Silver Md.
Minnesota
Reigh
Henshel
Mississppi R.
Convent
Knoll
Lake
Michigan
Wisconsin R.
Skare
Iowa
Turkey River
Osceola
Illinois
Kenosha
Mammoth-
Mastodons

THE HEBIOR MAMMOTH

Figure 4.3. Paleo-Indian spear points from the Skare site, near Madison, Wisconsin. Points a, b, and c are fluted and date to around eleven thousand years ago; points b and c are made from Hixton Silicified Sandstone. Points d, e, and f date to the later Paleo-Indian; points e and f are made from Illinois Moline Chert.

migrations of caribou in Canada are known to take them across bodies of water instead of around them, and the swimming animals can easily be dispatched from boats.

Among the items used and exchanged at the Skare site were special types of colored stone used to make spear points, knives, and other tools (figure 4.3). Such stone was much preferred by people of that time and sometimes came from geological sources many hundreds of miles from where the tools were later found. The Paleo-Indians probably believed that these stones were imbued with special magical or supernatural characteristics, explaining their wide distribution. One type of stone found at the

Figure 4.1 (*top left*). Location of sites mentioned in text.

Figure 4.2 (*bottom left*). Reconstructed Kenosha County mammoth on display at the Milwaukee Public Museum.

Skare site and at many other places in Wisconsin is called Moline chert because of its source at Moline, Illinois, near the confluence of the Rock and Mississippi Rivers. It is dark blue and often banded with light and dark colors.[4] Paleo-Indians in the Upper Midwest, especially in northeastern Illinois and Wisconsin, also extracted different kinds of chert from narrow stream valleys where erosion of softer rock has left harder tool stone exposed in shelves. People carried the raw stone to adjacent camps where they worked the stone into rough forms that could be easily transported and later formed into appropriate implements. Fluted points of Moline chert are much more numerous in Wisconsin than in Illinois, where the chert originated, indicating that the significance of the stone increased with distance.[5]

A second stone heavily used and exchanged in Wisconsin and in nearby areas is Hixton Silicified Sandstone, a grainy quartzite-like stone that is often white, honey colored, or red. Hixton Silicified Sandstone is found only at a small Jackson County mountain called Silver Mound, near Hixton, Wisconsin, where there are numerous quarries. The surrounding landscape is strewn with dense workshop sites with artifacts from many cultural periods, including Paleo-Indian. A study of several hundred early Paleo-Indian fluted points from throughout Wisconsin and northern Illinois shows that nearly 40 percent were made from this rock.[6] Hixton Silicified Sandstone continued to play an important role in the belief systems of Wisconsin people over the next ten thousand years, as indicated by the use and wide distribution of artifacts made from this rock during certain time periods.

Like all human beings, the Paleo-Indians therefore undoubtedly had a rich and elaborate spiritual life. Like that of later Native people, the world of the Paleo-Indians probably was shared with a number of spirit beings, deities, and supernatural forces. And, like those of their descendants, these were surely inspired by the animal life around them: birds, aquatic life, and mammals, including the huge mastodon and mammoth. The Paleo-Indians undoubtedly believed in some sort of afterlife, as did all humans of the time, and they engaged in special ceremonies upon the death of a member of the group. The oldest burial in Wisconsin thus far discovered is that of a single individual who was cremated approximately nine thousand years ago and buried in a pit in Brown County, near Green Bay.[7] The burial pit, called the Renier site, included a number of heat-shattered spear points meant to accompany the individual to the afterlife and/or to honor the dead individual. Many of these points were made from Hixton Silicified Sandstone obtained from Silver Mound, 125 miles to the west.

Cremation is a custom shared by many people of the world, past and present, and has many different meanings. For the highly mobile Paleo-Indians, the cremation of corpses may have provided a convenient way to transport the remains over long distances to the desired place of burial. Whatever the reason, there is evidence that the custom of ritual burning was widespread. At three other locations in northern Wisconsin, clusters of burned spear points similar to those found at Renier have been recovered.[8] Human bone was not found with these artifacts, but archaeologists suspect that it long ago disintegrated.

The Archaic Tradition: Territories, Trade, and Cemeteries

Over the next several thousand years, climatic change continued to alter the landscape of Wisconsin. The climate warmed, and the North American glacial environment retreated north into present-day Canada. Many animals, such as the mammoth and mastodon, became extinct, but other more familiar and easily hunted species, such as moose, elk, and, especially, deer, proliferated. Deciduous forests and grasslands replaced the relatively unproductive spruce forests, providing a variety of edible plants and supporting abundant game. Warmer rivers and streams replaced the rapidly running and frigid glacial discharge streams and offered abundant aquatic life, including many species of fish and mussels. The many lakes and wetlands left in the wake of the glaciers also provided habitat for fish, waterfowl, and aquatic mammals.

Over time, the descendants of the Paleo-Indians adapted to these resource-rich environments by developing new hunting and gathering strategies and by introducing a number of technological innovations: axes for chopping wood, stone implements for grinding and processing plant foods, specialized gear for fishing, and a long wooden spear thrower or atlatl for increasing the effectiveness of hunting by increasing velocity and precision. This long period of cultural change has been called the Archaic period or tradition and has been dated between circa 8000 and 500 B.C.[9]

As with the Paleo-Indian period, much of the early part of the Archaic period is shrouded in mystery, again because of the very low population density. Like the Paleo-Indians, people of the early parts of the Archaic era are known primarily for their distinctive spear points and knives. From the locations of these, it is surmised that early Archaic people lived much like their Paleo-Indian ancestors, ranging widely over the landscape.

There is better evidence for the later part of the Archaic, as the increasing availability of seasonally recurring food resources promoted tremendous growth in population and important changes in economic strategies. It no longer was necessary to travel vast distances to find food. By scheduling hunting and collecting activities to coincide with the maximum availability of the food—such as spawning fish, herding animals, seeding plants, and migrating birds—families and bands were able to inhabit much smaller territories. A typical year in the life of people at the end of the Archaic in southeastern Wisconsin may have found them on lake shores and river terraces in summer, where many different plant and animal foods, including fish, could be found; near oak-hickory groves in autumn, where protein-rich nuts and acorns could be gathered; and, in winter, under rock overhangs in sheltered valleys, where deer could be hunted. As a consequence of shrinking band territories, clear regional cultural differences among peoples began to emerge about three thousand years ago, as indicated by differing subsistence strategies, artifact styles, and other customs.

A tendency to stay in one area for longer periods of time stimulated other important social and economic changes. One was experimentation with plant cultivation, which led to the domestication of certain wild plant species that provided starchy seeds for consumption. Among them were marsh elder, chenopodium or goosefoot, and sunflower. Native Americans began to control their food sources by planting and encouraging the growth of these plants near major camps rather than gathering wild seeds over large areas. Although these local plants never became a major part of the diet, they were a significant and reliable supplement. Most important, the cultivation of these plants predisposed people in the Midwest to adopt plants that had been domesticated elsewhere—squash from the Gulf coast, corn and beans from Mexico—and that would much later revolutionize Native American life.

Another important development was the expansion of trade. Not all band territories were comparable in the types of resources they supplied to meet the needs of daily life, including food, stone for tools, and animal skins for clothing. Furthermore, it can be expected that local shortages in critical resources, such as food, occurred from time to time. Without a mechanism for evening out these disparities, the potential for conflict between groups, even warfare, was very real. Formal trade relationships among neighboring bands helped reduce conflict by guaranteeing the flow of critical resources, although apparently this did not always work. To keep trade networks open and continually running, special items of great symbolic value were exchanged. The ceremonial exchange of such items no doubt facilitated the trade of more commonplace items when they were needed. In one spectacular development, called the Old Copper Complex, people in the eastern part of the state exchanged objects of supernatural power, but mostly among themselves.

Over time, other exotic goods were exchanged that ultimately linked much of eastern North America in one vast trade network. Trade items found at Archaic sites in Wisconsin include seashells from the Atlantic Ocean, blue-gray "hornstone" chert from Indiana, and obsidian or volcanic glass from the Yellowstone area of Wyoming.

A third trend that grew out of the development of smaller, fixed territories was the elaboration of rituals related to the burial of the dead and the selection of places within these territories as permanent symbols of the rights of the social group to the land and its resources. Cemeteries become territorial markers in which social groups staked their claim to a place in the world by virtue of links to the ancestors buried there.

The Great Warming

These trends, however, were not continuous and spread gradually over the state as a whole. A global climate shift beginning about 4000 B.C. caused a several-thousand-year drought called the Hypsithermal or Mid-Holocene Warm climate, characterized by temperatures much warmer than those of today.[10] Large areas of the Midwest were affected as water tables dropped, streams dried up, and grasslands expanded at the expense of forests. The effect was to restrict humans and animals to better-watered areas. Some upland areas were virtually abandoned except for special purposes such as the extraction of stone for making implements.[11] Many sites established along water courses during this time would have been destroyed or covered by water when the rains returned much later. Excavations at the few identified habitation sites occupied between 4000 and 3000 B.C. in south-central and southwestern Wisconsin show that these were short-term camps located near wooded areas in wetter places. At the Crow Hollow site near the Kickapoo River, charred fragments of walnuts and hickory nuts were found in ancient shallow pits.[12] Protein- rich nuts and acorns, gathered in fall, would remain an extremely important part of the diet and subsistence for peoples of the Upper Midwest up to historic times. Evidence for hunting comes from deer remains as well as the discovery of projectile points for hunting and scrapers used for hide preparation.

The Old Copper Complex

A completely different environment developed along and near the shores of Lake Michigan because of a dramatic rise in the lake level. This was not the result of increased rainfall here but rather the effects of geological events associated with the end of the Ice Age. As glaciers retreated north, the land depressed by the great burden rebounded, sending water in Lake Superior southward and expanding Lake Michigan and raising its water level to a point twenty feet higher than today's level,[13] creating an environment along and near the lake that was much moister than the dry conditions that prevailed elsewhere. The expanded lake would have affected inland climates, as Lake Michigan does today, moderating the climate, making it moister, and providing a richer variety of plant and animal foods. This, in turn, attracted an enormous human population. The expansion of the lake over shallower areas provided easy access to fish, stimulating a fishing complex along the lake. Among the fish species sought would have been the huge bottom-dwelling sturgeon, which came into the shallow areas and swam upriver to spawn, where they could be easily speared or harpooned in great quantity. The long-lived sturgeon can attain lengths of more than six feet and weigh up to 200 pounds. Sturgeon fishing played a major role in the traditional economy of the Menominee, who have long occupied northeastern Wisconsin along Lake Michigan, and it continues to be a practice of ceremonial and economic importance today. Sturgeon is also one of the Menominee clans.

As populations grew along the lake and in adjacent areas, an extraordinary material culture developed that included the trade of vast numbers of copper implements, exchanged mostly as finished items. Some of these were related to fishing, but there were many different objects: axes, adzes, gouges, many types of spear points, knives, and ornaments (figure 4.4). There are no copper deposits in the bedrock of the region, although chunks of copper, small and large, are still occasionally found in eastern Wisconsin that have been ripped up from northerly sources and redeposited by glaciers. Copper was mined in northern Michigan and Isle Royale in Lake Superior, where thousands of quarry pits can still be seen. After extraction from veins, copper was worked into implements by hammering it with hard stones and then heating and cooling it with water, a process called annealing. This process was repeated until the desired implement was completed.

The use of copper dates back as early as 5500 B.C. in Wisconsin, making it among the earliest metallurgies in the world.[14] Copper cannot be directly dated, but occasionally remnants of wooden shafts and other organic matter that have adhered to the copper implements are preserved by copper salts that are toxic to bacteria that would normally cause decay of the wood, allowing the use of radiocarbon dating.

From 4000 B.C. to 1500 B.C., exchange and trade in copper became so common that archaeologists once referred to the phenomenon as the Old Copper Culture. In recognition of the fact that the use and trade of copper probably involved people of different cultural backgrounds, they are now known as the Old Copper Complex, the word "complex" referring to a shared customs.

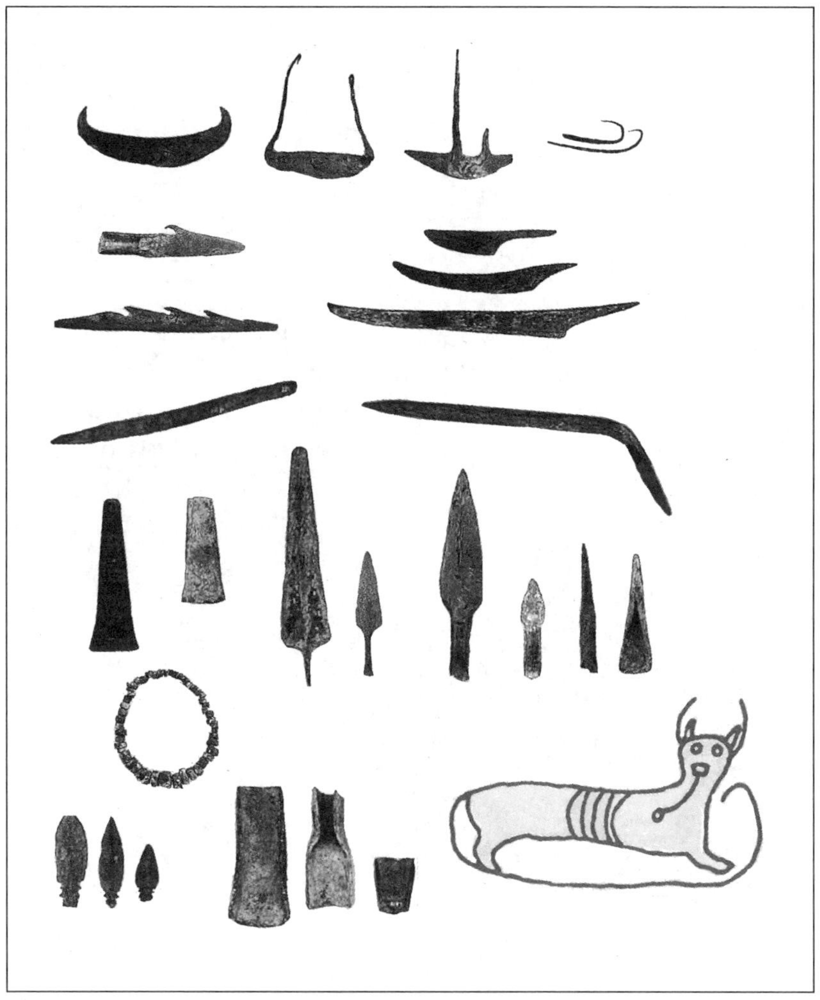

Figure 4.4. Old Copper Complex weapons and tools from the collections of the Milwaukee Public Museum. *Bottom right*: drawing of Mishipizheu on an 1830 Ojibwe birchbark song scroll.

Tens of thousands of copper artifacts have been found over the years (figure 4.5). Many are surface finds turned up by artifact collectors, but now collectors use modern metal detectors and unfortunately damage many potentially important copper artifacts by digging them out. Most of this trade and exchange occurred between local populations in northern, central, and eastern Wisconsin and parts of Michigan, but similar copper artifacts have been found in more distant places such as the eastern Great

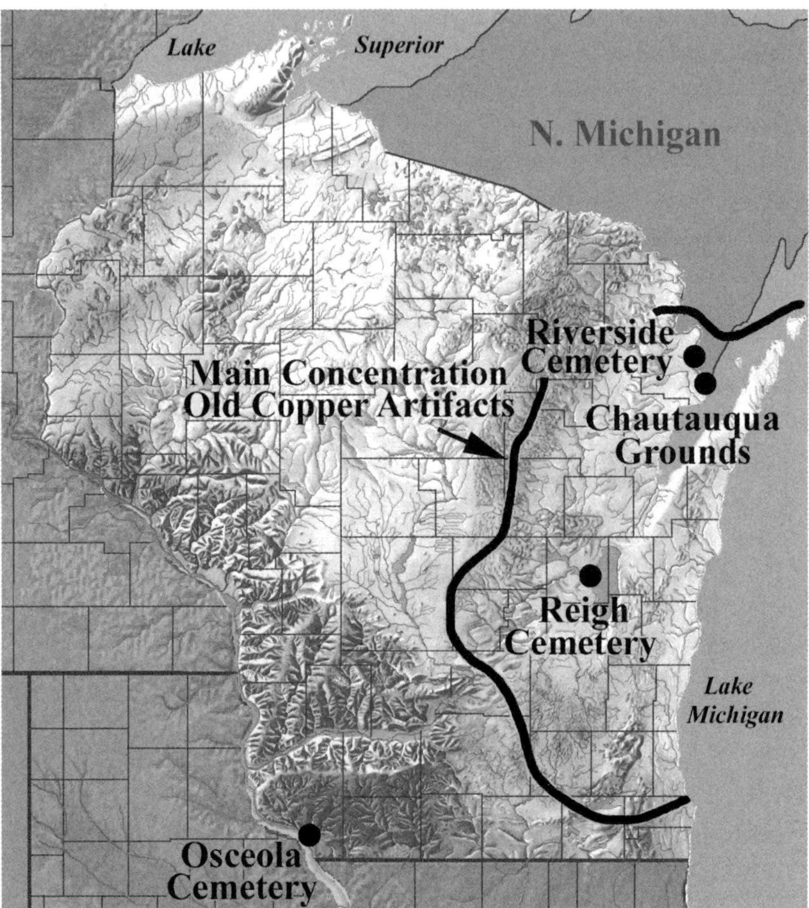

Figure 4.5. Large numbers of Old Copper artifacts have been found in Wisconsin and Upper Michigan. This map shows the main concentration of Old Copper artifacts in Wisconsin along with sites mentioned in the text.

Plains, Canada, and the eastern seaboard, indicating the development of vast trade networks among Archaic peoples.[15] Copper objects also have been found at a series of sites in Wisconsin along the Mississippi and lower Wisconsin Rivers, well away from the main Old Copper region to the east; perhaps this area, with its strategic location on North America's main transportation route for people, goods, and ideas, served as an early external trade center. Among the sites here is the earliest cemetery known in Wisconsin, called the Osceola site.

Some Old Copper implements were directly related to fishing, reflecting the growth of this enterprise. They include socketed harpoons for catching large fish, such as sturgeon, and even fishhooks. Some long, heavy bars with wear at the ends may have been used to make holes in the lake ice for winter fishing. Woodworking tools such as adzes and gouges would have been useful in making dug-out canoes from logs. Preserved dugout canoes have been dated back several thousand years in the western Great Lake areas and were used by the peoples of the area along with birch-bark canoes into the nineteenth century. The Kenosha Public Museum in Wisconsin displays a dugout radiocarbon-dated to two thousand years ago. Some Old Copper artifacts are almost identical to slate or metal ulus used by the much later Arctic-dwelling Inuit for slicing fish and other meat. One of the few excavated Old Copper settlements or camps, the Chautauqua Grounds site, is located at the mouth of the Menominee River and produced a variety of fishing-related copper artifacts.[16]

The mystery of the Old Copper Complex is why copper was so important for the people in this particular region, so far from its major sources. At first glance it would seem that use of metal would have a technological advantage over the stone and bone generally used for the production of implements, and certainly it is true that the ease of working the soft metal made it possible to form some objects that could not easily have been made with stone, such as gouges used for woodworking, socketed harpoons for fishing, and some ornamental objects. However, copper is much less durable than stone, and the crafting of copper into implements is much more labor intensive, as described earlier. Moreover, stone tools, such as spears, knives, and axes that parallel many copper implements, continued to be made at the same time. An overall technological advantage also does not explain the drop in the use of copper even as societies in the area became more complex. After about 1200 B.C., the use of copper in the region was largely restricted to the manufacture of ornaments, objects of ritual importance, and sharp pointed awls useful in turning hides into clothing.

If copper offered no real technological and economic advantages over the more easily obtained and worked stone and bone, then why was it so important to the people at this time? This question is similar in some respects to the question of why the Paleo-Indian people made their spear points from certain exotic stones when other easily chipped stone was abundant. In recent decades, archaeologists have focused on the symbolic qualities of copper in traditional Native beliefs, which associate it with supernatural forces; therefore, it was believed, copper items were imbued with "wonderful power," in the words of the archaeologist Susan Martin.[17]

Martin cites the tradition of the northerly peoples such as the Ojibwe and the Menominee that evoked the powers of the watery underworld and in particular a great horned monster called Mishipeshu, Mishipizheu, or

Gitche-anah-bezhe, alternately translated as the Great Lynx, the Great Underground, or the Underwater Wildcat and often described as having a long copper tail.[18] In the seventeenth century, the Ottawa told the Jesuit missionary Claude Allouez that they made sacrifices to Mishipeshu in order to calm lake waters and bring sturgeon and that they carried power-leaden copper nuggets in their medicine bags.[19] Painted images of Mishipeshu can be found on ancient art panels that adorn rock ledges overlooking the waters of lakes across the north. The Menominee, who still reside in the area of the Old Copper Complex in northeastern Wisconsin, also trace their ancestral roots to an underground bear with a copper tail.

The exchange of copper involved not useful items—often identical types of implements appear to have been swapped in the trades—but the offering and receipt of gifts of power. Gift exchanges of such power-charged objects to secure friendly relations among different groups of people makes sense in an area so packed with people that violent conflict over resources would otherwise be inevitable.

First Cemeteries

The earliest cemeteries recorded in Wisconsin appeared between 4000 and 1500 B.C. and were linked to the Old Copper Complex. One is the aforementioned Osceola site on the Mississippi River in Grant County, in which five hundred people were buried at various times in a large grave pit.[20] Few grave offerings accompanied burial rituals, but there were some copper objects. The dead were interred at Osceola as bundles of bones or, in a few cases, as cremated bone. The bone bundles take the form of "secondary burials" or "reburials," which continued to be common practice among some Native peoples in North America right up to the time of European contact. After death, the body was left out on a scaffold or sometimes even buried in the ground until it decomposed (figure 4.6). At an appointed time, the bones of all those who had died during a certain interval were gathered, carefully scraped clean, and buried together in one place amidst great ceremony.

A similar ritual was recorded with a fair amount of disgust in the seventeenth century by Jesuit missionaries living among the Huron of the eastern Great Lakes region.[21] Their descriptions of the "Feast of the Dead" celebrated by the Huron provide insight into what might have happened at Archaic cemeteries thousands of years earlier. The Feast of the Dead lasted for several days but was conducted only once every eight to twelve years by a host village. The purpose of the ceremony was to rebury in a common grave all those who had died in years past. Relatives disinterred or otherwise collected

Figure 4.6. Many Native peoples placed the dead on scaffolds until the bodies decomposed, eventually gathering and burying the bones.

the remains of their kin, cleaned the bones, and hung the robe-covered bone bundles on poles surrounding the large pit. After a time, all the bone bundles, along with grave offerings, were placed in the pit so that the spirits of friends and relatives could be together. The grave was then covered.

The Feast of the Dead was more than a mortuary ritual. It reinforced the common identity of the Huron and even helped create alliances with others. Feasts and other social activities accompanied the reburial, and neighboring villagers were invited to participate in ceremonies and festivities. In a version of the ceremony, later documented for the western Great Lakes, several tribes formed important political and economic alliances by participating in this mortuary ritual.[22]

Other large Old Copper–period cemeteries are located within the main area of copper use and exchange in eastern Wisconsin. These contain copper objects intended as grave offerings as well as other symbolic objects from other regions of North America. These cemeteries include the Reigh site on Lake Winnebago near Oshkosh and the Oconto site near Lake Michigan.[23] These contrast with Osceola sites in that they contained multiple ossuaries containing the remains of several individuals, and the bodies were usually fully articulated and extended "in the flesh," indicating that they were buried soon after death, although there were also some bone bundles and cremations. The fact that most people were buried as they died suggests that their settlements were located nearby. Grave goods, including numerous copper objects, accompanied specific individuals, suggesting the rise of social differences. One individual at Reigh was interred with a sandal-shaped ornament called a gorget, made from seashell, and another was accompanied by a feathered headdress like those worn by "chiefs" in later Plains societies but entirely made of copper.

The Red Ochre Complex

By 1200 B.C. the climate had changed again, bringing both cooler and much wetter weather to Wisconsin and even leading to periodic flooding of water courses.[24] In response, populations spread out and continued to grow. Artifacts from the Late Archaic are commonly found throughout the southern Wisconsin landscape in all environmental zones. The Mid-Holocene Warm climate had ended, and so had the Old Copper Complex, which was gradually replaced by another ceremonial movement spreading from the east called the Red Ochre Complex, dated between 1200 and 500 B.C.[25] The new complex takes its name from the new custom of spreading layers of red ochre in graves. Red ochre was made by grinding hematite, an iron oxide, into a powder. By adding fluid to the powder, Native people also used red ochre as a pigment for paint into the period of European contact. The use of copper decreased and was now largely restricted to the manufacture of such ornaments as beads. At the same time there was an increase in burials of exotic and beautiful objects obtained through long-distance trade (figure 4.7). There is strong evidence of social ranking but also of increasing intergroup violence and warfare as territories became smaller and better defined.

Figure 4.7. Red Ochre Complex ceremonial blades. The one on the right has been called a "Turkey Tail."

The Riverside cemetery, located on the Menominee River along the Wisconsin/Michigan border near its mouth at Lake Michigan, shows the transition between the Old Copper and the Red Ochre ceremonial complexes.[26] The cemetery, excavated in the late 1950s, is very near the earlier Old Copper Chautauqua Grounds habitation site, and some of the copper items interred with the dead are also fishing oriented, such as ulu-like crescents. Other grave objects included copper celts, small axe-like tools and weapons; copper projectile points; and a large number of ceremonial chert blades from far-off places but typical of the Red Ochre Complex, as were layers of red ochre found in some graves. One particularly notable artifact found in the cemetery was a block of black obsidian or volcanic glass from the Yellowstone area of Wyoming.

Both adults and children were buried at the site with high-status items. This indicates that inherited status passed through lineages and families and marks, for the first time in Wisconsin, the presence of social ranking in which some kinship groups were considered more important then others.[27] For example, a red ochre–covered human fetus was buried wrapped in a long string of copper beads and accompanied by a copper celt.

Violence and warfare erupted during this time as is apparent from a grave complex with red ochre and distinctive Red Ochre Complex artifacts discovered during building construction at the Convent Knoll site in Elm Grove, Wisconsin.[28] In one of the graves, a young girl had been interred with prestige articles: a large ceremonial knife and a string of shell beads. However, nearby were the haphazardly arranged skeletons of eight adult men, all of whom had probably been killed in a single battle or attack. Spear points were embedded in the bones, and some bodies were partially dismembered and scalped.[29]

Cemeteries into Mounds

Old Copper Complex and Red Ochre Complex cemeteries of the Archaic tend to be located on hills and knolls or other prominent places that easily could have functioned as territorial markers for the people who created the cemeteries. The next step was the construction of more visible markers in the form of mounds of dirt placed over the cemeteries. Conspicuous mortuary structures containing the bones of honored ancestors would have been particularly important if ancestral territories and resources were being contested.

Sometime just before 500 B.C., the first burial mounds appeared on the Wisconsin landscape, growing out of the Red Ochre Ceremonial Complex. The construction of these mounds reflected the elaboration of rituals surrounding death and the desire to create visual and symbolic links among human beings, the land, and the supernatural world. The mounds also reflected the continued social and cultural complexity among the Native people of Wisconsin.

5

Early Burial Mound Builders

The Early and Middle Woodland Stages

Until recently, the construction of burial mounds, along with the introduction of pottery vessels after about 1000 B.C., was used to mark the beginning of the Woodland period and the birth of a new Woodland tradition way of life in eastern North America. It is now clear that the custom of mound building is much older and the result of social and economic changes already under way during the Archaic.

The First Earthworks in North America

Mound building seems to have begun independently in several regions of North America. Along the Atlantic coast in Labrador, a complex maritime culture of caribou and sea-mammal hunters had begun to bury their kin, covered with red ochre, in low earthen and rock mounds by 5600 B.C. Near the Gulf of Mexico, larger earthen burial mounds excavated in such places as Louisiana and Florida have recently been radiocarbon dated to between 4000 and 2000 B.C.[1]

The mound-building tradition in Louisiana eventually led to the construction of the imposing Poverty Point site on the Bayou Macon in the Mississippi River valley (figure 5.1). Poverty Point is considered to be the first major civic, ceremonial, and trade center in North America. Around 1200 B.C., ancient Native Americans built huge concentric earthen

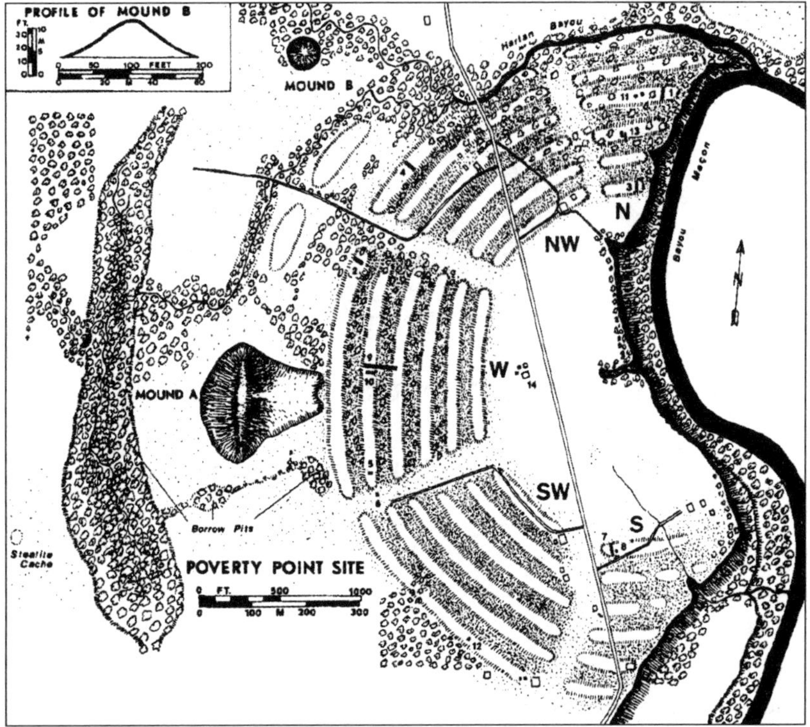

Figure 5.1. The Poverty Point site, on the Bayou Macon in Louisiana, is the remains of the major earthen ceremonial center in North America.

embankments that enclosed a large plaza.[2] Immediately to the west of the complex is a mound in the shape of a bird that is 710 feet long and more than 70 feet high. Bird imagery, representing the upper world in the cosmology of Native peoples, carries through to the modern day, appearing in such forms as thunderbirds. As we shall see, birds of various sorts, particularly raptors, played a prominent role in the artwork and belief systems of Woodland and Mississippian peoples in the Midwest.

The First Burial Mounds in Wisconsin

Traditionally the construction of burial mounds, along with the introduction of pottery vessels after about 500 B.C., was used to mark the point at which Woodland period ways of life spread to Wisconsin. As in other areas of the eastern United States, it is now clear that the custom of mound building is a bit older, having arrived in Wisconsin after it had been established elsewhere, and was the result of social and economic changes already under way during the end of the Archaic associated with a local evolution of the Red Ochre Complex. These first transitional mounds are large conical or round mounds that are few in number and cover the graves of only a part of the population—those individuals with high social status. Where the rest of the population was buried is largely unknown but presumably they were interred in grave pits unmarked by mounds such as that at Convent Knoll.

The burials in pits below these first mounds are accompanied by prestige goods acquired from distant places and are covered by layers of red ochre. In contrast to earlier burials, the offerings include locally made pottery, marking the first use of ceramic vessels in Wisconsin. The appearance of pottery reflected people's tendency to spend longer periods of time at one place. For obvious reasons, easily broken and unwieldy clay pots intended to be used for storing and cooking are of questionable value to a highly mobile society. In earlier times, skins, baskets made from woven grasses or bark, and bark containers were commonly used. As people increasingly settled down in relatively long-lasting camps, however, the advantages of hard-walled, comparatively leak-proof containers for cooking and storage became more apparent.

As noted, in the Upper Midwest the first burial mound sites are directly linked to the Red Ochre Complex. One example in Wisconsin is the Henschel site, which once included three large conical mounds arranged around a spring on a hill overlooking the huge Sheboygan Marsh in Sheboygan County (figures 5.2, 5.3). To the east of the conical mounds were a linear mound and a group of "panther" or water-spirit effigy mounds, all of which were built during a later period. The Sheboygan Marsh provided an extraordinary abundance of food resources—waterfowl, fish, mammals, and a wide variety of plants—to the people who used the Henschel mounds. It must have been a place where people gathered frequently and thus was a logical location for periodic ceremonial activities. The construction of the Henschel mounds around a spring is also significant because springs issue life-giving water and are the sources of special earth, fine sands, and muck, all of which are associated with concepts of rebirth and fertility in Native belief systems. Springs are believed to be entrances to the watery underworld, the residence of the great and powerful water spirits, and mound groups were constructed on or near springs throughout the entire period of mound building. At Henschel the later water-spirit mounds seem to be oriented to the spring itself.

Like those of many other mounds in Wisconsin, the aboveground portions of the three conical mounds at the Henschel site were leveled by farming. However, a map made in 1920 by Alphonse Gerend, a Sheboygan dentist, preserved the locations of the mounds.[3] The largest of them found

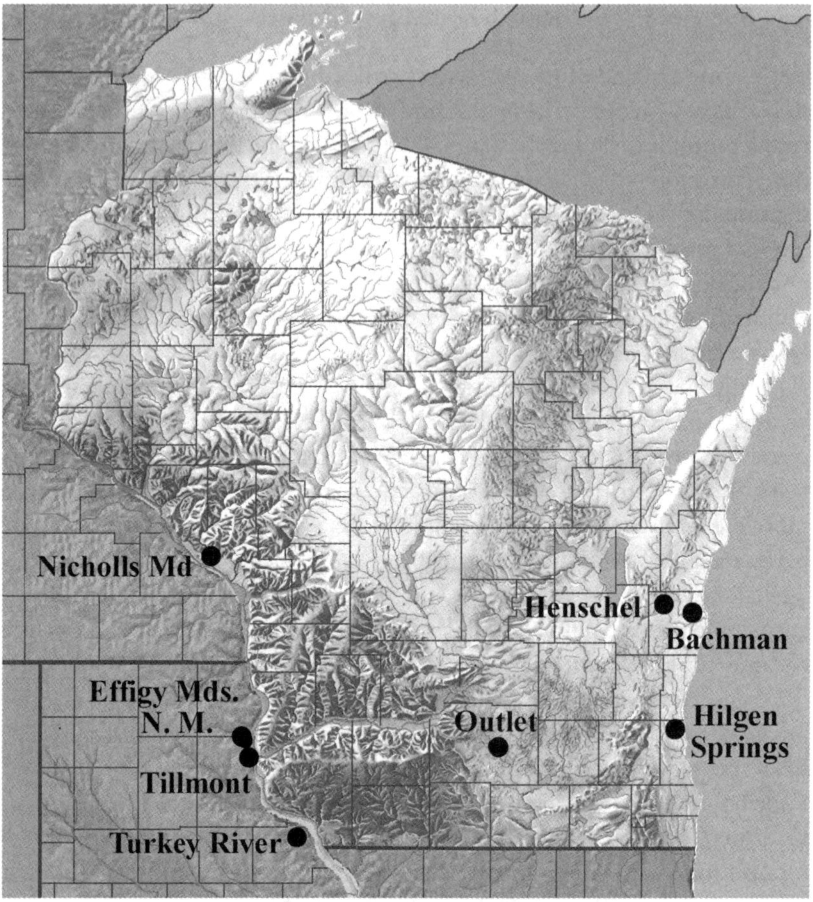

Figure 5.2. Mound groups and other archaeological sites mentioned in text.

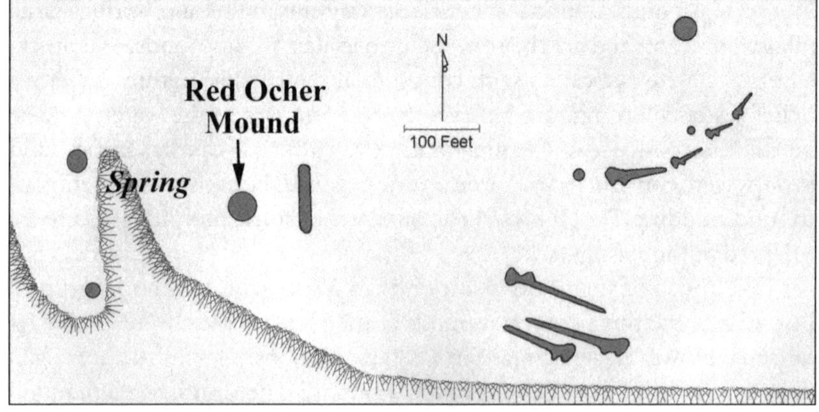

Figure 5.3. The Henschel mound group on the Sheboygan Marsh.

its way into Cyrus Thomas's report for the Bureau of Ethnology.[4] Evidently, the digger had found a large boulder vault or enclosure within which many skeletons were arranged around a large marine conch shell. More than a century later in the 1990s, heavy machinery inadvertently exposed part of a burial pit that had been beneath another of the leveled mounds, and this was carefully examined by an archaeologist. This portion of the below-ground chamber also contained a concentration of large rocks, possibly a cairn or vault, and an unknown number of burials covered with red ochre. Grave offerings included copper and conch-shell beads as well as knives and spear points made of hornstone from Indiana, in a style similar to those made by earlier pre-mound-building adherents to the Red Ochre Complex. This part of the chamber was covered by a layer of black soil. Charcoal from the pit dates the funerary activities to about 600 B.C., a date consistent with the last phases of the Red Ochre Complex in Wisconsin. Pottery sherds were also found the mound fill.[5]

Other Red Ochre mound sites that were excavated include the Turkey River mound group, located on a high bluff overlooking the confluence of the Turkey and Mississippi Rivers in Iowa.[6] Mound building began at the site with the Red Ochre Complex but expanded over several centuries as cultures and customs changed. Several of these early conical mounds are located within and around a roughly circular ditch enclosure. Bone-bundle burials and a cremation within the mounds were found in circular limestone enclosures, one capped by limestone slabs and accompanied by exotic ceremonial items typical of the period—a "Turkey Tail" blade of Indiana hornstone chert and Marine shell beads. Artifacts found in mound fill included pottery sherds representing the first types of pottery made in the Upper Midwest.

The human remains at Turkey River show evidence of the widespread violence that spread at the time, as is evident at the earlier-mentioned Convent Knoll site. These included one individual who had apparently been stabbed with a copper awl and another who had a spear point lodged in his rib cage or sternum. Four other skeletons were headless, possibly decapitated, and one of these had a "Turkey Tail" ceremonial blade in place of his head. Later Woodland peoples added burials and earth to the tops of the Red Ochre mounds and expanded mound building along the bluff edge to the northwest.

Adena and Hopewell

After 1000 B.C., the custom of building burial mounds was also practiced by people living in the Ohio River valley, where it marked the beginning of their local Early Woodland stage, known as the Adena Complex.[7] Like the Old Copper and Red Ochre Complexes in Wisconsin and adjacent regions, Adena was not one culture but a cluster of rituals shared by a number of different peoples. One ritual was the erection of large conical mounds over burial pits or chambers dug into the ground; sometimes these elaborate chambers were lined with logs and lay beneath the floors of pole-and-thatch grave shelters that were burned to the ground before the mounds were constructed. Mounds grew in size through time by the addition of more burials and earth. One Adena mound in Moundsville, West Virginia, right across the river from Ohio, was more than sixty-seven feet high. Near the burial mounds, the Adena people also built large earthen enclosures that possibly served as sacred spaces for conducting ceremonies related to the burials.

The burial of relatively few people in pits below the mounds reflects the growing complexity of Native societies in eastern North America, in which differences in social status were becoming even more evident. Simultaneously, long-distance trade networks grew even more elaborate, and important people buried in the mounds were often accompanied by symbolic items of great prestige value acquired from distant places, such as seashells, sheets of mica from North Carolina, pipestone from Minnesota, blue-gray hornstone chert from Indiana, lead (for white pigment) from southwestern Wisconsin or northern Illinois, and copper from around Lake Superior. Adena and the following Hopewell were artistic complexes that provide substantial insights into the worldview and supernatural beliefs of the time in the form of statuettes and images on pottery and other art that features animals and supernatural beings.

Around 200 B.C., Adena climaxed with the development of the phenomenal ceremonial complex in the Ohio River and lower Illinois River valleys called Hopewell.[8] Archaeologists date Hopewell in these areas to between 200 B.C. and A.D. 300 and assign it to the Middle Woodland stage or period. In Wisconsin, during this time, trade networks continued to expand, moving around great quantities of exotic items and raw materials and ultimately linking much of North America east of the Rocky Mountains. This vast ceremonial trade network and the associated rituals have sometimes been called the Hopewell Interaction Sphere, but now, more accurately, it is known as the Hopewell Ceremonial Complex, since it represented a ceremonial movement much more extensive than the Old Copper and Red Ochre Complexes. Through this interaction, local peoples throughout midwestern and eastern North America adopted Hopewell customs and religious beliefs. In areas to the west of Ohio, Hopewell centers grew in

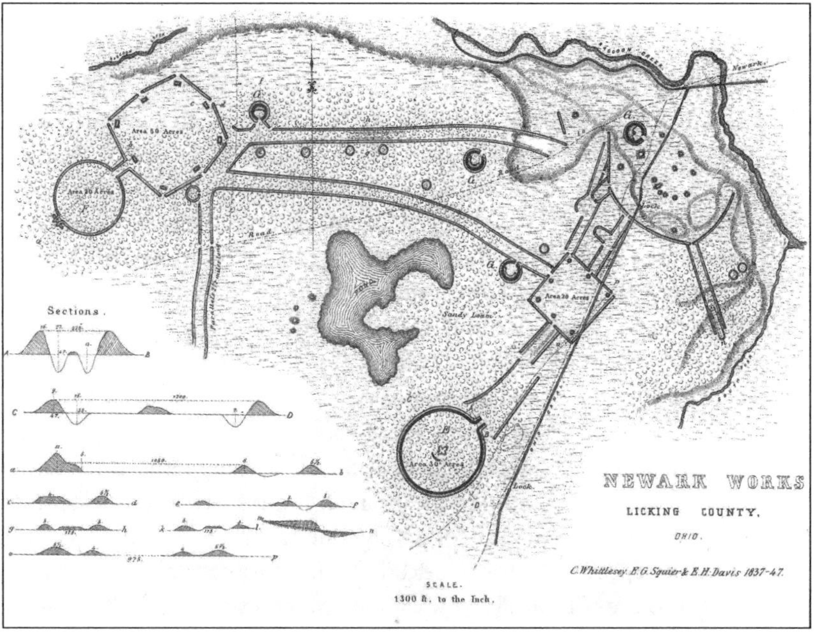

Figure 5.4. The Hopewell Newark earthworks site in Ohio.

Indiana, Illinois (where it was called Havana Hopewell), and along the Mississippi River in Wisconsin and Iowa.

During Hopewell times, the construction of earthworks in Ohio reached awe-inspiring dimensions. Massive geometric earthworks—squares, circles, and octagons—covered vast tracts of land, sometimes hundreds of acres (figure 5.4).[9] Large, wide "sacred roads" seem to have connected some of these ceremonial areas, and analysis has linked alignment among the earthworks to observations of solar and lunar cycles. These spectacular structures required sophisticated engineering and architectural skills and thus were the special focus of the adherents of the myth of the Lost Race in the nineteenth century. The scale and engineering complexity of Hopewell earthworks still excite the imagination.

Relying on the rich and diverse array of Hopewell art and iconography, David Penny described the cosmology of the Ohio Hopewell culture as a vertically layered universe with bird imagery representing the upper world and serpent imagery, the lower.[10] The bear, representing the earth plane of the lower world in later Native cultures of the Midwest, was also a particular focus of veneration and was evidently considered a great medicine animal.

One carved stone figurine from Ohio is of a medicine man wearing a bearskin that retains its head.[11]

Dualism is apparent in the layout of many Hopewell ceremonial centers, with large pairs of square and circular or octagonal enclosures, although sometimes there are three enclosures.[12] These have been interpreted logically as representing ritual places for different segments of Hopewell society. The dual arrangements could well reflect the existence of a two-part or moiety social structure representing clans of the upper and lower worlds. Martin Byers alternatively proposes that ceremonial activities of both clans and cults, specialized internal organizations devoted to world renewal ceremonies, took place at the ceremonial centers. Clan ceremonies transformed the deceased into ancestors, but the cults saw their deceased members as offerings to enhance the sacred powers of nature.[13]

Hopewell earthworks often enclose clusters of large burial mounds. Like those of the Adena Complex, the mounds frequently cover the elaborate log-lined crypts of important people. The burial chambers appear to have functioned as repositories for the dead for quite some time before being covered by mounds. Typically, one or sometimes several individuals were placed in a subterranean and roofed-over crypt not long after death. As other deaths occurred in the family or clan, the bones of the decomposed bodies that had been interred earlier were moved to one side in carefully arranged bundles and the newly dead were placed in the center of the chamber. Some of the burials were in the form of cremations. Eventually, the crypt was covered by a mound—undoubtedly with great ceremony—and some burials were occasionally added to the mound at later times. Other Hopewell mounds covered the burned remains of charnel houses. These were large aboveground wood-and-thatch crypts in which members of a family or clan were placed after death, either "in the flesh" or as cremations, and that sheltered a variety of rituals attending burial ceremonies. At some point, possibly when it was full, the structure was ritually burned, and a mound was built over the spot to mark its location.

Offerings of great prestige value accompanied people buried in Hopewell mounds. Beautifully crafted ornaments and objects of copper, mica, slate, fine chert, obsidian, and silver were typically placed in these special burials, as were exquisitely crafted pottery vessels with intricate designs. Also usually included were platform pipes made from a variety of stones from various places throughout the Midwest, sometimes carved in the form of beautiful animals. Smoking had become an important part of ritual life, and tobacco, a plant originally domesticated in Mexico, was grown for ceremonial purposes. In Ohio and southern Illinois, subsistence was based on plentiful natural resources and small gardens of domesticated local plants that were enhanced by squash and small amounts of corn.

The complexity of Hopewell burial customs and the elaborate nature of their earthworks have led some archaeologists to believe that some Hopewell societies had arranged themselves into social aggregates called chiefdoms. Like bands and tribes, chiefdoms are integrated by networks of kinship relations, but, unlike these simpler forms of social organization, chiefdoms are hierarchical. Social power is concentrated in certain family lineages or clans that control the distribution of food and resources to the rest of the population. The presence of the immense earthworks themselves attest to great social complexity.

It is clear that the construction of burial mounds and associated earthworks played an important role in Hopewell societies. They functioned as ceremonial centers for small nearby settlements and helped reinforce the identity of the social group as a whole. Perhaps, as with the Feast of the Dead conducted by the Huron, neighboring tribes and chiefdoms were invited to bring gifts and grave offerings and to participate in ceremonies, thus helping to reinforce or create alliances. The exchange of gifts during these periodic burial rituals was probably one of the many ways that the vast Hopewell trade network moved goods around eastern North America. Certainly, the burial of important people in prominent structures with symbols of prestige not only emphasized the status of the chiefly families but also created a continuing demand for exotic goods that kept the trade networks operating.

The construction of mounds in Hopewell times also reflected spiritual concerns. Robert Hall observed that many Middle Woodland mounds, including some in Wisconsin, contained offerings that are symbols of or metaphors for rebirth, world renewal, and fertility in many Native belief systems. They include layers or pockets of white sands, mucky soils, puddled clays, and clam shells.[14] For the Woodland mound builders, the most important aspect of the ceremonial of mound burials may have been that they provided an opportunity to associate the deaths of prominent people with the rebirth and renewal of the world and all its living things. This concept was clearly present as the first mounds were being built in Wisconsin.

The Early Woodland in Wisconsin

The first burial mounds in Wisconsin appeared during the transition from the Archaic to the Early Woodland about 600 B.C. and continued through the Early Woodland stage or period, dated in Wisconsin to between 500 B.C.

and A.D. 100. Life in Wisconsin during the Early Woodland period appears to have been much like that during the Late Archaic. Social groups occupied defined territories, shifting locations occasionally to take full advantage of nature's bounty. Several examples of Early Woodland camps have been found at various places in the state, and they provide insights into how people adapted to different environments.[15] At the Bachman site, near Sheboygan, archaeologists found the seeds of domesticated sumpweed at a deer-hunting camp, the first evidence of cultivation in the state. The Beach site, on Lake Waubesa near Madison, was a warm-weather camp from which Early Woodland people collected a wide variety of foods, including fish, mammals, waterfowl, plant seeds, nuts, and acorns. On the Mississippi River floodplain, a late-summer camp called the Mill Pond site produced evidence of intensive clam gathering as well as fishing and hunting of riverside animals.

The use of ceramic containers for storing and cooking food expanded during the Early Woodland. Of all the artifact classes that archaeologists study, pottery is the most useful because different societies made pottery in different ways and decorated the pots with distinctive designs. Even within one group or culture, ceramic characteristics and decorations changed over time. Once a ceramic type is dated by radiocarbon or other means, the discovery of similar sherds can reveal much about where specific cultures lived and with whom they interacted.

Woodland pottery in Wisconsin was made with local clays mixed with crushed rock. As was the case with most Native American groups, the potters were probably women. The surfaces of clay pots made in Woodland times were first roughened or marked with cords or fabrics. Decorations were then stamped, impressed, incised, or trailed on this surface. Although there is much individual variation, the decorative motifs found on pottery were not based on the fanciful whim of the potters or selected for purely aesthetic reasons. Pottery designs appear to have included symbols that represented the underlying structure of the people's belief systems. David Benn, who has specialized in the study of design symbolism on Woodland pottery, suggests that chevrons found on Woodland pots are bird symbols that denote the "upper world" in Native American cosmology, while other designs, such as some arrangements of parallel lines, represent the "lower world," which includes earth and water (figure 5.5).[16] Many Native cultural traditions in North America conceptualize the earth itself as lying between the upper world, which contains the sun, the moon, and celestial birds, and the watery underworld, which is inhabited by various powerful water spirits and monsters.[17] In many instances, the upper world and the lower world are viewed in direct opposition to each other but are depicted together in

Figure 5.5. Early Woodland pot decorated with chevron and linear designs, possibly denoting the upper world and the lower world.

symbols in order to conceptualize harmony. Variations on this upper-world/lower-world theme appear in decorations on pottery made in the Midwest throughout the rest of the prehistoric period. Such symbolism provides invaluable clues to ideology and possibly even the social divisions of ancient cultures and assists in the interpretation of the meaning of other customs, such as mound building.

Early Woodland Mounds

One Early Woodland mound group near Cedarburg consisted of just three conical mounds, like the slightly earlier Henschel mound group made during the late Archaic. The Hilgen Spring mound group overlooks Cedar Creek, a tributary of the Milwaukee River, which, as its name implies, is also associated with prominent springs. Two of the Hilgen Spring mounds were excavated in 1968 by the Public Museum of the City of Milwaukee just before the construction of a subdivision on the site.[18] The larger of these mounds was forty feet in diameter and six feet high. Construction destroyed the third mound. The two excavated mounds were similar in construction and had much in common with other Early Woodland mounds in eastern North America. Both were built over large grave pits, one containing the remnants of an extended, presumably "in the flesh" burial and the other, three reburials in the form of bone bundles. Over the pits, a layer of black organic soil was placed in a mound; on top of the black soil were the burial mounds, consisting of soil and sand from the surrounding area. The black soil was apparently taken from a nearby camp, since it included such debris as chips from stone-tool making, food remains, broken artifacts, and charcoal. In one of the two mounds, an infant burial was placed in the mound fill, and sometime later a bone bundle was placed in a pit dug into the mound surface.

No grave goods were found, but there were other features in the pits that were the remnants of burial rituals and that probably symbolized the concept of the renewal of the earth. Pieces of limestone and brightly colored fieldstone were concentrated alongside the burial pit in one mound, and around it, at roughly the cardinal directions, were four other such concentrations. Robert Hall has identified an identical arrangement, but made of earth, in a Woodland mound in Iowa and relates it to the widespread "Earth-Diver" origin stories and the ritual re-creation of the earth.[19] Variations of the Earth-Diver stories are found among many Native American tribes and, indeed, in some Old World cultures, suggesting that the structure of the tale goes back to extreme antiquity. The essence of the stories is that a water creature dives deep into a primordial ocean to retrieve some mud, from which the earth is made. In a Cheyenne version, a mud hen brings up sediment that is divided by the creator to form the earth. The Cheyenne have a ceremony that recapitulates this act of creation for the purpose of promoting "the fertility of all living things upon which the Cheyenne depended." Called the Sun Dance or Lodge of New Life, the rite includes the cutting of sod into five blocks, representing the creation of the earth, and then the placing of the sod pieces around a buffalo-skull altar near a central Sun Dance pole. Closer to Wisconsin, Hall highlighted a Ho-Chunk belief that after the earth was created, it was in constant motion, so attempts were made to secure it at the four cardinal directions with four islands, water spirits, and snakes. It is also tempting to tie the four concentrations of stones surrounding the Hilgen Spring burial pit to this earth creation concept, particularly because of the association of the mound group with springs, the entrance to the underworld for water spirits.

The Middle Woodland Stage: Interaction with Hopewell

The construction of mounds increased in Wisconsin during the Middle Woodland period, dated in Wisconsin to between about 100 B.C. and

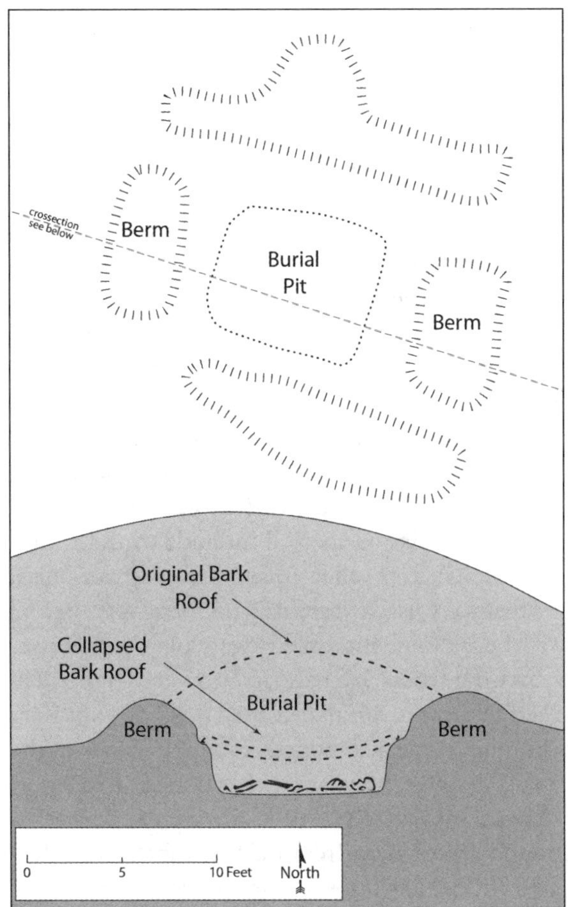

Figure 5.6. Plan view and profile through the central portion of the Nicholls Mound, showing the central burial pit, embankments, and grave shelter.

A.D. 500.[20] Several dozen locations, largely in the southern part of the state, have now been identified, almost all on terraces or bluff tops overlooking major bodies of water. Middle Woodland mounds sometimes occur singly, but most frequently they are found in small groups. At many locations, later mound builders added their own mounds to the groups, so it is difficult to determine just how many were constructed during the Middle Woodland period. Like earlier mounds, Middle Woodland mounds are conical in form and are very large by Wisconsin standards. The Nicholls Mound, near Trempealeau, measured about ninety feet in diameter and was twelve feet high, making it among the largest burial mounds ever built in Wisconsin (figures 5.6, 5.7).

The ceremonies, rituals, and artifacts associated with this major wave of mound building show influences from Hopewell centers in Illinois and

Ohio, particularly at those Wisconsin mound centers along the major midcontinental transportation route, the Mississippi River. Along the Mississippi, many Middle Woodland mound centers were built on river terraces between the mouth of the Wisconsin River near Prairie du Chien, to the south, and the mouth of the Trempealeau River, to the north. Mound groups are found at virtually every major drainage valley, called hollows or coulees in southwestern Wisconsin. The mound centers typically consist of clusters of mound groups or several mound groups within a short distance of one another. This pattern suggests that several social groups, such as families or clans, were involved in the construction of the centers and/or that the focus of mortuary and other ritual activities shifted location over time.

Most of what is known about the mound groups along the Mississippi River derives from the excavations conducted in the nineteenth century by the Smithsonian Institution and, especially, from the work undertaken between 1928 and 1930 by the Milwaukee Public Museum.[21] Excavations of selected mounds revealed that, like Hopewell mounds to the south, mounds in the upper Mississippi River valley covered rectangular burial pits or subterranean crypts that were used continually for many years before a mound was erected over them. Some interments were placed in aboveground stone crypts or encircled by rocks, later also to be covered by earthen mounds. The dead were laid in these crypts in extended positions not long after they had died or as bundles of cleaned bones. As with mounds in the Ohio and Illinois River valleys, there is evidence that bones, decayed of flesh, were set aside as new corpses were placed in the crypts. Beneath a mound at the Schwert mound group, near Trempealeau, a shallow twelve- by eight-foot pit contained the remains of seven extended "in the flesh" burials and many more bone bundles. On an earthen shelf framing the pit was a continuous line of bundled bones. The remains of at least forty-six people lay buried in the pit beneath the Nichols Mound, and a thick layer of bark covered the area of the tomb, suggesting that before its construction, the chamber was sheltered by a building or roof of some kind (figure 5.6).

Careful excavation of some of these Mississippi River mounds by the Milwaukee Public Museum added other details about burial rituals. When the Middle Woodland people dug the rectangular grave pits for several of the mounds in the Trempealeau area, they were careful to pile the dirt in four separate embankments paralleling the sides of the pit. This arrangement is reminiscent of that of the stone piles at the Hilgen Spring mound group, although the association with the cardinal directions is not exact. The Nicholls Mound has also offered a rare glimpse at the actual mound-building methods. A cut through the mound revealed that it was built up by what had been thought to be hundreds of small dumpings of dirt but

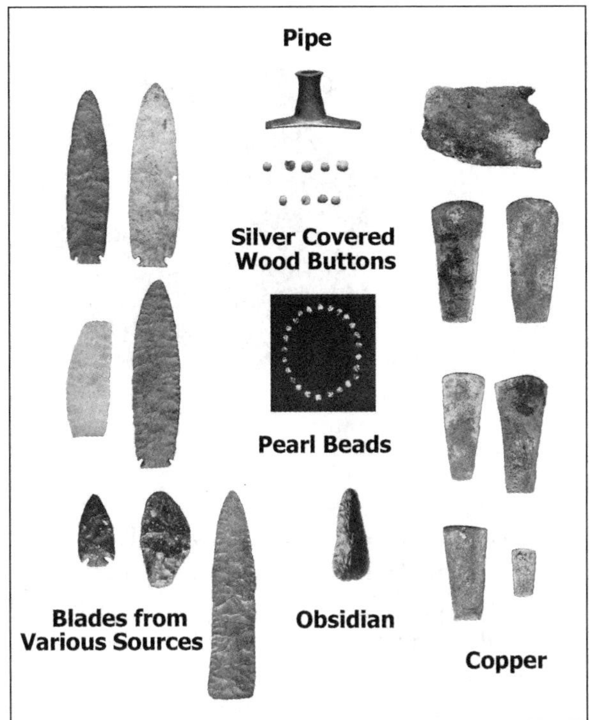

Figure 5.7. Exotic Hopewell period artifacts found in the Nicholls Mound in western Wisconsin.

which are now recognized as blocks of prairie sod, a mound-building practice also found among Hopewell-related people in Illinois.[22]

Grave offerings in the mounds along the Mississippi River attest to both the status of the people buried in the mounds and their close interaction with other Hopewell centers in the Midwest. In the large Nicholls Mound, a central burial pit contained several reburials of bone and the remains of seven individuals laid out in extended position, one of whom was accompanied by silver-covered wooden beads, copper celts, a copper plate, freshwater pearls, shell beads, a platform pipe, and chipped-stone blades made from fine cherts from western North America and Hixton Silicified Sandstone from nearby west-central Wisconsin (figure 5.7). Offerings and ornaments found in other western Wisconsin Hopewell mounds include ceremonial blades and other chipped-stone tools, platform pipes, pottery vessels that appear to have been traded up from Hopewell communities in Illinois, and bear canine-teeth pendants.

Overall, the Middle Woodland people of west-central Wisconsin appear to have been middlemen in the Hopewell exchange network, handling exotic materials that flowed from the far west such as grizzly bear teeth, blades

Figure 5.8. Middle Woodland Hopewell–style pot probably acquired from the Illinois Hopewell.

made from a type of translucent, honey-colored stone called Knife River flint, pieces of obsidian, and, from Minnesota, catlinite, a soft red stone especially important to Native peoples even now for fashioning ceremonial pipes. An analogy for this middleman role during the Middle Woodland period is the historic-period fur trade, during which some Native people in Wisconsin and elsewhere operated as intermediaries between European fur traders living on the east coast of North America and Native peoples living far in the interior. Native middlemen obtained European-made goods to be exchanged for beaver and other pelts supplied by tribes living further west and delivered the pelts back to the European traders in the east. Some trade goods were given to the middlemen as profit, and these not only served as useful objects but also brought status to the Native traders in their own cultures.

Blades made from Hixton Silicified Sandstone have been found as grave offerings in western and south-central Wisconsin mounds, indicating use of status-related or symbolic material. The elaborate Middle Woodland mounds in the Trempealeau area are located within twenty-five miles of the quarries at Silver Mound, and it is possible that the people interred in these mounds belonged to families or clans that controlled access to and distribution of this long-prized and sacred western Wisconsin rock during the Hopewell period.

If only certain people were interred beneath mounds in these important ceremonial centers, where were other people buried? In 1948 road construction between conical mounds of the Outlet site in south-central Wisconsin, built as early as the Middle Woodland period, exposed a large grave pit, unmarked by a mound, that contained the remains of thirteen individuals placed in the pit as they died.[23] The pit was later filled, but no mound was placed over it. Grayish-white marl had been applied to the face of one individual, forming a mask-like covering. Marl is a clay-like calcium precipitate formed in lake sediments such as in the adjacent Lake Monona. According to Ho-Chunk traditions, water spirits live in marl caves, so the association of the deceased with the watery underworld is quite probable. By extension, those buried beneath high mounds would belong to the upper world in a two-part social scheme. In contrast to several of the excavated Hopewell mound burials from Wisconsin sites, including one at Outlet, no grave goods accompanied the people in the grave pit at the Outlet site, implying a lower social status.

Exploring an ancient campsite on a small, low Mississippi River island, James Stoltman of the University of Wisconsin uncovered even more dramatic evidence for the existence of a two-part social structure reflected by mortuary customs during the Middle Woodland. While mounds for the upper-world elite are found along mainland bluffs, Stoltman's archaeological crew encountered a large unmounded Middle Woodland grave pit at the Tillmont site with the remains of as many as thirty people who had been placed in the facility soon after each death and with few grave offerings.[24] As with the smaller grave pit at the Outlet site, these may be people associated with the watery lower world, given that the grave pit is located in a low area surrounded by water. The grave pit, located on federal lands, was exposed and documented, but, in accordance with federal procedures, which include consultation with Native American representatives, the remains were not removed. The same type of social dualism, or moiety social structure, is reflected by burial customs at Illinois Middle Woodland sites. Burial mounds for the upper division occupy higher places, while other people were buried in grave pits in lower areas on the landscape and covered by low, broad mounds of earth.[25]

Small groups of large conical mounds were built elsewhere in southern Wisconsin along major bodies of water during the Middle Woodland period, but they show lesser degrees of Hopewell influence.[26] Middle Woodland mounds are found on the Rock River, Lake Koshkonong, Lake Mendota, Lake Monona, and the lower Fox River, among other places. Burials are usually in pits beneath the mounds, which are sometimes covered with rock or layers of burned or organic soils. Grave offerings similar to those in Hopewell mounds are occasionally found, but are not nearly as common. Among these rare exotic objects are Hixton ceremonial blades, freshwater pearls, shell beads, bear canines, copper artifacts, and platform pipes.

Mound building was not a common custom in northern Wisconsin at this time. A mound center from the Middle Woodland period, however, may have been the Cyrus Thomas mound group, located on Rice Lake in Barron County, although some archaeologists feel that it could date to much later in time. Excavations done by the Public Museum in the 1930s at the Cyrus Thomas group found burials associated with local pottery, two white clay "death masks" reminiscent of that found at the Outlet site, and a bear canine-tooth pendant typical of Hopewell ceremonial activity.[27] Occasional discoveries of Hopewell trade objects at campsites at other locations in northern Wisconsin indicate that people in this region participated in long-distance trade networks to some extent.

The lifestyle of Middle Woodland peoples included hunting, gathering, fishing, and gardening, and there are hints that settlements were becoming more concentrated and long-lived. At the end of the Middle Woodland period in Wisconsin, during the transition to the Late Woodland period, the first formal villages with wigwam-like houses appeared in the southwestern part of the state.[28] As well, smaller groups used rockshelters and camps for short periods while hunting deer or acquiring other resources.

Enclosures

Middle Woodland peoples in Wisconsin did not build ceremonial centers with immense earthen enclosures like those in Ohio, but they may have used smaller rectangular, octagonal, and circular embankments as sacred places. Earthen enclosures and circular ditches were built as early as the Late Archaic period in Iowa, so it is certainly a possibility that the custom continued into later times but was influenced by Hopewell ritual. However, the few known examples at mound groups in Wisconsin are in some instances associated with effigy mounds classified as belonging to the later Late Woodland tradition, suggesting a number of alternative possibilities. The custom may have continued into later times, the enclosures may have been built prior to the effigy mounds at these sites, or the effigy mounds may even have begun to appear in small numbers as early as the Middle Woodland period, growing directly out of Hopewell influence. One example may be a circular earthen berm mapped in the late nineteenth century by Theodore H. Lewis near the Kickapoo River in southwestern Wisconsin that enclosed a central bird effigy. This enclosure/bird mound combination is remarkably similar to a seeming bird enclosure documented at the Hopewell Newark earthworks in Ohio, mapped in the 1840s by Squier and Davis (figure 5.9).[29] While the possibility is tantalizing, a connection between the two cannot be proved. The Kickapoo River site is now plowed away, and modern archaeologists are uncertain whether the earthwork in the Ohio enclosure was meant to represent a bird at all. Excavations in the

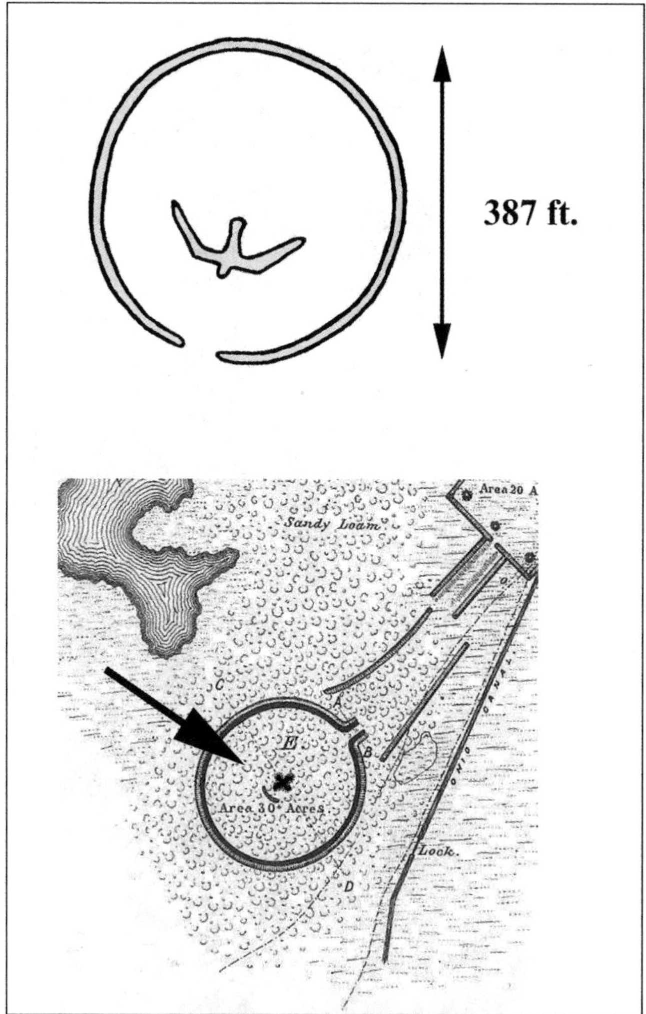

Figure 5.9. *Above*: drawing of enclosure near the Kickapoo River in Wisconsin from an 1886 map made by T. H. Lewis. *Below*: bird enclosure at the Newark earthworks in Ohio mapped by Squier and Davis.

1920s revealed instead that the supposed bird mound covered a large ceremonial structure.

Middle Woodland Effigy Mounds?

There is other, more substantial evidence that the building of effigies of supernatural beings or spirits had roots in Hopewell ceremonial customs, if

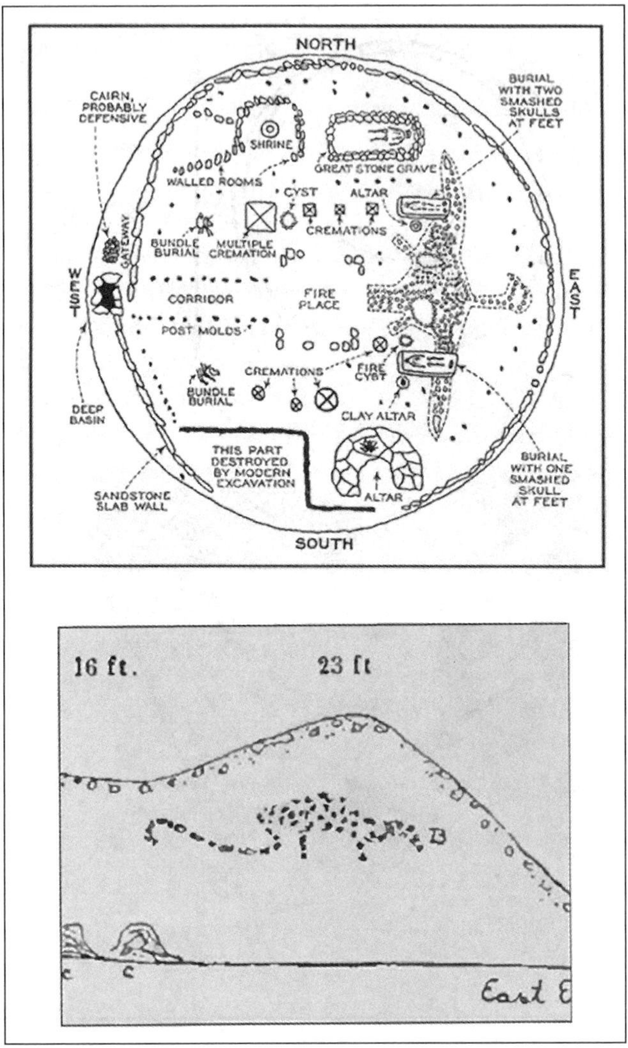

Figure 5.10. *Above*: excavation map of the North Benton Hopewell mound showing stone effigy of a bird. *Below*: Moorehead sketch of stone effigy water-spirit-like creature from an Ohio Hopewell mound.

not in earlier traditions, and that these customs could have spread to the Hopewell centers in the Wisconsin area, leading to the later explosion of effigy mound building found there. Early excavations of the Hopewell North Benton Mound in Ohio uncovered a boulder outline of a great bird and central fireplace, amid other rock ritual constructions and within a circular rock enclosure (figure 5.10).[30] In the early twentieth century, the

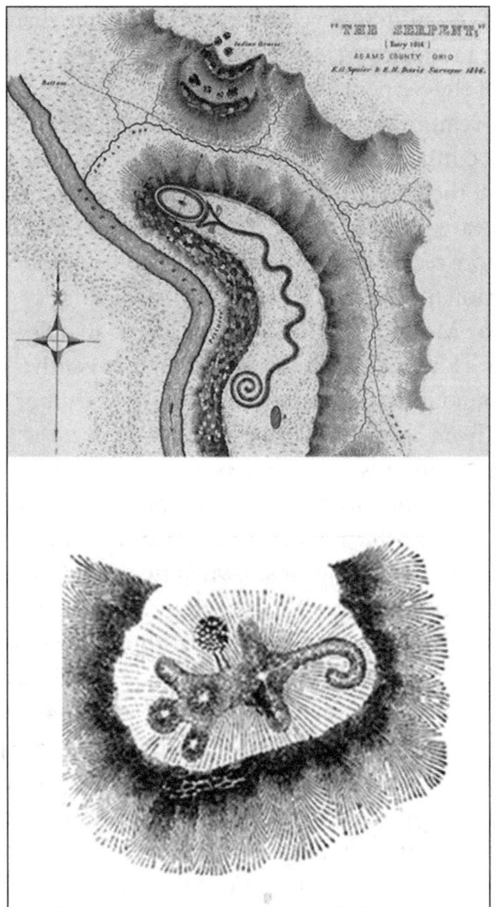

Figure 5.11. Ohio effigy mounds rendered by Squier and Davis in 1848. *Above*: the Serpent Mound. *Below*: the Alligator Mound.

pioneering archaeologist Warren Moorehead found another creature made of boulders that looks very much like a long-tailed underworld water spirit in an Ohio Hopewell mound. Unfortunately, only a sketch survives from his excavation (figure 5.10).[31] Much further west, a Hopewell mound at Utica, Illinois, covered burials and a boulder effigy of either a snake or a long-necked bird.[32] It would seem only one step from these boulder effigies to aboveground earthen effigies of the same types of creatures that were obviously important in the supernatural beliefs of the time.

Two famous earthen effigy mounds are in Ohio—the great Serpent Mound and the so-called Alligator Mound (figure 5.11)—but both have been attributed to cultural developments much later than the Hopewell period through radiocarbon samples extracted from the mounds. However, redating of the Serpent Mound using new experimental radiocarbon techniques that require extracting small bits of charcoal from the dirt now places its initial construction much earlier—back to Adena times—which would mean that the earthen effigy mounds were being made in Ohio long before they appeared in Wisconsin. The earlier date remains controversial since an even more recent radiocarbon date taken from the Serpent Mound places construction much later, as originally believed.[33]

The Alligator Mound is unlikely to represent an alligator and instead appears to show a long-tailed "Underground Water Panther" or water spirit as commonly found in Native tradition and cosmology, but it is flattened as though viewed from above.[34] It too has been dated to the period after the Middle Woodland, but it is interesting because the form is very similar to a long-tailed creature, but with horns, etched on a Middle Woodland stone pipe found in southeastern Minnesota by an artifact collector (figure 5.12).[35] The creature on the pipe is shown in two perspectives, as is the case with many of the artifacts found in later effigy mounds. On the side of the pipe, it is shown in profile as a horned panther-like animal with a long looped tail. On top, the same animal is shown, as indicated by the same interior decoration, but viewed from above, much as in the Alligator Mound. At the very least it can be said that the concept expressed by the Alligator Mound in monumental form was already present during the Middle Woodland in another type of ceremonial representational art. Interestingly, the pipe was made of purplish Baraboo pipestone from an outcrop near Devil's Lake, Wisconsin, a later effigy mound building center.

Comparatively few effigy mounds in the Wisconsin area have been radiocarbon dated, but those that have, along with dates from related habitation sites, mostly suggest a time span between A.D. 700 and 1100, or well after the Middle Woodland. However, the earliest radiocarbon date for an effigy mound in the Upper Midwest was obtained from a bear mound at Effigy Mounds National Monument on the Mississippi River in Iowa in the 1960s; this test seemed to indicate construction at A.D. 375 (± 100 years), well before the effigy mound era.[36] As mentioned, the bear was held in great reverence by the Hopewell people and was probably considered a provider of great medicine. Bear mounds are unusually common at the Monument and in the surrounding Mississippi Valley area, and there is much evidence of substantial Hopewell-related activity in the form of conical mounds with Hopewell-period burials and artifacts. Taken at face value, the early date seems to provide evidence of effigy mound building during the Middle Woodland, perhaps with roots in the Hopewell, but once again

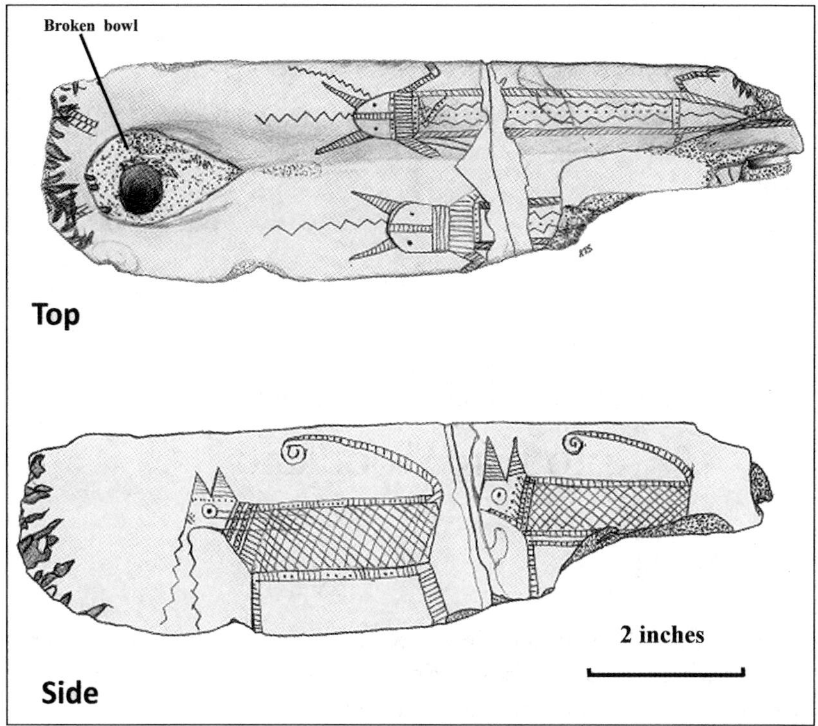

Figure 5.12. Drawing of Middle Woodland–style stone pipe with water spirit shown in two perspectives.

there is an issue. The same mound produced a second date that was 250 years later, greatly confusing the matter, and no artifacts were found in the mound excavation to clarify the situation. As it stands, archaeologists are understandably reluctant to accept the early date for the bear mound.

Despite such issues and problems, it remains feasible (and an interesting matter for future research) that the later effigy mound construction in Wisconsin and adjacent regions had its roots in the Hopewell Ceremonial Complex and eventually sparked development of the spectacular and unprecedented new ceremonial movement examined in the next chapters.

6

From Middle Woodland to Late Woodland

As the far-flung Hopewell trade and ceremonial complex waned, patterns of life in what is now the mid-continental United State again changed. In Wisconsin, communities turned inward toward more local social relationships. It is not yet possible to fully document changes in political and social organization during this transition, except to note that population numbers continued to rise, some groups began to settle down into more sedentary villages, the trend of expanding and intensifying the exploitation of food resources continued, and burial practices changed. The construction of burial mounds at special locations for a variety of social, economic, and ritual purposes accelerated, climaxing between A.D. 700 and 1100 in Wisconsin's spectacular Late Woodland ceremonial landscapes. Thousands of mounds were sculpted from the surrounding earth into sometime huge effigies of animals, supernatural beings, and even a few human beings.

This period of rapid change began circa A.D. 500, as new technologies and foods were introduced from elsewhere and integrated into existing Woodland tradition lifeways. The bow and arrow replaced the spear thrower as both a hunting and a fighting weapon. Better pottery vessels were made and were decorated with symbols drawn from an elaborate and ancient belief system. Most important, corn joined squash and local domesticated plants in the diets and economic strategies of people in the Midwest.[1] The spread of corn and other crops was facilitated by a climatic fluctuation beginning about A.D. 700 called the Atlantic or Medieval Warm Climate, which brought warm and moist weather. Corn or maize had been domesticated from a wild plant called *teocinte* and slowly diffused northward, reaching the Midwest by A.D. 900 (although one radiocarbon date taken from corn indicates an earlier initial appearance).[2]

As corn cultivation became common, populations in mid-continental North America began a shift to village-based farming as a way of life, though to a lesser degree in Wisconsin than in other regions. By a thousand years ago, virtually all people living in areas of the Midwest where agriculture could be successful were cultivating crops, especially corn, to one extent or another. This shift from an economy based on hunting and gathering to one centered on growing corn brought about enormous cultural change that affected not only economic and settlement patterns but also social relations between people and cultural beliefs. It is perhaps one of the most revolutionary developments to have occurred in the thirteen-thousand-plus-year cultural history of Native North America.

Many groups of people, small and large, adopted these changes, and archaeologists commonly collectively refer to societies of this time in the Midwest as "Late Woodland." As the term implies, the Late Woodland peoples are regarded as direct descendants of their Middle Woodland tradition forebears, and the Late Woodland is viewed as a later stage within the Woodland tradition.[3] Late Woodland populations shared broad similarities, but many different cultures and communities made up this tradition.

In the central Mississippi Valley, the Late Woodland stage was very short. Some Late Woodland villages in southern Illinois grew rapidly into large, settled, farming towns and evolved into a highly complex "Mississippian" culture centered on a city now called Cakokia.[4] The Mississippian way of life quickly spread, in some cases through direct colonization as Mississippian people moved north shortly after A.D. 1000 to settlements in northern Illinois and in far western Wisconsin.[5] Between A.D. 1050 and 1100, the Mississippians established a large fortified town, later known as Aztalan, along the Crawfish River in south-central Wisconsin.[6]

The Mississippian peoples who lived together with allied Late Woodland people at Aztalan and elsewhere in Wisconsin interacted with their new neighbors in a variety of ways. As a result of their cultural exchange, a new way of life, called Oneota, emerged in Wisconsin within generations, enduring until European contact.[7] The tangled relationship among all of these overlapping traditions is a matter of intense research and discussion in the archaeological world.

Transition from the Middle to the Late Woodland in Wisconsin

The transition from the Middle Woodland to the Late Woodland is best known from sites in western Wisconsin and northeastern Iowa along and near the Mississippi River, but even there the archaeological record is a bit cloudy. One reason may be wide-scale climatic shifts that brought drought to many areas. As modeled by the climatologists Reid Bryson and Robert Bryson of the University of Wisconsin Climatic Research Center, the archaeological Middle Woodland stage in Wisconsin ended with the onset of a sharp drought sometime between A.D. 400 and 500. They suggest that the drought may have been as intense as the Mid-Holocene dry period and comparable to the Dust Bowl years of the 1930s. They add that climatic change seems to have been rapid and "probably catastrophic for the established lifestyle."[8] A lack of radiocarbon dates for occupations and mound groups during this time has been noted by Wisconsin archaeology experts James Theler and Robert Boszhardt.[9] However, change had been occurring before the drought and continued after.

What is known about the Late Middle Woodland and the first part of the Late Woodland period comes mainly from floodplain camps and cave and rockshelter sites in northeastern Iowa and southwestern Wisconsin where there are thick layers of cultural deposits. Initial Late Woodland pottery decoration combined Middle Woodland notched "dentate" stamps with the impressions of twisted cords—a harbinger of the elaborate cord-decorated pottery of the effigy mound builders and other Late Woodland peoples in the Midwest.[10]

The first evidence of village life in Wisconsin appeared at the end of the Middle Woodland stage in the verdant Wisconsin River valley of southwestern Wisconsin, where wild foods were especially abundant. The Millville site, Wisconsin's oldest fully documented village to date, included fourteen wigwam-like houses and numerous pits for food storage (figure 6.1). Woodland people lived there during the autumn and winter seasons between A.D. 200 and 400, supporting themselves chiefly by hunting deer and elk.[11] There are no burial mounds at Millville, but several newborn infants and older women were buried there. The site produced many pottery sherds decorated with dentate stamps. Projectile points found at Millville were small, suggesting the use of the bow and arrow for hunting.

Woodland peoples elsewhere in Wisconsin were expanding their food alternatives by planting squash in their small gardens and gathering wild rice, which grew in abundance in shallow lakes and rivers.[12] Other food

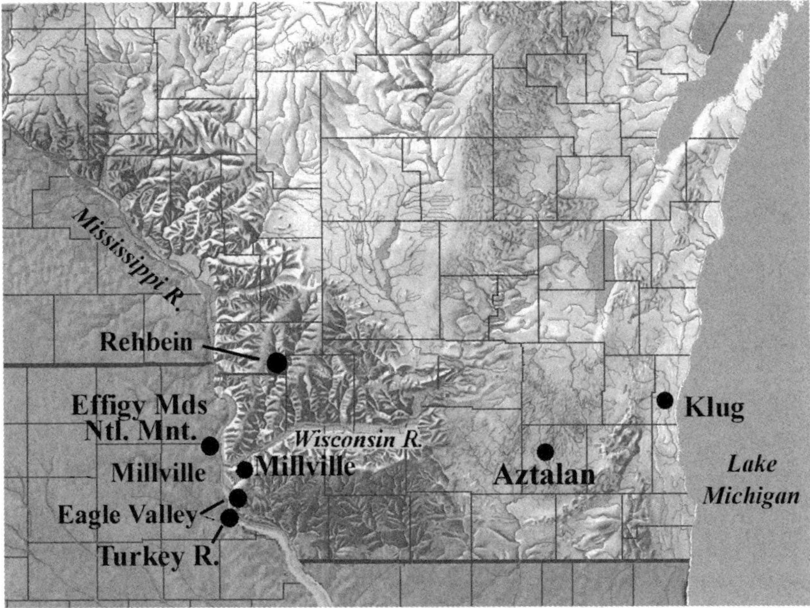

Figure 6.1. Location of Late Middle Woodland and Early Late Woodland sites mentioned in text.

during this time came from cultivating and gathering wild plants and collecting clams or mussels from rivers.

Mound Building

Cultural changes are reflected in mound building during this transitional period. People made smaller but more numerous mounds, covering grave pits containing extended "in the flesh" burials and/or bone bundles and cremations.[13] Burials were often enclosed by arrangements of rocks. Burial offerings were sparse and simple, such as pottery vessels. Missing are the types of exotic prestige goods from distant places found in previous Hopewell-related mounds.

Many of the mounds were conical forms, though smaller than earlier ones, but initial Late Woodland people also built numerous short, narrow linear mounds. Robert Hall suggests that conical and linear mounds represented a two-part social system (moiety), with the conical mounds representing the people of the upper world and the linear mounds people of the lower world.[14] As mentioned previously, a two-part social system had existed in

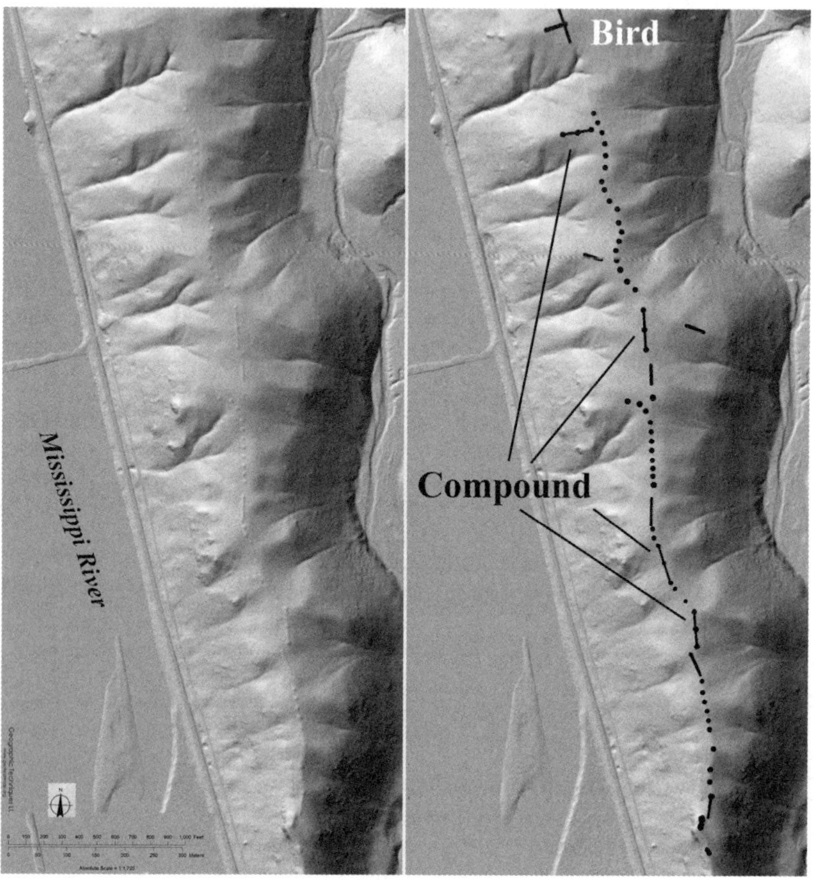

Figure 6.2. LiDAR images of the Eagle Valley mound group near Glen Haven on a high bluff overlooking the Mississippi River in Grant County, Wisconsin.

previous Middle Woodland societies, so the new division in mound forms probably represents a continuation of this social structure.

An analysis of mound arrangements also suggests that people of this time made other forms called compound mounds. Compound mounds are strings of conical mounds connected by short earthen ridges, symbolically joining the mound forms of the upper and lower worlds. Compound mounds may contain two to ten conical segments, but most common by far are strings of three, a variant found at more than a dozen mound sites along the Mississippi bluffs of Iowa and Wisconsin (figure 6.2).[15] A second, less common variant found at sites within Effigy Mounds National Monument and along the Turkey River in Iowa includes seven conical segments. The compound mounds at Effigy Mounds National Monument include both

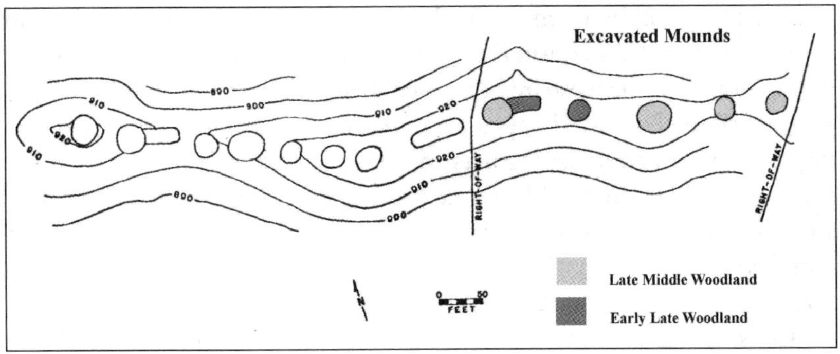

Figure 6.3. Map of the Rehbein I site.

three-segment and seven-segment variations. These numbers obviously had great meaning, but what that meaning could be remains a mystery.

At many sites in the western Driftless Area, various combinations of conical, linear, and compound mounds are arranged in lines or "processions" that follow the tops of bluffs. In some cases, the processions include one or a few effigy mounds at their ends or on adjacent bluff spurs: birds, bears, canines (fox or wolf), and the occasional rare long-tailed water spirit (figure 6.2). It could be that these effigy mounds were added later during the expansive era of effigy mound building, but it may also be that the first effigies depicting key spirit beings of the upper and lower worlds were being made at this time, as was proposed in chapter 5 for the earlier Hopewell-influenced Middle Woodland. However, a lack of radiocarbon dating hampers interpretation.

One site that does trace the transition between the Middle Woodland and the Late Woodland is called Rehbein I, located on a bluff near the Kickapoo River, a tributary of the Wisconsin River in southwestern Wisconsin (figure 6.3).[16] In the 1970s, archaeologists from the Wisconsin Historical Society excavated six mounds located along the planned route of new highway construction. The demolished mounds were later reconstructed nearby with their human remains reinterred at the request of the Great Lakes Intertribal Council. Some mounds were built in Middle Woodland styles but lacked the prestige grave offerings of the Hopewell period and contained newer pottery forms. One tomb, later covered by a mound, had been lined with logs and roofed with bark before it was burned, no doubt as a part of the ceremonial closure of the facility, as in earlier Middle Woodland customs. Sometime later, about A.D. 700, a short linear mound characteristic of the Late Woodland was attached to the Late Middle Woodland mound and another conical mound was probably added to the group.

From Middle Woodland to Late Woodland

The transition between the Middle and the Late Woodland periods in the eastern half of Wisconsin is even more poorly understood. The types of pottery found in the west are not generally found in the east; instead there was a curious short-lived appearance of pottery types decorated with the impressions of woven fishing nets and tempered either with grit (crushed rock) or crushed clam shell.[17] At one site next to the later town of Aztalan in south-central Wisconsin, net-impressed pottery was found with charred corn kernels. Similar pottery has been found as far east as the Klug site in Ozaukee County near Lake Michigan.[18]

Considering the symbolic importance of pottery decorations for Native peoples, it could well be that the water-related emphasis reflected by net impressions combined with the use of clam shells in the manufacture of some pots suggests an association with the watery underworld, a theme that continued later in the eastern part of the state with the dominance of water-related effigy mounds forms.

The next part of the Late Woodland period, which started around A.D. 700, is much better known, since populations greatly increased throughout southern Wisconsin at that time, leaving behind much evidence of their lifeways. It was a time when mound building greatly proliferated as a ceremonial complex emerged and swept over the region, resulting in the creation of many vast effigy mound landscapes.

7

The Effigy Mound Ceremonial Complex

The Late Woodland period, between A.D. 700 and 1100, was a revolutionary and dramatic period in the history of the mound-building cultures that occupied what is now the state of Wisconsin. Populations increased; food production intensified, leading to adoption of corn horticulture; and mound building exploded across the southern part of the state with the creation of many thousands of effigy mounds and other earthen forms at nearly a thousand different places, many times forming huge ceremonial landscapes. The reasons for this extraordinary effigy mound phenomenon, unique in the world, are still a mystery.

During this time, Late Woodland culture continued to push out of the main river valleys and lake shores, settling upland areas that had not been particularly attractive to earlier Woodland people and repeating to patterns of land use similar to those of Late Archaic peoples. By A.D. 900, warm-weather agricultural villages were established at rather small upland ponds in the Four Lakes area around modern Madison, well away from lakeshores occupied by other communities.[1] The southern part of the state's landscape became crowded with people, much as it had been during the Middle Archaic Old Copper Complex in eastern Wisconsin. However, this time the exchange of power-charged symbolic items did not bond together various local groups and societies. In fact, there appears to have been no significant trade in prestige items with other regions, although copper and tool stones circulated in small quantities.[2] Instead, the different Late Woodland peoples in Wisconsin and adjacent states were linked by a ceremonial complex or movement that led to the creation of dense groupings of effigy mounds (figure 7.1).

Figure 7.1. Aerial photo of the Shadewald effigy mound group, located on a high hill near the Wisconsin River in Richland County, also called "Frank's Hill" in memory of the late landowner, Frank Shadewald, who carefully preserved and maintained it.

Making a Living

Like peoples of earlier cultures, Late Woodland peoples moved within defined territories according to the rhythm of the seasons, relying heavily on hunting and on the gathering of wild food resources. Small seasonal villages and camps were established in different parts of each territory to take advantage of food at its time and place of optimum availability. In rugged southwestern Wisconsin, camps and villages near rivers broke into small groups of hunters and their families, who headed into the uplands to hunt deer in sheltered valleys and to seek winter refuge in caves and rock overhangs. In west-central Wisconsin, communities tended to stay near the Mississippi River, sending hunting and gathering parties into the uplands as needed.[3] In eastern Wisconsin, rock shelters and caves are scarce and populations tended to stay near large, food-rich wetlands and lakes.

Late Woodland people supplemented their diet with garden produce, including indigenous plants domesticated in former times. These included chenopodium, sunflower, and sumpweed, as well as squash, a cultigen introduced into Wisconsin from the south about two thousand years ago.[4] After A.D. 900, corn became increasingly important in the Late Woodland diet. The rise of corn horticulture among Late Woodland peoples seems to have

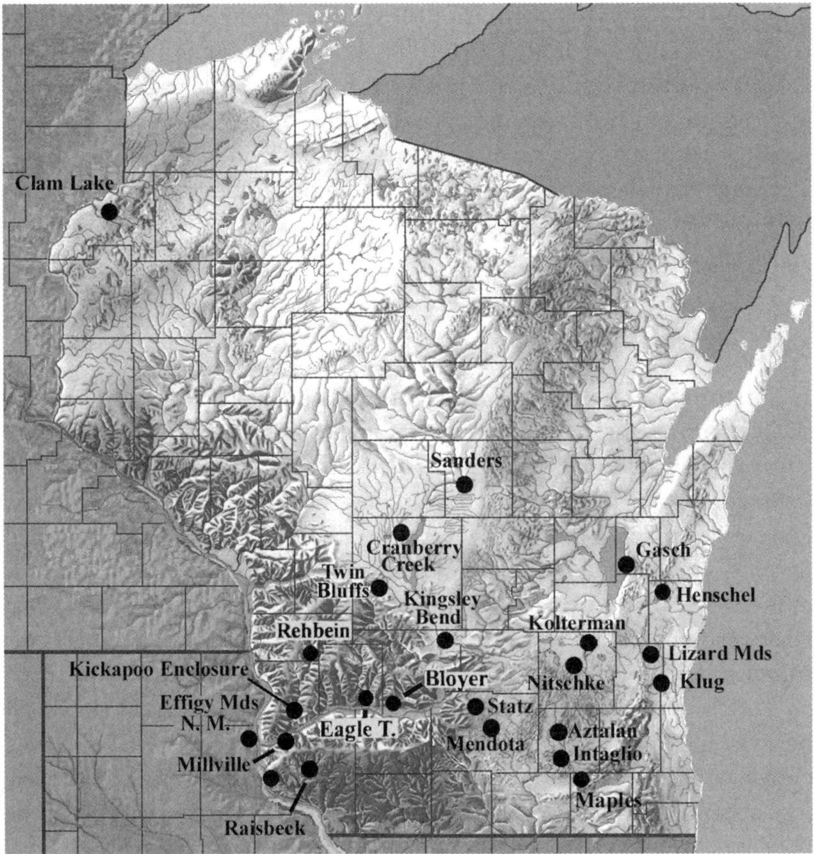

Figure 7.2. Location of sites mentioned in text.

been gradual and to have occurred at different rates in different areas. This may have to do with variations in the intensity of social contact between various Wisconsin communities and people living to the south who had made the transition to corn farming a bit earlier. Alternately, some groups of people may have been more willing to change long-established ways of life. Despite the increasing popularity of corn, wild plant foods such as nuts, berries, and wild rice continued to be relied on more than cultivated crops.[5]

Archaeologists document a dramatic growth of population in the Midwest throughout the Late Woodland, as reflected in the larger number of Late Woodland habitation and mound sites measured against those from earlier times.[6] As with the diffusion of southern crops, the settlement of marginal areas during this time also may have been stimulated by the climate of the time, which made upland areas better watered and lush. As populations grew, opportunities for conflict between individuals and communities increased. After A.D. 1000, for example, some Late Woodland villages were fortified by wooden walls or stockades.[7] Other signs of warfare at this time come from mound burials, where some human skulls bear cut marks closely resembling those made by scalping.[8] Evidence of violent death, including arrowheads and dart points embedded in bone, has been found in Wisconsin and at a number of later Late Woodland sites in Illinois, Iowa, and other places in the Midwest.[9]

Settlements and Housing

Habitation sites included small villages and special hunting, fishing, shellfish-processing, and resource-gathering camps of various types. Where larger villages appeared, there appears to have been a simultaneous increase in the amount of effort devoted to planting crops and to storing food. These few excavated Late Woodland villages were small and were never occupied for long—though there are signs of rebuilding at some, suggesting cycles of abandonment and reuse. As agricultural pursuits increased, more substantial villages appeared, and some were located at major ceremonial centers surrounded by effigy mounds.

Late Woodland houses consisted of wigwam-like structures and small pithouses, each accommodating perhaps only a single family. Pithouses, partially dug into the earth and covered with bark, matting, or other coverings attached to wooden poles, became common throughout much of the northeastern United States during the latter part of the Late Woodland. The living spaces in both kinds of houses varied from circular, to oval, to rectangular. Some pithouses boasted a long, narrow entrance way, giving the structure a keyhole-shaped appearance. Examples of these have been found in several places in southern Wisconsin, including the Statz site located at the headwaters of the Yahara River.[10] Late Woodland people intermittently occupied the small hamlet at Statz for some years between A.D. 800 and 1100, apparently during the autumn and winter (figure 7.3). Archaeologists from the Wisconsin Historical Society found the remains of three pairs of small keyhole houses at Statz, surrounded by refuse and storage pits. A single extended family probably occupied each pair of houses.

Pottery, People, and the Wider Cosmos

Late Woodland jars are thinner walled and more elaborately embellished than pots made in earlier periods. The finest and most widespread styles found in Wisconsin are known collectively to archaeologists as Madison

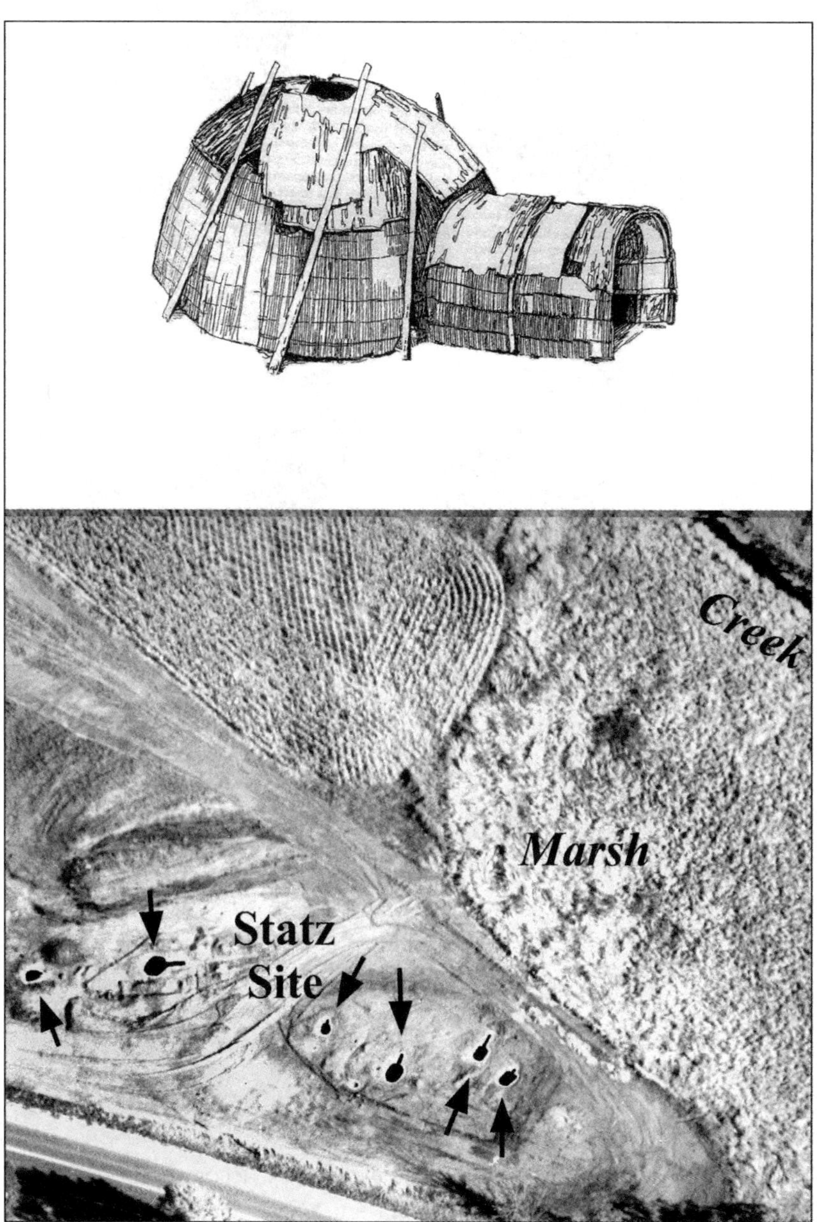

Figure 7.3. *Above*: artist's conception of a keyhole-shaped pithouse. *Below*: aerial photograph of the arrangement of pithouses at the Statz site.

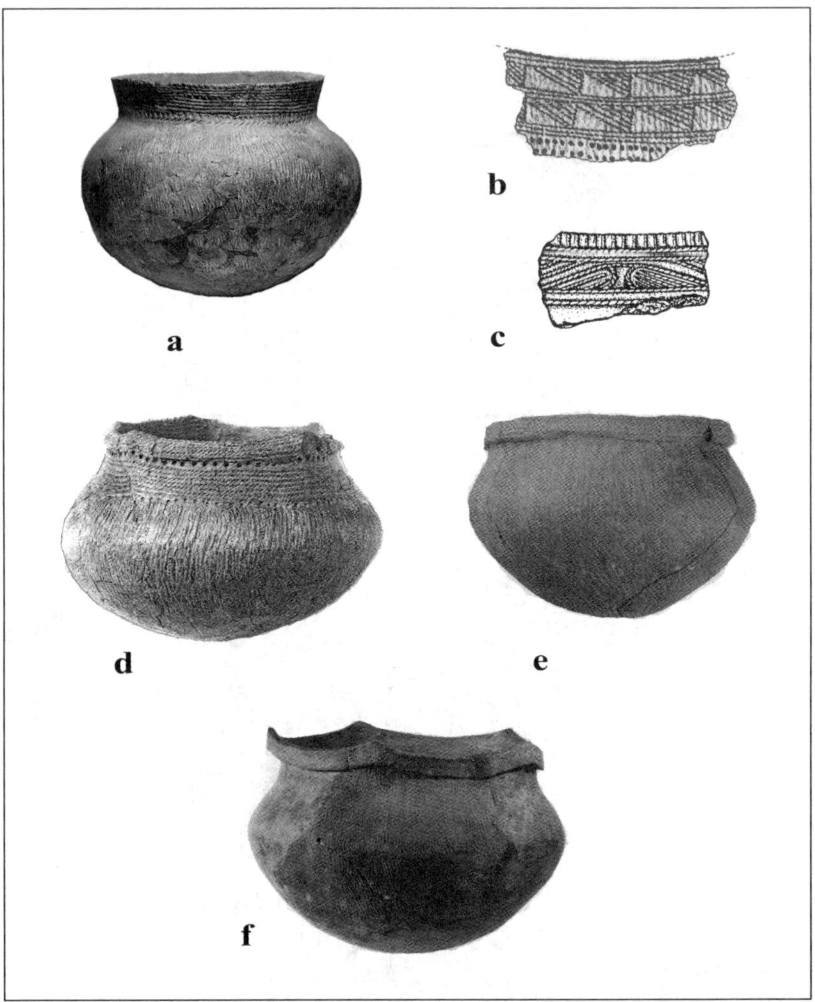

Figure 7.4. Late Woodland pottery: (a) Madison cord-impressed pot; (b) Madison cord-impressed rim sherd from the Gottschall Rockshelter; (c) cord-impressed bird from the Fred Edwards site in southwestern Wisconsin; (d) cord-impressed collared pot; (e) collared pot from the Nitschke mound group; (f) collared pot from Aztalan.

ware, and these rank among the most exquisitely decorated pottery ever made in the midwestern United States (figure 7.4). Madison ware jars are decorated with intricate geometric designs made by impressing woven fabrics, single cords, knotted cords, and stamps made from cords into the moist clay surfaces of the pots. A second style, known as "Angelo Punctated" and decorated with alternating bands of trailed lines and indentations rather than cord impressions, was made in west-central Wisconsin.[11] Angelo Punctated jars are very similar to other pottery made in Minnesota, suggesting that people in west-central Wisconsin had ties to residents further to the west on the eastern prairies.

After about A.D. 900, and coinciding with increases in corn horticulture, another Late Woodland pottery form, bearing a distinctive collar around the rim, became increasingly common. Collared ware, with its simplified cord-impressed decorations, replaced Madison ware as the predominant form of pottery found at Late Woodland sites in the region before the disappearance of the Late Woodland way of life from the archaeological record around A.D. 1200. Some archaeologists speculate that the appearance of collared, cord-impressed pottery signaled an invasion of new groups into southern Wisconsin: Late Woodland farming peoples from Illinois or the Eastern Great Lakes who began expanding or migrating into Wisconsin in the ninth century, at first living side by side with local effigy-mound-building people and then replacing or absorbing them completely.[12]

Recent studies show that collared pottery simply represents a style that became more popular over time among many Late Woodland peoples in the Midwest as they became increasingly horticultural.[13] Both Madison ware and collared styles were found mixed together at the Late Woodland Statz site, but the collared styles increased in frequency later in the site's history, and this pattern of slow replacement recurred across Wisconsin. Furthermore, collared wares have been found in effigy mounds themselves along with uncollared Late Woodland wares.[14]

Both decorated Madison ware and some collared ware jars bear designs similar to those on Early Woodland pottery in Wisconsin: chevrons, triangles, and horizontal, vertical, and diagonal lines. As noted earlier, this geometric imagery seems to represent the upper and lower levels of a tiered universe.[15] The dualistic concept of opposing but balanced forces inhabiting different levels of the cosmos is so widespread in the archaeological record and among living Native societies across the Americas that it must have considerable antiquity.

Sometimes the symbolism is clear, but often it occurs in more abstract forms. Clear upper-world and lower-world imagery appears on Late Woodland pots in Illinois in the form of cord-impressed figures (figure 7.5). The figures include birds and, in some examples, human beings dressed as birds. The bird impersonators depicted on the Illinois pots and in many other Native American art forms have been interpreted as medicine men or shamans calling on upper-world forces during rituals and dances.

The lower world was represented on the Illinois pottery by images of long-tailed water spirits, who, in Native belief systems, were often conceived

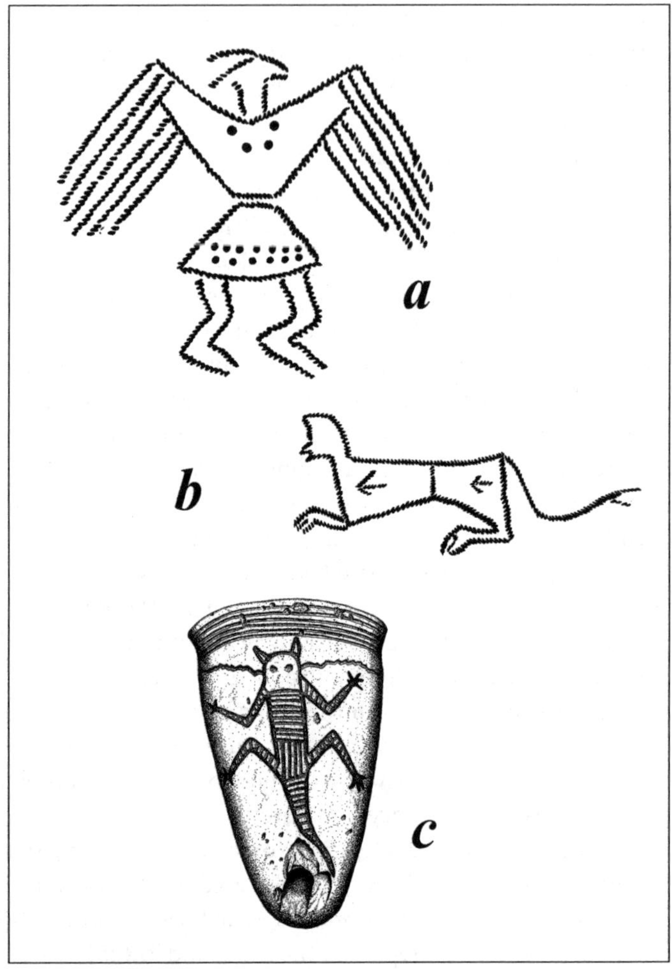

Figure 7.5. Upper-world and lower-world symbolism on Late Woodland pottery: (a) bird-dancer and (b) long-tailed water spirit on Late Woodland pottery from Illinois; (c) depiction of a horned water spirit on a Late Woodland pipe found near Mauston, Wisconsin, and documented by the Mississippi Valley Archaeological Research Center.

of as inhabiting a watery world under the earth. They both complemented and opposed upper-world beings, representing femininity, creation, darkness, death and rebirth, and chaos. Throughout the Americas, such spirit beings were thought of as taking the form of creatures that mixed the features of cougars, jaguars, snakes, deer, bison, fish, birds, other animals, and humans.[16] The powerful beings that the Ho-Chunk (Winnebago),

Figure 7.6. Thunderbirds at the Twin Bluffs rock-art site.

Menominee, Potawatomi, and Ojibwe called water spirits or water panthers were primarily feline in form, with long tails and horns or antlers, and they sometimes had scales and dorsal spikes. In historic times, Great Lakes tribes decorated twined bags with images of water panthers on one side and their complements the thunderbirds on the other side.[17]

As with earlier pottery designs, David Benn related chevrons and triangular designs on Late Woodland pottery to the upper world and parallel lines to the lower world.[18] Depictions of water spirits on one Late Woodland pipe found in the effigy mound region show that Late Woodland people perceived these powerful beings as horned, striped, or spotted creatures with long tails and clawed or taloned feet, almost identical to how earlier Middle Woodland perceived them. The image in figure 7.5 is very similar to the depiction of a water spirit as viewed from above, as shown on the Middle Woodland pipe described in chapter 5. Images of water spirits that may or may not date from the Late Woodland are also carved into and/or painted on the walls of caves and rockshelters. Other rock-art sites, those usually associated with bluffs or heights, bear clear images of thunderbirds as depicted in even modern Native art (figure 7.6). Similar beings, from both realms, appear in earthen form among the effigy mounds.

The Emergence and Spread of the Effigy Mound Ceremonial Complex

The Early and Middle Woodland custom of building earthen mounds to bury the dead, mark social territories, and ceremonially renew the world continued into the Late Woodland period, but with some stunning differences. Mound construction greatly accelerated, and Late Woodland people throughout southern Wisconsin and in parts of adjoining states engaged in a spectacular custom that involved the creation of sometimes massive earthen funerary sculptures of birds, mammals, supernatural beings, and even humans. Well over three thousand effigy mounds were erected across southern Wisconsin, usually together with many more thousands of conical and linear mound forms. A few prominent and select locations were transformed into huge ceremonial complexes containing hundreds of effigy mounds, conical mounds, and linear mounds. As previously discussed, the first effigy mounds may well have emerged from the Hopewell Ceremonial Complex as it faded, eventually giving birth to a new Effigy Mound Ceremonial Complex. The Effigy Mound Complex is unique in the world and certainly qualifies as an archaeological world wonder.

Wisconsin's effigy mounds are so linked to the Late Woodland period that until recently it was common to use the labels "Late Woodland" and "Effigy Mound Culture" interchangeably in Wisconsin. However, effigy mounds were not built by all of Wisconsin's Late Woodland peoples. As we shall see, people living in northern Wisconsin had their own distinct kinds of mound ceremony. Furthermore, the people who built effigy mounds in southern Wisconsin probably thought of themselves as members of many different, independent communities rather than as members of a single tribe or culture. Effigy construction was an idea shared by many people, much as people from many cultures around the world call themselves Roman Catholics or Buddhists today.

Some effigy mound builders returned to places used by earlier peoples, indicating a desire to associate themselves with ancestral peoples or sacred places, if not outright cultural links between the people of the different mound-building traditions. In contrast, in the vicinity of modern Waukesha, Wisconsin, local residents seem to have deliberately avoided places where older mounds stood.[19] Effigy mounds represented a ceremonial that was more narrowly regional in scope than Hopewell and that may have fostered harmony and interdependence among local populations. As with the much earlier Old Copper ritual exchanges, such ceremonials would have been a valuable uniting force among and within communities attempting to deal with the consequences of growing populations, increasingly sedentary and horticultural ways of life, and, later, frictions arising from the arrival of Middle Mississippian strangers and their customs. At some sites, ridged earthen enclosures accompanied the mound groups, defining spaces that might have been used for dances or related ceremonies.

Long a mysterious part of the Wisconsin landscape, the effigy mounds are now regarded as monumental representations of the same underlying belief structure and worldview encoded on Woodland pottery and other artwork; as long suspected, they almost certainly are a mirror of a clan-based social system. In the words of R. Clark Mallam, effigy mound ceremonialism represents ancient "ideology from the earth."[20] Likewise, Robert Hall characterized the effigy mounds as "monumental constructions of the cosmology of their builders."[21] Noting that many effigy mounds were clearly built to be in motion, Birmingham has more recently proposed that effigy mounds were not static monuments or simply elaborate tomb markers but rather ancestral or otherwise powerful spirits brought into visible existence by rituals at places on the natural landscape where those spirits were perceived to dwell.[22] In this view, the effigy mound landscapes were perceived to be alive.

Wisconsin is the heartland of the effigy mound phenomenon, although the effigy mound region also includes adjoining counties in Illinois, Iowa, and Minnesota (figure 7.7). To the south, it extends from Lake Michigan near the Wisconsin-Illinois border westward to the Rock River valley in Illinois and then northwest for a short distance into Iowa. To the west, the area runs along a north-south line that takes in corners of Iowa and Minnesota. Turning east just north of La Crosse, the boundary extends generally east to Green Bay, generally following the tension zone—the transition between southern plants and animals and the North Woods. There are some outliers, but these boundaries encompass the major concentrations of effigy mound groups.

In his environmental study of the distribution of effigy mounds in Iowa, Clark Mallam pointed out that this region generally corresponds to a distinct environmental area characterized by mixed southern hardwood forests, oak savannas, and some prairie. In addition to the abundant aquatic resources found in its many lakes, rivers, and wetlands, the region offered a great diversity of wild plant- and animal-food resources.[23] Among the most important of them were deer, whose population density is greatest in this large region. Immediately to the north lie the coniferous-hardwood forests, and to the west and south, broadly speaking, is prairie—environments with a much narrower selection of foods. Deer were not plentiful in those areas.

Within this extremely food-rich region, Late Woodland people built mound groups that ranged in size from a just a few to many hundreds of

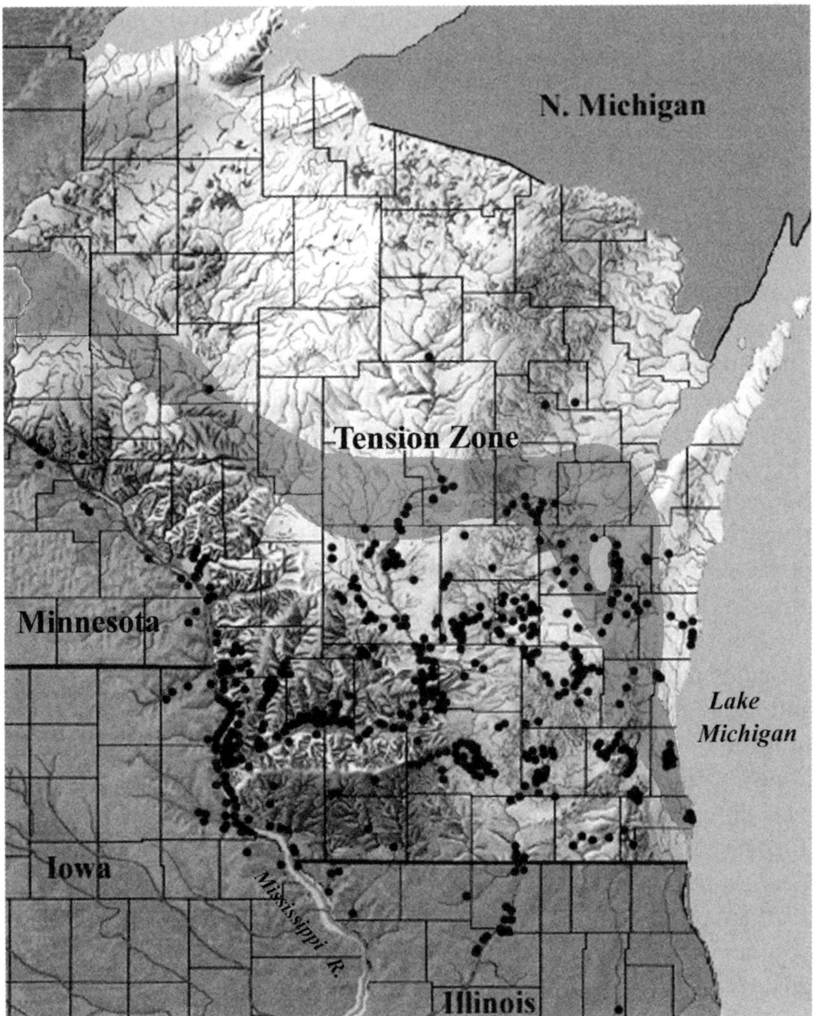

Figure 7.7. Distribution of effigy mound sites.

mounds. A typical group contains around a dozen mounds, with an average of three effigies, three linear mounds, and six conical mounds per site, though the size and composition of specific groups varies widely. Isolated effigy mounds occur, but rarely.

One of the largest mound groups in Wisconsin is the Cranberry Creek mound group, near Necedah on the Cranberry Creek, a tributary of the Wisconsin River. The Cranberry Creek group may trace changes within the Effigy Mound Ceremonial Complex through time, as the mound landscape

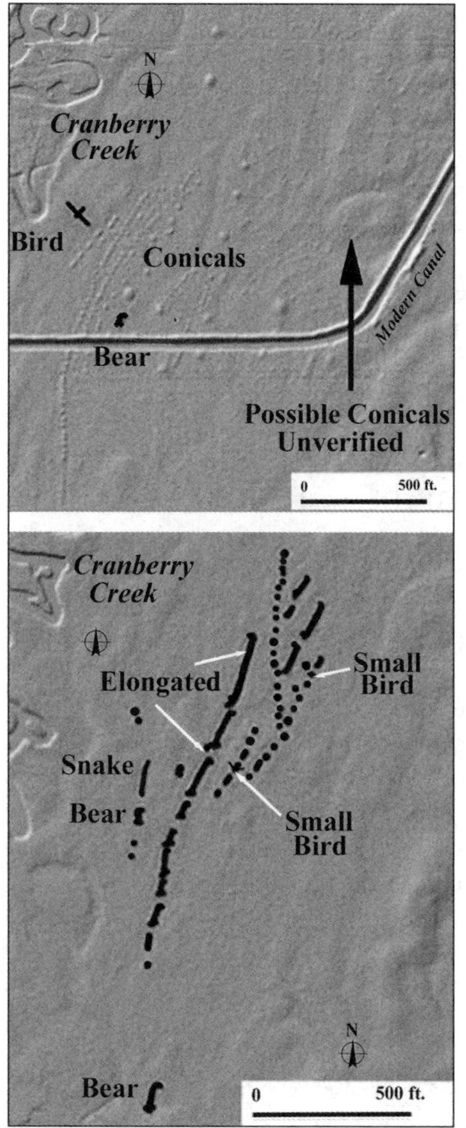

Figure 7.8. LiDAR images of Cranberry Creek mound landscape. *Above*: northern group with effigies highlighted. Recent LiDAR of this northern group shows many more possible mounds in dense vegetation on the western side that have not been previously documented and need to be verified. *Below*: southern group with mounds highlighted.

is divided into two parts (figure 7.8). The southern mounds are arranged in a broadly linear fashion, with rows of conical mounds and effigies of small birds, bears, and forms that are either unusually elongated animals or perhaps water spirits with a curious downward flip on the ends of their long tails. To the north, several hundred conical mounds are arranged in rows, along with a mere two effigies: a bird and a bear. Most of the conical mounds are small and low, like those found in other Late Woodland groups, but the group appears to have been built around several large conical mounds that might be earlier mounds or that might represent a type of Late Woodland mound that contains mass burials rather than the usual one or few. Just north of this grouping is a Late Woodland camp that produced examples of collared-ware pottery most commonly made after A.D. 900. The closeness of this camp may indicate that the northern grouping dates toward the end of the Late Woodland period.

Similar mound landscapes where only a few key effigy mounds are found among numerous conical mounds are located along the Mississippi River. At the Sny Magill site, in Iowa, a large number of conical mounds arranged in neat rows sit next to a few effigy mounds. Excavations at Sny McGill determined that mound building began there as early as the Late Archaic. At the Diamond Bluff site in northeast Wisconsin, dozens of conical mounds are joined by two effigies. The Diamond Bluff site, however, is a late site, with evidence of Woodland, Mississippian, and Oneota interaction.[24]

The largest effigy mound landscape ever recorded was located on the banks of the Mississippi River in northeastern Iowa. The Harper's Ferry "Great Group" (technically several immense mound groups very near one another) may have once contained 894 mounds, including 271 effigy mounds![25] Sadly, the Harper's Ferry mounds have mostly vanished. At the virtually intact Raisbeck mound complex in southwestern Wisconsin, there are a total of 40 effigies among the 125 mounds, the largest single concentration of effigy mounds left in existence (figure 7.9).[26]

These ceremonial landscapes are astonishing not only because of the number of mounds they contain but also because of the sheer number of mounds that were built within a comparatively short period of time. Before the custom of building effigy mounds ended between A.D. 1100 and 1200, more than one thousand effigy mound centers had been created in Wisconsin, home to more than twelve thousand individual mounds. Several thousand were recognizable effigies of animals or spirits, while the remainder were low conical, oval, linear, and other geometric forms. The actual number of mounds built by effigy builders during the Late Woodland period was even higher; not every Late Woodland ceremonial center built during the period of effigy construction contained effigy mounds, and many mound sites were destroyed before they could be recorded by nineteenth- and twentieth-century researchers.

Effigy mound groups were built in approximately twenty-five subregions, each containing several clusters of mound sites and each probably representing the home territory of one or more related bands of people.[27] One such territory was the "Four Lakes" region in and around the greater

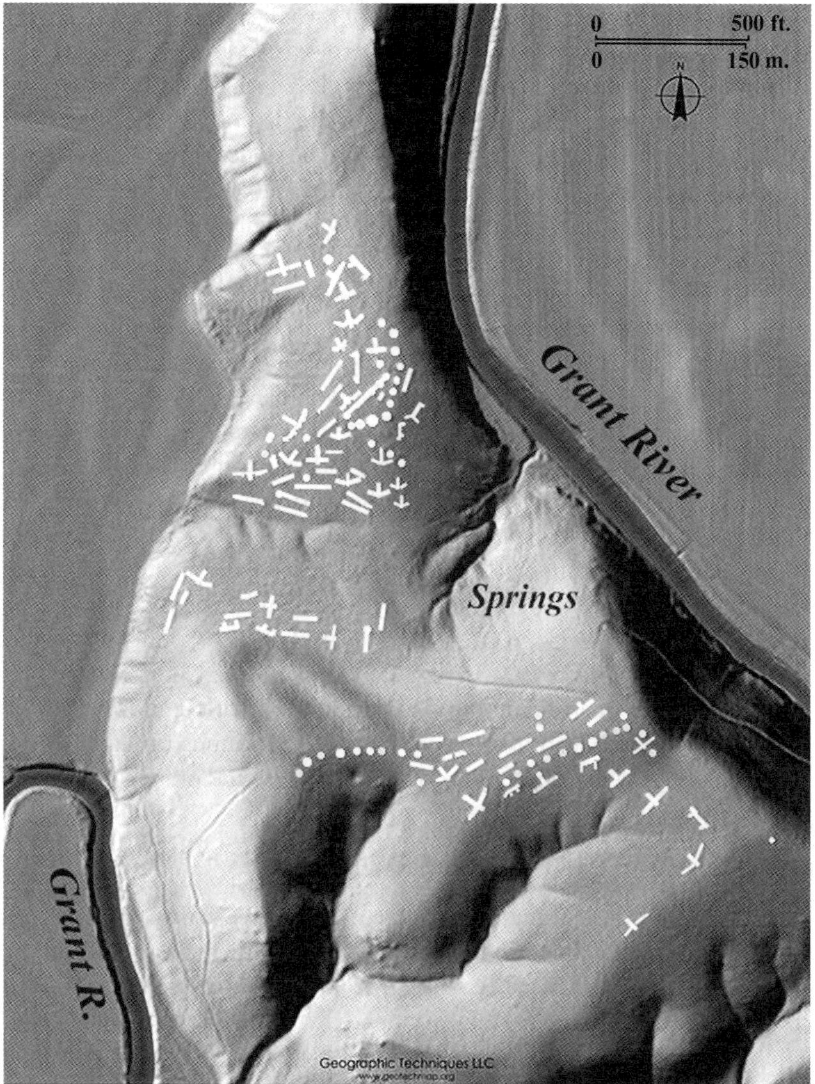

Figure 7.9. LiDAR image of the Raisbeck mound group with mounds highlighted for clarity.

Madison metropolitan area in south-central Wisconsin, where more than 100 groupings containing more than 1,200 individual mounds, most constructed during the Late Woodland, once existed.[28] Other areas with remarkable densities of effigy mound groups are along the lower Wisconsin River near its confluence with the Mississippi River, and along the Grant, Rock, and upper Fox Rivers.

With some notable exceptions, most of the effigy sites in each territory were located on high ground, bluffs, or terraces overlooking major rivers, streams, lakes, and large wetlands, though the specific land forms chosen varied from place to place. People living in the Bad Axe Valley of western Wisconsin preferred to put their mounds on the slopes at the bases of river bluffs. Further south, near modern Cassville, Wisconsin, effigy builders chose high ground on the summits of the towering bluffs overlooking the Mississippi and its tributaries.

Over the several-century span of effigy construction, each community would have needed to build at least one mound per year to account for just the known mounds, and a figure of two mounds per year per community is probably more accurate. While most Late Woodland mounds are low and many effigy and linear mounds are less than one hundred feet long, the amount of effort required to build a mound was sometimes substantial. The largest existing effigy mound in the Midwest—a huge bird with a wingspan of 624 feet—is located on the state-owned grounds of Mendota Mental Health Institute on Lake Mendota near Madison. An even larger bird effigy with a wingspan of a quarter-mile once existed as part of the remarkable Eagle Township effigy mounds in Richland County. Preserved in Man Mound County Park, near Baraboo, is an effigy in the shape of a 218-foot-long human being, now a National Historic Landmark, with horns or a horned headdress. Some snake-like mounds on lakes in the Madison area reached lengths of seven hundred feet and more.[29]

Mound Construction and Location

Much labor and investment of time went into construction of a mound. The rituals that went along with mound building in themselves could extend over long periods of time. The aboveground parts of effigy mounds seem to have been constructed in single (but perhaps lengthy) building episodes. The mounds are rarely layered or stratified, though some very elaborately layered mounds containing sequences of white, yellow, red, and black fills are known.[30] In many cases, there does not appear to have been any special preparation of the ground surface before the mounds were built, but again this is not a universal trait. In some cases, mound floors were carefully prepared with different colored soils or sediments. The methods used to build effigy mounds were similar throughout southern Wisconsin but varied in detail from community to community and from one mound designer to another. Effigies of different forms built at the same ceremonial center usually share the same construction techniques, suggesting that the person or persons responsible for directing a mound's construction did so for all the different social groups associated with effigy symbols in that community.

The dead were placed on the surface of the ground or in shallow pits in areas that would become the head or heart of the mound form, indicating an intimate association between the dead and the effigy. Occasionally mounds also contain rock arrangements, receptacles formed from clay, and evidence of ritual fires. Sometimes an intaglio or "reverse cameo" in the form of the effigy to be constructed was first dug several feet into the ground. The intaglio was later filled, forming a three-dimensional earth sculpture. In most cases, it appears that dirt from the surrounding area was scraped rather than dug out, with antler rakes and small stone tools. Large tools equivalent to shovels or hoes have not been identified among the implements of Late Woodland peoples, although it is possible that these were made of wood that would not have survived in the archaeological record.

Most mounds were built in harmony with the landscape. As was frequently observed in the past and as is very clear to all who have visited mound groups, the orientation and arrangement of mounds often follow the contours of the landforms on which they were built, apparently artistically inspired by the topography (figure 7.10). The landscape itself was used to bring the mounds to life. Birds fly gracefully across ridge tops and up and down slopes. Animals parade across ridge tops and slopes, changing direction, sometimes subtly, with the orientation of the terrain. Water spirits move up and down elevations, crawling to and from springs and other water sources. So closely do mounds relate to the landscape that it sometimes is difficult to see where the mounds end and the rest of the terrain begins. The concept of harmony is also illustrated by the absence of holes or borrow pits in the landscape, despite the mounds' having been built of dirt from the surrounding area. The effigy builders seem to have taken their mound fill from shallow scrapes or in ways that would heal quickly, leaving no scars behind. In all these regards, we are reminded of R. Clark Mallam's interpretation that effigy mounds were built to symbolize and ritually maintain balance and harmony with the natural world within the context of ceremonies of renewal and rebirth.

A small conical mound might take fifty adults one afternoon to build. An average effigy mound might take the same-size group a full day and the largest mounds almost two weeks working dawn to dusk. But mound building would have been only the tip of the iceberg. Analogy with modern Native funeral ritual suggests that the construction of every mound was accompanied by other ceremonies that required further investments of labor and time—feasts, dances, give-away ceremonies, speeches, and both public

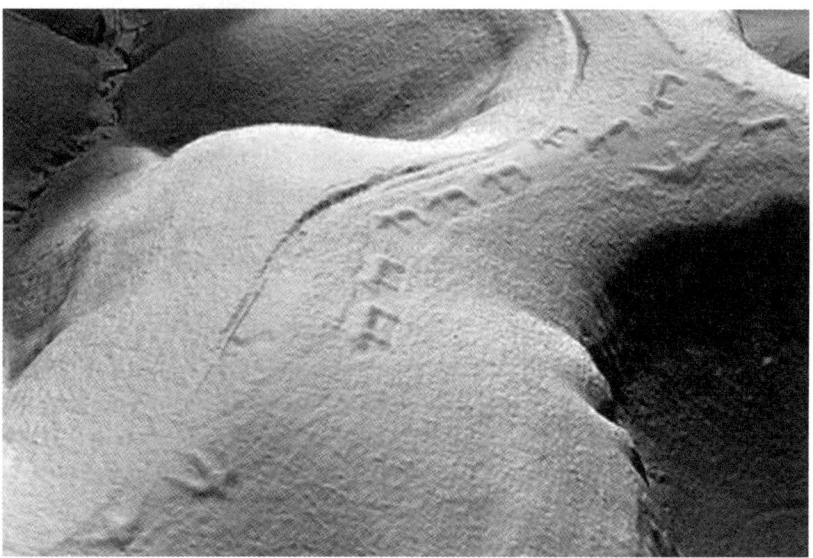

Figure 7.10. LiDAR image of the Marching Bear mound group at Effigy Mounds National Monument.

and private rituals designed to ease the passage of the dead to the next world, comfort family and friends, restore balance to the community and the universe at large, reaffirm ties between the living and the ancestors, and celebrate the eternal cycle of death and rebirth. At the Kolterman and Nitschke I mound groups in eastern Wisconsin, concentrations of butchered and burned animal bone accompanied the interments, suggesting that feasts were occasionally a part of the rituals and that the food remains were buried as offerings.[31] The scale of these efforts is beyond that usually associated with hunting and gathering societies on the edge of horticultural life, but the distribution of mounds may hold clues about how small communities managed to sustain mound ritual.

Despite great variations in mound forms, the sculpting of effigy mounds throughout each region generally followed the same basic ritual protocols. For example, there was a tendency for mounds to be situated consistent with the orientation of the natural feature upon which they were built, roughly parallel or perpendicular to the land form, and for animal mounds to be built with legs downslope and heads pointing downstream when located along streams and rivers (figure 7.11).

Effigy mounds and mound landscapes occupy prominent locations on the terrain and tend to be associated with the richest areas of plant and animal resources that could support the gathering of a large number of people on a

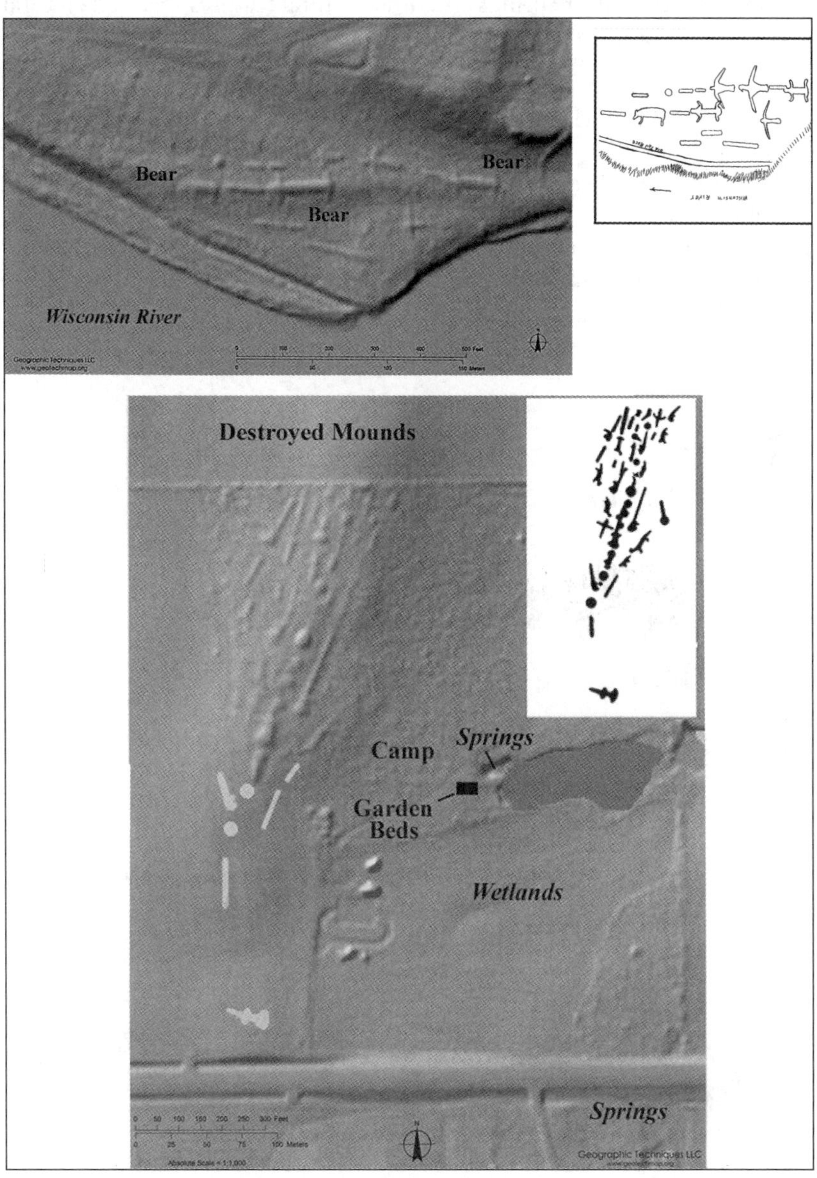

Figure 7.11. *Above*: LiDAR image of the Bloyer or Twin Lizard mound group on the Wisconsin River. *Below*: LiDAR image of the Nitschke mound group.

seasonal basis.[32] But the locations of effigy mound groups were not based solely on economic considerations. Like earlier mounds, many effigy groups were built near springs and other natural features that had cultural and spiritual connotations.

The Meaning of the Mound Forms

Effigy mounds come in many different forms. Most can be now recognized as animal-like spirits and supernatural beings long important to Native people. Adding to the variety of observed forms is the insight that effigy mound forms were made in one of two perspectives, either in profile or flattened, as though looking down on the form (or up in the case of flying birds) (figure 7.12).[33] Some birds are alternatively shown with wings

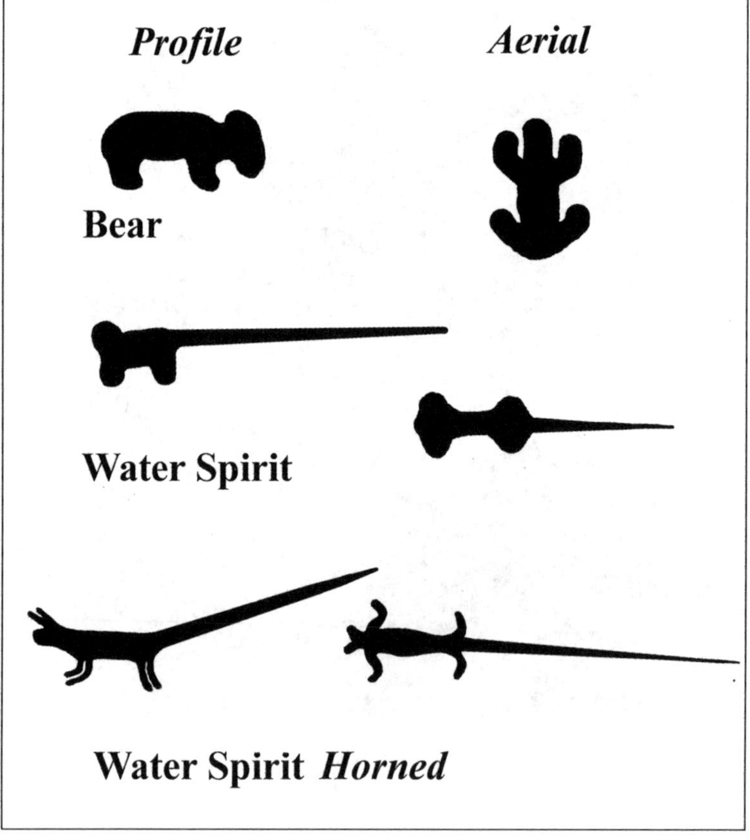

Figure 7.12. Examples of effigy mounds shown in two perspectives.

folded parallel to the body rather than outstretched in the way that thunderbirds are often depicted in a full frontal perspective in traditional art and iconography. Many other mound shapes defy easy identification.

In the center of the effigy mound region around the chain of lakes historically referred to as the "Four Lakes" (although there are five lakes), most, if not all, major animal-like forms appear to be present. At least ten basic forms can be identified, although some of these are of the same animal or spirit but shown in a different perspective (figure 7.13). There are birds of several

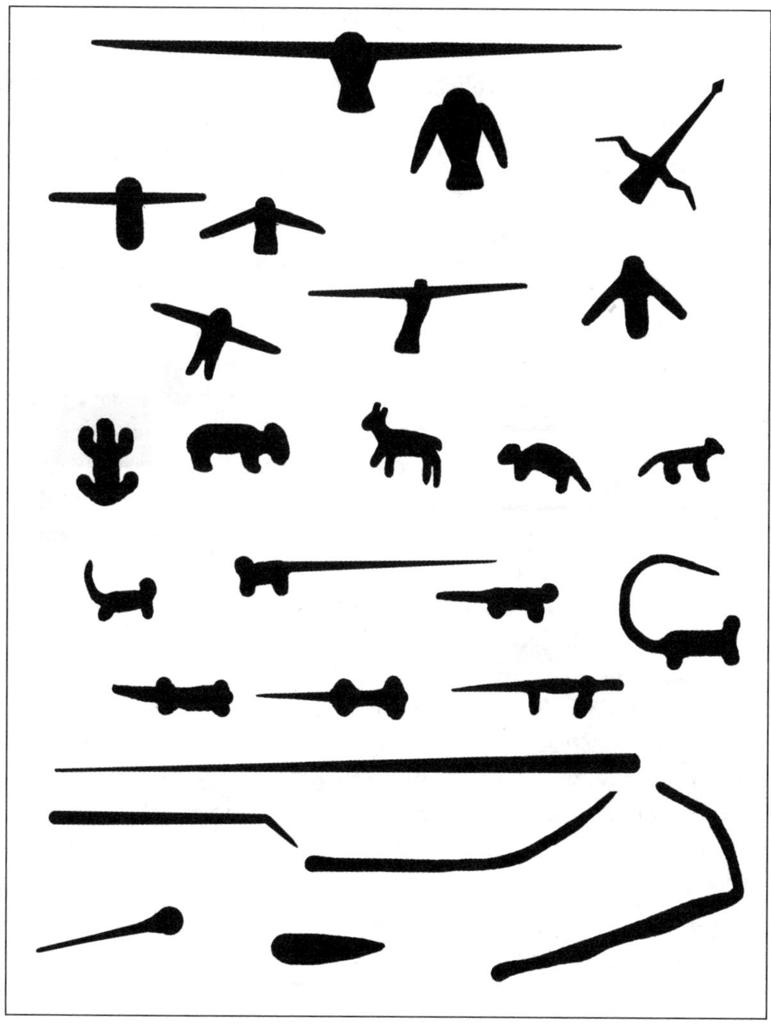

Figure 7.13. Common effigy mound forms in south-central Wisconsin.

types, including waterfowl, raptors, and what appear to be thunderbirds; bears and canines; water mammals (e.g., otter, mink, fisher, muskrat); long tailed panther-like water spirits; and what might be snakes.[34] Rosebrough identified many more effigy mound forms recorded over 175 years of previous mound research, including several unique and undecipherable forms.[35]

Different researchers have attempted to classify effigy forms, but even currently accepted categories are unlikely to fully and accurately represent how Late Woodland peoples perceived the mounds they built. Even so, mounds can be generally grouped into simple if probably overly broad categories. As with earlier burial mounds, the key to the meaning of the effigy mounds can be found in Native belief systems and cosmology.

In the 1970s, R. Clark Mallam provided the insight that most of the animals or spirits depicted in effigy form fall into three classes corresponding to the three natural realms—air, earth, and water—that provide the resources on which humans depend. Because of this, he theorized that mounds had been built to symbolize and ritually maintain balance and harmony with the natural world. He viewed the mound groups as "places to which people returned again and again for the purpose of life-way reinforcement and renewal."[36]

Robert Hall took this theory a step further. He noted a close parallel between the major forms of effigies and the depictions of powerful spirits that inhabit the upper world and the lower world in the cosmology of many Native American tribes of the Midwest and argued that the primary organizing principle for mound groups was these two major divisions.[37] Thunderbird and other bird effigies symbolized the air or upper world. The lower world was subdivided into earth and water and was represented by bears and water spirits, respectively. Hall made the convincing case that long-tailed effigies, variously known as panthers, lizards, and turtles, can be viewed as variable depictions of the water spirits important in midwestern belief systems and that appear in other Late Woodland art forms. Working from this Native worldview, Hall stated that effigy mound groups were "monumental constructions of the cosmology of their builders and represented the division of the world into earth/water and sky divisions."[38]

Some mound groups clearly depict this arrangement. The Woodward Shores mound group on the north shore of Lake Mendota, now partly destroyed, models the underlying structure of effigy mound ceremonialism in a horizontal and sequential fashion (figure 7.14). Birds, likely thunderbirds, begin the grouping and are followed by earth mammals, canines (foxes or wolves), and a bear. The grouping ends with water-related effigy mounds, most of which are oriented toward the lake: water spirits, a water mammal, and a linear mound that perhaps was meant to be a snake.

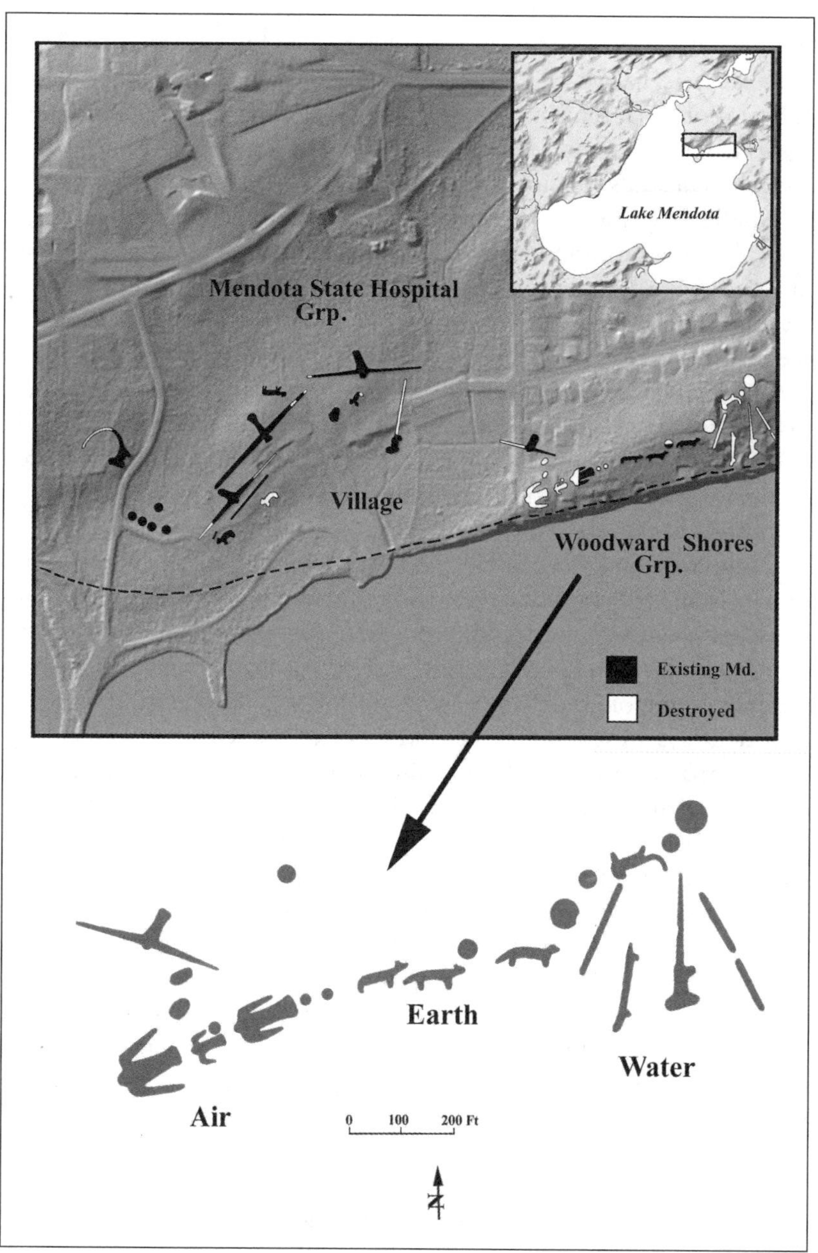

Figure 7.14. The Woodward Shores mound group on the north shore of Lake Mendota, based on a map by T. H. Lewis and surviving mounds.

Other data provide some support for Hall's observations. The most common classes of all identifiable effigy forms are birds (40 percent), bear and bear-like forms (21 percent), and long-tailed forms variously referred to as panthers, lizards, and turtles but that probably represent water spirits (18 percent). The remaining 21 percent are various kinds of animals and spirits that often cannot be easily identified, including canine-like mounds and different kinds of aquatic mammals.

Studies have found a substantial difference in the distribution of these key effigy mound forms.[39] In eastern Wisconsin, where rivers, lakes and marshes abound, water-related effigy mounds—especially water spirits—are found in high frequencies, whereas birds and bears are most common in the rugged Driftless Area, in southwest Wisconsin, with its high hills, cliffs, and bluffs. Between these two areas, birds, bears, and water spirits commonly occur together in mound groups (figures 7.15, 7.16). A case study of the Four Lakes area found a similar distribution of mound forms related to topography and geography within the large effigy mound landscape found around the lakes.[40]

A close examination conducted by Rosebrough of all effigy mound groups in the effigy mound region found that each of the twenty-five regions had its own unique blend of mound forms, with one or two forms far more common than the rest (figure 7.17).[41] No matter which effigy form was most common, forms from the complementary or opposing world are almost always present in the area and are often the second most common forms in that territory. Rosebrough also found that the more effigies present at a specific grouping, the more likely it was to have effigy forms representing both the upper world and the lower world. Smaller mound sites often contain only a single effigy form or mounds representing only one level of the cosmos. Earth animals such as bears and/or short-tailed animals are the dominant forms in the Mississippi Valley south of Prairie du Chien and in the area of modern Baraboo. Water spirits are prevalent in lake and wetland-rich eastern Wisconsin. Upper-world bird forms are the dominant type in interior portions of the rugged Driftless Area, where they are paired with earth animals, and portions of the Rock River valley in southern Wisconsin, where they are paired with water spirits.

Figure 7.15 (*top right*). *Above*: the bird-dominated Eagle Township mound group on the Wisconsin River in southwestern Wisconsin, based on mapping by T. H. Lewis. *Below*: LiDAR image of the Kingsley Bend mound group on the Wisconsin River in south-central Wisconsin.

Figure 7.16 (*bottom right*). Original map of water-themed mounds at the Hagner or Lizard effigy mound group, now part of Lizard Mound County Park.

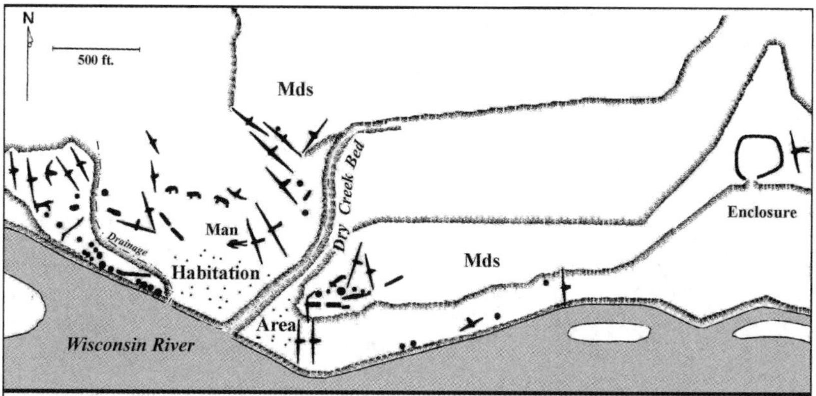

N
500 ft.
Mds
Dry Creek Bed
Drainage
Man
Habitation
Area
Mds
Enclosure
Wisconsin River

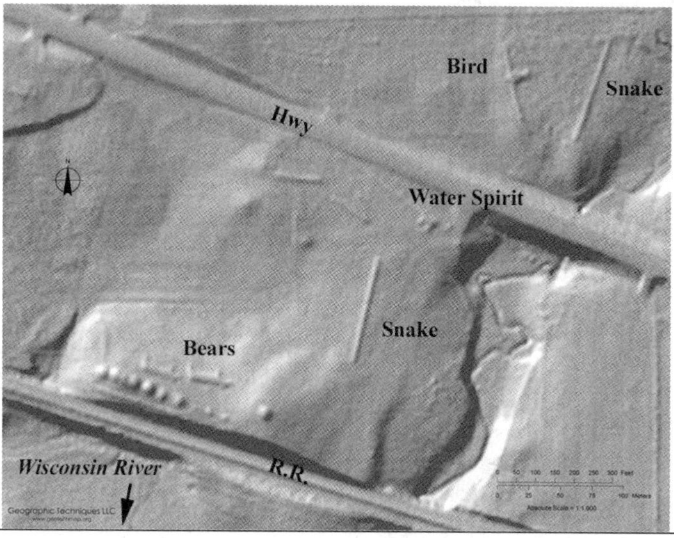

Bird
Snake
Hwy
Water Spirit
Snake
Bears
Wisconsin River
R.R.
Geographic Techniques LLC

WOODED AREA
HAGNER'S WOODS
MOUNDS DESTROYED BEFORE 1883
N
W
E
S
SCALE IN FEET
HAGNER INDIAN MOUNDS
FARMINGTON TOWNSHIP, WASHINGTON COUNTY, WIS.
SURVEYED BY
KERMIT FRECKMANN
1941

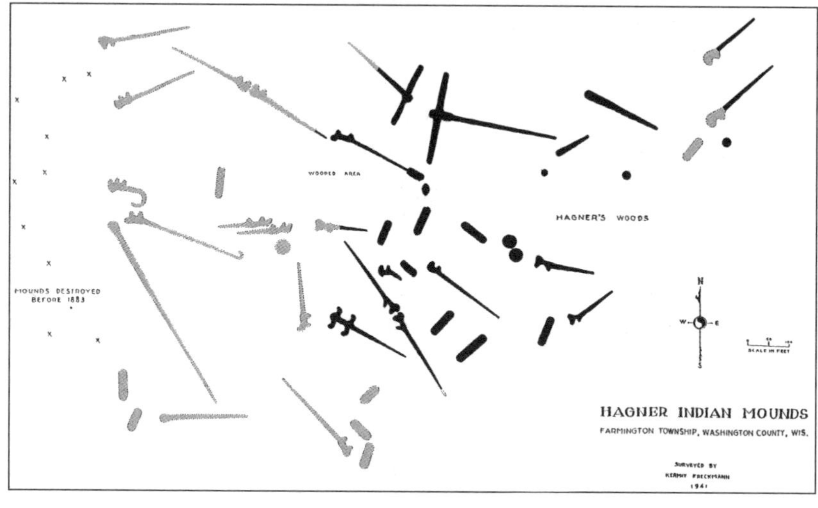

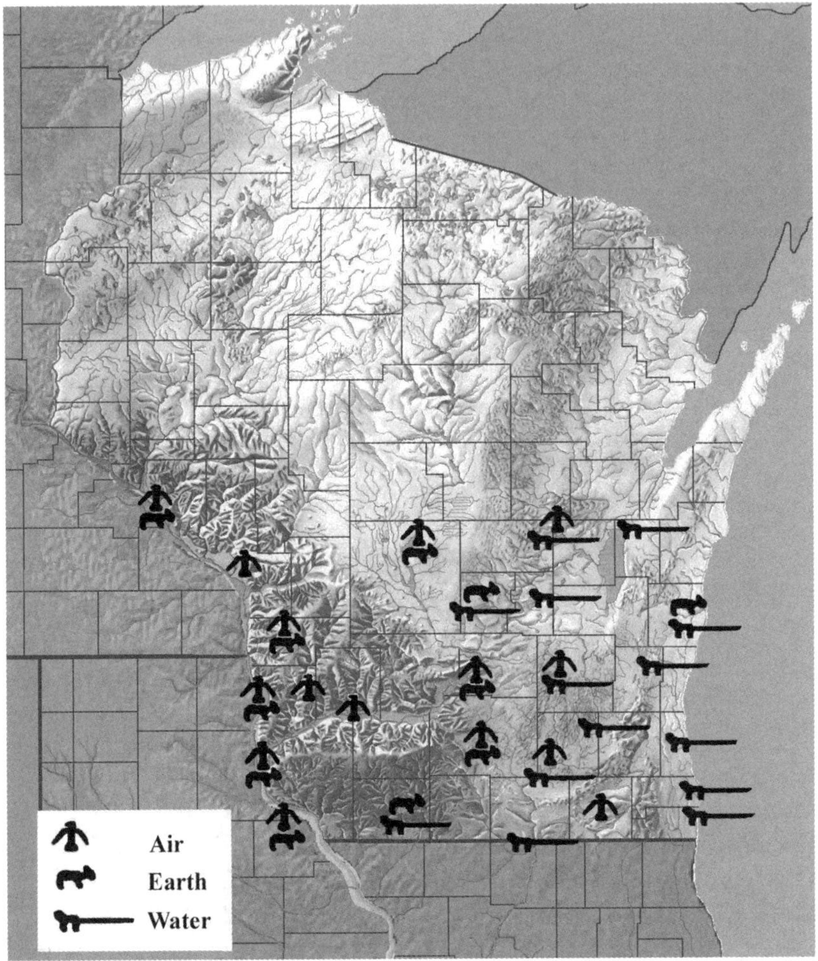

Figure 7.17. Subregions showing the most common forms of effigy mounds.

The fact that effigies representing the upper world and the lower world are found in every presumed Late Woodland community supports Mallam's contention that Late Woodland people were concerned with maintaining balance and harmony in the world. This is consistent with a deeply rooted and widespread pattern found in the Americas. Native societies from South America to the Great Lakes often divide themselves into two complementary but always slightly unequal parts.[42] Sometimes, as among the Ho-Chunk and the Menominee, those two parts are linked to the upper and lower worlds.

According to Radin, Ho-Chunk are divided into two groups: "those who are above" (*wangeregi herera*) and "those who are on earth" (*manegi herera*).[43] These divisions or "moieties," as anthropologists call them, are exogamous; that is, people cannot marry members of their own social division. Each moiety is subdivided into a number of clans, each with its own origin story and social responsibilities. The largest and most important clan in the upper division is Thunderbird. Thunderbirds are powerful spirits who are approachable by humans as guardians and helpmates. Lightning flashes from their eyes, and thunder is caused by the flapping of their wings. Other members of the upper division include the Warrior or War-People, Eagle, Hawk, and Pigeon. Ho-Chunk people told Radin that the Warrior clan is paired with the Hawk clan but could be symbolized by the depiction of a human being.

The lower division is represented by clans of the earth and water: Bear, Buffalo, Deer, Elk, Fish, Snake, Water Spirit, and Wolf. Of these, the Bear and the Water Spirit clans are the most important, with some Ho-Chunk maintaining that the Water Spirit clan ruled over the lower division in former times. Water spirits are in eternal opposition to the thunderbirds. While capable of malevolence, they are also "capable of bestowing great blessings on man."[44] Regarding the water spirit, Ho-Chunk people told Brown that "it is sometimes regarded as a 'bad spirit,' destroying men by overturning their canoes and in other ways. Its good must be gained by offerings."[45] Radin wrote that a constant theme in Ho-Chunk society was the renewal of order in a chaotic world, which was accomplished by the performance of certain rituals, and the maintenance of the balance of social power between the upper world and the lower world, as represented by the Thunderbird and Bear clans.[46]

The symbolism of the effigy mounds is a good match for the social system of the Ho-Chunk, but it is important to point out that other midwestern tribes are organized by similar concepts. For example, the Algonquian-speaking Menominee also have a dualistic belief system, with a multitiered universe organized into halves: an upper and a lower. As for other peoples, the denizens of the upper world are the thunderbirds and other avians. In the lower world live the Great White Bear and the Underground Water Panther. Menominee clans are grouped into two divisions: the Thunderers and the Bears.[47]

An interesting alternative to the two-division model was given to Radin by some Ho-Chunk who identified three clan groupings headed by the thunderbird, bear, and water spirit. What is significant about this arrangement is that it not only more finely defines the realms of the natural world (sky, earth, and water) but also represents the three most common types of effigy mounds.

The Upper World

In this cosmology, a class of mounds associated with the sky or upper world, are found a number of bird forms. This is one of the commonest classes of effigies. The bird category includes straight-winged, eagle-like figures that closely resemble modern Native depictions of the thunderbird. These eagle-like mounds are among the largest effigies ever constructed. As noted earlier, one of several large eagle-like birds arranged around a Late Woodland village on Lake Mendota has a wingspan of 624 feet. As also mentioned, an eagle-like straight-winged bird, probably a thunderbird, with a wingspan of more than nine hundred feet once flew across a terrace near the Wisconsin River in Richland County. A few rare bird mounds have projections or "horns" on their heads and may also represent thunderbirds, as horns are a common way to represent spiritual power in the art of the Americas. At the Gottschall Rockshelter in Iowa County, Robert Hall and Robert Salzer identified a one-thousand-year-old painting of a falcon with an object, probably a cedar bough, attached to its head as is characteristic of thunderbirds mentioned in Ho-Chunk and Ioway stories.[48] As we shall see, peregrine falcons emerged as powerful symbols in the later Mississippian and Oneota cultures. Alternately, horned-bird effigies might represent more common species such as the great horned owl. Not surprisingly waterfowl effigies such as geese are almost always found near lakes and large wetlands, such as the great Horicon Marsh, where waterfowl gather in large numbers today.

Some mounds in this upper-world class have the characteristics of both birds and human beings. These effigies typically have long, wing-like arms; long, forked tails that resemble human legs; and either human or bird-like heads. If these effigies represent birds, they probably depict avian spirits such as thunderbirds or swallow-tailed kites, a striking black-and-white raptor that is now endangered but once soared in Wisconsin's skies. Fork-tailed bird mounds also resemble depictions of "bird-men." Depictions of dancers dressed as birds (probably hawks or falcons) appear on Late Woodland pots in Illinois but are more common in Middle Mississippian and later Oneota iconography. As with other imagery, the presence of possible bird-man mounds in Wisconsin hints that aspects of effigy mound ideology might have been shared with Middle Mississippian and Oneota cultures. Bird imagery, particularly of the hawk and falcon, remained an important element in Native iconography in the Wisconsin region right up to European contact.

The Lower World: Earth

The most common earth-related effigy mounds are those referred to as bears or sometimes as buffalo; it sometimes is difficult to distinguish between the forms. Like thunderbirds and water spirits, bears are considered to be very special spirit beings and often figure prominently in origin stories and clan structures. In the Midwest, bear ceremonialism can be traced back in time as far as the Middle Woodland, when it was clearly associated with Hopewell-influenced ritual. The Menominee of northeastern Wisconsin believe that they are descended from an ancestral bear that emerged from the earth, and the bear stands as a symbol for the lower-world half of the Menominee people as a whole.[49] The Bear clan is the head of the lower-division Ho-Chunk earth clans.

Less common animals in this mound category are canine-like, perhaps representing wolf or fox, and antlered animals such as deer and elk. All these forms are subjective categories and represent the best guesses about the animal or spirit being represented. What they really are, unfortunately, was known only to the original builders. Animal effigies of this class, especially bear and buffalo, are found mainly in the western and central parts of Wisconsin but occasionally in other places.

The Lower World: Water

Water, one part of the lower world, is represented principally by long-tailed effigy forms that historically have been referred to as panthers, turtles, or lizards and that together compose the third-largest class of effigy mounds. As Robert Hall pointed out, so-called turtle mounds do not even look like turtles: they and some so-called lizard mounds appear to be panther or water-spirit mounds as viewed from above, with two legs depicted on each side of their bodies.[50] The real difference among these mound types may be only in the perspective that the builders wanted to provide. The association between long-tailed effigy mounds and water spirits was made quite some time ago and has long been a part of Wisconsin archaeological literature. In 1910, Arlow B. Stout of the Wisconsin Archeological Society asked Fred Dick, a Ho-Chunk man camping with his family near the Wisconsin Dells, about the long-tailed "panther mounds." After consulting with elders, Dick reported that the effigy represented a spirit animal that lived in water.[51] The following year, several well-informed Ho-Chunk men from Nebraska provided Charles E. Brown of the State Historical Society of Wisconsin with the same information: that long-tailed panther mounds were representations of water spirits.

Long-tailed water-spirit mounds are found throughout the effigy mound region but are concentrated in the low-lying eastern part of Wisconsin, where large lakes, swamps, and marshes abound. The association of the water spirits with water is quite obvious from this distribution. Moreover, water-spirit mounds tend to be near springs, which bubble up from beneath the earth and have been held in sacred reverence by ancient people around the world. They are the source of life-giving water, symbolic of rebirth and renewal. Fine sands, like those in springs, are occasionally found in mounds of all periods, perhaps as a symbol of this concept. For Native peoples springs are also entrances to the watery underworld used by powerful water spirits, shamans, and the spirits of the dead. Brown was told in 1926 by Oliver La Mere, a Ho-Chunk from Nebraska with ties to Wisconsin, that springs and other waters were under the care of the Water Spirit clan.[52] In Madison, an unusually dense arrangement of effigy mound groups that included water-spirit forms once existed on the shore of Lake Wingra, a small body of water off the main water transportation route. Such intense ritual interest in this small lake may be explained by the fact that it is fed by a number of large, prominent springs. Some of these springs were considered sacred by the later Ho-Chunk residents of the Madison area.[53]

The presence of sacred springs also may account for the location of the spectacular and enigmatic Lizard mound group near West Bend (see figure 7.16) The group once consisted of nearly eighty mounds, including a pair of goose or crane effigies and a large number of mounds erroneously referred to in the nineteenth century as lizards and not recognized as water spirits. The group is situated on a large low plateau far away from major bodies of water. This unusual location has long puzzled archaeologists. A close inspection of the environment of the group reveals a major clue in that the plateau is part of the headwaters of a branch of the Milwaukee River that flows to Lake Michigan. At several points surrounding the mound group are springs that provide sources of this water.

Snakes or serpents are found among water-related effigy mounds, although these have not been recognized as such in the past and generally are referred to simply as long, tapering mounds. In Native traditions, snakes are viewed as guardians of the underworld, and the Snake clan is one of the lower, water-related division of clans of the Ho-Chunk. Among the Mississippian people snakes had a logical connection to fertility because they are from the watery underworld and are "reborn" when they shed their skin. One stone figurine found in the Cahokia area, called the Birger figurine, is of a woman hoeing the body of a serpent that sprouts gourds from its back.[54] The Serpent Mound of Ohio is in the shape of a huge coiled snake, and snakes are featured in artwork of the Ohio Adena and Hopewell cultures.

Some linear mounds have forked ends that resemble the way horned water serpents are depicted in Native American art.

Several snake effigies in Wisconsin are serpentine in form, but a majority are depicted as straightened. This seems to relate to one of several versions of the world's creation recounted by the Ho-Chunk, in which Earth-Maker sent down snakes to anchor the earth after it continued spinning after being formed.[55] Snake forms are rare in the Driftless area of southwest Wisconsin and are more commonly found in the watery world further east, especially in the south-central part of the state.

Other common forms representative of water may be smaller, tapering linear mounds, sometimes curved, sometimes described as "catfish" or "sturgeon" mounds. These mounds are found within the area of effigy construction in southern Wisconsin but also to the north in Shawano and Oconto Counties. The interpretation that these mounds are fish is, of course, speculative.

Intaglios

Not all effigies associated with the lower world are mounds. In some cases, effigy forms were dug out from the earth to create intaglios, or the reverse of a mound that rises from the ground. Early mound researchers noted the presence of at least eleven open intaglios associated with mound groups near Baraboo, Fort Atkinson, and Milwaukee.[56] Nine of these were water spirits and two others, bears. Previous interpretations were that these were unfinished effigy mounds. However, four water-spirit intaglios were clustered at one site along the Milwaukee River, suggesting that the intaglios were indeed the desired product—effigies of lower-world animals created by excavation into the lower world (figure 7.18). Only one intaglio, a long-tailed water spirit on the Rock River in Fort Atkinson, has survived modern land development. Significantly, during very heavy rains the intaglio fills with water, literally forming a spirit of water, and this seems to be the point of the ritual construction.

Crosses

The intaglios indicate that the effigy mound ceremonials were not just about building forms related to the clans of the dead. This is supported by other effigy forms and mound arrangements. A small number of crosses with equal-sized arms, always oriented to the cardinal directions, are known to have been built in southeastern Wisconsin, including a huge one mapped by Increase Lapham (figure 7.19).[57] This symbol represents the earth and is

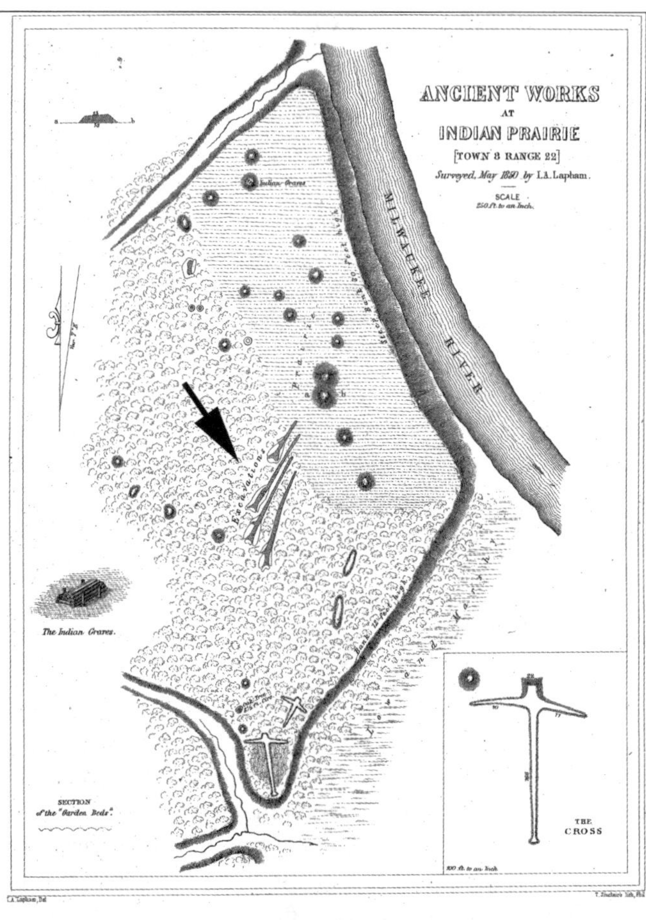
ANCIENT WORKS
AT
INDIAN PRAIRIE
[TOWN 8 RANGE 22]
Surveyed, May 1850 by I.A. Lapham.
SCALE
250 ft. to an Inch.
MILWAUKEE RIVER
Excavations
The Indian Graves.
SECTION
of the "Garden Beds".
THE
CROSS
100 ft. to an Inch.

Part of tail
Head
Legs
Flooded Rock River

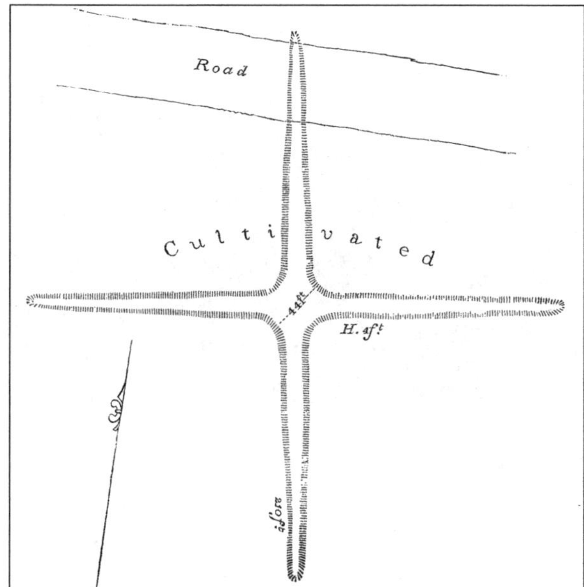

Figure 7.19. Large cross mound mapped by Increase Lapham on an eastern Wisconsin prairie.

a very old one. The arms represent the four directions, which are associated with different colors or attributes and are anchored by spirit beings to prevent the earth from shifting. This symbol—usually surrounded by a circle—also appears in Mississippian and later Oneota artwork and in the artistic traditions of many Native peoples. Among the Ho-Chunk, it is the symbol of Earth-Maker, creator of the earth and cosmos.[58]

Mound Pairs

Other types of dualism are present in effigy mounds arrangements that recur at some of the larger mound sites, mostly in eastern Wisconsin. Many times, especially with panther-like water-spirit mounds, virtually identical mounds are paired (figure 7.20; also see figure 7.16 for numerous examples at Lizard Mound Park). Some are side by side, whereas others nearly touch head to head or tail to tail. At the Kratz Creek mound group, a bear mound is found between a pair of water-spirit mounds. In a variation of this, sometimes nearly identical mounds are attached to one another. At some sites,

Figure 7.18 (*left*). *Above*: map by Increase Lapham of effigy mound group along the Milwaukee River with intaglios. *Below*: water-spirit intaglio in Fort Atkinson filled with water after a period of heavy rains.

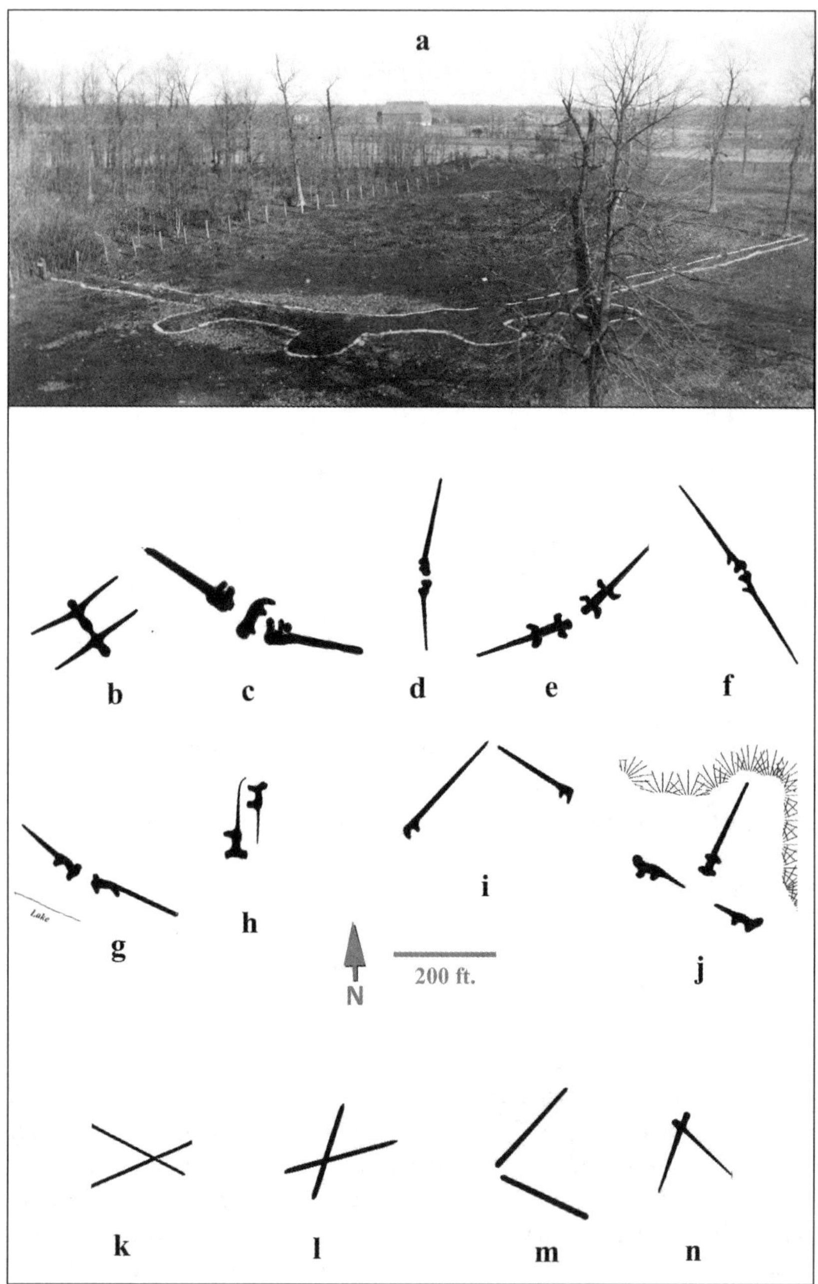

Figure 7.20. Joined, paired, and crossed mounds: (a) joined water-spirit mounds at the Ridge or Gasch mound group overlooking Lake Winnebago as photographed in 1915; (b–j) examples of effigy mound pairings from various sites; (k–n) crossed mounds from various sites in south-central Wisconsin.

pairing is in the form of long, crossed linear mounds, although with no consistent directional pattern. At the current time, we can only speculate as to the meaning of these occasional patterns.

Human Being Mounds

By far, most identifiable effigy mounds are animal-like, but in at least five instances human beings are depicted, and most of these are horned or wearing horned headdresses. Some are clearly in motion (figure 7.21). Along with key effigy forms such as thunderbirds, bears, and water spirits that relate the realms of air, earth, and water, so-called man mounds provide major clues to the overall meaning of the effigy mounds ceremonialism.

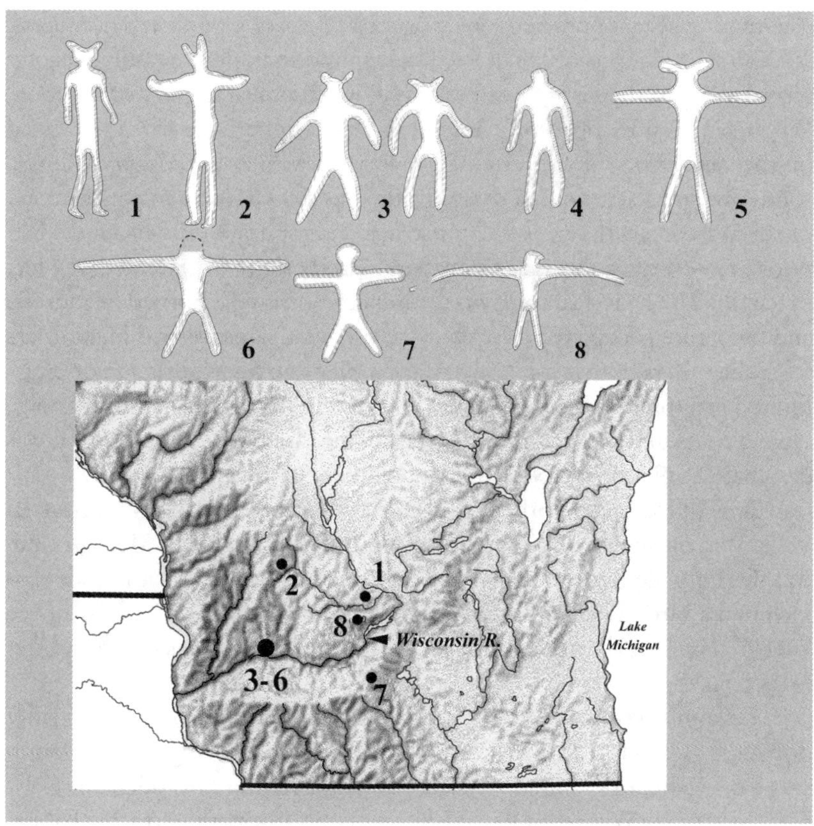

Figure 7.21. Human being and "bird-man" mounds: (1) Man Mound County Park, Sauk County; (2) La Valle Man Mound, Sauk County; (3–6) Eagle Township, Richland County; (7) near Mount Horeb, Dane County; (8) Devil's Lake State Park, Sauk County.

Further clues are derived from their limited distribution in the Wisconsin River valley and its tributaries in modern-day south-central Wisconsin.

Monumental depictions of human beings in North America are not confined to the Upper Midwestern effigy mound region and apparently have a long temporal span. Elsewhere in North America, images of human forms are made of stones, boulder outlines, arrangements of rock cobbles, or desert clearings[59] and seem to be singular expressions of ritual activity rather than a part of extensive ceremonial landscapes like those in the effigy region. Most also date later in time than the human earthen mounds of the Upper Midwest. Horned or antlered human beings occasionally appear among other symbols in carvings and paintings in caves and rockshelters in the Upper Midwest and resemble the human effigy mounds. Two human figures at Samuel's Cave and Gullickson's Glen in western Wisconsin show figures with arms raised and mouths open as though the figures were chanting, singing, or praying; one is horned or wearing a antlered headdress.

The most famous of the horned human mounds, and the only one preserved today, is the giant Greenfield Man Mound near the city of Baraboo, Wisconsin, first mapped by Canfield in 1842 (figure 7.21).[60] It is located on the valley floor at the base of a low ridge within the Baraboo Range, south of a small stream that drains to the Baraboo River, a major tributary of the Wisconsin River. Road construction amputated the mound's feet prior to its preservation as a county park, but it originally extended 214 feet in length. The head features two prominent horns or a horned headdress, and the figure is depicted as walking to the west. This horned man differs from the others in that it is solitary and well away from other major effigy mound groupings, although a linear mound is located on the bluff above. Owing to its uniqueness and importance, the Greenfield Man Mound was designated a National Historical Landmark in 2016.

Canfield mapped another large horned human effigy in 1872 near La Valle, Wisconsin, about twenty miles west of the Greenfield Man Mound, but the La Valle figure was part of a cluster of zoomorphic mounds that included a bird, a horned water spirit, and several linear mounds (figure 7.21).[61] The La Valle figure was also animated, with its arms raised and feet in motion.

The largest known concentration of human mounds occurred further down the Wisconsin River within the Eagle Township effigy mound landscape of Richland County, on a terrace and surrounding hills along the north side of the Wisconsin River. Radiocarbon dates from associated habitation areas show use of the area between A.D. 900 and 1000.[62] Spreading over several square miles, the Eagle Township effigy landscape once contained several hundred mounds in many subgroupings often dominated by bird effigies, along with habitation areas, possible ridged agricultural fields, and an earthen ceremonial enclosure. Most of the Eagle Township mounds have disappeared, but a significant part of the landscape was documented by Theodore H. Lewis before its destruction in the late nineteenth century

Among the Eagle Township mounds were at least three human mounds and possibly more. On the west side of the landscape, Lewis mapped a pair of clear human forms, in a subgrouping along with one bird and one bear (figure 7.21).[63] Smaller than the La Valle and Greenfield Man mounds (only about one hundred feet in length and fifty to sixty feet in maximum width), the "twin" human figures were horned and in obvious motion. Interestingly, and no doubt symbolically significant, their orientation contrasts with those of the bird and bear effigies; the heads of the humans are in an opposite direction and toward the Wisconsin River. They seem to have been created as if to face or oppose the other mounds representing the upper world (bird) and earth (bear), and one gets the definite impression that a story is being told here. Further east and along the Wisconsin River, Lewis mapped a third definite human figure—this time without horns—in the midst of the densest concentration of effigy mounds (mostly birds), which arcs around a habitation area (figure 7.21).

Other effigies in the broader Eagle Township ceremonial landscape have some human characteristics and may be fork-tailed birds or bird-men.[64] One, with outstretched arms and leg-like appendages, appears as a "soil shadow" on the aerial photograph shown in figure 1.6 along with similar soil disturbances marking the former location of a massive conical mound, a linear mound, and the 900-foot-long eagle or thunderbird previously mentioned in this chapter. The head region of the possible bird-man cannot be discerned. Another bird-like figure mapped by Lewis has an odd bi-lobed head that might or might not represent horns. The exact location of that mound is unknown, but certainly it is now gone.

Nearer modern Madison, in 1838 Richard Taylor found a 125-foot-long human-like figure within a long chain of effigy mounds paralleling an ancient trail near the "Four Lakes" to Blue Mound in Dane County (figure 7.21; also see figure 2.2). The effigy had outstretched arms, a round head, and appendages that might represent legs. However, this figure also could well be a fork-tailed bird or bird-man.[65] There have been other scattered reports of human mounds elsewhere, but they are even more dubious.

What the human mounds symbolize, and their purpose, is as yet uncertain, but the horns or horned headdresses on many lead to several possibilities. Paul Radin asked people living on the Winnebago Reservation in Nebraska about the human mounds, and a few elders said they represented the Warrior or Hawk clan.[66] Warriors among Great Plains people often

Figure 7.22. A photograph of Winnebago (Ho-Chunk) and Fox medicine men.

donned buffalo or bison horns that provided them with spirit powers. Some spirits themselves had horns.

In the eastern woodlands of North America, medicine people, frequently referred to as shamans, often wore bison horn or deer- or elk-antlered headdresses that conferred supernatural powers (figure 7.22). Such religious practitioners were in direct touch with the spirit world through dreams and visions. In many Native societies, including those of the Upper Midwest, medicine people belonged to ceremonial societies that cross-cut community boundaries. Such medicine societies provided years of training in holistic healing (both spiritual and practical) and were vested keepers of sacred knowledge not shared with other community members. Medicine Society members would have been the most likely to oversee effigy mound ceremonies, which would have required arcane knowledge and contacts with the supernatural.

The depiction of the La Valle man mound, with its arms raised, is consistent with depictions of ritual activity. Similar figures can be found in the rock art of the region, amid other ritual paintings and carvings, and medicine-man figures with upraised arms are common among rock-art sites in Canada, north of Lake Superior. Ethnographic accounts describe upraised arms as a position indicating the dispensing or receiving of spirit powers. Thus, the restricted distribution of the horned humans could indicate that this area was a center of a medicine society ritual and perhaps even its origin place. Geographic associations with medicine societies are not unusual. Ojibwe traditions place the origin of their medicine society, the Midewiwin, on Madeline Island near the south shore of Lake Superior.[67]

A third interpretation derives from the general theme of effigy mound ceremonial activity, related to ongoing re-creation of the world and its people. One Ho-Chunk story relates that Thunderbird and Water Spirit transformed themselves into humans and that other animals likewise underwent transformation, becoming the ancestors of the various clans at a place called Red Banks. The Ho-Chunk locate Red Banks on the shores of Green Bay on the Door Peninsula. The Greenfield Man Mound especially recalls a Ho-Chunk tradition, recorded by Radin, that the horned Water Spirit became human "and walked."[68] Likewise, at least some bird-man-like mounds of the area could record the transformation of the thunderbird into human form.

Purpose of the Mounds

Effigy mounds were probably created during a variety of ceremonials, but all drew upon the same cosmology and underlying belief structure. Effigy ceremonials could have been related to clan and lineage rituals, rituals of medicine and other societies, evocations for protections and blessings, or general world-renewal ceremonies. Whatever the rituals' other purposes, the burial of the dead was a prominent feature. Burials were placed in pits below mounds, on the former ground surfaces, or at different levels in the mounds themselves. Burials in effigies typically were placed at significant anatomical positions, such as hearts and heads. Burials in conical and linear mounds tended to be placed at the mound's center. Finally, burials were sometimes placed outside the mounds, indicating the broader use of mound sites as cemeteries.

Late Woodland mound burials differed in many respects from earlier Middle Woodland burials, in a way that has been interpreted as reflecting social differences. First, burial pits or chambers do not appear to have functioned as long-term family crypts, used continually for interments for a long time before mounds were built over them. Unlike in Middle Woodland crypt mounds, primary extended burials (that is, laid out in a prone position before the body decays) are rare to nonexistent in Late Woodland mounds. Late Woodland burials often occurred as cleaned bundles of bones, but "in the flesh" interments in the flexed or fetal position also were fairly common. Cremations occurred as well, but early excavation and analysis methods did not lend themselves to easy recognition of small fragments of burned human bone, so how commonly cremation was practiced is unclear.

The pattern of Late Woodland burials indicates that the mounds were not necessarily built immediately after a death. Rather, mounds were built at certain times when appropriate ceremonials were conducted. Corpses, bone bundles, and cremated remains would be brought from temporary resting places for final burial in a mound. Both the number of Late Woodland mounds and the presence of flexed burials indicate that mound ceremonials occurred at fairly frequent intervals, perhaps annually. These ceremonials might have coincided with important calendar and symbolic occasions, such as the summer or winter solstice and the spring or fall equinox, or with specific events such as the death of a prominent community member or strife within or between communities.

Effigy mounds, linear mounds, and most Late Woodland conical mounds usually contain the graves of only one person or a few people. A minority appear at first glance to include no burials at all, but whether this phenomenon is the result of a true lack of burials or the more likely explanations of poor bone preservation, incomplete excavation, or use of excavation methods that miss highly fragmented or cremated bone is unclear. Complicating this pattern is the occasional presence at a ceremonial site of one or two larger conical mounds containing many bone bundles or a mass of intermingled skeletal remains. For example, one conical mound at the Raisbeck mound group yielded the disarticulated remains of sixty-five people, and other smaller mass burials have been found in conical mounds surrounded by effigies at Kratz Creek and Nitschke in eastern Wisconsin.[69] These rare conical mounds indicate that burial for some portions of the community was delayed for an extended period of time. There have been occasional discoveries of Late Woodland burials far from any mound site. These burials may represent bodies that, for one reason or another, were never retrieved for reburial at mound sites or the burials of individuals never destined for mound burial in the first place.

Why so many different methods of burial, including effigy burial, individual burial in conical mounds, mass burial in conical mounds, nonmound burial, cremation, bone bundling, in-the-flesh burial, and so forth, were used by Late Woodland peoples is not yet well understood. However, later Native beliefs and traditions suggest some possible answers to the mystery. In several midwestern Native nations, the type of burial varied from clan to clan or from one time of year to another. Mass burials, such as those in the larger conical mounds, have parallels to the "feast of the dead," which united the exhumed dead of entire communities in a single grave.[70] The act of creating the mass grave brought the living closer to their ancestors and to one another at times of social stress. Perhaps Late Woodland peoples in the area of effigy construction practiced a blend of these traditions, giving mound burial to some people at some times of the year, depending on their clan, and retrieving the bodies of other community members for mass burial at other occasions.

The type of burial might also have varied according to the status or social role of the deceased. At first glance, and in contrast to many Middle Woodland mounds, the Late Woodland mounds do not appear to mark the burial places of important or "chiefly" families. Very few nonperishable objects were placed with the deceased in effigy mounds, and most burials lack identifiable grave offerings of any sort. The items that are present are simple in nature: pottery containers, smoking pipes, a stone knife, miscellaneous bone or copper tools—objects that could conceivably assist the spirit in the next world but do not mark elite status. That the grave goods do not have prestige value has been used to argue that the societies that built the effigy mounds were not marked by the types of social differences found earlier or at least that social status did not determine access to mound burial. However, this argument overlooks the most elaborate grave offerings of all: the effigy mounds themselves!

Further, analysis of the skeletal remains excavated from several effigy sites by the Milwaukee Public Museum has revealed some intriguing patterns. The people buried in effigy mounds were more likely to be buried in the flesh than people buried in conical mounds, suggesting that the mound ceremony was less likely to be postponed after their deaths. They were less likely to share their mound with other burials, whereas all of the "feast of the dead" types of burials were made in conical mounds. None of the individuals buried in effigy mounds exhibited signs of broken bones, indicating that they either lived lives of less risk or that deforming injuries excluded people from effigy burial.[71]

Astronomical Alignments

The arrangements of mounds discussed previously have no consistent orientations that would indicate anything other than local variation, and in general it has been shown that arrangements of mounds are consistent with the cultural meanings that the effigy mound builders attached to topography as a reflection of broader cosmological concepts. However, a great deal of public interest recently has centered on the idea that mounds are arranged so that their alignments can be used to predict or observe the movements of the sun, moon, and stars. Some investigators of astronomical alignments believe that "ancient geometries" shared by mound builders and other ancient peoples across the globe are encoded in the angles and alignments of the mounds.[72]

Ancient people the world over were attuned to the heavens and extremely knowledgeable about the movements of various celestial bodies. Furthermore, they attributed supernatural qualities to the sun, moon, stars, and planets, which often were perceived and personified as deities and spirit beings that played major roles in creation stories and cultural epics of mythic heroes. The Ho-Chunk of Wisconsin, for example, include Sun, Moon, and Morning Star in a pantheon of spirits and deities.

The use of astronomical references, particularly tracking the movements of the sun, moon, and major stars and planets, has been well documented in the ceremonial life of Native people of the Americas and other ancient peoples throughout the world. Various studies of the great Hopewell earthen enclosures in Ohio show compelling correlations with solar and lunar cycles, and similar alignments have been proposed for the great ancient city of Cahokia and associated Mississippian sites. Certainly the custom of using ceremonial structures to merge annual solar cycles and the seasons, the monthly death and rebirth of the moon, and the disappearance and reappearance of the morning and evening star (Venus) with the concept of death and rebirth of humanity is well demonstrated in other parts of the world, such as at megalithic structures such as Stonehenge in England and New Grange in Ireland.

One of the problems for researchers of such alignments is that, given the myriad possible sighting points and lines among the thousands of differently oriented effigy mounds and their appendages, almost any alignment that one is looking for can be found. In addition, finding a specific and common pattern for orientations to specific horizon events, such as sunrises and sunsets, is complicated by the fact that many effigy mounds do not have a view to a flat horizon because they are arranged on slopes and/or are in areas surrounded by hills or vegetation that would change the angles at which the sun and other bodies would appear to rise or set. Generalizations are therefore difficult to make without direct observation. Further, given the sheer number of different communities and mound designers involved in effigy construction over the four centuries of the effigy-building era, there were certainly different ideas about how effigies should be arranged.

Only a comparatively few mound groups have been completely studied, and some of these have resulted in equivocal, dubious, or negative results with regard to celestial alignments. One study examined the Maples mound group in Whitewater Effigy Mounds Preserve and found that only a few mounds there appear to have special orientations, such as to the cardinal directions and possible solstice points.[73] Another, at Lizard Mound County Park, among other places, asserted a variety of solar, lunar, and planetary alignments, but an independent expert review found that, while it is plausible that a few linear mounds in the Lizard mound group were used to observe or mark solar events such as the solstices, other conjectural alignments are arbitrary or, at best, not clear.[74]

Proposed orientations at the Henschel mound group on the Sheboygan Marsh links panther (or water-spirit) effigy mounds and earlier large conical mounds to observation of the solstices and equinoxes, as well as lunar movements. An alternative explanation (and these two are not mutually exclusive) is that the water-themed effigies are arranged to appear as if they were coming from a major spring that is now used as the source for several trout ponds on the property (see figure 5.3).[75]

Finally, a recent study of mound orientations was conducted at Effigy Mounds National Monument by William Romain, an expert in astro-archaeology who has written several books and articles on the topic. Romain found no celestial correlations but instead noted that mounds were precisely aligned to local topographic features. Most followed the trajectory of the ridge lines they were built upon.[76] His study echoes earlier observations that orientations, alignments, and arrangements had more to do with topography, geography, and the meanings that the mound builders attributed to features of the natural landscape than with celestial features.[77]

Nevertheless, it is still possible that, in certain cases, celestial alignments were incorporated into earthwork building at some key effigy mound ceremonial centers, since such knowledge had been used for ceremonial purposes in North America prior to the effigy mound era in the Upper Midwest. Given the complex, multilevel symbolism, metaphors, and allegories embedded in mound building by Native peoples, it is quite likely that mound arrangements owe their complexity to a variety of factors, including the relationship of effigies to actual and supernatural habitats, harmony with the landscape, the relationship of the effigies to one another, cardinal directions, and, feasibly at especially important ceremonial centers, the incorporation of celestial observations, such as the winter and summer solstices, into ceremonies that observed the death and rebirth of seasons and hence the ritualized cyclical renewal of the earth and its people.

Ceremonial Centers

In Early and Middle Woodland times, mound ceremonialism functioned on several levels. Mounds were burial places that marked territories and were the focus of ceremonials that integrated groups through the practice of rituals related to the renewal of the world and its resources. The effigy mound builders brought forward and elaborated these concepts. During the 1970s and 1980s, archaeologists began to hypothesize that effigy mound groups had been built as part of ceremonial activities that were directed primarily at socially integrating segments of Late Woodland society. In this view, effigy mound groups marked the places at which highly mobile hunting and gathering families periodically rendezvoused with one another during the year to undertake a number of social, economic, and ceremonial activities that linked the families in a band. The Middle Woodland burial mounds and, indeed, cemeteries in general functioned to integrate social groups, but directly through rituals that focused on the burial of the dead. During the era of the effigy mounds, burial of the dead and accompanying mortuary rituals may have been only one part of a complex and continual ceremonial.

At some effigy sites, mounds are accompanied by earthen enclosures or areas that might have functioned as dance rings. Rare excavation between and around mounds indicates that mounds may be surrounded by pits filled with burned stone and other materials, perhaps representing disposal of debris from bonfires and feasts. Historic funerary rituals of Native peoples often involve social gatherings, funeral orations, and ceremonies to assist the dead and protect the living, sometimes taking place at different times for years after a death, and there is no reason to believe that ceremony among the effigy builders was any different. Effigy mounds and other Late Woodland mounds are the tips of the ritual icebergs, representing much that is hidden from view or lost to time.

While the interpretation that effigy mound groups represent ceremonial centers has not changed, the view that the effigy mound people were hunters and gatherers who spent much of the year living in small family groups away from other members of the band is being challenged. Although this way of life may have characterized groups very early in Late Woodland times, the recent discovery of Late Woodland villages such as the Statz site indicate that at least some families were living in villages during portions of the year and, after A.D. 900, had turned increasingly to corn agriculture. Rather than linking families into bands, effigy mound ceremonialism and ceremonial centers may have integrated bands, lineages, and even villages into larger social groups.

The Effigy Mound Ceremonial Complex

The similarity of mound forms, mound arrangements, and other customs attending mound construction found throughout the large effigy mound area argues for a shared sacred knowledge that may have been controlled by a society (perhaps secret) of religious specialists, such as medicine people or shamans, who directed the mound-building ceremonials. Such societies are common in historic and modern Native cultures and cross-cut clans and village organizations. For example, members of the Grand Medicine Society, which is found among both Siouan and Algonquian-speaking tribes in the Midwest, are the keepers of origin stories and other sacred knowledge, especially that concerning medicine and healing rituals that frequently involve the restoration of balance and harmony in the world.

Quite obviously, larger mound groups served as ceremonial centers, but the relationship between the effigy mound ceremonial centers and the villages and populations they served is still being researched. In the past there have been few investigations around effigy mound groups, and until recently few Late Woodland major camps and villages had been identified. What evidence there is to date, however, suggests that the distance between effigy mound groups and associated habitations may have been determined by local geography. In many areas, such as the Four Lakes region around Madison, mound groups tend to have been built on high elevations, while villages or camps were located on the shores of the lakes, which were more suitable for living. One example is the Mendota State Hospital site, where a village is surrounded by effigy mounds that included huge eagle-birds, probably thunderbirds, that may have been perceived as great protectors of the village. Mound groups constructed along rivers might have habitation areas immediately adjacent. In the 1960s, William Hurley found evidence of a village or major seasonal camp at the Sanders site on the Wisconsin River. Farther down the river in Richland County, archaeologists from the Wisconsin Historical Society, working with staff from the Ho-Chunk Nation Cultural Resources Department, located a Late Woodland settlement that had been neatly enclosed by a spectacular effigy mound group first surveyed by Theodore H. Lewis in the 1890s.[78]

In other instances, habitations at groups away from major bodies of water were temporary or nonexistent. Surveys and test excavations around the large and complex Nitschke group, arranged along a glacial drumlin in Dodge County, found only a small, temporary camp, although a small plot of garden beds had been recorded nearby.[79] Extensive surveys around a small, isolated grouping of two effigy mounds along a creek near Lake Waubesa in south-central Wisconsin found no evidence of an associated habitation area contemporary with the mounds.[80] In areas of great mound density, it is not clear whether each mound center served a separate group of people or whether a single band or village of people was responsible for building a number of mound groups, shifting the location of mound construction from time to time as desired space (hilltops, for example) became filled.

The Rise and Fall of Effigy Mound Ceremonialism

Although it had its roots in earlier times, the precise beginning of the great effigy mound ceremonial landscape construction has not been established. Of the many thousands of effigy mounds recorded—and the several hundred excavated—only a few effigy mounds (excluding conical and linear mounds) have been radiocarbon dated, and these from only six mound groups spread across the effigy mound region.[81] Some of these dates were taken when the technique was not as accurate as it is now, resulting in possible errors of several hundred years and often yielding dates that were too early due to sampling of heartwood from trees that were a century or more old when they were cut and used. Recent and critical examinations of radiocarbon dates, along with data from habitation sites, suggest that the majority of effigy mounds were built during a comparatively brief period in the Late Woodland, beginning around A.D. 700 and ending, for the most part, sometime around A.D. 1100.[82]

At this point, two fundamental questions still have to be answered: Why did Late Woodland people begin building so many effigy mounds in the first place, displaying their ideology on the landscape in such an extraordinarily visible fashion? And why did they stop?

The expansion of the Effigy Mound Ceremonial Complex is most likely related to events taking place elsewhere in the Midwest at the time, as well as to the role of mound building in rituals of world renewal. The early years of the Late Woodland period were an unstable period of population growth, increasing warfare, and rapid technological, economic, and social change. Perhaps the Early Late Woodland people of southern Wisconsin began to perceive ideological and even physical threats that undermined their sense of cultural well-being. When faced with similar challenges brought about by continuing contact with Euro-Americans, Native Americans in the nineteenth century responded by developing new religious movements, such as the Ghost Dance and the Dream Dance, that cross-cut social boundaries and that redefined who they were and brought them hope of a better way of life: bringing the world back into balance and harmony.

The effigy mounds are monumental representations of the cosmology and ideology of their builders. Perhaps effigy ceremonialism began as an attempt by a people to define themselves and their homelands in relation to their ancestors, a tactic used by early agricultural peoples across the globe. Evidence for this idea might be found at the Raisbeck site in southwestern Wisconsin, where some people were buried with tools that were hundreds and even thousands of years older—picked up from the ground just as people pick up arrowheads today—and given to the dead to link them to those who came before. Perhaps, through the ritual act of world renewal at times of stress, the effigy mound people sought to call on the power of their ancestors and spirit beings to restore harmony to grieving communities within a quickly changing world.

If the beginnings and spread of the great wave of effigy mound construction remain unresolved issues, the demise of the ceremonial is less so. Mississippians began to visit Wisconsin between A.D. 1000 and 1100, establishing colonies along the Mississippi River and later establishing a large town, now called Aztalan, in south-central Wisconsin. Other villages exhibiting various blends of Middle Mississippian and Late Woodland influences appeared shortly afterwards. Finally, as both the Late Woodland and Mississippian traditions began to fade from the human landscape of Wisconsin, a new cultural tradition coalesced, identified by archaeologists as "Upper Mississippian" or "Oneota," likely composed of people carrying on a blend of Late Woodland and Mississippian cultural traditions. The singular term, however, obscures many and evolving variations of "Oneota" life. By A.D. 1200, most of the population of southern Wisconsin had gathered in a handful of large, horticultural villages that were occupied year round, leaving essentially abandoned many places where effigy building had thrived. Effigy construction ended, and so did the Late Woodland Effigy Mound Complex.

We believe that the effigy mound ceremonial helped bind people in Wisconsin and adjacent areas, easing the transition to settled village life. The loose array of clans or ritual societies whose identities were expressed through effigy symbolism likely crystallized into a formal clan organization capable of maintaining order in villages composed of previously independent bands. The system may have operated in a manner similar to that of the historic Ho-Chunk, where clan affiliation determines one's social roles and responsibilities, potential marriage partners, and even where one's house should be located in the village.

Though mound building persisted for a time among some Oneota and related communities, few effigies were built. The only known examples of Oneota (or Oneota-like) effigy mounds are located at an early village and ceremonial center on the Mississippi River at Diamond Bluff, dated to A.D. 1100–1200, where, among hundreds of conical mounds, there are three effigy mounds representing the three essential realms of air, earth, and water: a bird, a mammal, and a water spirit.[83] Early Oneota pottery found within one of the effigies confirms that they may have been among the last effigies built.

Robert Hall believed that the end of the period of burial mound construction, which saw a shift to large nonmounded cemeteries with individual graves and burials under house floors, occurred as ceremonialism shifted its emphasis from world renewal to new, agriculturally focused ceremonies and celebrations such as the Green Corn ceremony, which were tied to the fertility of the earth. These new rituals, which may have been introduced by the Mississippians, separated renewal from funeral ceremony, so that mound building was no longer needed.[84]

But the traditions of the effigy builders did not completely disappear after A.D. 1200 in Wisconsin. The descendants of the Oneota—the Ho-Chunk and Ioway (and probably others)—retained major aspects of an ancient belief system and social structure that can be traced back to the effigy mound builders and before.

Mounds in Northern Wisconsin

The region of the effigy mounds in Wisconsin corresponds to the highly productive deciduous forests and parklands south of an environmental transition known as "the tension zone." This zone, which consists of a mixture of southern and northern plants and animals, runs west across central Wisconsin and arcs north in the northwestern part of the state. Above the tension zone lie the coniferous forests of Wisconsin's "North Woods." Except for fish and wild rice, northern Wisconsin was not nearly as productive in wild food resources in the past as southern Wisconsin. Before the logging period of the nineteenth century, for example, the deer population was extremely low. In addition, because of the short growing season, horticulture never became an important part of the Native American economy, with a few notable exceptions.

Of the tens of thousands of mounds constructed in Wisconsin, only about 1,500 were built above the tension zone, most in two clusters: one near where the tension zone and its abundant resources and milder climate loop up into northwestern Wisconsin and another in and around modern Menominee County in northeastern Wisconsin. In the "snowbelt"—the northernmost tier of counties adjacent to Lake Superior and the Upper Peninsula of Michigan (Douglas, Bayfield, Ashland, and Iron)—fewer than three dozen mounds have been recorded.

Northeastern Wisconsin

The two areas of Late Woodland mound building in northern Wisconsin probably represent different cultural traditions or tribal groups. Of the two, our understanding of the mound-building traditions of northeastern Wisconsin is weakest and is hampered by a lack of dated mounds and the apparent persistence of the mound-building tradition into the post–Late Woodland period. For now, it can be said that at least some of the mounds in that region were built by Late Woodland peoples who practiced a way of life roughly similar to that of their southern counterparts and who were beginning to settle into larger communities near lakes and wild-rice beds. They made and used northern variants of Madison ware, as well as their own distinct kinds of pottery. Their sites yield more fishing gear than effigy-builder sites, as well as more evidence of copper working.

Mounds in northeastern Wisconsin outwardly resemble those of southern Wisconsin, save for the near absence of animal-shaped effigy mounds. They are found in isolation or in small groups. Most mounds in this area are conical, but oval and linear mounds occasionally can be found, as can tapering linear mounds and conical or oval mounds with linear or tapering linear "tails." These latter two mound types are sometimes called "catfish" mounds and may be a more abstract form of effigy mound. Flexed burials, cremations, and bone bundles were placed on the ground surface before mounds were built over them or in pits dug into completed or partially completed mounds. Some mounds contained large deposits of bone, similar to the mass burials found in conical mounds in southern Wisconsin. Not every resident of the region received mound burial. A nonmounded cemetery containing flexed burials and bone bundles was found at the Robinson site, again demonstrating the complexity of Late Woodland funeral traditions.[85]

Northwestern Wisconsin

More is known about Late Woodland mound ritual in northwestern Wisconsin, but less is known about the everyday lives of the mound builders because few excavations have been carried out at village sites in this region. Pottery found in some mounds is very different from pottery made by people in southern and northeastern Wisconsin. Instead, it bears similarities to jars found at sites extending along the southern and northwestern shores of Lake Superior, from the Upper Peninsula of Michigan into northern Minnesota and southern Manitoba. Mounds in this part of Wisconsin are

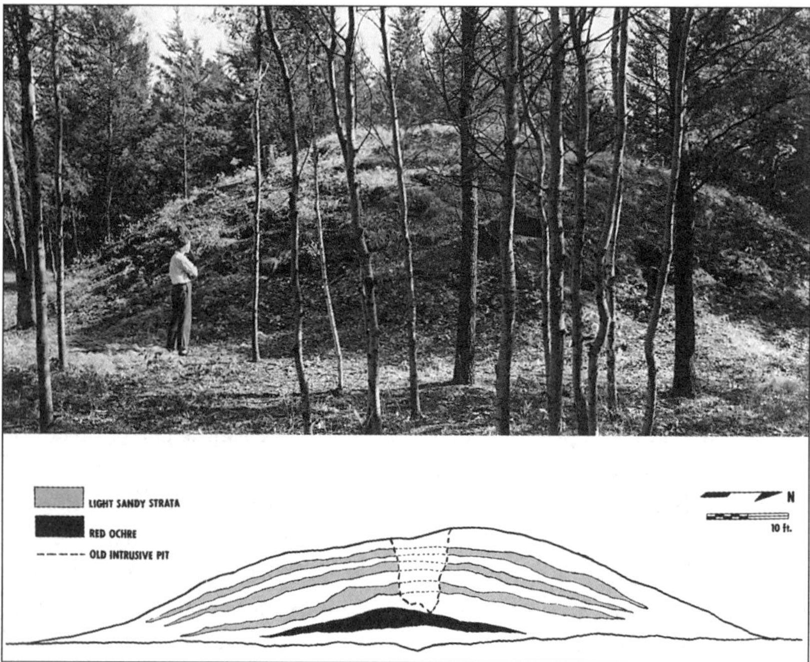

Figure 7.23. *Above*: large conical mound on Clam Lake in northern Wisconsin, built in stages over a long period of time, before its excavation in the 1930s. *Below*: profile of the Clam Lake mound.

usually conical or oval in form, but some short linear mounds are known. They are sometimes higher and more pronounced than mounds in southern and northeastern Wisconsin. Most are part of small groups, but a considerable number of mound locations (about 30 percent) consist of a single huge conical mound, often reaching heights of more than twelve feet.

Early archaeological excavations at a few of the largest conical mounds revealed that they are "accretionary" mounds, built in stages over a long time—perhaps many generations—and containing layer after layer of soil and human remains. This pattern of periodic mass burial is typical of "feast of the dead" ceremonies and may be yet another variation of Late Woodland mass burial. The Late Woodland mound builders of northwestern Wisconsin, however, returned to particular mounds to add to them rather than building new mounds as did their southern neighbors.

At the Clam Lake mound, William McKern of the Public Museum of the City of Milwaukee documented a sequence of periodic ceremonial activities that eventually created a mound fourteen feet high and ninety feet in diameter (figure 7.23).[86] The initial mound had been only four feet high and thirty-four feet in diameter. Either no burials were placed in this first mound or none survived to be documented, but it was covered with red ochre, a symbol of death and burial ceremonialism for Native Americans since ancient times. After an unknown span of time, beach sand and six bundles of cleaned human bones, wrapped in birch bark, were added. This second level was capped by dirt, and as time passed two more layers were built on top, each one containing many bone bundles.

McKern and many others believed that such bone bundles represented the remains of people brought down from mortuary scaffolds much like those maintained by the Dakota and other tribes in this region. In fact, McKern theorized that this mound had been built by the historic Dakota, but radiocarbon dates obtained later from the nearby and similar Spencer Lake mound, as well as the type of pottery found in the Clam Lake mound, indicate that the mound had been constructed hundreds of years earlier. It could well be that the mound builders were the ancestors of the historic Dakota. However, the pottery of this region is more like the pottery associated with speakers of Algonquian languages, like the Cree and Cheyenne, than to the pottery of the Dakota. Just which groups descend from the mound builders of northwestern Wisconsin is unresolved.

The Late Woodland Mound Builders of Wisconsin

The various Late Woodland mound builders of Wisconsin adapted long-standing traditions and deeply rooted belief systems to help them navigate a changing world. Mound builders in southern, northeastern, and northwestern Wisconsin walked different paths but faced the same challenges—increasing populations, rising conflict, a slow turning away from mobile life styles, and the later arrival of new ideas, trading partners, and potential enemies from far to the south. They adapted by creating mounds in new forms and in new ways and used mound ceremonies to bring stability to their lives. Mounds and the rituals that went with them connected them to their societies, their ancestors, and the universe in which they lived.

Though the mound builders in each region responded differently to these challenges, one commonality among them is particularly intriguing. In each area, a variety of mound forms were built. In each area, the bodies of some dead were treated in different ways from others: as bone bundles, cremated, or buried "in the flesh" not long after death. In each area, some people were buried alone in mounds while others were mingled in mass graves that call to mind the historic feasts of the dead. In each area, people returned to particular sites to build multiple mounds while building only one mound at other sites. These patterns, submerged within variation at regional, local, and even site-level scales, hint at the complexity of Late Woodland social systems and beliefs, which in turn merged with new ideas to herald the final period of mound building in Wisconsin.

8

Platform Mound Builders

The Mississippians

The Mississippian Tradition

The fate of the Late Woodland mound builders and the emergence of the Oneota culture in Wisconsin were inextricably tied to the appearance of a new civilization that was springing from the vast fertile Mississippi River floodplains of southern Illinois. Around A.D. 800, local Late Woodland people in this "American Bottom" made the shift to corn horticulture and within a few hundred years had organized one of the most complex societies in ancient North America north of Mexico. This new culture has been referred to as the Middle Mississippian because it developed in the central part of the Mississippi River valley, but hereafter in this volume it is called simply Mississippian.

Because of its spectacular nature, the Mississippian culture or tradition is exceptionally well studied. In addition, this remarkable society was documented in the writings of early explorers. The last vestiges of Mississippian cultural traditions were still thriving in parts of the present-day southeastern United States when Spanish and French explorers arrived.[1] Native nation names associated with the Mississippian civilization in the historic period include the Cherokee, Natchez, Choctaw, Creek, and Chickasaw. These were later referred to as the "civilized tribes" by Europeans because of their social complexity. Members of the sixteenth-century Spanish de Soto expedition even referred to the female leader of one town as a "queen." Among the many distinctive characteristics of the Mississippian cultural tradition was its monumental architecture: the raising of large earthen mounds used as platforms for special structures such as a temples, mausoleums for dead nobles, and houses of leaders and nobles.

Cahokia

At the heart of the early Mississippian tradition is the largest native settlement ever to have been constructed in what is now the United States, a place that is now called Cahokia. Many archaeologists would trade their careers to learn by what name it was known to most of the people of eastern North America one thousand years ago—for there resided America's first great lords.

Cahokia is situated on the Mississippi River floodplain in Illinois, across the river from St. Louis, Missouri. The site draws its modern name from a tribe that lived in the area in the eighteenth century, although the tribe had little to do with the site itself. Archaeologists traced Cahokia's development from a concentration of agricultural villages and mound ceremonial centers to a dense city. At its greatest power, about nine hundred years ago, this city covered more than five square miles and accommodated a population consisting of many thousands (figure 8.1).[2] More people lived right across the river on the site of modern-day St. Louis; development of the modern city destroyed much of the settlement that had undoubtedly been a part of the Cahokia urban area.

Cahokia was a fabulously vital and complex community. A huge wall of timber and clay, complete with watchtowers, enclosed the central two hundred acres of the city. Within this central precinct, the seat of Cahokia civic and religious power, lay a public plaza and a number of very large earthen mounds and a flat-topped platform, on top of which apparently stood ceremonial structures and the houses of the ruling families. At one end loomed Monk's Mound, a flat-topped stepped pyramid that was one hundred feet high and that covered fourteen acres at its base. It is the largest prehistoric earthen structure constructed in the Americas, and on top lived the great ruler of the city. According to European observers, leaders among the southwestern Natchez belonged to the Sun clan and were believed to have descended from the sun, one of the principal deities of the Mississippians.[3] Cahokian leaders may have believed the same.

Many members of Cahokia's ruling class were buried in an elaborate tomb complex contained in a low ridged-topped mound, called mound 72, excavated in the 1970s.[4] Extraordinary offerings accompanied the burials, including hundreds of human sacrifices, and these tell us a great deal about

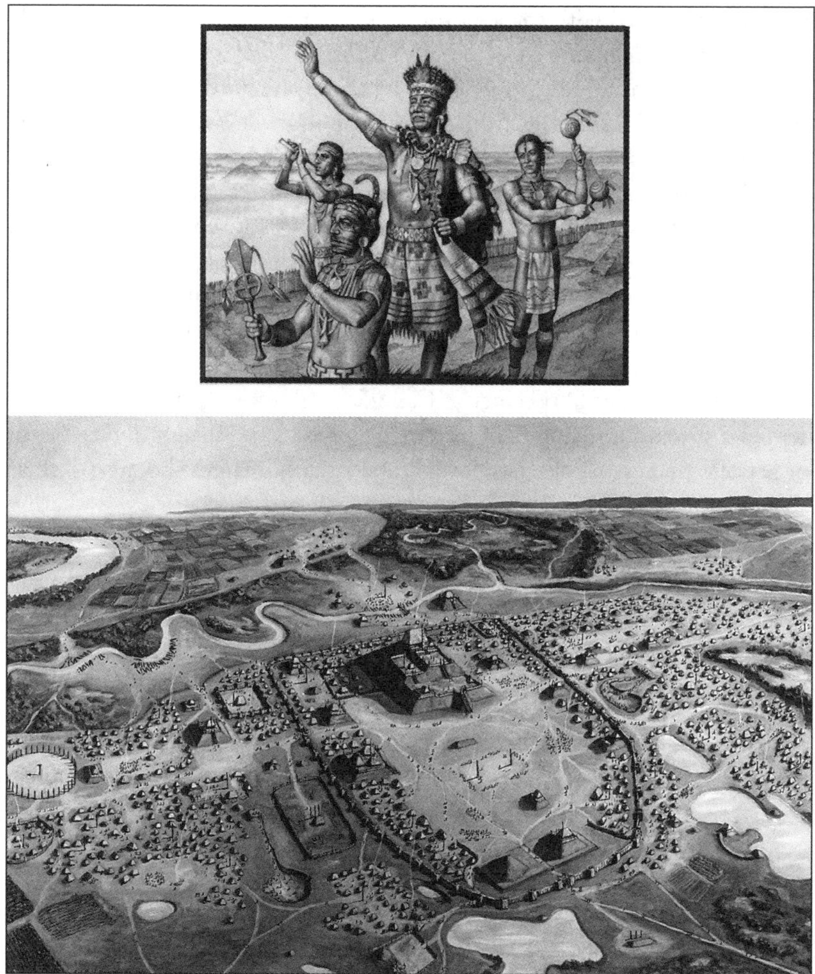

Figure 8.1. *Above*: artist's conception of the Mississippian elite by Lloyd Kenneth Townsend. *Below*: Cahokia, around A.D. 1150, by William R. Iseminger.

the power of both the rulers and Cahokia from the tenth through the thirteen centuries. One such individual, almost certainly a great ruler himself, lay on a death bed of twenty thousand shell beads, and below him a woman was interred.[5] Perhaps this was his wife: an eyewitness account by Le Page du Pratz, an early French settler in the southwest, tells of the funeral procession of a Natchez war chief, Tattooed Serpent, during which retainers and members of his family were strangled to join him in death.[6]

The great leader in Mound 72 was surrounded by the corpses of human sacrifices as well as by a variety of exotic goods such as clusters of arrows, each cluster tipped with stone points in styles representative of the widely dispersed regions that had come under Mississippian influence or control. Among them was a bundle of arrows whose stone heads were made from Hixton Silicified Sandstone from Silver Mound in west-central Wisconsin.

Even more dramatic representations found in Mound 72 of the power of the lords of Cahokia were several large burial pits containing hundreds of human sacrifices. One contained the remains of more than fifty people, mostly young women, laid in neat rows. Another, located below a row of people buried on wooden litters used by Mississippians to carry elites, contained the remains of adults who appeared to have been herded into the hole and killed there, some obviously by arrows.

Outside the central precinct of Cahokia were more large mounds, residential districts consisting of houses made of poles and thatch, and circles of large poles that archaeologists have dubbed "woodhenges" because of their probable function as calendrical or astronomical observatories. Radiating from Cahokia itself were smaller subordinate towns and ceremonial centers as well as dozens of hamlets and farmsteads. Thousands of acres of farm fields surrounded these places and produced much of the Mississippian food.

Cahokia and Mississippian society was so vast and so complex at about A.D. 1100 that some archaeologists believe that it formed the first formal state-level society in North America, much like other early civilizations of the world such as those in Mesopotamia, Egypt, and China, as well as the Maya, Inca, and Aztecs in the Americas, that had urban centers, monumental architecture, a state religion, and a stratified society with hereditary royalty on top.

Others view the social and political structure at Mississippian society at Cahokia as a kinship-based chiefdom, although in this case much more elaborate than those of Hopewell times.

Unlike state-level societies that have markets, chiefdoms distribute food and other necessities during the course of important ceremonies and feasts controlled by the chief. These were giveaway ceremonies that reflected well on the chief, increasing that person's prestige and influence, although the food and goods distributed had been originally collected from the general population. This process of redistribution functioned to help even out inequalities that might arise as the result of uneven access to resources. One important ceremony of this kind, found among the later Mississippian cultures of southeastern United States in the historic period, was the Green Corn Ceremony or Busk, an annual fertility or "first fruits" celebration.[7]

As it formed, the Mississippian culture expanded. Feeding and clothing many thousands of people would have quickly strained the local resource base. The Mississippians turned thousands of acres of fertile bottomlands into farmland and soon occupied upland areas further away from the Mississippi River. But there must have been a continuing need for other staples such as meat, hide for clothing, stone for tools, and wood for construction, as well as for goods that were symbols of prestige for the ruling families. The acquisition of such goods required a vast trade network that, like the ancient Hopewell Ceremonial Complex or Interaction Sphere, reached out into much of North America. Given Cahokia's massive fortifications around the center of the city and the militaristic imaginary in its art, including men dressed as hawks and dancing with severed heads, this probably was not always a cooperative venture. Furthermore, Cahokia itself may have been competing with other powerful Mississippian political entities that developed throughout the lower Mississippi River valley. Eventually, the Mississippian culture in many forms became a fierce and dominating presence throughout most of the Mississippi River drainage system.

The Mississippians in Wisconsin

Mississippians expanded far to the north into what is now the state of Wisconsin, establishing small colonies along the Mississippi River about A.D. 1050 (figure 8.2). These were short lived, but within decades another wave of Mississippian immigrants came into the region; their presence has been documented throughout Wisconsin but especially the southern part and the western area near the Mississippi River. Among the settlements was the large Mississippian town now called Aztalan along the Crawfish River in present-day Jefferson County.[8]

What brought the Mississippians north is unclear, but there may have been a number of factors. It can be broadly observed that expansions are characteristic of early urban-based civilizations throughout the world, which need to acquire resources and land for growing populations, to conquer potential enemies, to demonstrate the power and status of individual rulers and their lineages, and even to spread religious beliefs. Military incursions often accompany such expansions, but so do mutually beneficial trading and diplomatic alliances. It is possible that some of these factors were at work in the northward Mississippian expansions.

Trempealeau

The initial migration of the Mississippians to Wisconsin appears to have related not to the need to acquire land or practical necessities but to a totally different kind of resource—supernatural power! Important and surprising

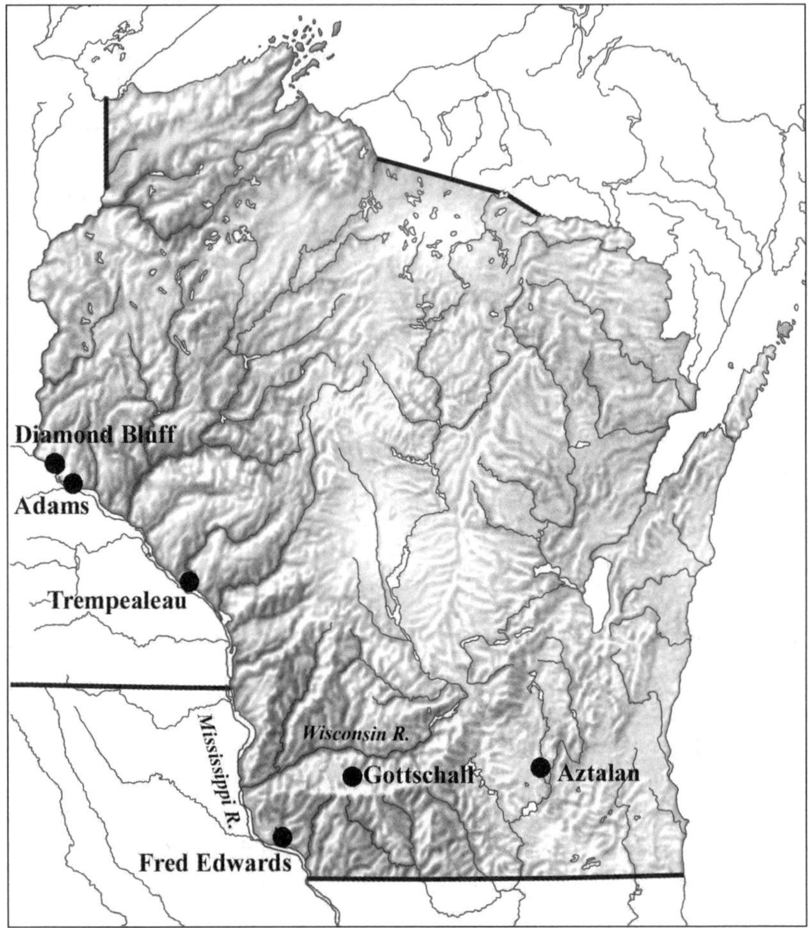

Figure 8.2. Mississippian-related sites mentioned in text.

discoveries made in recent years show that the first peoples from the emerging Mississippian culture in southern Illinois established short-lived colonies along the Mississippi River in modern-day Vernon and Trempealeau Counties, even as Cahokia first formed as a city and ceremonial center between A.D. 1000 and 1050. At several places archaeologists found small villages with houses made in Mississippian style with typical early Mississippian artifacts such as pottery made in the Cahokia area and hoes and exquisitely made arrow points made from stone found only in southern Illinois.[9] The Mississippians at these settlements seem to have brought with them all the cultural necessities from back home.

Curiously, there is no evidence of interaction with the local Woodland people who had long occupied the same locales, building considerable numbers of burial mounds, including effigies, but they may have not been present in any numbers by the time of the Mississippian migration. Theler and Boszhardt propose that the population of deer had collapsed at A.D. 1000 in the region as result of hunting pressure by the large and growing Late Woodland populations.[10] Subsequently, the Late Woodland people vacated the region. The deer population would have rebounded by the time the Mississippians arrived, fifty years later, and, along with corn agriculture, would have permitted a sustainable existence.

In the center of the modern river town of Trempealeau, the Mississippian newcomers built three platform mounds into a high bluff overlooking both the Mississippi River and the main Mississippian village on the river banks. The platform mounds, first documented in the nineteenth century, obviously formed the ceremonial heart of that community (figure 8.3). Among other things, the Mississippians brought their religious practices.

The attraction of the area, far from home, appears to have been not the opportunity to acquire what would be considered practical necessities but rather the attainment of supernatural powers, as proposed by investigating archaeologists. A dominant feature of the area is an unusual mountain-in-a-river, a local landmark today called Trempealeau Mountain. The mountain is an erosional remnant of a large ancient ridge cut off from the mainland by the river (figure 8.3). The mountain was a significant part of the natural landscape for the Ho-Chunk, who occupied this area in the nineteenth century, and a large group of Woodland mounds was built on the summit and slopes of the hill, attesting to its significance in earlier times. The archaeologists investigating the Trempealeau colony—Timothy Pauketat, Robert Boszhardt, and Danielle Benden—believe that the mountain, as the most prominent feature in the Upper Mississippi River valley, would have been perceived as a place of supernatural powers and possibly even as a shrine.[11] Considering that the Trempealeau colony dates to the very time that the city of Cahokia was forming, they propose that, in order to establish the city as a ceremonial and cosmic center of the world, the Mississippians desired to appropriate special places at the limits of their world that they believed were imbued with supernatural powers.

It may also be added that twenty-five miles to the east of Trempealeau is Silver Mound, the source of Hixton Silicified Sandstone, which had been viewed as a culturally important, if not sacred, rock for Native peoples from the time they first came to the region thirteen thousand years ago. As mentioned, a large cluster of arrows tipped with Hixton was buried with

Figure 8.3. *Above*: platform mounds on a high hill overlooking the town of Trempealeau as they appeared in the early twentieth century. *Below*: Trempealeau Mountain.

the great lord of Cahokia in Mound 72, and this burial took place around the same time that the Mississippian colonies in Wisconsin were developing.

Gottschall Rockshelter

There is evidence of early contact between Mississippians and indigenous Late Woodland/effigy mound people further to the south at the Gottschall

Figure 8.4. Mississippi-style paintings and sandstone head from the Gottschall Rockshelter.

Rockshelter in the upland bluffs south of the Wisconsin River in modern-day Iowa County. The site is a sandstone cave that occupies a deep ravine seven miles from the river, a cave that had been used for thousands of years by area people. About one thousand years ago or slightly thereafter, Mississippian people painted the sandstone walls with figures of people and animals that tell a story still recounted by Ho-Chunk and closely related Ioway people in modern times (figure 8.4).[12] The paintings are clearly made in a Mississippian style that is foreign to Wisconsin, but excavations in the cave floor found no unequivocal evidence of Mississippian artifacts. Instead, it appears that Late Woodland people were the principal occupants of the cave at the time the paintings were made. These were probably the same people who maintained the villages surrounded by large numbers of effigy mounds along the Wisconsin River in modern-day Eagle Township of Richland County, mentioned in the preceding chapter.

Robert Salzer of Beloit College first documented the paintings in the 1980s and subsequently conducted excavations into the floor of the cave, revealing neat layers of archaeological deposits that had accumulated during the many years the cave was in use. The main panel of the paintings depicts two large human beings with disks or orbs on their heads opposing a turtle, a peregrine falcon, and a smaller individual elaborately dressed and decorated as a Mississippian warrior. All of the humans have typical "forked-eye" faces in imitation of the markings around the eyes of the peregrine falcon. The falcon was much revered by the Mississippians, no doubt because of its hunting process: the bird swoops down at high speeds and immobilizes its prey with a blow much like that dealt by a war club in battle. At the bottom of the main composition and off to the side is a small human figure smoking a long pipe who appears to be the transmitter or storyteller of the story being told by the paintings.

The late Robert Hall, an expert on Native traditions and belief systems, recognized the composition of the paintings and related them to a series of sacred stories that recount the life and exploits of a mythic culture hero named Red Horn that were obtained by the anthropologists Paul Radin and Allison Skinner from the keepers of such esoteric knowledge among the Ho-Chunk and closely related Ioway in the early twentieth century.[13] These oral traditions are long and complex, but the parts that relate to the paintings are those that recount how a race of giants attacks the people but is defeated in contests by Red Horn, assisted by his friends Thunderbird and Turtle. In later contests Red Horn and others are killed. The death of Red Horn is subsequently avenged by his sons, who seek out and kill the giants with the help of magic. They bring back the bones of Red Horn and others, who are magically brought back to life.

While the smaller figure opposing the giants could be Red Horn, Hall interpreted the person to be one of Red Horn's sons and suggested that the paintings pertained to the later part of the Red Horn story.[14] Significantly, excavations into the floor of the cave discovered a nine-inch-high human head carved from sandstone that may be a representation of Red Horn himself (figure 8.4). The face of the head was painted with vertical stripes similar to those on a human figure identified as Red Horn that was found among other Mississippian paintings in a cave in Missouri.[15]

There have since been other interpretations of the story on the cave walls, but Salzer, Rajnovich, and Hall are undoubtedly correct in identifying the Gottschall Rockshelter as a ritual cave or shrine at which the transmission of a sacred story between Mississippians and Indigenous people was used to create an alliance through bonds of kinship. The paintings have not been directly dated, but Salzer traced them to a layer in the floor dated between A.D. 900 and 1000 through drops of paints found in deposits under the paintings. Reexamining the detailed archaeological data published by Salzer and Rajnovich, another archaeologist, Robert Boszhardt, came to the conclusion that paintings were instead made after A.D. 1000, perhaps as late as 1060.[16] Nevertheless, the site still represents another early

Mississippian presence in Wisconsin, as at Trempealeau. What happened next in the area of the Gottschall site is unknown, for the current evidence suggests that all people subsequently abandoned the region and that Mississippian activity moved elsewhere in Wisconsin.

Fred Edwards Site

The Fred Edwards site represents a second wave of Mississippian-related activity in Wisconsin. It is a large village in southwestern Wisconsin along the Grant River, a tributary of the Mississippi. Like the Trempealeau settlements, the village contains Mississippian-style houses and Mississippian artifacts. Unlike the Trempealeau settlements, Fred Edwards is surrounded by effigy mounds and its inhabitants used both Mississippian-style pottery and variations of Late Woodland cord-decorated pottery that blends Woodland and Mississippian elements. Fred Edwards also had a sturdy stockade, suggesting that its residents were expecting trouble. The village was occupied between A.D. 1050 and 1150 by people with Mississippian connections, newcomers from Iowa and/or northern Illinois, and quite probably by the effigy-building residents of the Grant River valley. No Mississippian platform mounds were built at the Fred Edwards site. Lead, deer bones, and stone hide scrapers were found in comparatively large quantities, leading the site investigator, Fred Finney, initially to conclude that the site was founded by newcomers who had come to acquire lead and deer hides.[17] Lead was used by both Native people and later white settlers as a base for white paint. The Native people probably focused on white paint for body decoration, which, judging from the Mississippians' artistic renditions of themselves, was elaborate and could include tattooing. The southwestern part of Wisconsin contains extensive lead deposits and drew thousands of American miners in the early nineteenth century. This area, along with southern Wisconsin in general, also supported a large deer population. However, the recent discovery of many effigy and other mounds immediately surrounding the site, in a fashion reminiscent of the Eagle Township and Diamond Bluff settlements described earlier, raises the possibility that Fred Edwards may be a Late Woodland village whose residents were beginning to settle down and, in this case, establish strong trade connections with Mississippian and other populations.

Aztalan: A Mississippian Outpost

The largest and most famous Mississippian site in Wisconsin is Aztalan, located on the Crawfish River near the town of Lake Mills (figure 8.5).[18]

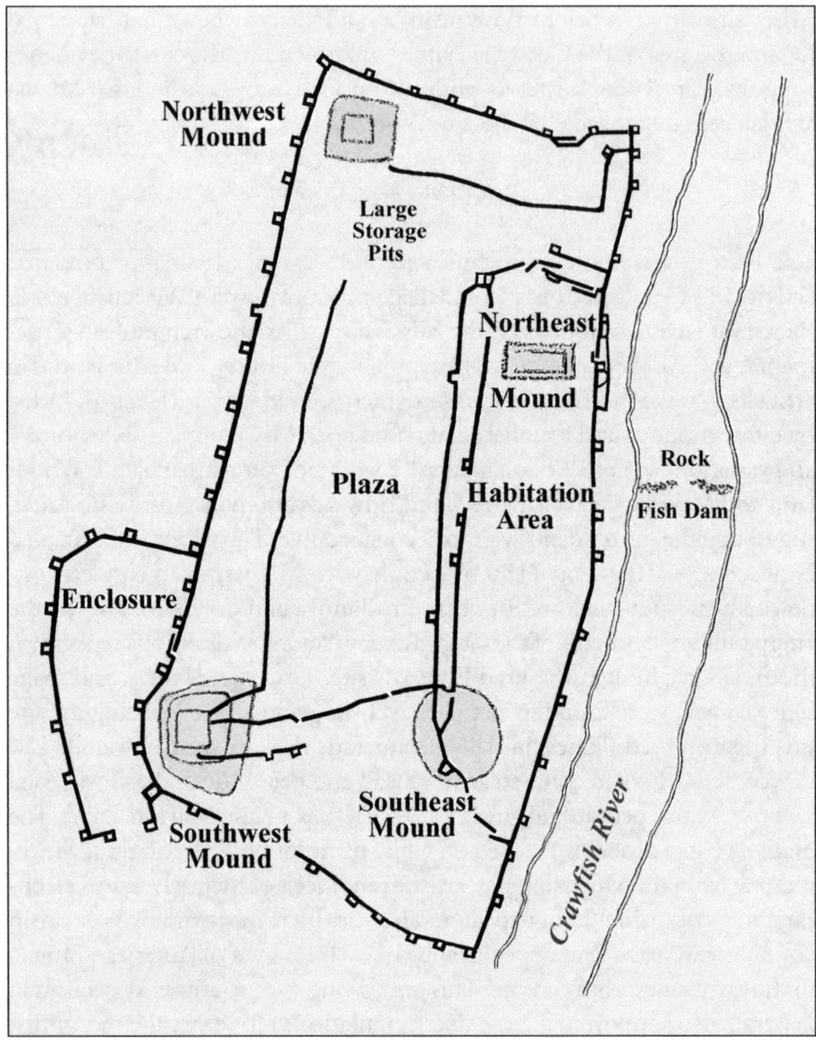

Figure 8.5. Layout of Aztalan based on archaeological research.

The name Aztalan comes from a greatly mistaken idea prevalent in the early nineteenth century that the site was the place of origin of the Aztecs of Mexico. Because of its uniqueness in Wisconsin, the site has been the focus of intensive archaeological investigations beginning in the nineteenth century. Increase A. Lapham mapped the site and examined some mounds before 1855, and Samuel Barrett of the Public Museum of the City of Milwaukee conducted the first professional excavations beginning in 1919.[19]

Later archaeologists from the Wisconsin Archaeological Survey and the Wisconsin Historical Society examined parts of the site from the 1940s through the 1960s. The later work resulted in the reconstruction of two platform mounds and segments of a defensive wall. Beginning in the 1980s and continuing through the present, researchers from the University of Wisconsin–Milwaukee, the University of Wisconsin–Madison, and Michigan State University have conducted more limited and focused investigations at the site that continue to contribute important data.

At its heyday around A.D. 1150, Aztalan covered fifteen acres and was enclosed by a formidable wall made of huge posts interwoven with willow branches and thickly plastered with clay and mixed grass, a type of construction known as wattle and daub. Large buttresses located at intervals along the wall not only helped support the massive structure but also probably served as watchtowers and defensive positions for warriors. Two sets of progressively smaller enclosures subdivided the town, separating it into different social spaces.

At roughly the four corners of the town are earthen mounds, three of which are smaller versions of the kind of platform mounds found at Cahokia and other Mississippian sites. The platform mounds supported civic and religious structures, and each appears to have played a distinct role in Aztalan life. The southwestern mound—the largest at the site—was two-tiered and built in several stages over time (figure 8.6). The top surface was covered with a white clay facing, enhancing the dramatic appearance of the mound. On top of the mound, there was a large structure or house, measuring forty-two feet on a side and built of upright posts. Inside the structure, archaeologists found storage pits containing the remains of corn. The structure almost certainly was the house where the ruling Mississippian family lived.

The northwestern mound functioned as a platform for a mausoleum for Mississippian elite (figure 8.6). It was built in three stages, and atop the second stage archaeologists who sampled the mound with trenches found the remains of a burned mausoleum, also called a charnel house, containing the bones of ten people, who had been placed side by side in the five-by-twelve-foot structure.[20] The long bones of an eleventh individual were bundled and held together by a cord.

Charnel houses were common repositories for the remains of important Mississippian families. After learning of this custom, Hernando de Soto and his conquistadors raided mound-top charnel houses in the southeastern United States in search of valuables, enraging the local Indian inhabitants. Like those of Hopewell times, the Mississippian mortuary structures were

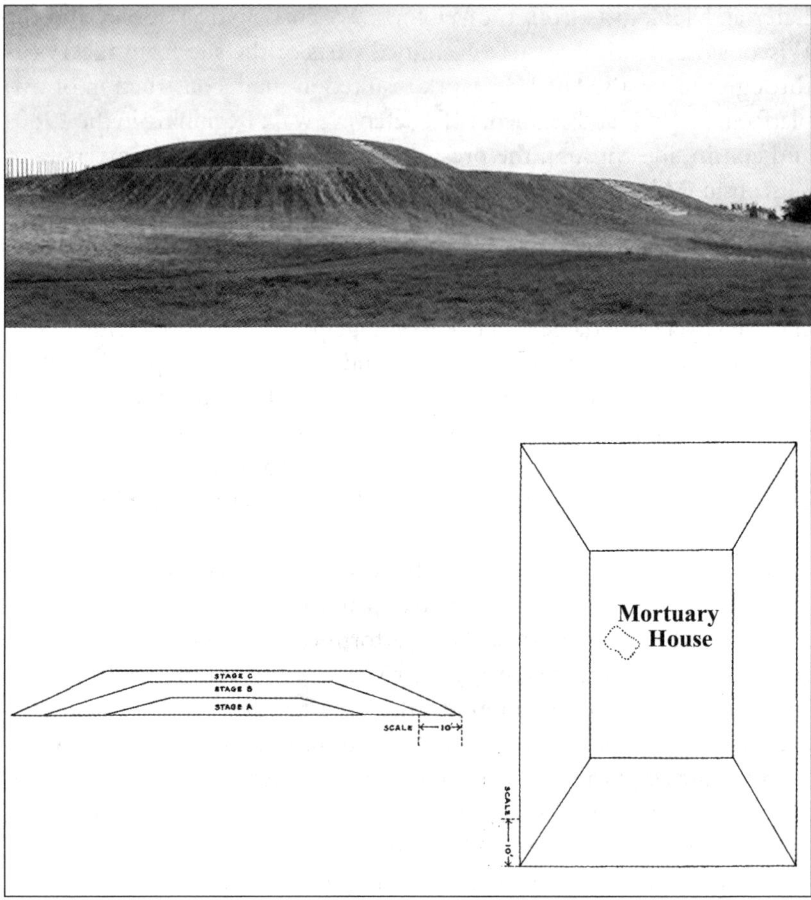

Figure 8.6. *Above*: southwestern mound. *Below*: drawing showing location of mortuary structure on northwest platform mound at Aztalan.

periodically burned or dismantled, which stimulated a phase of new mound construction. The remnants of a second charnel house may have existed on the top of the northwestern mound or elsewhere on the site. According to a report written in 1838, mound diggers excavated the top of a large "oval" mound somewhere within the enclosure at Aztalan and recovered the charred remains of more than fifty bundles of human bones still tied by cords.[21]

The northeastern platform mound at Aztalan was first excavated in the 1960s, but, unlike the southwestern and northwestern mounds, it was never reconstructed. It apparently functioned as a platform for a temple or religious structure. The mound was built in one stage, but it was raised over the remains of a large building, measuring forty-five by ninety feet, that had been constructed on the ground surface. Another building was built on top of the mound; this building was open walled and constructed of upright posts. Inside the structure, the Aztalan people maintained sacred fires in large pits. Periodically, the fires were extinguished and the pits were cleansed or reconsecrated by lining them with pure white sand.[22] Eyewitness accounts by Europeans tell us that sacred fires were carefully maintained in temples by Mississippian peoples in the Southeast, where they were perceived as the personification of the sun deity. The ritual fires would have been extinguished and rekindled during a version of the annual Green Corn Ceremony.[23]

Recent analysis of unpublished information obtained during the 1960s excavations has supplied many more details about this ceremonial structure complex. Thomas Zych of the University of Wisconsin–Milwaukee found that the original structure had been built by previous Late Woodland people living at the site but that it contained indications of early Mississippian contact in the form of locally made pottery with Mississippian characteristics.[24] The later mound-top building was built by the Mississippian themselves, but five different pots were found in the mound, four of them placed upside down. The different pottery styles demonstrate a multiethnic presence at Aztalan, which was occupied by both Mississippian and Late Woodland peoples.

The oblong southeastern mound had previously been thought to have been a natural landscape feature incorporated into the town plan, and at one time it even supported a corner of an interior stockade. Recent archaeological excavations conducted by Lynne Goldstein of Michigan State University have now determined that much of the knoll was enhanced with earth by the Mississippians, although the purpose of this newly discovered mound is still unknown.[25]

Aztalan's residential district occupied the eastern side of the town along the river. It accommodated several hundred people who lived in small but substantial single-family pithouses built of wattle and daub. Some were circular and others rectangular, with pronounced entranceways, much like the keyhole houses of the Late Woodland. The residential area was set off from the rest of the site, but another stout wall with watchtowers and bastions was built, possibly as a backup in case the town walls were breached.

Down the center of the site is the plaza, characteristic of Mississippian settlements, where public gatherings, ceremonies, and feasts would have been held. The city of Cahokia had several such plazas. In the 1990s, investigators from the University of Wisconsin–Milwaukee discovered a specialized precinct at the northern end of the plaza with a large number of huge clay-lined pits in which food was stored. The existence of a centralized food depot suggests that food distribution was controlled by the town leader.

Extending out from the town wall at the southwest part of Aztalan is a mysterious walled enclosure surrounding five acres of land. This kind of enclosure has not been documented at other Mississippian sites. Excavations by Barrett in the early twentieth century followed the enclosure wall and showed that, like the town itself, it consisted of clay-covered wood timbers and was complete with watchtowers. Subsequent excavations determined that the enclosure was connected to the town in the area of the principal platform mound by two narrow passageways. Some ideas expressed in the past about the enclosure's functions are that it may have served as an extra fortification protecting the elite who lived on the main mound or that perhaps it was used as a sacred place for ceremonies conducted by the leaders or for special religious activities that were not to be viewed by the rest of Aztalan's population.

But excavation maps made by Barrett suggest that there was a wide entrance or a gate-like gap on the south end of the enclosure that led to the outside world, and this has been recently confirmed by modern excavations.[26] Most of the area of the enclosure has not yet been examined, so archaeologists are uncertain about the activities conducted within the enclosure, but the large entranceway suggests that it might have been a secure place for outside visitors who were not allowed into the town, such as traders bringing needed goods to the town or those seeking to form alliances and agreements. The narrow entrances to the town and the narrow passageways from the enclosure into the town, as well as the watchtowers, indicate that the use of the space was tightly controlled.

Ceremonial Post Mounds and the "Princess Burial"

Early visitors to Aztalan described about forty-five acres of land immediately north of the town proper that were used for growing crops, since the ridged agricultural fields were still visible. To the west and overlooking the crop fields originally stood a line of at least twenty-nine large conical mounds that followed a high ridge that trended north-south (figure 8.7). A line of ten smaller conical mounds was situated on a slope just below this. Even farther to the west was a third group of about a dozen conical mounds that has been called the Greenwood mound group. By the twentieth century, many of the Greenwood mounds had been obliterated by farming, but

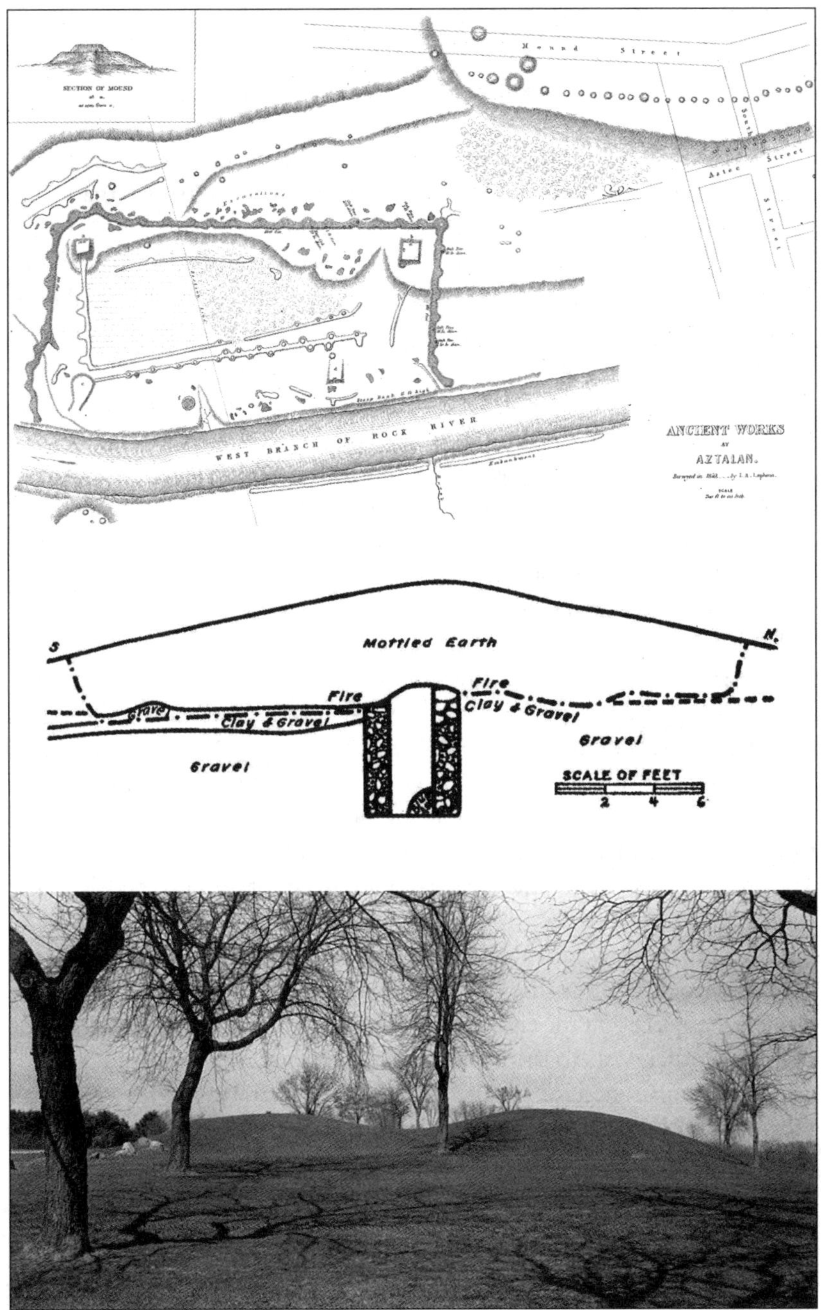

Figure 8.7. Conical mounds above the town of Aztalan: (*above*) 1855 map by Increase A. Lapham; (*center*) profile of conical mound showing hole for ceremonial post beneath; (*below*) photo of surviving ceremonial post mounds in Aztalan State Park.

Barrett examined some of those that remained and found that they contained large central pits with cremated human remains and bundle burials. No grave goods were found, so the connection of the group to the Mississippian town is as yet unclear.

Barrett explored the large conical mounds in the long central line on the ridge top, and his findings resulted in two surprises. The first was that many of the mounds were not burial mounds at all but covered deep pits in which large and presumably very high wooden posts once stood. The diameter of the posts was approximately fifteen inches. In one mound, the basal remnants of a large oak post were still in place. The function of these posts is not obvious, nor is the reason that their locations were covered by high, prominent mounds. Barrett suggested that the annual Green Corn Ceremony, as widely practiced by southeastern Mississippian peoples in the historic period, was a possible reason for the erection of large poles. European observers described dances associated with the ceremony as taking place around a special pole erected for the purpose.[27] The post mounds in part overlook Aztalan's cornfields. Alternatively, the posts could have played a role in year-round calendrical observations, as did the woodhenges at Cahokia.

The second surprise came toward the northern end of this unusual line of mounds. In a grave pit beneath a low conical mound nearly fifty feet in diameter Barrett discovered one of the most lavish Native burials ever found in Wisconsin: the famous "princess" burial. This was a woman in her early twenties whose corpse had been wrapped in three belts of several thousand beads made from local river clams and Gulf Coast marine shell. The presence of so many shell beads is reminiscent of the bead bed found in the burial of the great lord in mound 72 at Cahokia. From this, it can be presumed that this woman was from an elite Mississippian family.

Whatever her status, the important young Aztalan woman was buried in a peculiar place—at the end of a line of mounds that marked the locations of former ritual posts to the northwest of the town. One possibility is that she was a human sacrifice. The abandonment of Aztalan is correlated with the intense drought that occurred sometime between A.D. 1100 and 1200 as modeled for the region by the University of Wisconsin Climatic Research Center.[28] If crops could not be grown successfully any longer, perhaps the mound-covered ritual post holes representing Green Corn Ceremonies were replaced by an appeal to the supernatural for relief that included the offering of a precious gift—the life of a young woman, representing fertility, from the most important lineages in the community. Modern analysis of the skeletal remains, however, showed no evidence of violent death.

History of Aztalan

The history of the town of Aztalan is becoming clearer as a result of continuing archaeological work at the site. This early village was situated at a place that had been used by previous Woodland people for quite some time, and Middle Woodland artifacts are commonly found at the site. Effigy mound and earlier peoples of the Middle Woodland people also used the locale for ceremonial purposes. Directly across the river from Aztalan are the remains of earthen and conical burial mounds, one of which yielded a stone platform pipe typical of the Middle Woodland Hopewell culture in the region. Nearby, Barrett mapped a long-tailed water-spirit mound characteristic of the Late Woodland effigy mound builders, but the presence of such a mound is uncertain since an earlier map by Theodore H. Lewis showed no effigy but instead a long earth ridge and the possible remnants of another enclosure.[29]

Excavating layered middens, or garbage deposits, along the bank of the Crawfish River, John Richards of the University of Wisconsin–Milwaukee was able to piece together a chronology of events that showed the evolution of the town from its beginning as a Late Woodland village between A.D. 800 and 1000.[30] The village subsequently developed some sort of connections to the emerging Mississippian society in southern Illinois; early Mississippian pottery began to appear in the archaeological deposits, but it was made by local people rather than imported. There is unmistakable later evidence, in the form of pottery from Cahokia and extensive modifications to the site, that the Mississippians themselves were present, although Late Woodland people continued to live in the town. At this time, sometime just before A.D. 1100, Aztalan was expanded and rebuilt along the lines of Cahokia and other Mississippian communities; changes included platform mounds as well as a formidable wall around the town. Mississippian peoples no doubt also introduced new ceremonies and rituals to the indigenous Late Woodland people. Evidence from the earlier excavations of the platform mounds and walls as well as ongoing research indicates that Aztalan underwent several major waves of reconstruction by the Mississippians.

Throughout the history of the town, many of its residents were drawn from Late Woodland populations. Much of the ceramic assemblage found at the site, even pieces dated to after the arrival of the Mississippians, are Late Woodland collared types, although earlier Late Woodland ceramics that preceded the collared types are also present. The social composition of Aztalan brings to mind the fur-trading posts and centers during the historic period, where the European traders lived surrounded by communities of

Native Americans who were drawn to the posts because of the access it provided to European-made goods.

But if Aztalan was a trading outpost, and this has *not* been established, for what could the Mississippians and their close allies have been trading? The Cahokia scholar Melvin Fowler once speculated that copper acquired from northerly sources in Michigan might have been involved, and a copper workshop has recently been identified at Cahokia, although there are no copper deposits in that region.[31] Copper was highly prized by Mississippian people but was largely reserved for special objects such as ceremonial plaques embossed with symbols and figures that had religious significance. Only small quantities of copper have been found at Aztalan, largely in the form of beads and awls, but early excavations by Samuel Barrett of the Milwaukee Public Museum located a small area of the site where he believed that copper had been worked and stored.[32] The Milwaukee Public Museum also has in its possession a pair of large copper earrings called "long-nosed god maskettes" found at the site, apparently by Barrett. At other Mississippian sites, including Cahokia, these rare ceremonial objects were made of shell.

Among the arrow points found at Aztalan are an unusual number made of quartz, a rock that is much harder to work than chert but that is abundant in the area. Quartz was rarely used by ancient societies of southern Wisconsin. Arrow points and other small implements made of quartz are commonly used in northern Wisconsin, where there is no chert but plentiful quartz deposits. The presence of the quartz artifacts could be the result of trading contacts with peoples from further north, much closer to copper sources. Nevertheless, copper has not been found at Aztalan in sufficient quantities to convince most researchers that it was anything but an incidental trade item.

The archaeologists Lynne Goldstein and John Richards have pointed out that Aztalan is located immediately adjacent to large wetland areas that could have produced any number of food resources.[33] Furthermore, Aztalan lies in a region characterized by mixed forest and prairie. This environment would have supported (and still does) a large deer population. Perhaps, as at the Fred Edwards site, the acquisition of deer hides was a major focus of Mississippian trading activity.

The function of Aztalan as trading center has not been proved, and there are any number of other reasons that the Mississippians might have established Aztalan as a town in Wisconsin. For example, John Richards and Robert Jeske speculate that it could have been home to a group of Mississippians and allies who fled north as result of internal friction at Cahokia and among the peoples of southern Illinois.[34] Almost certainly the continuing excavations at the site will help soon solve what is for now the town's greatest mystery.

Aztalan and Its Neighbors

The presence of several types of Late Woodland pottery, including that of local peoples, certainly indicates that the Mississippians at Aztalan enjoyed peaceful relationships with at least some of the Indigenous people. This possibility is reinforced by the presence of contemporaneous Late Woodland villages and sites in southern Wisconsin, including those within a short distance of Aztalan, where artifacts such as pottery have been found that indicate direct contact and interaction and perhaps even intermarriage between the Late Woodland and the Mississippian people. But Aztalan itself has provided undeniable evidence of a town at war, by its massive fortifications as well as other evidence of violence.

Throughout the town proper, early archaeological excavations exhumed discarded, burned, and butchered human body parts in refuse pits, fireplaces, and refuse middens that led the pioneering Aztalan archaeologist Samuel Barrett to conclude that the Aztalan people were cannibals.[35] Modern analyses of the Aztalan remains found that they did not fit the pattern of documented examples of cannibalism to obtain food, but many are consistent with intensive warfare.[36] Historical accounts describe instances where warriors cut apart the bodies of dead enemies, bringing home body parts such as limbs and heads as war trophies to be displayed during festivities. Tribes such as the Huron, Creek, and Tunica also tortured, burned, cut into pieces, and sometimes even ate their prisoners in order to gain their power and courage.[37] Modern analyses also suggests that many of the disarticulated remains could also have been the result of Mississippian mortuary practices, which included dismembering of corpses, cleaning and bundling of bones, and the final burial or storage of some the bones, as well as cremation.[38] During these rituals, some bone, notably skulls, were saved for ancestor veneration and some other bones were simply discarded. One bone bundle found in the Northwestern mound mausoleum or charnel house consisted only of long bones.[39]

The Mississippians and their allies at Aztalan clearly had enemies. Among them could have been other Late Woodland people who were not allied with the Mississippians. Conflict among many bands and tribes may have arisen from competition for natural resources, creating an unstable situation in which alliances frequently shifted. There is some evidence that one enemy could have the Oneota people at nearby Lake Koshkonong, about fifteen miles away. These Oneota were part of an agriculturally based cultural tradition that developed fully after the Mississippian culture and dominated the Wisconsin human landscape to the time of European contact.

But whether the Oneota were contemporaneous with the Mississippians at Aztalan is a matter of debate. On the basis of radiocarbon dates, the archaeologists John Richard and Robert Jesse argue that the Oneota were present on Lake Koshkonong at the same time that the Mississippians were at Aztalan, and another prominent archaeologist, David Overstreet, believes that the Oneota emerged before the Mississippians were present at Aztalan.[40] Another view is that Oneota did not emerge in Wisconsin as a cultural tradition until later as result of the rapid cultural transformation of Late Woodland people through Mississippian influence.

One thing that is generally agreed is that the town of Aztalan was abandoned about A.D. 1200 as the Mississippian culture went into an eclipse in the northern parts of North America and as people eventually left the once great city of Cahokia itself.

The Red Wing Locality

Other important evidence relating to the complicated history involving the Late Woodland, the Mississippians, and the Oneota comes from a place much further north along the banks of the Mississippi River in what are now Goodhue County, Minnesota, and Pierce County in northwestern Wisconsin, which had been another center of Mississippian activity. Here, a series of large fortified villages surrounded by dense Late Woodland–like burial-mound complexes once existed at what has been called the Red Wing Locality.[41] More than two thousand mounds were built in the two-state area over several hundred years. Two small Mississippian-style platform mounds at sites in Minnesota suggest a Mississippian presence. In Wisconsin, the village and mound complexes include the Diamond Bluff site, where Mississippian and Oneota pottery has been found in Late Woodland villages and in burial mounds. Researchers see Diamond Bluff and the other Red Wing Locality sites as places to which Late Woodland people from throughout the region were drawn by the Mississippians, giving birth in that area to the Oneota lifeway or tradition. James B. Stoltman and George Christiansen argue that effigy mound people vacated the whole of southwestern Wisconsin and migrated to the Red Wing area.[42] Their theory is that the rapid cultural transformation of the Late Woodland effigy mound builders into Oneota was accomplished through their intense interaction with the Middle Mississippians at places such as Red Wing. Along with characteristic pottery, a Late Woodland presence there is indicated by three effigy mounds among the hundreds of small conical burial mounds constructed around village areas (figure 8.8). These show a bird, a canine-like animal, and a water spirit: key representations of sky, earth, and water for the effigy mound people.

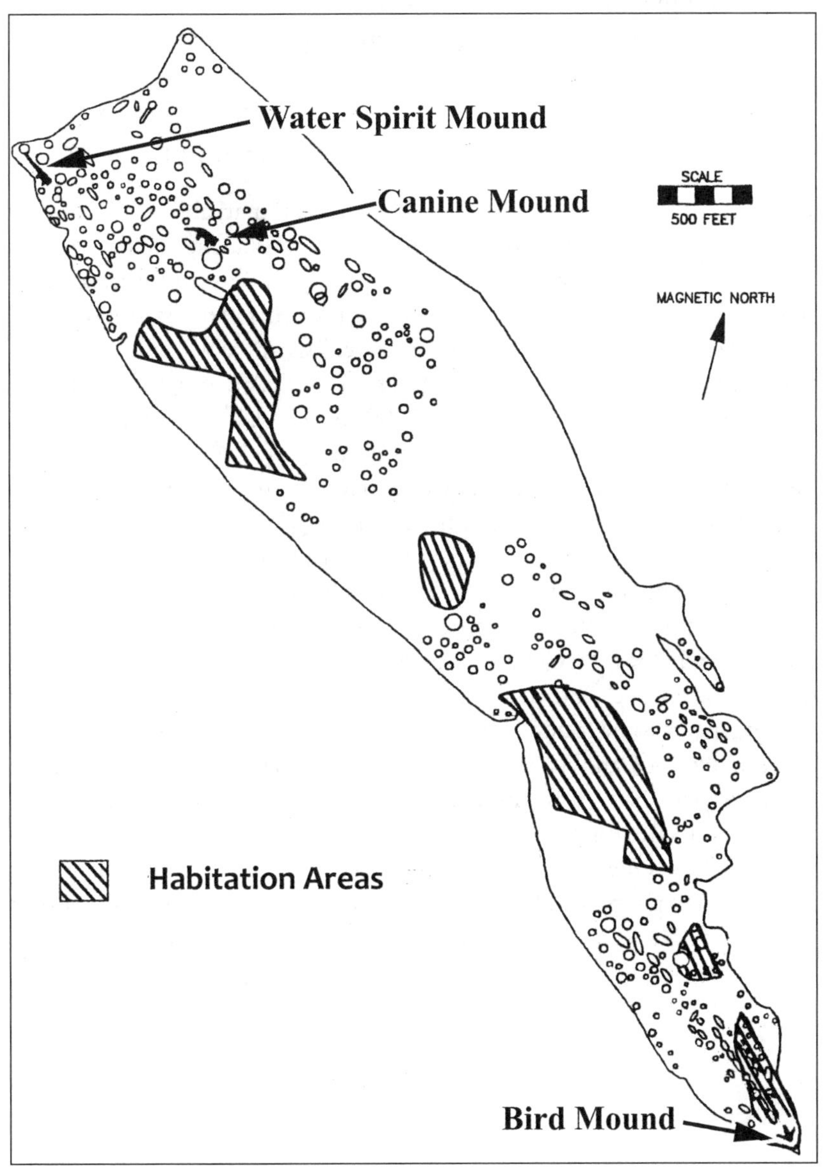

Figure 8.8. Plan of the Diamond Bluff site, also known as the Mero Complex, showing mounds and habitation areas.

These may have been the very last expressions of the effigy mound tradition. Excavated in the 1940s, the water-spirit mound provided supporting evidence for the transition of Late Woodland to Oneota through Mississippian influence. Both Mississippian and Oneota pottery accompanied burials in the Late Woodland mound form.[43]

The Demise of the Mississippian Culture

Between A.D. 1200 and 1300, Cahokia and its remarkable society disappeared from the mid-continent. The city itself was abandoned, as was its daughter community of Aztalan in Wisconsin. The reasons for the demise of Cahokia may have been varied and included overexploitation of local resources, internal political friction, warfare, loss of ideological power, and widely fluctuating climatic swings. Areas of North America were visited by a long, severe drought between A.D. 1100 and 1200, immediately followed by a lengthy period of much colder weather, now evocatively called the Neo-Boreal or Little Ice Age, that would have affected agricultural pursuits. Alternatively, new evidence published in 2015 indicates that the city of Cahokia was flooded after a sharp rise in the Mississippi River about A.D. 1200, rendering much of the ancient city inhabitable.[44]

Mississippian culture continued to flourish in many forms in the South, including what is now Georgia, Alabama, Louisiana, and even Oklahoma on the eastern Great Plains, until the appearance of the Europeans, but it no longer was to be found further north. And North America never again saw the likes of Cahokia, the ancient Mississippian capital. However, the Mississippians had great influence on the indigenous Wisconsin people, and this influence can be seen in the development of the new cultural tradition called the Oneota, likely the descendants of both Late Woodland and Mississippian peoples and the ancestors of some of the modern Wisconsin Native nations.

9

Burial Mound Construction and Use in Later Times

After the collapse of the Mississippian civilization in the Midwest and the apparent disappearance of the ubiquitous Late Woodland people, including the effigy mound builders, what is now central and southern Wisconsin appears to have been populated mainly by somewhat culturally similar peoples called Oneota by archaeologists.[1] The Oneota are distinguished in the archaeological record from other and earlier peoples by their use of characteristic forms of pottery tempered by crushed clam shell, the prevalence of large villages occupied during much of the year, and a subsistence pattern based on agriculture. Unlike the Mississippians, the Oneota did not build temple mounds, and, unlike the Late Woodland people, they did not typically build burial mounds, except early in their history when conical mounds served as burial places. Also unlike Late Woodland people, who had widely dispersed camps and villages, the Oneota were concentrated in widely separated village clusters in various parts of Wisconsin. Similar Oneota population centers emerged elsewhere in what are now Michigan, Illinois, Iowa, Minnesota, South Dakota, Nebraska, and Missouri.

Who Were the Oneota?

The origin of the Oneota in Wisconsin is another archaeological issue that has been heavily researched and hotly debated.[2] Noting a similarity between some Oneota and Mississippian customs, one early but now discarded hypothesis was that the Oneota were simply the descendants of Mississippian migrants to Wisconsin who had replaced the Indigenous population. Another proposed that the Oneota developed independent of the Late Woodland and Middle Mississippian cultures from a common Woodland base as part of the same broad trajectory toward increasing agricultural life. According to one version, the Oneota then migrated north into Wisconsin, eventually eliminating or displacing the Late Woodland people. Some Oneota became briefly allied with the contemporaneous Middle Mississippians, while others were not as much affected by culture contact.

We follow many others in the view that most likely the Oneota in Wisconsin were the descendants of Late Woodland effigy mound builders whose lifestyle had been transformed both by the adoption of corn agriculture and by contact, even intermarriage, with the Mississippian people and that the modern descendants of the Oneota are the Ho-Chunk and others. This view is supported by other lines of circumstantial evidence, such as linguistic and geographic continuity of the various cultural entities, evidence that Oneota ways of life persisted into the period of European contact, and secondhand accounts of the peoples of Wisconsin transmitted to the French.

The nature and intensity of cultural contacts between the Late Woodland and the Mississippian peoples varied from region to region, ranging from indirect contacts to cohabitation, such as at Aztalan.[3] This accounts for the different rates at which the transition was made and the fact that some Late Woodland populations persisted in certain areas of Wisconsin for a short time after the appearance of Oneota culture in other areas. It is also possible that some Late Woodland people may have even fled the region, passing through Minnesota and heading west to the Great Plains.[4]

The name Oneota is drawn from the Oneota River in Iowa, now called the Upper Iowa River, where this cultural tradition was first identified. It has also been known in archaeological literature as the Upper Mississippian tradition, as opposed to Middle Mississippian. As with all these matters, archaeologists do not know for sure the name or names by which the people referred to themselves, although most scholars are fairly certain of the many tribal names by which their midwestern descendants were known by Euro-Americans in historic times: the Siouan-speaking Ho-Chunk, Ioway, Kansa, Missouria, Omaha, Osage, and Otoe, and perhaps the Santee or Dakota Sioux. Recent archaeological work in northeastern Wisconsin has even hinted that the ancestors of the Algonquian-speaking Menominee may be included in the broad Oneota classification.[5] It is clear that what archaeologists call Oneota includes many different Native peoples and languages. Therefore, like the previous Late Woodland tradition, Oneota should not be thought of as a single "culture" but rather as a category that groups together the residents of many independent villages who adopted roughly similar but not identical ways of life.

Settlements

The first communities that archaeologists call Oneota appeared sometime after A.D. 1000, several in areas that had been centers of intense Mississippian activity. Carcajou Point, at Lake Koshkonong, and villages near modern Diamond Bluff, Wisconsin, may have been among the earliest settlements, as some pottery and other features found there clearly derive from the Mississippian tradition but in the context of Late Woodland and/or Oneota occupations. At later Oneota sites, the blending of styles and lifeways was more complete. Soon, Oneota farming villages were established on river terraces and lakes on or near easily tillable light sandy soils.

Most aspects of Oneota life were similar to those of Late Woodland peoples, but changed to accommodate a more sedentary way of living and the introduction of new Mississippian technologies and ideas. Like that of the Mississippians, the economy of the Oneota was based on farming. Corn, beans, squash, and other crops were cultivated around large villages that were occupied mainly during the warmer months. High-protein beans, first domesticated in Mexico, were apparently not cultivated by the earlier Mississippians and represent a new addition to the economy. The combination of corn, beans, and squash would come to be known among Native peoples as the "three sisters" because they complement one another nutritionally and continuously enrich the soil when planted together. The Oneota also relied heavily on river and lake resources, such as fish, clams, and wild rice. The Oneota hunted deer and elk as well as a variety of small animals for meat, hides, and bone that could be fabricated into tools. Some Oneota apparently traveled to the eastern Great Plains to hunt bison or buffalo.

Oneota people never developed large towns like Aztalan. Instead, the evolution of Oneota society over its six-hundred-year history is reflected in changing household patterns. The first identifiable Oneota communities consisted of small villages of single-family pole- and bark-covered pithouses similar to those of the earlier Late Woodland and Mississippian people.[6] Later, many of the Oneota appear to have lived in large communities with longhouses, sometimes 150 feet in length, that accommodated many families of a single lineage or clan (figure 9.1).[7]

After A.D. 1300, the Oneota consolidated into several densely populated principal centers in the southern and western areas of Wisconsin: a western

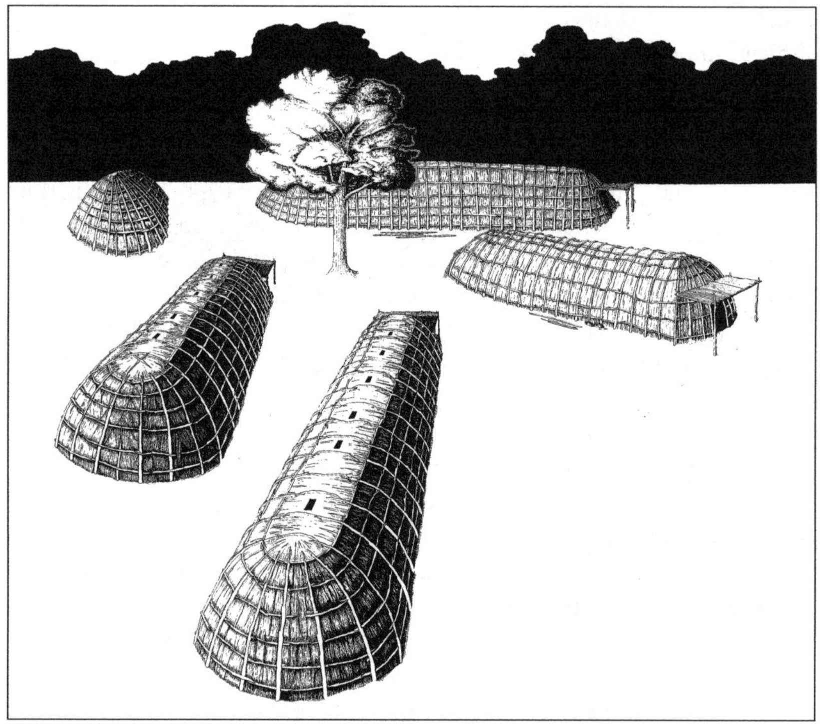

Figure 9.1. Oneota village scene in Wisconsin, around A.D. 1450.

concentration on the sandy Mississippi River terraces around present-day La Crosse, an eastern concentration along the Middle Fox River, including Lake Winnebago, as well as at nearby Green Bay and on the Door Peninsula; and a dense concentration of villages around Lake Koshkonong, a site that has been the focus of ongoing investigations by the University of Wisconsin–Milwaukee (figure 9.2).[8] There is some evidence, as yet unconfirmed, that the Oneota at Lake Koshkonong may have been somewhat insulated from the tumult of European contact and that they may have continued their way of life after Oneota ways were disrupted along the Fox River.[9] In recent decades, archaeologists have shown that Oneota-like farming villages also existed in the north woods, outside the main areas previously recognized as territory of the Oneota.[10]

In northern Illinois and far southeast Wisconsin, another related cultural group, called Langford, emerged and adapted to life on the prairies through a mixture of hunting, gathering, and agriculture.[11] It is dated mainly between 1200 and 1350, making it partly contemporaneous with Oneota. Langford people made pottery with design motifs similar to those used by the Oneota

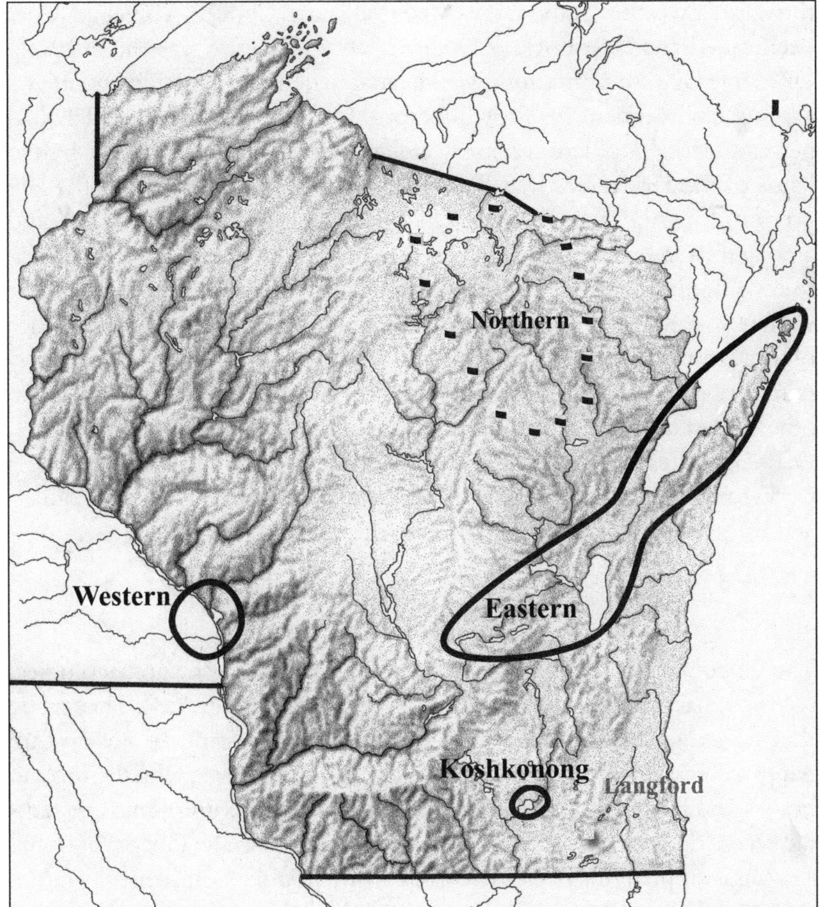

Figure 9.2. The distribution of Oneota population centers in Wisconsin.

but on pots reminiscent of those of the Late Woodland people in their use of cordage to roughen surfaces and crushed rock as a tempering agent. Langford people typically buried their dead in low mounded cemeteries. The relationship between the Langford and the surrounding Oneota neighbors is still in question, but analysis of human remains from burials in northern Illinois shows traumas consistent with a high level of warfare,[12] and the Langford tradition disappeared from the archaeological record prior to European contact.

Through most of Oneota history, the climate in Wisconsin, as in many parts of the America and elsewhere in the world, was characterized by much cooler temperatures than we experience today and much cooler also than the warmer weather of the earlier Medieval Warm Climate. This climate has been called the Neo-Boreal or "Little Ice Age."[13] Perhaps the far-flung Oneota village concentrations were in areas where the local climate offered a better environment for growing crops. Outside Wisconsin, widely dispersed Oneota population centers similarly have been linked to the homelands of modern tribes that lived in these areas.[14] Throughout the late prehistoric period, the areas between the Oneota enclaves in Wisconsin and among the Oneota settlements elsewhere in the Midwest seem to have been thinly populated, suggesting the maintenance of vast buffer zones. That warfare was part of life throughout this period is evident from the presence of some fortified villages, signs of violence consistent with warfare on many human remains, and the persistence of war-related imagery on pottery and in other art. At the same time, there is evidence that expanded trade connected Oneota villages in Wisconsin with one another, with other Oneota villages further south and west on the eastern Great Plains, and with Algonquian- and Iroquoian-speaking populations in the eastern Great Lakes.

Pottery

The Oneota are distinguished from other cultures in the archaeological record in part by their distinctive styles of pottery (figure 9.3). They made thin-walled globular pottery vessels that, like Mississippian pottery, are tempered with crushed shell. The form of the jars, however, with their round bodies and high rims, comes from Late Woodland pottery-making techniques, as do the notched lips of many Oneota pots. The Oneota adopted the Mississippian practice of decorating the shoulders of their pots rather than limiting decoration to the rims and lips as did the Late Woodland people. Oneota pottery is often decorated with designs made by trailing a blunt tool, incising with a sharp tool, or punching the end of a narrow tool into wet clay to create punctates. With some notable and early exceptions, the Woodland practice of impressing cords into the clay was not employed.

Early Oneota decorations were also clearly inspired by Mississippian motifs such as a circle and cross motif, interlocking scrolls, curved lines, chevrons, and other geometric patterns applied to a smooth surface (figure 9.3). These Mississippian designs appear to be elaborations of the upper-world and lower-world themes and would have been easily understood and absorbed by Late Woodland people who shared a similar worldview.

After Cahokia's power waned and Mississippian settlements in Wisconsin were abandoned, Oneota decorations took on a more distinctive flavor but continued to deal with ancient upper-world and lower-world themes that, like those used for the earlier effigy mounds, seem to have had geographic

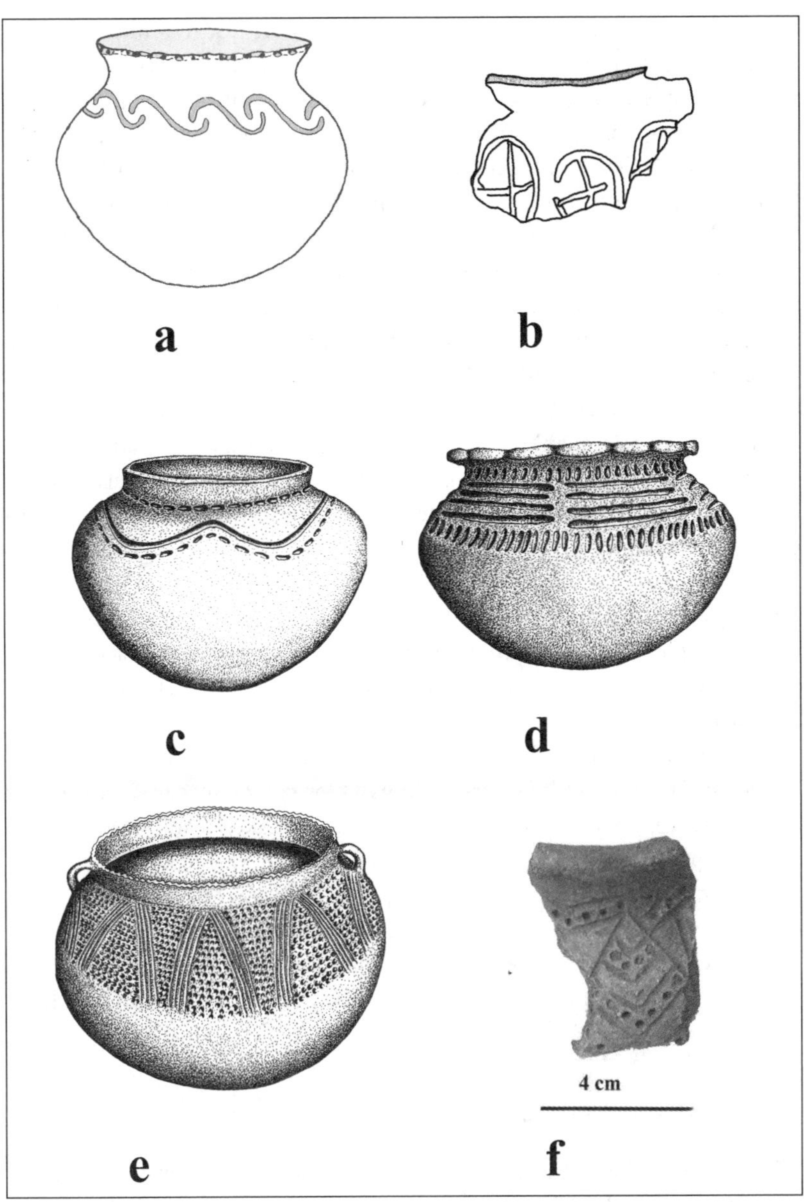

Figure 9.3. Oneota pottery: (a) drawing of Oneota pot with Mississippian motifs from the Carcajou Point site; (b) drawing of circle and cross motif from the Grand Village site in central Wisconsin; (c) curvilinear designs from eastern Wisconsin circa A.D. 1150 to 1350 with probable water symbolism; (d) trailed designs on pottery from eastern Wisconsin circa A.D. 1350 that may be lower-world (earth) symbolism; (e) upper-world (falcon) symbolism characteristic of western Wisconsin circa a.d. 1400; (f) photograph of a hawk or falcon tail on a miniature pot from the collection of James Bussey from the Crabapple Point site on Lake Koshkonong.

associations. Like the ancestral effigy mounds in the form of birds, Oneota upper-world symbolism has been found largely, although not exclusively, in western Wisconsin. A legacy of both the Mississippian ideology and continuing warfare, one prominent upper-world image was a stylized peregrine falcon or hawk; hawk or falcon symbolism on pottery and other art has been found further south and west in Wisconsin and is associated with Oneota population concentrations in Illinois, Iowa, Minnesota, and Missouri.[15]

Lower-world symbolism seems to predominate on Oneota pottery from eastern Wisconsin, as it did on the earlier water spirit-shaped mounds of this region. Curvilinear designs, probably water motifs, were common on pottery from the thirteenth and early fourteenth centuries; after A.D. 1350, these gave way to rectilinear patterns of vertical and, especially, horizontal lines that may be general representations of the earth, as they appear to be on Woodland pottery (figure 9.3). Interestingly, the Ho-Chunk, also known as the Winnebago and widely believed to be descended from the eastern Oneota, were known to be associated with water by others. Winnebago is an Algonquian name for the Ho-Chunk that probably refers to dirty or muddy water, and the Ho-Chunk were known to the French as "people of the sea."[16] However, these associations may have reflected the fact the Ho-Chunk lived near large bodies of water such as Lake Winnebago and Lake Michigan.

Although lower-world symbolism appears to predominate in eastern Wisconsin, pottery with upper-world hawk or falcon imagery, very similar to western Oneota pottery, has been found at Lake Koshkonong and in small quantities at eastern Oneota sites on Green Bay, on the Door Peninsula, and at other sites in the region.[17] The upper-world and lower-world iconography may reflect the existence among the Oneota of moieties (dual-clan social divisions) and/or perhaps phratries (groups of related clans), which were present in many Native cultures such as the Ho-Chunk and the Menominee.

Burial Mounds

Like their Woodland ancestors, some early Oneota (or emerging Oneota) continued to build small conical burial mounds around their villages, sometimes in great numbers. This appears to have been a transitional phase as most later Oneota abandoned the custom of burying the dead in mounds, at least with any frequency. Among these transitional sites are the Diamond Bluff and Adams sites on the Upper Mississippi River, which are among the places where the Oneota culture appeared, and the later Armstrong site, farther downstream in Trempealeau County. Elsewhere in Wisconsin, mounds do not appear to have been common, even at early Oneota sites. Some Oneota—for example, those at the Grand Village site in Green Lake County—enhanced natural knolls by adding dirt to accommodate ongoing burials.[18] These hills took on the appearance of large low burial mounds. Interestingly, one motif found on pottery from a Grand Village mound is a circle enclosing a cross, a pattern that also appears in Mississippian iconography and that is interpreted as a symbol of the world (figure 9.3). Among North American cultures the cross represented the four sacred directions. For Ho-Chunk people, this cross was also the symbol for Earth-Maker who created the world.[19]

After about A.D. 1300, most Oneota interred people right after death in individual graves in cemeteries at their villages, although the custom of building burial mounds lingered among some Oneota-related people elsewhere in the Midwest. In addition, people often were buried beneath the floors of their houses, a practice that, in the case of young children, was already present at the appearance of the first Oneota communities.[20] The change from burial in mounds to burial in cemeteries seems to have been related to the appearance of the more sedentary farming lifestyles of the first Oneota communities. Ceremonies of world renewal, which had been part of burial mound ritual, became associated with crop fertility rather than mortuary rites, and other ceremonies and institutions evolved to integrate segments of society socially.[21] Among the new ceremonials was one that appeared later in the evolution of the Oneota and that was specifically directed at social integration: the Calumet Ceremony. In the Calumet Ceremony, as documented in the historic period, outsiders are symbolically adopted into the tribe, taking the name of a deceased member. The ceremony involves dancing and smoking a calumet pipe, which consists of a special, elaborately carved wooden stem and a bowl of red pipestone. Robert Hall has drawn a parallel between the Calumet Ceremony and earlier mound ceremonialism, pointing out that during the Calumet Ceremony the dead are symbolically reborn.[22] Red pipestone "disk" pipe bowls believed to be from calumets and dated to after A.D. 1350 are commonly found at Oneota sites.

Northern Wisconsin

Although the custom of building burial mounds gradually disappeared over most of Wisconsin, there is evidence that mound-building rituals persisted in the northern part of the state among some Native people who continued to follow a mobile hunting and gathering lifestyle through the time of contact with Europeans. As William McKern observed many years ago, the people appear to have been the Santee or Dakota Sioux, who occupied northwestern Wisconsin until the Ojibwe drove them further west beginning in the early eighteenth century.[23]

In the 1950s, Leland Cooper excavated a large conical mound in the Rice Lake mound group and found some European trade items that may have accompanied burials. The mound was one of fifty-one original mounds, making the group one of the largest in northern Wisconsin. Earlier excavations had been done at the group under the direction of Cyrus Thomas of the Smithsonian Institution in the late nineteenth century during his quest for the "mound builders." The mound that Cooper excavated had been badly disturbed.[24]

Like the Clam Lake and Spencer Lake mounds in Burnett County, the mound at Rice Lake appears to have been built in stages over time. Cooper suggested that the remains of people buried in the mound, like those buried in the Clam Lake and Spencer Lake mounds, had been brought down from nearby scaffolds, where they had awaited periodic mass burials in a mound. Few grave goods accompanied the burials, but among them were a steel spring and a lead button. The spring may have been a component of a "hair puller," a device for removing facial hair that was a popular European trade item during the fur-trading period in northern Wisconsin. Since such objects were not available until after European contact, the burials and the mound itself, Cooper believed, must necessarily date to after that time. As McKern did in reference to the Clam Lake and Spencer Lake mounds, Cooper identified the inhabitants of northwestern Wisconsin during the early historic period, the Dakota, as the people likely to have built at least some of the mounds at Rice Lake.

Cooper did not believe that the historic items in the Rice Lake Mound were intrusive—introduced into an ancient mound after the mound had been completed—but the fact that the mound had been heavily disturbed before being excavated by Cooper has led archaeologists to be cautious about accepting it as historic rather than prehistoric and ascribing a specific tribal affiliation to its builders. Minnesota provides better evidence that burial mounds were occasionally built in the historic period and specifically by the Dakota, who also occupied parts of Minnesota until being displaced in the eighteenth century by the Ojibwe. The Cooper mound site, located at Mille Lacs, Minnesota, has a series of three conical mounds. One, excavated in 1967, covered a grave pit that contained a vessel of Ogechie ware, a style that archaeologists feel certain was made by a branch of the Dakota known as the Mdewakanton. Other offerings in the grave pit were trade goods acquired from French fur traders between 1670 and 1740, consisting of glass beads, copper cone-shaped "tinkling" ornaments, and a copper ring.[25]

Where Did the Oneota Go?

The first European accounts of the inhabitants of Wisconsin describe a powerful, numerous, and sedentary people who spoke a language unknown to the French and whom the Algonquian-speaking allies of the French called the "Ouinipigou" (Winnebago/Ho-Chunk). Archaeology reveals that Wisconsin in the years immediately prior to French contact was home to clusters of Oneota settlements, making it likely that at least some Oneota and the Ouinipigou were one and the same. After Jean Nicolet's visit to the western Great Lakes in 1634, a series of catastrophic wars and epidemics broke out, nearly annihilating the indigenous peoples of Wisconsin. That time also marks the end of the archaeological record of Oneota ways of life in Wisconsin.

The western Oneota at La Crosse migrated across the Mississippi River into Iowa, where scholars, on the basis of combined archaeological and historical evidence, believe they came into history as the Ioway.[26] Archaeological evidence shows that the eastern Oneota had already been reduced to a few villages in the sixteenth century: most of the large sites seem to have been abandoned at that time. Both warfare and the spread of infectious diseases carried by the Europeans may have been responsible.[27] The descendants of the eastern Oneota almost certainly include the Ho-Chunk.

Although there is not as yet unequivocal archaeological evidence for this link, there is much circumstantial documentary evidence as well as the evidence of oral history. Contemporary French accounts obtained from their allies and survivors of the tumultuous period place the Ho-Chunk in the same area as the late eastern Oneota, and oral traditions of the Ho-Chunk state that eastern Wisconsin was always a part of their homeland. Furthermore, Ho-Chunk oral traditions as well as early historical documents support archaeological evidence of a catastrophic population decline. The Ho-Chunk told the ethnographer Paul Radin that they had been a populous tribe but had been almost exterminated by disease and by wars with the more southerly Illinois nations.[28] Outside Wisconsin, widely dispersed Oneota population centers similarly have been linked to the homelands of modern tribes that lived in these areas.[29]

If the Oneota-Ho-Chunk/Ioway connection can be confirmed, then both the Ho-Chunk and the Ioway could likely trace their ancestry back to the Late Woodland populations that transformed themselves into the Oneota. Both Ho-Chunk and Ioway traditions relate that they were once part of one tribe, separating in some distant past, with the Ioway traveling west while the Ho-Chunk stayed near Lake Michigan. The languages of the two nations are very similar, as are aspects of their social structures, belief systems, and other cultural traditions. It is possible that the single tribal entity remembered in oral history and reflected in the similarities in language and culture is the population of Late Woodland people who built effigy mounds.

This view is supported by some linguistic data. Employing glottochronology, a technique that dates divergence of languages by using known rates of changes in words, James Springer and Stanley Witkowski estimated that a language group that includes Ho-Chunk, Ioway, Missouria, and Otoe separated from other Central Siouan language groups sometime between A.D. 700 and 1000.[30] Significantly, these dates coincide with the coalescence of the effigy mound culture and immediately predate the appearance in the archaeological record of the Oneota in Wisconsin. The subsequent separation of at least Ho-Chunk and Ioway within this common language group can be traced in the archaeological record of the Wisconsin Oneota to between A.D. 1300 and 1500.

Reuse of the Ancient Mounds

Of everything that occurred in the eventful and dramatic history of Native peoples, contact with Europeans was the most catastrophic. Within a comparatively brief period, as much as 80 percent of the Indigenous population of North America died from infectious diseases. Whole tribes disappeared, and entirely new tribes were created by the survivors. In Wisconsin, Native peoples engaged in economic enterprises with Europeans, such as the fur trade, that changed their material cultures and eventually led to a dependence on European goods and the market system. Ceramic pots, with their ancient and deep symbolism, were supplanted by generic brass and copper containers. Iron implements and weapons replaced stone tools. By the mid-seventeenth century, the material cultures of the different tribes that occupied the western Great Lakes region were indistinguishable from one another. On the Great Plains, the introduction of the horse created a buffalo-oriented culture that drew tribes to the plains in great numbers. Competition and the westward migration of Euro-Americans led to great tribal movements, exacerbating intertribal warfare that further changed traditional societies and reduced populations. So much cultural disruption occurred during the early part of the historic period that it is frequently difficult to connect known tribes to their prehistoric ancestors. The archaeologist Carol Mason characterized this break in the record as an "archaeological Grand Canyon, more easily looked across than spanned or jumped."[31]

According to early historical documents and tribal oral traditions, people living in what is now Wisconsin when the Europeans arrived were the Ho-Chunk, Menominee, and the Santee or Dakota Sioux.[32] The Ioway, close relatives of the Ho-Chunk, apparently also resided in western Wisconsin until just before European contact but migrated west. Other people may have lived in Wisconsin, but they were pushed out, drawn to the Great Plains to hunt buffalo on horseback, or completely wiped out by disease and warfare before their existence could be documented.[33]

In the late seventeenth century, the Siouan-speaking Ho-Chunk lived in villages in eastern Wisconsin and the Algonquian-speaking Menominee lived to the north of them. The Sioux originally occupied northwestern Wisconsin. Also, by the late seventeenth century, waves of new Algonquian-speaking people were moving into Wisconsin. In the north, bands of Ojibwe migrated west from the eastern end of Lake Superior, leading to an extended period of warfare with the Sioux and forcing the latter further west into Minnesota. The more southerly areas of Wisconsin were briefly occupied by tribes that had expanded or pushed into Wisconsin after intertribal wars in the east during the early part of the historic period. Among these were the Sauk, Fox, Kickapoo, and Miami. In northern Illinois and southeastern Wisconsin, the Potawatomi, who appear to have originated in Michigan and are closely related to the Ojibwe and Ottawa, settled vast tracts of land, and there were also scattered mixed settlements of other tribes that had originated elsewhere in Wisconsin and the Midwest, such as the Sauk, Ojibwe, and Menominee.

Of all these, the Dakota or Santee Sioux may have been the only (and last) tribe to build burial mounds in Wisconsin. As the first European explorers and settlers swept into the state, they made note of the ubiquitous mounds on the Wisconsin landscape but repeatedly stated that they never saw local Native people making burial mounds, although cultural customs, including those related to burials, were often noted. In addition, later anthropological studies, based on historical accounts and oral histories, described in detail the mortuary practices in the historic period. All these studies document in-ground burial, unmarked by earthen mounds, or, as with the Potawatomi, Ojibwe, and some other groups, occasional placement of dead on scaffolds or in trees. When asked about mounds in more recent times, Wisconsin Native people themselves generally ascribed them to customs that were practiced in some distant past.

One interesting exception to tribal oral history is found in an article written by John Blackhawk, a Ho-Chunk from Black River Falls. Blackhawk was asked by Charles E. Brown, of the State Historical Society of Wisconsin, to give an account of Ho-Chunk beliefs concerning mound building. In the article, Blackhawk repeated information published by Paul Radin earlier in the century but added: "My grandfather related once of an instance where he saw a bird mound being built in front of a chieftain's lodge. This was perhaps the last of the custom. He noted that it was placed to the east of the lodge or lodges."[34] Taken at face value, this uncorroborated report would indicate that effigy mounds were also occasionally built, in imitation of existing mounds and unnoticed by neighboring white settlers, well into the nineteenth century. But there are other, more likely explanations. One is that the oral information was garbled and that what John Blackhawk meant to transmit was that the village was simply located near an ancient bird effigy mound. Throughout the chaotic historic period, bands of Native Americans settled or resettled on the very same sites that had been used by the mound builders, choosing them for the same reasons that the ancients had had for selecting them—access to critical food resources or to transportation and trade routes. The reoccupation of desirable locations is a pattern that was repeated over several thousand years, often leading to stratified archaeological sites that have provided a record of human occupation in Wisconsin. Early maps of mound groups by Increase A. Lapham and others depict corn, cultivated by Native people in the historic period, running up and over low effigy mounds, and even the ancient site of Aztalan was apparently occupied or used briefly in the late eighteenth or early nineteenth century by a Ho-Chunk family, since Lapham observed and mapped corn hills superimposed on the remains of the ancient site in the mid-nineteenth century.[35]

An even more likely explanation is that in his story Blackhawk recorded not the construction but the use of an existing mound for a burial, a common practice in many parts of southern Wisconsin during the nineteenth century that is well documented in both the historical and the archaeological records. Nineteenth-century observers made frequent mention of the custom as practiced by various tribes, especially those living in central and southern Wisconsin, such as the Ho-Chunk, Menominee, and Potawatomi.[36] Richard C. Taylor, observed, for example:

> Successive tribes have occupied, by turns, the region of the country where these apparent animal and human effigies abound. The Winnebago have held possession of that part of the Wisconsin Territory that lies immediately south of the Wisconsin River, and east of the Mississippi, only from sixty to eighty years. Previous to this time the district was in the hands of the Sauk and Fox Indians who dug and smelted the lead ore, but were driven out by the Winnebagos. Neither of these tribes now erect monuments of this character, to the memory of their dead. *We have seen them, it is true, in numerous places, excavate graves, and deposit the remains of the deceased on the summits of the ancient circular tumuli, which they appear to conceive were constructed for such purposes.*[37]

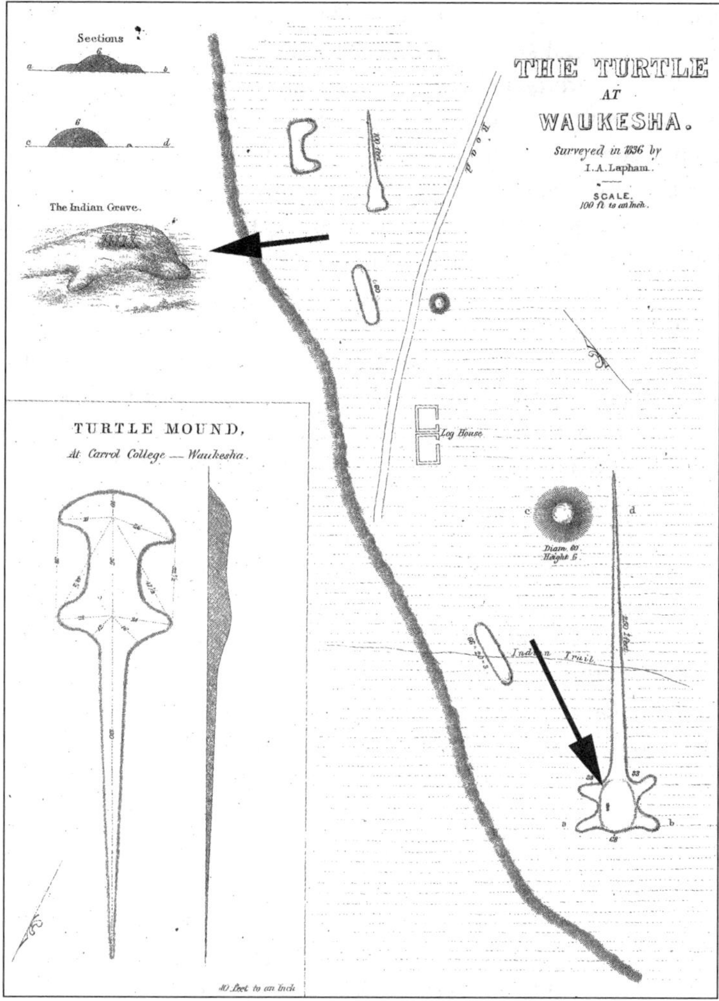

Figure 9.4. Effigy mound in present-day Waukesha, mapped by Increase A. Lapham in 1836, with a recently made grave and grave house, probably Potawatomi. A detailed rendering of the grave structure is at the upper left.

The reuse of these mounds for graves often involved the erection of small wooden structures such as log grave houses, in which were left offerings of food and tobacco, as was customary among the Potawatomi (figure 9.4). Archaeological reports and records, some dating back to the nineteenth-century mound-digging era, contain many references to the diggers encountering "intrusive burials"—graves dug into the mounds—accompanied by

European or American trade goods, such as silver ornaments, glass beads, iron axes, and metal kettles. Before the time of detailed soil observation, this misled some to conclude that the mounds themselves were of recent origin. The reuse of mounds for burials seems to have been primarily a nineteenth-century phenomenon, but the custom apparently continued into the early twentieth century in some areas.

The practice appears to have been related to the removal of Native tribes through treaties and Euro-American settlement. The earliest treaties, such as those signed at Prairie du Chien, were directed at establishing the land claims of the various tribes. After the 1830s, treaties divested Native Americans of their land for white settlement, restricting some tribes, like the Menominee and Ojibwe, to small reservations in northern Wisconsin and forcibly removing others, notably the Potawatomi and the Ho-Chunk, to western "Indian lands," ultimately in Nebraska and Kansas. Many Ho-Chunk and Potawatomi simply refused to move and continued to live where they could as fugitives and refugees until white settlement drove them to remoter areas, where they were joined by relatives who fled the western reservations. These "stray bands" and "lost tribes," as they were referred to, fiercely resisted repeated attempts at removal and were formally recognized by the federal government in the twentieth century.[38]

With the sudden loss of family or tribal burial grounds brought about by the treaties and white settlement, the refugees may have perceived the ancient mounds, especially the effigy mounds, imbued with spiritual and ancestral symbolism, as eternally sacred and sanctified places where their relatives could be most appropriately and safely interred. Lapham encountered many new Native graves on mounds in Milwaukee, Waukesha, and Dodge Counties during his survey of mounds in the mid-nineteenth century, after all the Native people in this area were supposed to have been relocated. Despite the increasing white settlement of the region, Lapham observed that families, probably Potawatomi, continued to visit these mound-top graves in Milwaukee annually. At Theresa in Dodge County, Lapham noted a mound entirely covered by graves, apparently from a small nearby Ho-Chunk and Menominee community.[39] As a sad footnote, most of the ancient mounds used much later by Native people as burial places have been obliterated by urban and residential development, road building, and modern farming. It would not be until the late twentieth century that federal and state laws would be enacted to protect mounds and other burial places.

10

Indian Mounds in the Modern World

The great era of burial-mound building began in Wisconsin around 800 B.C. and lasted for about another two thousand years. The earliest mounds, large and round or conical, were built as crypts in which to inter community leaders and their families and as landmarks to visually anchor mobile bands and tribes in the natural and supernatural worlds. Rituals that attended periodic mound building sought to renew the world and the resources on which people depended, eventually linking people over wide areas by means of shared ceremonials.

During the spectacular effigy mound period, between roughly A.D. 700 and 1100, people in Wisconsin and adjacent states created sometimes vast earthen ceremonial landscapes that modeled the underlying structure of their belief systems and social structure. These earthen effigies of powerful spirits also served as tombs. What stimulated monumental construction in this particular form and in this relatively small region of earth remains a matter for further research, but its uniqueness qualifies the phenomenon to be considered an archaeological world wonder on a par with the megalithic sites in Europe, England, and Ireland and the giant and mysterious Nazca desert drawings and lines in South America.

After A.D. 1000, the Mississippians briefly appeared on the stage, building on the Wisconsin landscape great "temple" mounds in their communities at Aztalan and Trempealeau: high earth platforms for important buildings and ritual activities. And then quite suddenly, in relative terms, the era of mound building came to an end, except perhaps in some places in the north. By A.D. 1200 economic and social changes that attended corn cultivation swept through the Midwest, leading to a new, agricultural way of life. New customs relating to death and burial evolved that replaced the practices that had required the construction of imposing earthen tombs and ceremonial centers.

The custom of building burial mounds and other earthworks was shared by many ancient peoples throughout eastern North America. In Wisconsin, mounds were found everywhere. Accordingly, it is almost certain that all of the indigenous Wisconsin tribes are descendants of the mound builders. A large body of evidence—archaeological, historical, ethnographic, linguistic, and oral—supports a conclusion that the Ho-Chunk and their close tribal relatives are distantly descended from the effigy mound builders. Some, like the Dakota or Santee Sioux in the north, may have built burial mounds into the time of European contact.

Sadly, about 80 percent of the 15,000 to 20,000 mounds built in Wisconsin during the mound-building era have been destroyed by recent agricultural activities, urban and residential development, and looting. Nevertheless, due both to early and aggressive preservation activities led by Charles E. Brown and his colleagues at the Wisconsin Archeological Society and to burial- and archaeological-site protection laws, several thousand mounds have been preserved in Wisconsin, more than in any other state. The appendix of this book lists numerous places where the public can experience these fascinating ancient earthworks.

Legislation to Preserve Mounds

Archaeological and historic sites have had some protection under state and federal laws, beginning in the late 1960s, but this legislation usually applied only to public lands or to significant historical and cultural sites that would be destroyed as a result of projects undertaken by the federal or state governments. In 1985, however, Wisconsin joined thirty-one other states with the passage of a law designed specifically to protect marked and unmarked burial places, including those used by ancient Native people. Most of the nationwide legislation was enacted in the 1970s and 1980s, when sensibilities were heightened about the treatment of grave sites of Indigenous peoples and the human remains recovered from them, including gratuitous displays in museums. The legislation was stimulated by the realization that, unlike modern cemeteries, ancient burial grounds had no protection and were being lost to modern development and other land-use practices. Input from the Native, academic, legislative, and broader communities was incorporated into Wisconsin Statute 157.70, the Burial Sites Preservation Law. Since Indian mounds are burial places, they were viewed as entitled to protection from disturbance. The first mound to be cataloged and protected under the law was a long-tailed effigy mound on the shore of Lake Monona in the community of Monona that was to be replaced by building.

The Burial Sites Preservation Law protects all burial sites on public and private land from disturbance, regardless of age and cultural, ethnic, or religious affiliation. Burial sites are defined simply as any places where human remains are buried and include marked and unmarked recent cemeteries, the often forgotten and overlooked family grave plots of early settlers, ancient Native graves, and Indian mounds. These burial places receive their greatest protection after they are "cataloged"—when the boundaries of the cemetery, grave site, or mound are identified so that they can be recorded on the deed for the property at the county Register of Deeds.

By law, Indian mounds and other defined grave sites are surrounded by a buffer zone of at least five feet, but sometimes more, within which disturbance cannot take place. Once cataloged and filed with the Register of Deeds, these burial locations "run with the land" and are identified in every title search of the property. Landowners of burial sites are entitled to a property-tax exemption on the basis of the area cataloged. Even though sites may be officially cataloged by the state, privately owned mounds are still private property, and visitors still have to obtain the landowners' permission to see the sites.

A provision of the Burial Sites Preservation Law permits the disturbance of a catalogued burial site with the prior approval of the director of the Wisconsin Historical Society. In some cases, the director or applicant may draw upon the advice of a Burial Sites Preservation Board consisting of representatives of Native nations, archaeologists, and Wisconsin Historical Society staff. It was foreseen that there might be circumstances when disturbance is unavoidable. When the graves of Native people are concerned, such decisions are made in consultation with interested Native nations. Occasionally, human burials from unrecorded or uncatalogued burial places are accidentally disturbed by earth-moving activities, ranging from small-scale gardening to excavation for new houses. Under the Burial Sites Preservation Law, work must immediately stop and the Burial Sites Preservation Office of the Wisconsin Historical Society must be notified. After a careful and considered evaluation, officials may order the remains and associated grave goods removed so that the project can proceed. The remains and grave goods are then returned to the appropriate parties for reburial. However, *preservation in place* is always the first alternative to be considered in these situations.

The Wisconsin Burial Sites Preservation Law has saved many hundreds of grave sites and cemeteries from potential disturbance or destruction, including a considerable number of ancient mounds. Today, most landowners are proud to have an Indian mound or mound group on their property and consider themselves to be stewards of a special part of Wisconsin history. They take mound preservation very seriously and often consult Native nations and other experts for advice on proper maintenance of the ancient monuments.

Despite a growing enthusiasm for mound preservation, concerns regarding the balance between preservation for the public good and private-property rights continue to be raised. Over the years, there have been some legal challenges, and in January 2016 one legislative proposal to modify the law was met by a peaceful "Save the Mounds" demonstration at the state capitol led by hundreds of Native people from different Native nations and accompanied by the beating of ceremonial drums.[1] Subsequently, the Wisconsin legislature convened a special study committee to thoughtfully examine the issue. Over the course of several weeks, they heard the testimony of Native peoples, commercial interests, archaeologists, and landowners. In the end, the committee proposed no substantial changes to the law, reaffirming the importance of mounds and other burial sites to Wisconsin's people.

Burial places on federally administered lands, such as national parks and reservation lands held in trust by the U.S. government for Native nations, are protected by the Native American Graves Protection and Repatriation Act of 1990 (NAGPRA). This federal law also provides procedures to follow when the graves or remains of Native people are inadvertently discovered and addresses issues that arise from the possession of human remains, grave offerings, and sacred objects by museums, universities, and other federally financed institutions. A major aim of NAGPRA has been to ensure that the human remains and funerary objects, as well as sacred items used in former or ongoing ceremonies, are returned or repatriated to the appropriate Native nations. For federally supported institutions, this process involves the inventories of relevant collections. These procedures have not been followed without difficulty, but the effort has provided new and exciting opportunities for dialogue and close cooperation between people of different cultures and has promoted close working relationships. It has also led to increasing sensitivity on the part of the general public toward human remains and objects that Native peoples hold in great reverence.

Since the enactment of the federal law, thousands of human remains and objects of cultural importance have been repatriated. But here, too, controversies still occur, as with the remains of the famous 8,500-year-old Kennewick Man, found in 1996 on federally administered lands in Washington State and thus subject to the requirements of NAGPRA. The discovery led to a lengthy legal dispute between Native nations of the region who wanted the remains for immediate reburial and scientists who argued that the find was so vital to the understanding of the origins of Native peoples of the Americas that first the remains had to be studied.[2] A federal court ruled in favor of the scientists, who among other things conducted DNA analysis from small bone samples that determined that Kennewick Man shared some distinctive genes with later Native peoples of the area and therefore was indeed an ancestor, despite being physically dissimilar. Thereafter, the remains were returned to the local Native people for burial.

Native and Scientific Perspectives on the Mounds

Kennewick Man illustrates the cultural differences and worldview that have long divided Native people and scientists, especially in the past, when archaeological excavation of burial mounds and other Native graves was common, as in Wisconsin. From a scientific perspective, the study of human remains and burial places can provide information about social status, family relationships, diet, daily activities, place of origin, disease, life expectancy, and even the evolution of warfare. Bones and teeth can help determine the ancestry, sex, social status, and age at and cause of death of an individual who lived in the distant past. As with Kennewick Man, DNA analysis now can reveal much about ancestry. Much of the information on ancient people in this book derived from the early excavations of burials and burial mounds. New scientific advances have greatly increased the potential for the study of human remains to answer important archaeological questions.

But from the perspective of many Native peoples, the scientific rationale for the study of human remains carries no weight. It is not only illegal to disturb the remains of their ancestors but also immoral. Once an individual dies and is buried, many argue, this sacred site should not be touched. Some Native people believe that the disturbance of graves interrupts the journey of the dead to the spirit land and at the very least dishonors the ancestors of the living. Many traditional people say that they know who their ancestors are and that oral traditions preserve the important and necessary elements of their history, so further analysis is unnecessary. For most, research on human remains and burials places Native people and their ancestors in the humiliating role of "laboratory specimens," a practice with roots in the racist attitudes common in the nineteenth century, when Native people were considered to be less than human.

It is not likely that these two different cultural views on burial places and human remains can be completely reconciled. From the standpoint of Native peoples, deeply held spiritual beliefs cannot be negotiated. Consequently, the philosophy adopted by most archaeologists, academics, and museum curators has been to respect the concerns of Native peoples and to make special efforts to involve Native nations in archaeological studies and educational exhibits that do not involve the disruption of sacred areas but still provide information on the ancient past. Today in Wisconsin, Native and archaeological communities work together on the basis of one principle that has wide agreement: burial places such as the mounds must be saved from destruction. This collaboration has resulted in many joint projects to locate and catalog Indian mounds and other burial sites, as well as places where ancient people lived, and this collaboration has led to the sharing of much information and perspectives. As we have seen, the incorporation of Native viewpoints and knowledge has proved critical to the unraveling of ancient mysteries, such as those of the Indian mounds.

Legacy of the Mounds

The construction and ceremonial use of burial mounds played an important role in integrating segments of ancient societies into larger communities. That is why this book emphasizes their function as ceremonial centers. We can image that, even when burials were not taking place, people gathered at these prominent places to take part in a wide variety of social celebrations, economic activities, and religious events that reinforced social bonds. Some Indian mounds in Wisconsin continue to play a similar role in the modern world. In 1998, the Monona Landmarks Commission hosted the dedication of a historic marker at a large two-thousand-year-old conical mound preserved on a small piece of public land in a suburban neighborhood. The mound is one of the last of the Outlet mound group, which once covered many acres of land. Fittingly, this mound was one of those saved from destruction by residential development by Charles E. Brown and the Wisconsin Archeological Society in 1938. Through an ambitious fund-raising campaign, the mound was purchased from developers by the Wisconsin Archeological Society and was given to the city of Monona.[3] The dedication was attended by a large crowd of neighborhood people as well as by members of the local Native American community. Speeches were made, food was shared, and people talked and visited. The highlight of the event came when most of those present participated in a Native celebration dance, led by Art Shegonee of the Potawatomi and Menominee nations. For the afternoon, this ancient mound functioned much as it had two thousand years ago—as the focal point of a community. A similar ceremony to honor the mounds took place later at another mound grouping at Woodland Park on a high ridge overlooking a Monona commercial district and was attended by state and local officials and representatives of Native nations (figure 10.1).

Figure 10.1. Speakers and representatives at the dedication of the Woodland Park mounds in 2002 in Monona, Wisconsin. *From left*: state archaeologist Robert Birmingham, Ada Deer (Menominee), Art Shegonee (Menominee/Potawatomi), Mary Lou Burczyk (Monona Landmarks Commission), and Dalles Whitewing (Ho-Chunk).

At Madison's Elmside Park, along the shore of Lake Monona, stands *Let the Great Spirits Soar*, a sculpture cast in bronze by Harry Whitehorse, a Ho-Chunk artist who lives in the area, as did his ancestors. The sculpture overlooks a pair of effigy mounds, a bear and a deer, part of a once-large mound group destroyed by residential development (figure 10.2). The artwork replaced a decaying wooden sculpture made earlier from a tree stump and depicts a Native man along with a wolf, an eagle, and bears—powerful cultural symbols for the Ho-Chunk. The park has become a popular gathering spot for small groups of people who come to view the sculpture and the mounds and to learn more about the heritage of their community. The Ho-Chunk Nation is currently working with many municipalities, such as the City of Monona, the City of Madison, as well as the Dane County Parks, to

Figure 10.2. *Above*: Harry Whitehorse and family at dedication of the Outlet Mound in Monona. *Below left*: Harry Whitehorse tree stump sculpture. *Below right*: bronze replacement.

ensure their parks and greenspace plans encompass an enhanced burial mounds site preservation component.

Elsewhere in Wisconsin, a new appreciation of ancient earthen monuments has also resulted in the celebration of their existence as community landmarks. In more recent years, the Wisconsin Archeological Society hosted several rededications of mounds throughout the state to mark the

Figure 10.3. Bill Quackenbush, Ho-Chunk Nation Tribal Heritage Preservation Officer, at the 2016 dedication of the bird mound at Devil's Lake State Park.

centennial anniversary of their dedication during public gatherings. Among these were the rededication of the famous Man mound, now a National Historic Landmark, near Baraboo in 2008, and that of a bird mound at Devil's Lake in 2016 that included presentations and inspiring comments by Ho-Chunk Nation officials (figure 10.3).

The Indian mounds and the other ancient earthworks preserved on the Wisconsin landscape are not just silent reminders of a long-ago people. The earthen monuments, representing different mound-building periods and sometimes different Native peoples, are valuable teaching devices. They teach us that, like all peoples and societies, Native customs continually changed in response to social and environmental changes and that contemporaneous Native nations are very different from one another, as they were in the past, each with its unique language, customs, and beliefs. The mounds teach us that there is not one "traditional" Indigenous culture with which later people should be compared, any more than there is one time in European or American history in which the "traditional" European or American culture can be identified. The Indian mounds of Wisconsin also remind us that, like all peoples and societies, Native peoples are a "historical" people in the sense that their history is deep, dramatic, and complex, spanning thousands of generations. As with different societies the world over, theirs is a history filled with legendary heroes, migrations, alliances, elaborate ceremonies and rituals, religious movements, powerful families, peaceful villages, beautiful and monumental artworks, wars, the rise and fall of spectacular societies, technological innovations, and economic and social revolutions. This story is far from the simplistic and stereotyped history constructed for Native peoples of the Americas in the past.

If the mounds represent change in one sense, they also represent cultural continuity in another. For Native peoples the mounds are eternally sacred places, the graves of ancestors that connect them to the land and the spirit world. But the mounds have also become highly visible and powerful symbols of the persistence into the modern era of uniquely Native values and beliefs. Indeed, when thunder and lightning move across the Wisconsin skies and water roils in the lakes and streams, there are still some who know that thunderbirds and water spirits are about their ancient struggle, which brings harmony to an unsettled world.

APPENDIX

Mound Sites Open to the Public

Following is a selection of Indian mound groups in Wisconsin that can be viewed by the public. These have been selected both because of ease of access and because they illustrate the different mound forms and arrangements found throughout the state, reflecting different cultures and periods of mound building. Many other mounds are on private lands or, if on public lands, are more difficult to view. The sites are listed by county. Unless otherwise noted, there are no admission fees.

BARRON COUNTY

Indian Mounds Park

Lakeshore Drive, Rice Lake

Twelve mounds of the Rice Lake mound group are preserved in Indian Mounds Park, a city park on the shore of Rice Lake. The group once consisted of fifty-one conical burial mounds, apparently built after about A.D. 500. Some mounds were excavated in the nineteenth century by the Smithsonian Institution during its search for the identity of the mound builders, while others were excavated in the 1950s. Many were obliterated by city expansion.

CALUMET COUNTY

Calumet County Park

Highway EE, off Highway 55, Stockbridge

Calumet County Park, located on the eastern shore of Lake Winnebago, is approximately two miles north of the community of Stockbridge. Six effigy mounds with lower-world water iconography—panthers or water spirits—are situated on top of a high escarpment that overlooks the lake.

High Cliff State Park

Highway 55, Sherwood
dnr.wi.gov/topic/parks/name/highcliff

High Cliff State Park is situated along the scenic limestone cliffs of the Niagara Escarpment, paralleling the eastern shore of Lake Winnebago, south of the community of Sherwood. The central portion of a once far more extensive effigy mound group—which included a bird, an animal (probably a bear), a large concentration of water spirits or panthers, and small conical mounds—is on the edge of the escarpment overlooking the lake. Some mounds at High Cliff were first featured in Increase A. Lapham's 1855 book, *Antiquities of Wisconsin*. The large number of water-spirit mounds is characteristic of the many mound groups built on the eastern shore of Lake Winnebago and in eastern Wisconsin in general. Six of these long-tailed effigies, as well as several conical mounds, may be seen along an interpretive trail at the park. State park and recreation fees; campsites are available.

Chippewa County

Lake Wissota State Park

Highway O, Chippewa Falls
dnr.wi.gov/topic/parks/name/lakewissota

The lone long-tailed water-spirit or panther effigy located here is very unusual because it is located far to the north of where effigy mounds are generally found in Wisconsin. The mound is low and difficult to distinguish, situated near Campsite #24. The park is located on Lake Wissota, seven miles west of Chippewa Falls. State park and recreation fees; campsites are available.

Columbia County

Kingsley Bend Mound Group

Highway 16, Wisconsin Dells
devilslakewisconsin.com/kingsley-bend-indian-mounds

Overlooking the Wisconsin River in south-central Wisconsin, the well-preserved and maintained Kingsley Bend mound group is owned and managed by the Ho-Chunk Nation. These mounds formerly were preserved within a Wisconsin Department of Transportation wayside along State Highway 16 but were transferred to the care of the Ho-Chunk Nation in 2006. The Ho-Chunk view these mounds, like all mounds, as an important cultural and sacred place but welcome respectful visitation.

The mounds extend down the slopes of a hill to the Wisconsin River, bordered on the south by a spring-fed creek. A huge, classic water-spirit mound that is oriented toward nearby springs and long linear mounds are located next to the parking area, while a line of large conical mounds, two bear effigies, and a short linear occupy the bluff top overlooking the Wisconsin River. A large eagle-like bird effigy and a long, straight, tapering linear mound sometimes interpreted as a snake are situated on the opposite side of Highway 16 and are not as easily visited.

Crawford County

Indian Mounds Park

Crawford County Highway Wayside, Highway 60 east of Bridgeport

Three linear and six conical mounds of the Cipra mound group can be viewed on this highway wayside along Highway 60 near the Wisconsin River, five miles east of Bridgeport. This site may be an example of the type of mound group built just prior to the appearance of effigy mounds.

Dane County

Madison, with its surrounding lakes, was the center of mound building in Wisconsin. Between 800 B.C. and A.D. 1200, Native Americans built more than 1,500 mounds in the Four Lakes area. A large number of them were preserved over the years through the efforts of Charles E. Brown of the State Historical Society of Wisconsin and other area residents.

Blackhawk Country Club

Blackhawk Drive, Madison

Arranged on the top and base of a drumlin along the shore of Lake Mendota, the mounds of the Black Hawk County Club illustrate the basic symbolism of effigy mounds and the use of the natural landscape to emphasize that symbolism. Now part of a golf course, three conicals occupy the highest elevation. A bird effigy on the top of the hill was destroyed during golf course construction but is memorialized by a half-scale replica built next to the clubhouse parking lot. A huge and impressive Madison-style zigzag winged goose flies across the upper slopes, between the top of the hill and Lake Mendota. Long linear mounds extend up the slope as though moving from the lake. One stretches two hundred feet up from the base of the hill to the conical mounds on top. At the base of the hill and across Lake Mendota Drive, a cluster of three small bear effigy mounds, representing the earth, can be found near the golf course practice range. A long-tailed water-spirit mound survives on private property along the lakeshore and is not publicly accessible. An excavation into the heart of the mound in the 1950s revealed the flexed remains of a young woman.

For personal safety and to avoid interference with golfers, visitors should get permission to visit the mounds at the golf course clubhouse on Blackhawk Drive.

Burrows Park

Burrows Road, off Sherman Avenue, Madison

Burrows Park, a small park on the shore of Lake Mendota, contains a bird effigy mound with a wingspan of 128 feet. A second effigy—a fox or canine-like animal—once stood alongside the bird but was destroyed. The bird was damaged by early looters but was restored by workers for the Works Progress Administration under the direction of Charles E. Brown.

Elmside and Hudson Parks

Lakeland Avenue, Madison

Elmside Park and Hudson Park were created in the early twentieth century to preserve three effigy mounds. The mounds are the only survivors of two large mound groups that formed part of a dense cluster of mounds that extended from the Yahara River to Olbrich Park. Most of the mounds were on higher ground in areas now occupied by houses; among them were many conical and linear mounds, bear effigies, a Madison-style goose with zigzag wings, and several birds—one with a wingspan reported to have been 568 feet. Elmside Park preserves two animal effigies: a bear and what has been referred to as a lynx. It also contains *Let the Great Spirits Soar*, a bronze casting of a beautiful tree-stump sculpture by Harry Whitehorse, a local Ho-Chunk (Winnebago) artist. An unusual water-spirit or panther mound with a crooked tail is found on lower ground, just to the west in nearby Hudson Park.

Forest Hill Cemetery

Regent Street and Speedway Drive, Madison
foresthill.williamcronon.net/effigy-mounds/mounds-in-madison/

Established in 1858, historic Forest Hill Cemetery is the final resting place of many of Wisconsin's most prominent citizens, including eight governors. Among the more modern graves is an effigy mound group that consists of most of a Madison-style, zigzag winged goose, two water spirits or panthers, and a linear mound. The head of the goose effigy, which is on a slope that leads (appropriately) to adjacent wetlands, was removed when a railroad was built through the area in the nineteenth century. Part of the tail of one panther and three additional linear mounds were destroyed during the early development of the cemetery. Efforts by Charles E. Brown of the State Historical Society saved the remaining mounds. Fittingly, Brown himself is interred at Forest Hill. His grave can be found in Lot 1 next to a large granite monolith bearing a single word: ARCHAEOLOGIST. A brochure for a self-guided walking tour of Forest Hill Cemetery is available at the cemetery office on Speedway Drive.

Governor Nelson State Park

Highway M, Waunakee
dnr.wi.gov/topic/parks/name/govnelson/

The 422-acre Governor Nelson State Park is located on the northern shore of Lake Mendota. A group of five conical mounds and a large panther or water spirit effigy mound can be found along trails that wind south of the main parking area and boat landing. The conical mounds may have been built during the Middle Woodland stage, while the effigy seems to have been added later. A stockaded Late Woodland village was located to the north of the mounds, in the vicinity of the showers and toilet near the beach. Native American cornfields were planted in this area, which also was the site of an early nineteenth-century Ho-Chunk village. State park and recreation fees.

Heim Mound

Mound Street, Middleton

The solitary Heim effigy mound is located on a small, wooded lot in a subdivision of Middleton on the outskirts of Madison. The mound depicts a 147-foot-long canine such as a fox or wolf. The property is owned and maintained by the Wisconsin Archeological Society and was donated to the society by Ferdinand Heim at the urging of the archaeologist and mound preservationist Charles E. Brown. Brown and the Wisconsin Archeological Society excavated a small part of the mound in the early twentieth century. Though not a public park, the Wisconsin Archeological Society welcomes quiet visitation. Please make sure not to block the narrow road that leads to it and take care not to disturb the neighbors on adjacent lots or any of the many ephemeral wildflowers that grow on and near the mound.

Indian Mound Park

Burma Road, McFarland

This Late Woodland mound group is located on a hill overlooking Lake Waubesa in Indian Mound Park. Called the Lewis mound group, after Tollef Lewis, the nineteenth-century owner, it formerly consisted of a canine effigy, four linear mounds, two conical mounds, and one oval mound. A long, curved earthwork sometimes identified as a "snake" effigy crawls down a steep slope to wetlands. Portions of some mounds were damaged by the construction of a water tower on the hill. Local volunteers have cleared the mounds and rerouted trails so that they no longer pass over the mounds.

Mendota Mental Health Institute

Troy Drive, Madison
dhs.wisconsin.gov/mendota/

Portions of two large mound groups are preserved on the grounds of Mendota Mental Health Institute, on the northern shore of Lake Mendota. The Farwell's Point mound group includes a number of immense conical mounds, portions of linear mounds, and bird and water-spirit effigies. These mounds were built over a span of more than one thousand years, with the large conical mounds possibly built during the Early or Middle Woodland stages about two thousand years ago. The effigy, linear, and smaller conical mounds date to the subsequent Late Woodland stage and are only about one thousand years old.

The Mendota State Hospital mound group, located to the east of the Farwell's Point mound group, between the main administration building and Lake Mendota, contains some of the finest, rarest, and largest effigy mounds preserved anywhere. Included are three large birds, two panthers (one with an unusual curved tail), two bears, a deer, several conical mounds, and one mound of indeterminate shape. One of the bird effigies has a wingspan of 624 feet. The deer effigy is unusual because four legs are depicted; it is the only known surviving effigy to show four legs in profile view.

The Mendota Mental Health Institute is an active medical facility, and there is security on the grounds. To protect the privacy of patients, it is necessary for visitors to gain permission to tour the mounds in advance from institute staff at the administration building, which is the first building on the right after entering the grounds.

Observatory Hill Mounds

Observatory Drive, Madison
https://lakeshorepreserve.wisc.edu/native-americans.htm

Directly to the west of the observatory on the campus of the University of Wisconsin, overlooking Lake Mendota, are the Observatory Hill mounds: a bird effigy and the only known two-tailed water-spirit effigy. One tail of the water spirit is barely visible and the other was partly destroyed by a sidewalk. The unusual two-tailed mound may represent two water spirits placed back to back, as paired effigies are found at several other mound groups. Other mounds at this site, including a long-tailed panther or water spirit, a linear mound, and conical mounds, were destroyed during development of the campus. Sidewalks that passed over portions of the mounds have been removed in recent years.

Outlet Mound

Midwood and Ridgewood Avenues, Monona

The large, conical Outlet Mound was one of nineteen conical, oval, and linear mounds arranged on the top and sides of a hill overlooking the Yahara River outlet of Lake Monona. Built two thousand years ago during the Middle Woodland stage, it is a good example of a mound of that era. Most of the other mounds in the group were destroyed, but several were professionally excavated prior to their destruction. One of the excavated mounds produced a stone knife characteristic of Middle Woodland Hopewell artistic traditions. Road grading near the mounds exposed a large tomb unmarked by a mound, also characteristic of Hopewell-related mortuary customs. It contained the remains of thirteen people. The Outlet Mound was purchased with funds raised by Charles E. Brown and the Wisconsin Archeological Society to save it from residential development and then was donated to the city of Monona.

Pheasant Branch Conservancy

Pheasant Branch Road, Middleton
parks-lwrd.countyofdane.com/park/PheasantBranchCreekConservancy

At the northwestern curve of Lake Mendota, Pheasant Branch Creek flows from a large bubbling sand spring, appropriately called "Mau e pinah" (beautiful spring) by the Ho-Chunk and now "Belle Fontaine," through wetlands to the lake where there was a Ho-Chunk village in the early nineteenth century. The Pheasant Branch Hill mounds overlook the spring from the top of nearby Frederick's Hill, just to the north. This mound group is another example of mound construction completed just prior to the creation of zoomorphic effigy mounds, in that it consists only of conical and short linear mounds. A later group—two bird effigy mounds and several linear mounds—was once found on a plateau partway down the hill and adjacent to the springs, but all traces of those mounds were plowed away when the land was farmed. The entrance to the county-run conservancy is located on Pheasant Branch Road about one-half mile north of County Highway M in Middleton. Trails lead to the spring and the hilltop mounds.

Picnic Point

University Bay Drive, Madison

On the eastern shore of Picnic Point, toward the tip of the peninsula, are one linear and one conical mound. On the western shore is a conical mound.

University of Wisconsin Arboretum

McCaffrey Road, Madison
arboretum.wisc.edu

Two Late Woodland effigy mound groups, including a bird, a panther, and linear and conical mounds, are located on both sides of McCaffrey Road at the University of Wisconsin Arboretum. One group is situated right above a prominent spring that was considered sacred by Ho-Chunk who camped nearby into the twentieth century. Among other things, springs were considered entrances to the watery underworld realm of the water spirits. These groups were restored by Charles E. Brown of the State Historical Society of Wisconsin. A map is available at the McKay Center at the arboretum.

Vilas Park

Erin and Wingra Streets, Madison

The Late Woodland effigy mound group in Vilas Park consists of a bird effigy, a linear mound, and six conical mounds. Two additional conical mounds and another bird effigy were destroyed when nearby houses were constructed. The plaque at the site is an example of the preservation efforts undertaken by Charles E. Brown and his colleagues at the Wisconsin Archeological Society.

Vilas Park Circle

Vilas Avenue, Madison

The small Vilas Park Circle was created to preserve a large effigy mound of a bear, which is located on the west side of the circular park. This mound was once part of a larger group that included seven linear mounds and a conical mound.

Woodland Park

Monona Drive, Monona

Two linear mounds, remnants of the long Tompkins-Brindler/Nichols group, follow the crest of the drumlin ridge just northeast of the water tower. The park, once covered by dense undergrowth, is being restored to an oak savanna. A pedestrian entrance to the park is on Monona Drive, but parking can be found near the Aldo Leopold Center off Femrite Drive. The entrance is about one-quarter mile east of Monona Drive on Femrite. A trail leads up to Woodland Park.

Yahara Heights County Park and Cherokee Marsh

Catfish Court off Highway 113/Northpoint Road, Westport
parks-lwrd.countyofdane.com/park/YaharaCherokee

Located along a large wetland called the Cherokee Marsh, north of Lake Mendota, this Dane County park preserves two effigy mounds: a bear and a long-tailed water spirit that is oriented to the marsh. The mounds are a part of the Yahara Heights mound group, which once included a short linear mound, a small conical mound, and a canine (fox or wolf) mound that were plowed when the area was farmland. The effigies of the group are all lower-world forms, but upper-world bird mounds were once found on hills further to the west. The bear and water spirit are easily viewed since park volunteers cleared brush and undergrowth over the area and returned it to oak savanna. The main entrance to the park and parking lot is on Catfish Court off Highway 113/Northpoint Road. Follow the trail northeast along the marsh for a little over a half-mile. A second entrance is located in a subdivision on Canton Lane, where a short trail marked by a gate leads east a short distance to the mounds.

Dodge County

Nitschke Mounds Park

Highway E, east of Highway 26, Burnett
http://www.co.dodge.wi.gov/community/visitors/parks-and-recreation/nitschke-mounds-park

The Nitschke I mound group occupies a glacial drumlin several miles east of the great Horicon Marsh. It is now located in a Dodge County park, created in the 1990s to preserve the large mound group for public interpretation. Another large mound group, Nitschke II, occupied an adjacent elevation a short distance to the southeast but was plowed away by farming. This two-part ceremonial mound landscape is unusual in both its remoteness and the fact that it is away from major bodies of water. Instead, the two mound groups were arranged near two large springs.

Once consisting of at least sixty-two mounds crowded together to fit the narrow, low, southwest/northeast-trending drumlin, the Nitschke I group now has forty-six mounds. Many others were leveled by farming, including numerous undocumented mounds north of the present park. These effigy types are mainly water and earth related, but Nitschke II once included a single bird that was not a water bird. Effigy mounds preserved at Nitschke I include straight-winged geese, water spirits, a bear, and short-tailed canine-like mounds, all with heads pointing to the southwest, following the direction of the drumlin. The group also featured several linear and unidentified mounds. As at many other effigy mound sites, a string of conical mounds extended along the very top of the ridge; several of these are superimposed on the long tail of the water-spirit mound.

Many of the mounds of both groups were partly excavated by the Milwaukee Public Museum, revealing burials and a strikingly unusual number of ceremonial offerings—largely clay pots, arrows, tools, and food remains from a feast. Recent work by the University of Wisconsin–Milwaukee just east of the mounds in an area where a small plot of ancient garden beds was recorded in the early twentieth century identified a small campsite used by Late Woodland people during mound construction. On the basis of the ceramics recovered by the Milwaukee Public Museum and modern radiocarbon dates derived from organic residue on the pots, the Nitschke mounds have been dated to the very end of the effigy mound era. The park has a trail, signage, and an interpretive display.

Dunn County

Wakanda Park

Pine Street, Menomonie

The Upper Wakanda Park mound group consists of three large oval mounds located in Wakanda Park on a ridge overlooking Lake Menomin, a widening of the Red Cedar River. Seventeen other mounds were located below this ridge but were flooded when the construction of a dam in the 1950s elevated the water level of the lake. Before their inundation, fourteen of the mounds were excavated and radiocarbon dated to sometime between A.D. 1000 and 1400. Burials and stone concentrations, or "altars," were found in them, and one of the burials was of an individual who had been cremated while wearing a clay face covering or mask. The custom of placing clay coverings or masks on the faces of the dead has been documented at two other mound sites in Wisconsin: the Cyrus Thomas mound group on Rice Lake and the Outlet mound group on Lake Monona.

Grant County

Cassville Bluffs Natural Area

Sand Lake Road, Cassville

A large bird effigy with a wingspan of 270 feet flies down a bluff slope edge high above the Mississippi River at the Cassville Bluffs Natural Area. It was documented in the late nineteenth century by Theodore H. Lewis, who did not mention any other associated mounds. The Natural Area is located at the end of Sand Lake Road, off Highway 133, southeast of Cassville.

Nelson Dewey State Park

Highway VV, Cassville
dnr.wi.gov/topic/parks/name/nelsondewey/

Several groups of mounds can be viewed at Nelson Dewey State Park overlooking the Mississippi River and opposite Stonefield Village Historic Site near Cassville. The most prominent are located along the main park drive and include several massive compound mounds that were probably built just prior to the expansion of effigy mound groups and landscapes.

Wyalusing State Park

Highway C, Prairie du Chien
dnr.wi.gov/topic/parks/name/wyalusing/

Wyalusing State Park is located near Prairie du Chien on the high bluffs overlooking the confluence of the Mississippi and Wisconsin Rivers. High vistas offer spectacular views of the rivers and surrounding countryside. More than 130 mounds have been recorded within the park boundaries by various surveyors since the 1880s. Before the park was established by the state, many of the mounds were destroyed by farming or stone quarrying. However, sixty-nine mounds survived and are carefully preserved, including the Sentinel Hill mound group and the Procession mound groups, which are composed of single lines of twenty-eight mounds each that follow the crests of bluffs: small conicals, short linears, bears, and a single-tailed effigy. There also examples of compound mounds at the park.

The mounds have not been professionally excavated but at least two separate periods of mound building seem to be represented at the park. Cyrus Thomas's crews investigated several large conical mounds in the area during the late nineteenth century and found burials in stone crypts, one with shell beads, a copper celt, and a stone platform pipe characteristic of the Hopewell-influenced Middle Woodland stage. Most of the other mounds in the park, however, appear to have been built during the early part of the Late Woodland stage. State park and recreation fees.

Iowa County

Lake Side Park

East Lake Shore Drive, Avoca

The Avoca mound group is located in Lake Side Park and campground on the shores of Avoca Lake, a backwater slough of the Wisconsin River. This mound group includes seven linear and four conical mounds that were once part of a larger group.

Jefferson County

Aztalan State Park

Highway Q, Aztalan/Lake Mills
dnr.wi.gov/topic/parks/name/aztalan/

Located on the Crawfish River, one mile east of Lake Mills, Aztalan is Wisconsin's premiere archaeological site. Prior to A.D. 1050, this site was the location of a Late Woodland village. Between A.D. 1050 and 1200, the site blossomed into a large Native American town, home to a group of Mississippian people who had migrated from Cahokia, in what is now southern Illinois. The Mississippians settled alongside the Late Woodland residents of Aztalan, built earthen platform mounds, and fortified the site with a huge timber and clay wall. Just northeast of the publicly accessible portion of Aztalan is a line of large conical mounds that mark the locations of ceremonial posts and the burial of a young woman who apparently was a member of the Mississippian elite.

Since 1919 the site has been extensively excavated by archaeologists, revealing the history of the town. Archaeological work by major universities continues at the site. A brochure for a self-guided walking tour is available at the site. The Friends of Aztalan State Park offer tours of the site and arrange special events. See the Friends website (Aztalanfriends.org) for information. A short video about the site made by Wisconsin Public Television can be viewed on either the park or Friends website. State park and recreation fees.

Dorothy Carnes County Park/Rose Lake State Natural Area

Radloff Lane, Fort Atkinson
http://www.jeffersoncountywi.gov/departments/departments_f-r/dorothy_carnes_park.php

A short-tailed "turtle" mound depicting an unknown animal in an aerial or flattened perspective is located along a trail overlooking Rose Lake. It is marked by a sign.

Garman Nature Preserve

Fox Lane, Waterloo
http://www.jeffersoncountywi.gov/departments/departments_f-r/dr_j_s_garman_nature_preserve.php

A line of twenty-two burial mounds, mainly small conicals, extends along the top of the ridge in this nature preserve and county park. The mounds were recently cleared of brush and restored to stop erosion within old looters' pits. The entrance to the preserve can be found off Highway 19 on the western edge of Waterloo. Turn east on McKay Way and then south on Fox Lane, where you will find a new park building and shelter with displays. A trail from the building leads southeast to the mounds.

Jefferson County Indian Mounds and Trail Park

Koshkonong Mounds Road, off Highway 26, Fort Atkinson
http://www.jeffersoncountywi.gov/departments/departments_f-r/indian_mounds_park.php

The southern part of the General Atkinson mound group is preserved in the Jefferson County Indian Mounds and Trail Park, south of the community of Fort Atkinson. These eleven mounds consist of tapering linear, conical, bird, and "turtle" mounds that represent panthers or water spirits as viewed from above, rather than from the side. The mounds range in length from 75 to 222 feet. The General Atkinson mound group originally consisted of seventy-two mounds, many of which were destroyed. The park includes one of the only surviving segments of the ancient trail system that once connected Wisconsin's mound-building communities. The trail was documented by a land surveyor in 1835 and is identified by signage within the park. In 1993 the late Hugh Highsmith of Fort Atkinson purchased the land containing the eleven mounds and, in cooperation with the Fort Atkinson Historical Society, donated the land to Jefferson County.

Panther Intaglio

Highway 106, Fort Atkinson

Just west of downtown Fort Atkinson, along the northern side of the Rock River, is the last remaining intaglio in Wisconsin. It was discovered by Increase A. Lapham in 1850 and is the only survivor of about a dozen intaglios recorded. It was once part of a large effigy mound group that was destroyed by residential development. The 125-foot intaglio is a scooped-out area in the form of a water spirit or panther about two feet deep. The excavation of this reverse image of a panther mound may be related to the fact that such water spirits were believed to originate in a watery realm below the surface of the earth. In 1919 the Fort Atkinson chapter of the Daughters of the American Revolution leased the land to preserve the intaglio, and it is now a small city park.

Juneau County

Cranberry Creek Archaeological District and State Natural Area

Highway G, east of Necedah
dnr.wi.gov/topic/Lands/naturalareas/index.asp?SNA=203

The largest remaining effigy mound landscape in Wisconsin open to visitors is located along the meandering Cranberry Creek, west of the community of Necedah and bordered on the west by vast wetlands. This intriguingly remote effigy mound landscape consists of two adjacent mound groupings now managed by the Wisconsin Department of Natural Resources as a State Natural Area. On the north is the Max Andrae I mound group, with more than two hundred mounds, mainly conical forms arranged in lines but also single bird and bear effigies and several short linear mounds. Many more mounds were destroyed by the operation of a commercial pine plantation and by the excavation of an irrigation canal, but recent LiDAR suggests the presence of undocumented mounds. This group is now largely covered by a tangle of vegetation, but the adventurous can find it by taking County G north from Highway 21, just east of Necedah. Go north about ten miles to the intersection of County Highways G and F and 7th Street. Look for a large sign. Park at the northwest corner of the intersection.

Further south is the Max Andrae II group, totaling another sixty mounds. Straight and curving lines of conical mounds are also found here, along with seventeen effigies of bears and small birds and effigies with the elongated bodies common to central Wisconsin. This southern group is harder to find because it is surrounded by forest and is not identified by signs. It can be found by taking 8th Street E west from County G. A path can be found on the north side of 8th Street about nine hundred feet east of its junction with 13th Avenue N. Take the path about five hundred feet north to where the mounds can be found in clearings.

Indian Mounds Park

Indian Mound Road, New Lisbon

Indian Mounds Park, on the Lemonweir River on the south side of New Lisbon, preserves a mound group that consists of three conical mounds, one linear mound, a compound or chain mound, and a water-spirit or panther effigy. Originally, there were at least ten other mounds, which have been destroyed. Chain or compound mounds are rarely found outside the Mississippi River valley. Some of the mounds were reconstructed by the Lion's Club of New Lisbon. Closed in winter.

Milwaukee County

Lake Park

Kenwood Boulevard and Lake Drive, Milwaukee

Lake Park, on Lake Michigan, preserves one of the few remaining mounds in Milwaukee. The low conical mound is located on a high bluff overlooking the lake in the northeastern corner of the park. It is two feet high and forty feet in diameter and was one of a number of like-sized mounds that once existed in the park area. The mound is undated but is typical of mounds built during the Woodland period.

Oneida County

Northern Highland American Legion State Forest

Highway 47, Lake Tomahawk
dnr.wi.gov/topic/StateForests/nhal/

Four conical burial mounds are located within the Indian Mounds Campground in the Northern Highland American Legion State Forest, about two miles north of the community of Lake Tomahawk, where they can be viewed in the picnic area adjacent to Lake Tomahawk. These are typical of northern Wisconsin for the Woodland period. State park and recreation fees.

Portage County

Lake Emily County Park

Lake Drive, Amherst Junction

Several small groups of conical, oval, and short linear forms are located within this scenic park, situated on Lake Emily in Portage County. A group of six oval mounds, four conical mounds, and one linear mound crosses Lake Drive on the east end of

Lake Emily. Two more oval mounds stand to the south, just northwest of the intersection of Lake Drive and Lake Emily Road. Another small group of two oval mounds and one conical mound is located near the park shelter, southwest of the intersection of Lake Drive and Old Highway 18.

Racine County

Mound Cemetery

West Boulevard, Racine

Fourteen conical mounds are found between modern graves in the northwestern portion of this historic landscaped cemetery.

Richland County

Eagle Township Mounds

Highways 60 and 193, Muscoda
3-eagles.org

Along the Wisconsin River, vestiges of the once-giant Eagle Township ceremonial landscape are preserved northwest and across the river from modern Muscoda in Richland County. Virtually intact mound groups, called the Shadewald I and II mound groups, occupy two high adjacent hills separated by Highway 193 just north of its intersection with Highway 60. They were once part of the giant Eagle Township effigy mound landscape along the Wisconsin River, most of which was destroyed by farming. The late landowner Frank Shadewald carefully preserved and maintained the mounds and encouraged visitors. On the top of the westernmost hill, twelve conical mounds of the Shadewald I grouping are arranged in a line that follows the contours of the hilltop in a roughly north/south direction. Shadewald II occupies the eastern hill with effigies of a bird, a bear, and a canine, as well as unidentified forms, and these also follow the contours of the top of the hilltop, in this case in an east/west direction. The two groups are now managed by the Three Eagles Foundation of Muscoda. Public access is allowed, but the foundation asks to be contacted first if large groups wish to visit.

To the south and overlooking the north bank of the Wisconsin River, the Schaeffer bird effigy is located on Department of Natural Resources land along Highway 60, a short distance west of its intersection with Highway 80. The bird flies south to the river and is marked by a small sign. It is the last survivor of a grouping that also included bear and linear mounds and that was part of the broad Eagle Township ceremonial landscape. The mound is visible from the highway, but visitors should park on Effigy Mound Lane, off Highway 60, and follow a trail to the mound.

Rock County

Beloit College Mounds

College Street, Beloit
beloit.edu/logan/mounds/

Twenty mounds dating to the Late Woodland period are located in the lawns in the heart of historic and private Beloit College. This total includes conicals, short linears, and a flattened effigy that resembles a turtle. The latter is used as a symbol for the college. The Logan Museum, located on campus near the mounds, also features rare and unique archaeological objects from around the world and has interesting interpretative displays.

Totem Mound Park

Totem Road, Beloit

Four mounds can be found in this city park along the Turtle River: an oval mound, two conical mounds, and a "turtle" mound depicting a long-tailed water-spirit effigy from above. The effigy is one of the finest remaining in Rock County. The other mounds, particularly one of the conical mounds, are lower and may be difficult to find.

St. Croix County

Birkmose Park

Coulee Road, Hudson

Overlooking the scenic St. Croix River valley, the Hudson mound group in Birkmose Park has six high conical mounds believed to have been built during the Middle Woodland period, about two thousand years ago.

Sauk County

Devil's Lake State Park

Highway 33, Baraboo
dnr.wi.gov/topic/parks/name/devilslake/

Devil's Lake State Park, located three miles south of Baraboo, preserves a number of effigy mounds that represent both the upper world and the lower world. A 150-foot-long "fork-tailed" bird effigy is located on the southeastern shore of the lake. It is also possible that this mound form represents a "bird-man," combining characteristics of a bird and a human being. Effigy mounds at the northern end of the lake are from the opposing lower world and include a bear, an unidentified animal, and a once-huge water spirit or panther. State park and recreation fees; campsites are available.

Man Mound County Park

Man Mound Road, Baraboo

Only one effigy mound in the shape of a human being has survived nearly intact. It is located near the base of a high hill in Man Mound County Park, to the northeast of Baraboo. Probably built more than one thousand years ago, this huge mound is in the form of a walking man who has horns or is wearing a horned headdress. The mound was first reported by W. H. Canfield in 1859 during a land survey. It was originally 214 feet long, but road construction in 1905 destroyed the feet and lower legs of the figure. The remainder of the mound was saved from further damage by the Wisconsin Archeological Society and the Sauk County Historical Society, which purchased the mound in 1907. It is now the centerpiece of a small county park. The Man Mound was designated as a National Historic Landmark in 2016.

Sheboygan County

Sheboygan Indian Mound County Park

South Ninth Street, Sheboygan
http://www.townandcountrygardenclub.org/sheboygan-indian-mound-park

Sheboygan Indian Mound County Park preserves what was first known as the Kletzien mound group. The group originally consisted of thirty-three conical and effigy mounds, primarily deer and panthers, as well as one panther or water-spirit intaglio. A number of mounds were excavated in 1926 by the Milwaukee Public Museum. Local garden clubs saved the mound group from development in the late 1950s by raising money to purchase the site. The land was subsequently donated to the city for an archaeological park, and sixteen of the eighteen existing mounds were restored under the supervision of the Milwaukee Public Museum. The Town and Country Garden Club developed a nature trail with signage and a guide to the trail that is available at the park and on their website. Open April 1 to November 1.

Trempealeau County

Perrot State Park

Sullivan Road, Trempealeau
dnr.wi.gov/topic/parks/name/perrot/

Just north of the town of Trempealeau, mounds from the Trowbridge mound group can be found at Perrot State Park. The large group once consisted of thirty-four conical and oval mounds, two short-tailed mammal effigies, a water-spirit effigy in an aerial or flattened perspective, and a bird effigy. Most have been destroyed by previous land use, but the park today preserves sixteen mounds, including one of the tailed mammal effigies. Displays about area archaeology can be found at the nature center. State park and recreation fees; campsites are available.

Trempealeau Platform Mounds

Main Street, Trempealeau
tremptrip.com/little-bluff-trail.html

The area around the modern Mississippi River town of Trempealeau was used as a ritual and mound-building center for more than two thousand years. On a high hill in Trempealeau itself are three descending platform mounds used by Mississippians from the Cahokia area in southern Illinois. Not far from the hill, called Little Bluff, archaeologists recently discovered a Mississippian village or colony occupied for a short time about 1050 A.D. A walking trail up to the platform mounds opened in 2016, with a trailhead and information kiosk on Main Street near the Little Bluff Motel.

Walworth County

Whitewater Effigy Mounds Preserve

Indian Mounds Parkway and Wildwood Road, Whitewater
http://www.whitewater-wi.gov/images/stories/agendas/landmarks/Effigy_Mounds_Preserve_Brochure.pdf

On the western side of the city of Whitewater, the municipally owned Effigy Mounds Preserve encompasses the Maples mound group. Thirteen mounds are found here: two types of birds, three water spirits, one water mammal, three linears, two conical mounds, and two oval mounds. An additional mound of uncertain form is also in the area. The group is arranged along a small creek with adjacent spring-fed wetlands. The preserve has informative signage and a trail map.

Washington County

Lizard Mound County Park

Highway A, east of Highway 111, West Bend
http://www.co.washington.wi.us/departments.iml?Detail=1023

This mound group originally contained approximately sixty mounds dominated by long-tailed effigy forms that early investigators thought were lizards. They are undoubtedly versions of water spirits or panthers. Over the years, many of the mounds were obliterated by continued cultivation, and others were reduced to a point where they are no longer visible. There are now twenty-nine mounds: conical and oval shaped, short linears, tapering linears, water spirits (panther), and two symmetrically paired water-bird effigies that fly away from each other.

The location of the group is unusual. It is on a low, level plateau far from any major body of water. The plateau is, however, surrounded by springs, which have many spiritual associations for Native peoples, being the entrances to the underworld of the water spirits. Thus the location and the underworld theme of the group may have been determined primarily by landscape features that have spiritual connotations. An interpretive kiosk and shelter stands near the park entrance. A sign-posted trail winds around the mounds. Open April 1 to November 1.

Quaas Creek Park

County Circle, West Bend

Near the Milwaukee River in West Bend are two bird mounds flying west together on a low ridge in the modern Quaas Creek Park. The birds have wingspans of 93 and 134 feet and are visible along a walking trail. Across the creek and lower on the landscape along the river once stood effigies that had water and lower-world symbolism: long-necked water birds similar to those at Lizard Mound County Park, a long linear, and two probable water-spirit mounds.

Waukesha County

Cutler Park

Maple Avenue, Waukesha

Three conical mounds preserved in Cutler Park are typical of those built during the Middle Woodland stage, approximately two thousand years ago. The large central mound is nine feet high and sixty-five feet in diameter. Excavations conducted by Increase A. Lapham in the 1840s found that the mound had been built over a large rock-lined burial chamber dug into the ground. In 1902 the city of Waukesha purchased the group to preserve it. The park is located next to the public library in downtown Waukesha.

Waushara County

Whistler Mounds Park

Highway FF, Hancock

The Whistler mound group, located in Whistler Mounds Park on Fish Lake, just east of the village of Hancock, contains one of the few surviving earthen enclosures in Wisconsin, as well as two straight lines of low conical mounds. The low, double-walled oval enclosure measures 120 feet by 51 feet. Such enclosures undoubtedly defined sacred spaces where periodic ceremonies were held. The site is undated but may date to the Late Woodland period.

Winnebago County

Smith Park

Park Street, Menasha

At least seventeen mounds once spread across an area on Doty Island, which sits along the Fox River at the point where it exits Lake Winnebago in the city of Menasha. Most were destroyed by farming and urban development, but three long-tailed water-spirit mounds are preserved in the south end of Smith Park.

State of Iowa

Effigy Mounds National Monument

State Highway 76, Marquette, Iowa
nps.gov/efmo

The best interpreted effigy mound landscape is Effigy Mounds National Monument, along the Mississippi River on the western periphery of the effigy mound region, located north of McGregor, Iowa. This large, scenic national park contains lines of "marching" bear effigies, bird effigies, conical and chain or compound mounds, linear mounds, and one conical mound dating to the early Hopewell-Middle Woodland stage. A total of ninety-six mounds have been preserved in the north and south units of the park. One effigy mound, the Great Bear, is 137 feet long, and one unusually long compound or chain mound links seven mounds. The mounds are arranged in clusters along the tops of bluffs overlooking the Mississippi extending north and south from the Yellow River, a major tributary of the Mississippi. Excavations of some mounds established that mound building began during the Middle Woodland stage and expanded during the Late Woodland period. A visitor center located off Highway 76 north of McGregor has informative displays and trail maps. Admission fee.

Notes

Chapter 1. The Mystery of the Mounds

1. Stephen H. Long, "Long Journal 1817—Down the Mississippi to Belle Fontaine, July 10 through August 15, 1817," 85–86.

2. Richard C. Taylor, "Notes Respecting Certain Indian Mounds and Earthworks in the Form of Animal Effigies, Chiefly in Wisconsin Territory, U.S.," 88, 90.

3. Increase A. Lapham, *Wisconsin: Its Geography, Topography, History, Minerology: Together with Brief Sketches of Its Antiquities, Natural History, Soil, Productions, Population and Government*.

4. William E. Whittaker and William Green, "Early and Middle Woodland Enclosures in Iowa."

5. Some of these erroneous reports even made the pages of the *New York Times*: "Wisconsin Mound Opened, Skeleton Found of a Man over Nine Feet High with an Enormous Skull," *New York Times*, December 20, 1897; "Strange Skeletons Found, Indications That Tribe Hitherto Unknown Once Lived in Wisconsin," *New York Times*, May 4, 1912.

Chapter 2. In Search of the Mound Builders

1. Robert Silverberg, *The Mound Builders of Ancient America*; Gordon R. Willey and Jeremy A. Sabloff, *A History of American Archaeology*.

2. Willey and Sabloff, *History of American Archaeology*, 14.

3. Willey and Sabloff, *History of American Archaeology*, 15.

4. Willey and Sabloff, *History of American Archaeology*, 28.

5. For an erudite discussion of American views pertaining to earthworks in the nineteenth century, see Roger G. Kennedy, *Hidden Cities: The Discovery and Loss of Ancient North American Civilization*.

6. Silverberg, *Mound Builders of Ancient America*, 159–160.

7. Silverberg, *Mound Builders of Ancient America*, 28.

8. Stephen D. Peet, "The Mound Builders," 188.

9. Edward G. Bourne, *Narratives of the Career of Hernando de Soto*.

10. Gloria Deák, *Discovering America's Southeast: A Sixteenth Century View Based on the Mannerist Engravings of Theodore de Bry*, 126–127.

11. Bourne, *Narratives of the Career of Hernando de Soto*.

12. Silverberg, *Mound Builders of Ancient America*, 6.

13. Caleb Atwater, *Descriptions of the Antiquities Discovered in the State of Ohio and Other Western States*.

14. Ephraim G. Squier and Edgar H. Davis, *Ancient Monuments of the Mississippi Valley*.

15. Willey and Sabloff, *History of American Archaeology*, 36.

16. William Green, "Examining Protohistoric Depopulation in the Upper Midwest."

17. Nancy O. Lurie, "Winnebago," 702–705; James A. Clifton, "Potawatomi," 736–741.

18. [Increase A. Lapham], "Antiquities of Wisconsin," 2.

19. Nathaniel F. Hyer, "Ruins of the Ancient City of Aztalan," n.p.

20. Richard C. Taylor, "Notes Respecting Certain Indian Mounds and Earthworks in the Form of Animal Effigies, Chiefly in Wisconsin Territory, U.S.," 88.

21. Taylor, "Notes Respecting Certain Indian Mounds and Earthworks," 104.

22. Increase Lapham, *The Antiquities of Wisconsin, as Surveyed and Described*.

23. Lapham, *Antiquities of Wisconsin*, 90.

24. Lapham, *Antiquities of Wisconsin*, 29.

25. William Pidgeon, *Traditions of De-coo-dah and Antiquarian Researches: Comprising Extensive Explorations, Surveys, and Excavations of the Wonderful and Mysterious Earthen Remains of the Mound-Builders in America; the Traditions of the Last Prophet of the Elk Nation Relative to Their Origin and Use; and the Evidences of an Ancient Population More Numerous Than the Present Aborigines*.

26. Pidgeon, *Traditions of De-coo-dah*, 44.

27. Silverberg, *Mound Builders of Ancient America*, 150.

28. Theodore H. Lewis, "The 'Monumental' Tortoise Mounds of De-coo-dah," 69.

29. Steven D. Peet, *Prehistoric America*.

30. Theodore H. Lewis, *The Northwestern Archaeological Survey*. The field notebooks and related documents from the survey are curated by the Minnesota Historical Society, St. Paul.

31. Fred Finney, "The Archaeological Legacy of Theodore H. Lewis: Letters, Papers, and Articles."

32. Quoted in Silverberg, *Mound Builders of Ancient America*, 170.

33. Bruce D. Smith, "Introduction" to *Report on the Mound Explorations of the Bureau of Ethnology*, 6.

34. Cyrus Thomas, *Report on the Mound Explorations of the Bureau of Ethnology*.

35. Marshall McKusick, *The Davenport Conspiracy* and "A Disturbed Bear That

Bears Watching and Other Remarks on an Iowa Effigy Mound Interpretive Model," 355; Thomas, *Report on the Mound Explorations*, 91–93, 531.

36. Thomas, *Report on the Mound Explorations*, 659.

37. The mound on Lake Butte des Morts probably dates to the Middle Woodland and was destroyed in the 1850s. Late-nineteenth-century researchers assumed that there was a connection between this mound and a famous series of eighteenth-century battles between the French and the Sac and Fox, and this error was repeated by subsequent investigators.

38. R. Clark Mallam, "The Mound Builders: An American Myth," 170–171.

Chapter 3. Excavation, Chronology, and Meanings of the Mounds

1. Walter Hoffman, *The Menominee Indians*, 38; S. A. Barrett and Alanson Skinner, "Certain Mounds and Village Sites of Shawano and Oconto Counties, Wisconsin," 503–504. Barrett and Skinner note that the published story is only part of a more elaborate one that accounts for the origin of the Menominee and the identity and disappearance of the mound builders.

2. Pliny Warriner, "Legend of the Winnebagos."

3. George A. West, "Indian Authorship of Wisconsin Antiquities," 253.

4. Arlow B. Stout, "Prehistoric Earthworks in Wisconsin."

5. Arlow B. Stout, "The Winnebago and the Mounds."

6. Charles E. Brown, "The Winnebago as Builders of Wisconsin Earthworks."

7. Brown, "Winnebago as Builders of Wisconsin Earthworks," 129.

8. Paul Radin, "Some Aspects of Winnebago Archaeology" and *The Winnebago Tribe*.

9. Carol I. Mason, "Archaeological Analogy and Ethnographic Example: A Case from the Winnebago."

10. W. C. McKern, "The Neale and McCaughry Mound Groups."

11. Detailed information on Brown's life can be found in Robert A. Birmingham, "Charles E. Brown: Wisconsin Archaeologist," 15–24.

12. Charles E. Brown, "The Preservation of the Man Mound."

13. Charles E. Brown, "Archaeological Items."

14. Itineraries for the Lake Mendota Historical Excursions, 1936 and 1939, box 21, Charles E. Brown Papers.

15. Charles E. Brown, "Lake Wingra," 91–92.

16. Charles E. Brown, "The Arboretum: Notes and Reminiscences by Charles E. Brown."

17. S. A. Barrett and E. W. Hawkes, "The Kratz Creek Mound Group."

18. S. A. Barrett, "Ancient Aztalan."

19. Charles E. Brown, "Superstitions about Indian Mounds."

20. Alice Kehoe, "The History of Wisconsin Archaeology," 13.

21. W. C. McKern, "The Kletzien and Nitschke Mound Groups," 462–463.

22. W. C. McKern, "Preliminary Report on the Upper Mississippi Phase in Wisconsin."

23. Chandler Rowe, *The Effigy Mound Culture of Wisconsin*.

24. Warren L. Wittry, "The Kolterman Mound 18 Radiocarbon Date."

25. William M. Hurley, *An Analysis of Effigy Mound Complexes in Wisconsin*.

26. Warren L. Wittry, "Archaeological Studies of Four Wisconsin Rockshelters."

27. Julian H. Steward, *Theory of Cultural Change*.

28. R. Clark Mallam, "The Mound Builders: An American Myth."

29. Morten Rasmussen et al., "The Ancestry and Affiliation of Kennewick Man."

30. Lynne G. Goldstein, "Landscapes and Mortuary Practices: A Case for Regional Perspectives," 101–120; Peter Mires, Jennifer L. Kolb, and Edgar S. Oerichbauer, "The Archaeological Resources of Northwestern Wisconsin: Region 1 Program, 1988–1989."

31. Steven Hackenberger, He Ping, and Larry A. Johns, "Final Report of the Rock County Indian Mounds Project."

32. Robert J. Salzer and Larry A. Johns, *Final Report of the Dane County Indian Mounds Identification Project*.

33. Barbara Mead, "The Rehbein I Site (47-Ri-81)."

34. John T. Penman, "Late Woodland Sites in Southwestern Grant County, Wisconsin."

35. Ultimately, the cemetery was saved when surrounding landowners who opposed development purchased the property. It is now public land.

36. William M. Hurley, "The Late Woodland Stage: Effigy Mound Culture," 298.

37. Robert Hall, "Ghosts, Water Barriers, Corn, and Sacred Enclosures in the Eastern Woodlands," 363.

38. Robert Hall, *Archaeology of the Soul: North American Belief and Ritual*.

39. Robert Hall, "Red Banks, Oneota, and the Winnebago: Views from a Distant Rock," 42.

40. Robert Salzer and Grace Rajnovich, *The Gottschall Rockshelter: An Archaeological Mystery*; Hall, *Archaeology of the Soul*. There are other interpretations of the paintings that are also derived from Ho-Chunk traditions as recorded by Radin. See Richard Dieterle, "The Gottschall Head," and Robert F. Boszhardt, "The Lady in Red (Horn)."

41. Paul Radin, *Winnebago Hero Cycles: A Study in Aboriginal Literature*.

42. Carol Diaz-Grandos, James Duncan, and F. Kent Reilly, *Picture Cave: Unraveling the Mysteries of the Mississippian Cosmos*.

43. David Benn, Arthur Bettis III, and R. Clark Mallam, "Cultural Transformations in the Keller and Bluff Top Mounds."

44. R. Clark Mallam, "Ideology from the Earth: Effigy Mounds in the Midwest."

45. Robert A. Birmingham and Amy L. Rosebrough, "On the Meaning of Effigy Mounds."

46. Robert A. Birmingham, *Spirits of Earth: The Effigy Mound Landscape of Madison and the Four Lakes*.

47. Jeffrey Quilter, "Introduction," in *The Pre-Columbian World*.

48. Andrew Newberg, Eugene G. d'Aguili, and Vubce Rause, *Why God Won't Go Away: Brain Science and the Biology of Belief*.

49. Ronald J. Mason, "Oneota and Winnebago Ethnogenesis: An Overview," 418. For a critique of the use of oral traditions, see also Ronald J. Mason, *Inconstant Companions: Archaeology and North American Indian Oral Traditions*.

50. John Broihahn and Amy Rosebrough, "Reconstructing Raisbeck: A Multi-Component Mound and Ritual Center in the Southern Driftless Area, Grant County, Wisconsin."

51. Amy L. Rosebrough, "Every Family a Nation: A Deconstruction and Reconstruction of the Effigy Mound 'Culture' of the Western Great Lakes of North America"; Amy L. Rosebrough, "Monuments and Mysteries: Social Geography of the Effigy Builders."

52. Some examples are Angela M. Zamencnik, "An Osteological Investigation of Lake Woodland Raisbeck Effigy Mound Group, Grant County, Wisconsin"; Christine Ella Ruth, "Death, Decay and Reconstruction: An Osteological Analysis of Effigy Mound Material from Wisconsin"; Wendy Lackey-Cornelison, "Constructing Community and Cosmos: A BioArchaeological Analysis of Wisconsin Effigy Mound Mortuary Practices and Mound Construction."

Chapter 4. Wisconsin before the Mound Builders

1. Archaeologists classify Native American cultures in Wisconsin into stages of cultural development within very broad traditions known as Paleo-Indian, Archaic, Woodland, and Mississippian. Stages and traditions are composed of cultural complexes that are generally similar to one another, reflecting very broad patterns in lifestyle. They are not necessarily the same as periods, although the terms "stage" and "period" are used interchangeably in this book for simplicity. One tradition or stage may persist in one area although it has disappeared in another. For example, the Paleo-Indian survived for more time in northern Wisconsin than in southern Wisconsin. Finally, stages are generally subdivided into phases, or archaeological sites in a particular area that were occupied for a short time by people who shared many customs, such as those in a tribe or band.

2. David F. Overstreet et al., *FY 1992 Historic Preservation Survey and Planning Grant: Early Holocene Megafaunal Exploitation, Kenosha County, Wisconsin*; Daniel J. Joyce, "Chronology and New Research on the Schaefer Mammoth (*Mammuthus primigenius*) Site, Kenosha County, Wisconsin, USA"; Eileen Johnson et al., "The Mud Lake Mammoth and People in Southeastern Wisconsin."

3. David F. Barton, "Skare Site Projectile Points"; Sissel Schroeder, "Evidence for Paleoindians in Wisconsin and the Skare Site."

4. Robert A. Birmingham and Allen P. Van Dyke, "Chert and Chert Resources in the Lower Rock River Valley."

5. Thomas J. Loebel, "A Survey of Wisconsin Fluted Points."

6. Loebel, "A Survey of Wisconsin Fluted Points."

7. Ronald J. Mason and Carol Irwin, "An Eden-Scottsbluff Burial in Northeastern Wisconsin."

8. Norman M. Meinholz and Stephen Kuehn, *The Deadman Slough Site: Late Paleoindian/Early Archaic and Woodland Occupations along the Flambeau River, Price County, Wisconsin*, 183–184.

9. Thomas C. Pleger and James Stoltman, "The Archaic Tradition in Wisconsin."

10. Reid A. Bryson and Robert U. Bryson, "The History of Woodland Climatic Environments: As Simulated with Archaeoclimatic Models"; Marjorie Green Winkler, "Late Quaternary Climate, Fire, and Vegetation Dynamics"; M. G. Winkler, A. M. Swain, and J. E. Kutzbach, "Middle Holocene Dry Period in the Northern Midwestern United States: Lake Levels and Pollen Stratigraphy."

11. Wendy G. Harris, "Upland Abandonment during the Middle Archaic Period: A View from Northeastern Illinois."

12. Steven R. Kuehn, "The Crow Hollow Site: A Middle Woodland Archaic Campsite in Southwestern Wisconsin."

13. Ardith K. Hansel and David M. Mickelson, "A Reevaluation of the Timing and Causes of High Lake Phases in the Lake Michigan Basin"; Curtis E. Larsen, "Geoarchaeological Interpretation of Great Lakes Coastal Environments."

14. Pleger and Stoltman, "The Archaic Tradition in Wisconsin"; Bill Reardon, "Oldest Carbon-14 Dated Copper Projectile Points from Wisconsin."

15. Pleger and Stoltman, "The Archaic Tradition in Wisconsin."

16. Thomas C. Pleger, "A Functional and Temporal Analysis of Copper Implements at the Chautauqua Grounds Site (47-Mt-71): A Multicomponent Site at the Mouth of the Menominee River."

17. Susan Martin, *Wonderful Power: The Story of Ancient Copper Working in the Lake Superior Basin*.

18. Grace Rajnovich, *Reading Rock Art: Interpreting the Indian Rock Paintings of the Canadian Shield*, 102–103.

19. Rajnovich, *Reading Rock Art*, 104.

20. Robert Ritzenthaler, "The Osceola Site: An 'Old Copper' Site Near Potosi, Wisconsin."

21. Bruce Trigger, *The Children of Aataentsic: A History of the Huron People to 1660*.

22. Harold Hickerson, "The Feast of the Dead among the Seventeenth Century Algonkians of the Upper Great Lakes."

23. David A. Baerreis, Hiroshi Daifuku, and James E. Lundsted, "The Burial Complex of the Reigh Site, Winnebago County, Wisconsin"; Neil J. Ostberg, "Additional Material from the Reigh Site, Winnebago County"; Robert E. Ritzenthaler and Warren Wittry, "The Oconto Site: Old Copper Manifestation"; Warren L. Wittry and Robert E. Ritzenthaler, "The Old Copper Complex: An Archaic Manifestation in Wisconsin."

24. James C. Knox, "Climatic Influence on Upper Mississippi Valley Floods."

25. Katherine P. Stevenson, Robert F. Boszhardt, Charles R. Moffat, Philip H. Salkin, Thomas C. Pleger, James L. Theler, and Constance M. Arzigian, "The Woodland Tradition."

26. Robert Hruska, "The Riverside Site: A Late Archaic Manifestation in Michigan."

27. Thomas C. Pleger, "Old Copper and Red Ochre Social Complexity."

28. David F. Overstreet, "The Convent Knoll Site (47Wk327): A Red Ochre Cemetery in Waukesha, Wisconsin."

29. Contrary to some sources of information, the practice of scalping was not first introduced to the Native peoples of the Americas by Europeans and Americans but goes back thousands of years along with the taking of whole heads as war trophies or for other purposes.

Chapter 5. Early Burial Mound Builders

1. For an overview of mounds constructed during the Archaic, see *Southeastern Archaeology* 13, no. 2 (1994), special issue, "Archaic Mounds in the Southeast."

2. Jon L. Gibson, *Poverty Point: A Terminal Archaic Culture of the Lower Mississippi Valley*.

3. Alphonse Gerend, "Sheboygan County."

4. Cyrus Thomas, *Report on the Mound Explorations of the Bureau of Ethnology*, 93–94.

5. David F. Overstreet et al., "Two Red Ocher Mortuary Contexts from Southeastern Wisconsin: The Henschel Site (47 SB 29), Jefferson County, Wisconsin."

6. William Green and Shirley Schermer, "The Turkey River Mound Group (13CT1)."

7. Brian Fagan, *Ancient North America: Archaeology of a Continent*, 403–410.

8. Fagan, *Ancient North America*, 411–422.

9. Mark J. Lynott, *Hopewell Ceremonial Landscapes of Ohio: More Than Mounds and Geometric Earthworks*.

10. David W. Penny, "Continuities in Imagery and Symbolism in the Art of the Woodlands."

11. Don W. Dragoo and Charles F. Wray, "Hopewell Figurine Rediscovered."

12. Bradley T. Lepper, "The Newark Earthworks: Monumental Geometry and Astronomy at a Hopewellian Pilgrimage Center."

13. Martin A. Byers, *The Ohio Hopewell Episode: Paradigm Lost and Paradigm Gained*.

14. Robert Hall, "In Search of the Ideology of the Adena-Hopewell Climax" and *Archaeology of the Soul: North American Belief and Ritual*, 18–23.

15. Constance Arzigian, "The Emergence of Horticultural Economies in Southwestern Wisconsin"; Lynn A. Rusch, "The Early and Late Woodland Occupations at the Bachman Site in East Central Wisconsin"; Philip H. Salkin, "The Lake

Farms Phase: The Early Woodland Stage in South Central Wisconsin as Seen from the Lake Farms Archaeological District"; James L. Theler, "The Early Woodland Component at the Mill Pond Site, Wisconsin."

16. David W. Benn, "The Woodland People and the Roots of Oneota," 103.

17. Kelvin W. Sampson, "Conventionalized Figures on Woodland Ceramics."

18. Howard Van Langen and Thomas F. Kehoe, "Hilgen Spring Park Mounds."

19. Hall, *Archaeology of the Soul*, 17–23.

20. Katherine P. Stevenson, Robert F. Boszhardt, Charles R. Moffat, Philip H. Salkin, Thomas C. Pleger, James L. Theler, and Constance M. Arzigian, "The Woodland Tradition."

21. W. C. McKern, "A Wisconsin Variant of the Hopewell Culture."

22. Julieann Van Nest, Douglas K. Charles, Jane Buikstra, and David L. Asch, "Sod Blocks in Illinois Hopewell Mounds."

23. Charlotte T. Bakken, "Preliminary Investigations at the Outlet Site."

24. James B. Stoltman, "Tillmont (47CR460): A Stratified Prehistoric Site in the Upper Mississippi River Valley."

25. Jane E. Buikstra and Douglas K. Charles, "Centering the Ancestors: Cemeteries, Mounds and Landscapes of the Ancient North American Continent."

26. Robert J. Salzer, "The Wisconsin North Lakes Project: A Preliminary Report" and "The Woodland Tradition: An Introduction"; Stevenson et al., "Woodland Tradition."

27. Leland Cooper, "The Red Cedar River Variant of the Wisconsin Hopewell Culture."

28. Joan Freeman, "The Millville Site: A Middle Woodland Village in Grant County, Wisconsin."

29. Squier and Davis, *Ancient Monuments of the Mississippi Valley*.

30. Willis H. McGrath, "The North Benton Mound in Ohio."

31. Bradley Lepper, Ohio History Connection, personal communication.

32. Harry C. Henriksen, "Utica Hopewell: A Study of Early Hopewellian Occupation in the Illinois River Valley."

33. Lepper, personal communication.

34. Bradley T. Lepper and Tod A. Frolking, "Alligator Mound: Geographical and Iconographical Interpretations of a Late Prehistoric Effigy Mound in Central Ohio."

35. Robert F. Boszhardt, "An Etched Pipe form Southeastern Minnesota."

36. James B. Stoltman and George W. Christiansen III, "The Late Woodland Stage in the Driftless Area of the Upper Mississippi Valley."

Chapter 6. From Middle Woodland to Late Woodland

1. Thomas Emerson, Dale McElrath, and Andrew Fortier, eds., *Late Woodland Societies: Tradition and Transformation across the Mid-Continent*.

2. Lynne Goldstein and Donald H. Gaff, "Recasting the Past: Examining Assumptions about Aztalan."

3. Katherine P. Stevenson, Robert F. Boszhardt, Charles R. Moffat, Philip H. Salkin, Thomas C. Pleger, James L. Theler, and Constance M. Arzigian, "The Woodland Tradition."

4. William Iseminger, *Cahokia Mounds: America's First City*.

5. James Stoltman, Danielle M. Benden, and Robert F. Boszhardt, "New Evidence in the Upper Mississippi Valley for Premississippian Cultural Interaction with the American Bottom"; Timothy Pauketat, Robert F. Boszhardt, and Danielle M. Benden, "Trempealeau Entanglements: An Ancient Colony's Causes and Effects."

6. Robert A. Birmingham and Lynne Goldstein, *Aztalan: Mysteries of an Ancient Indian Town*.

7. James Stoltman, "The Appearance of the Mississippian Tradition in the Upper Mississippi Valley."

8. Reid A. Bryson and Robert U. Bryson, "The History of Woodland Climatic Environments: As Simulated with Archaeoclimatic Models."

9. James L. Theler and Robert E. Boszhardt, *Twelve Millennia: Archaeology of the Upper Mississippi Valley*.

10. James B. Stoltman and George W. Christiansen III, "The Late Woodland Stage in the Driftless Area of the Upper Mississippi Valley."

11. Joan Freeman, "The Millville Site: A Middle Woodland Village in Grant County, Wisconsin."

12. Stevenson et al., "Woodland Tradition"; Stoltman and Christiansen, "The Late Woodland Stage in the Driftless Area," 499–500.

13. Stevenson et al., "Woodland Tradition"; Stoltman and Christiansen, "The Late Woodland Stage in the Driftless Area," 499–500; David Benn, "Some Trends and Traditions in Wisconsin Cultures of the Quad-State Region in the Upper Mississippi River Basin."

14. Robert Hall, "Red Banks, Oneota, and the Winnebago: Views from a Distant Rock."

15. Amy L. Rosebrough, "Every Family a Nation: A Deconstruction and Reconstruction of the Effigy Mound 'Culture' of the Western Great Lakes of North America," Appendix: Driftless Area.

16. Barbara Mead, "The Rehbein I Site (47-Ri-81)."

17. Robert Hall, *The Archaeology of Carajou Point*, 114–115; Charles R. Moffat and Robert F. Boszhardt, "Sand Country Prehistory: The Late Woodland Settlement of the Central River Drainage," 68–69; Goldstein and Gaff, "Recasting the Past," 105.

18. Lynne Goldstein, Cynthia Klink, Ellen Ghere, Jeffrey Logsdon, Mary Imam, and Neil C. Tappen, "The Klug Island Site (47-Oz-67), Ozaukee County, Wisconsin: A Report on Test Excavations and Preliminary Analysis."

Chapter 7. The Effigy Mound Ceremonial Complex

1. Philip H. Salkin, *Archaeological Mitigation Excavation Excavations at the Sticker Pond I Site (47DA424) in Middleton, Dane County, Wisconsin*.

2. James B. Stoltman and George W. Christiansen III, "The Late Woodland Stage in the Driftless Area of the Upper Mississippi Valley."

3. Katherine P. Stevenson, Robert F. Boszhardt, Charles R. Moffat, Philip H. Salkin, Thomas C. Pleger, James L. Theler, and Constance M. Arzigian, "The Woodland Tradition"; Dan Wendt, *Late Woodland Site Distribution in Far Western Wisconsin*.

4. Stevenson et al., "Woodland Tradition"; Jennifer Picard, "Northern Flint, Southern Roots: A Diachronic Analysis of Paleoethnobotanical Remains and Maize Race at the Aztalan Site (47-JE-0001)."

5. Picard, "Northern Flint, Southern Roots."

6. William Green, "Prehistoric Woodland Peoples in the Upper Mississippi Valley."

7. Victoria Dirst, "Stockbridge Harbor: A Late Woodland Village on Lake Winnebago."

8. Rodney E. Riggs, "Human Skeletal Remains from the Poor Man's Farrah (47-Gt-365) and the Bade (47-Gt-365) Sites in Southwestern Wisconsin."

9. George R. Milner, "An Osteological Perspective on Prehistoric Warfare."

10. Norman Meinholz and Jennifer Kolb, *The Statz Site: A Late Woodland Community and Archaic Workshop in Dane County, Wisconsin*.

11. Robert F. Boszhardt, "Angelo Punctated: A Late Woodland Ceramic Type in Western Wisconsin."

12. Philip H. Salkin, "The Horicon and Kekosgee Phases: Cultural Complexity in the Woodland Stage in Southwestern Wisconsin."

13. John Martin Kelly, "Delineating the Spatial and Temporal Boundaries of Late Woodland Collared Wares from Wisconsin and Illinois"; Stoltman and Christiansen, "The Late Woodland Stage in the Driftless Area."

14. Judy A. Clauter, "Ceramic Analysis from the Nitschke Mound Group (47DO27) and the Nitschke Garden Beds (47DO518) Sites."

15. David K. Benn, "The Woodland People and the Roots of Oneota."

16. Kelvin W. Sampson, "Conventionalized Figures on Woodland Ceramics."

17. Ruth Bliss Philips, "Dreams and Designs: Iconographic Problems in Great Lakes Twined Bags."

18. Benn, "The Woodland People and the Roots of Oneota."

19. Amy L. Rosebrough, "Every Family a Nation: A Deconstruction and Reconstruction of the Effigy Mound 'Culture' of the Western Great Lakes of North America," 463.

20. R. Clark Mallam, "Ideology from the Earth: Effigy Mounds in the Midwest."

21. Robert Hall, "Red Banks, Oneota, and the Winnebago: Views from a Distant Rock."

22. Robert A. Birmingham, *Spirits of Earth: The Effigy Mound Landscape of Madison and the Four Lakes*.

23. Clark R. Mallam, *The Iowa Effigy Mound Manifestation: An Interpretative Model*, 76.

24. Roland Rodell, "The Diamond Bluff Site Complex and Cahokia Influence in the Red Wing Locality."

25. Mallam, *Iowa Effigy Mound Manifestation*, 76.

26. John Broihahn and Amy Rosebrough, "Reconstructing Raisbeck: A Multi-Component Mound and Ritual Center in the Southern Driftless Area, Grant County, Wisconsin."

27. Amy Rosebrough, "Monuments and Mysteries: Social Geography of the Effigy Builders."

28. Birmingham, *Spirits of Earth*.

29. Birmingham, *Spirits of Earth*.

30. S. A. Barrett and E. W. Hawkes, "The Kratz Creek Mound Group."

31. Clauter, "Ceramic Analysis"; Warren Wittry and Edgar G. Bruder, "Salvage Operations at the Kolterman Mound Group, Dodge County, Wisconsin."

32. Mallam, *Iowa Effigy Mound Manifestation*; Lynne G. Goldstein, "Landscapes and Mortuary Practices: A Case for Regional Perspectives."

33. Hall, "Red Banks, Oneota, and the Winnebago"; Birmingham, *Spirits of Earth*.

34. Birmingham, *Spirits of Earth*.

35. Rosebrough, "Every Family a Nation."

36. Mallam, *Iowa Effigy Mound Manifestation*.

37. Hall, "Red Banks, Oneota, and the Winnebago."

38. Hall, "Red Banks, Oneota, and the Winnebago," 51.

39. George Christiansen III, "Burial Mound and Earthwork Research Project."

40. Birmingham, *Spirits of Earth*.

41. Rosebrough, "Every Family a Nation"; Rosebrough, "Monuments and Mysteries."

42. Jeffrey Quilter, "Introduction."

43. Paul Radin, *The Winnebago Tribe*, 137.

44. Radin, *Winnebago Tribe*, 239–240.

45. Charles E. Brown, "Water Spirit Legend, Told by Winnebago Indians."

46. Paul Radin, *The Road of Life and Death*, 54–55.

47. Louise S. Spindler, "The Menominee."

48. Robert Salzer and Grace Rajnovich, *The Gottschall Rockshelter: An Archaeological Mystery*.

49. Spindler, "Menominee."

50. Hall, "Red Banks, Oneota, and the Winnebago."

51. Stout, "The Winnebago and the Mounds"; Charles E. Brown, "The Springs of Lake Wingra."

52. Oliver La Mere to Charles E. Brown, November 27, 1926, box 3, Charles E. Brown Papers.

53. Charles E. Brown, "The Springs of Lake Wingra."

54. S. C. Power, *Early Art of the Southeastern Indians: Feathered Serpents and Winged Beings*.

55. Radin, *Winnebago Tribe*, 164.

56. Charles E. Brown, "The Intaglio Mounds of Wisconsin."

57. Increase Lapham, *Antiquities of Wisconsin, as Surveyed and Described*.

58. Radin, *Winnebago Tribe*.

59. G. J. Hudak, "Boulder Outlines in Southwestern Minnesota"; Thomas F. Kehoe and Alice B. Kehoe, "Boulder Effigy Monuments in the Northern Plains."

60. William Canfield, "Survey Notebook."

61. Canfield, "Survey Notebook."

62. Robert A. Birmingham, "An Archaeological Survey of Wisconsin Winnebago Land in Eagle Township, Richland County, Wisconsin"; George W. Christiansen III, *Archaeological Investigations along STH 60 between CTH W and STH 80 in Richwood and Eagle Townships in Richland County, Wisconsin*.

63. Theodore H. Lewis, *The Northwestern Archaeological Survey: Fieldbooks and Related Volumes, 1880–1895*, 26–28, 47–50.

64. Amy L. Rosebrough, "National Historic Landmark Nomination for Greenfield Man Mound."

65. Richard C. Taylor, "Notes Respecting Certain Indian Mounds and Earthworks in the Form of Animal Effigies, Chiefly in Wisconsin Territory, U.S."

66. Radin, *Winnebago Tribe*, 33.

67. Selwyn Dewdney, *The Sacred Scrolls of the Southern Ojibway*.

68. Radin, *Winnebago Tribe*, 194.

69. Wittry and Bruder, "Salvage Operations at the Kolterman Mound Group"; McKern, "The Kletzien and Nitschke Mound Groups."

70. Erik Seeman, *The Huron-Wendat Feast of the Dead: Indian-European Encounters in Early North America*.

71. Wendy Lackey-Cornelison, "Constructing Community and Cosmos: A BioArchaeological Analysis of Wisconsin Effigy Mound Mortuary Practices and Mound Construction."

72. James P. Scherz, "Pertinent Aspects of Geometry, Astronomy, Distance, and Time."

73. Frank D. Stekel, Larry A. Johns, and James P. Scherz, "Whitewater Effigy Mounds Park: The Maple Mounds Group."

74. Scherz, "Pertinent Aspects"; Letter from E. C. Krupp to Robert A. Birmingham, Office of the State Archaeologist, Wisconsin Historical Society, October 31, 1991.

75. Gary Henschel, "Henschel Mounds (47 Sb 29) as Possible Solstice Markers: A Progress Report."

76. William Romain, *LiDAR Assessment of Earthworks at Effigy Mound National Monument*.

77. Robert A. Birmingham and Amy Rosebrough, "On the Meaning of Effigy Mounds"; Birmingham, *Spirits of Earth*.

78. William M. Hurley, *Analysis of Effigy Mound Complexes in Wisconsin*; Birmingham, "An Archaeological Survey of Wisconsin Winnebago Land in Eagle Township."

79. Clauter, "Ceramic Analysis."

80. Robert A. Birmingham, "Archaeological Investigation of a Proposed Dog Park and Disk Golf Course at Capital Springs Park, Dane County, Wisconsin."

81. Paul L. Beaubien, "Some Hopewellian Mounds at Effigy Mound National Monument, Iowa"; Hurley, *Analysis of Effigy Mound Complexes in Wisconsin*; Warren L. Wittry, "The Kolterman Mound 18 Radiocarbon Date."

82. Stoltman and Christiansen, "The Late Woodland Stage in the Driftless Area."

83. Moreau Maxwell, "A Change in the Interpretation of Wisconsin's Prehistory."

84. Hall, "Red Banks, Oneota, and the Winnebago," 51–52.

85. Robert J. Salzer, "The Wisconsin North Lakes Project: A Preliminary Report."

86. W. C. McKern, *The Clam River Focus*.

Chapter 8. Platform Mound Builders

1. Edward G. Bourne, *Narratives of the Career of Hernando de Soto*; John R. Swanton, *Indian Tribes of the Lower Mississippi Valley and Adjacent Coast of the Gulf of Mexico*. For a highly readable account of the de Soto expedition, see David Ewing Duncan, *Hernando de Soto: A Savage Quest in the Americas*.

2. William Iseminger, *Cahokia Mounds: America's First City*.

3. Antoine-Simon Le Page du Pratz, *Histoire de Lousiane*.

4. Melvin Fowler, Jerome Rose, Barbara Vander Leest, and Steven R. Ahler, *The Mound 72 Area: Dedicated Space in Early Cahokia*.

5. Thomas E. Emerson, K. Hedman, E. Hargrave, D. Cobb, and A. Thompson, "Paradigms Lost: Reconfiguring Cahokia's Mound 72 Beaded Burial."

6. Le Page du Pratz, *Histoire de Lousiane*, 758.

7. J. Witthoft, *Green Corn Ceremonialism in Eastern Woodlands*.

8. Robert A. Birmingham and Lynne Goldstein, *Aztalan: Mysteries of an Ancient Indian Town*.

9. James B. Stoltman, Danielle M. Benden, and Robert F. Boszhardt, "New Evidence in the Upper Mississippi Valley for Pre-Mississippian Cultural Interaction with the American Bottom"; Timothy R. Pauketat, Robert F. Boszhardt, and Danielle M. Benden, "Trempealeau Entanglements: An Ancient Colony's Causes and Effects."

10. James L. Theler and Robert E. Boszhardt, "Collapse of Critical Resources and Culture Change: A Model for the Woodland to Oneota Transformation in the Upper Midwest."

11. Pauketat, Boszhardt, and Benden, "Trempealeau Entanglements."

12. Salzer and Rajnovich, *The Gottschall Rockshelter*.

13. Paul Radin, *Winnebago Myth Cycles: A Study in Aboriginal Myth Cycles*; Alanson Skinner, *Ethnology of the Ioway Indians*.

14. Robert Hall, *Archaeology of the Soul: North American Belief and Ritual*.

15. James R. Duncan and Carol Diaz-Granados, "Of Myths and Masks."

16. Robert J. Salzer, "A Preliminary Report on the Gottschall Rockshelter (47Ia80)"; Robert F. Boszhardt, "Oneota Horizons: A La Crosse Perspective," 211.

17. Fred Finney, "Intrasite and Regional Perspectives on the Fred Edwards Site and the Stirling Horizon in the Upper Mississippian Valley."

18. Birmingham and Goldstein, *Aztalan*.

19. S. A. Barrett, "Ancient Aztalan."

20. Chandler W. Rowe, "A Crematorium at Aztalan."

21. William T. Sterling, "A Visit to Aztalan in 1838."

22. Lynne G. Goldstein and Joan Freeman, "Aztalan: A Middle Mississippian Village."

23. Witthoft, *Green Corn Ceremonialism in the Eastern Woodlands*.

24. Thomas Zych, "Aztalan's Northeast Mound: The Construction of Community."

25. Lynne G. Goldstein, ed., *2013 Aztalan Excavations: Work on the Gravel Knoll and West of the Stockade*.

26. Goldstein, *2013 Aztalan Excavations*.

27. Barrett, "Ancient Aztalan," 232–233; Witthoft, *Green Corn Ceremonialism in the Eastern Woodlands*, 62.

28. Reid A. Bryson and Robert U. Bryson, "The History of Woodland Climatic Environments: As Simulated with Archaeoclimatic Models."

29. Theodore H. Lewis, "Enclosures in Wisconsin."

30. John D. Richards, "Ceramics and Culture at Aztalan: A Late Prehistoric Village in Southeastern Wisconsin"; John D. Richards, "Collars, Castellations, and Cahokia: A Regional Perspective on the Aztalan Ceramic Assemblage."

31. Biloine Whiting Young and Melvin L. Fowler, *Cahokia: The Great Native American Metropolis*, 294; Matthew L. Chastin, Alix C. Deymeir-Black, John E. Kelly, James A. Brown, and David C. Dunand, "Metallurgical Analysis of Copper Artifacts from Cahokia."

32. Barrett, "Ancient Aztalan."

33. Lynne G. Goldstein and John D. Richards, "Ancient Aztalan: The Cultural and Ecological Context of a Late Prehistoric Site in the Midwest."

34. John D. Richards and Robert Jeske, "Location, Location, Location: The Temporal and Cultural Context of Late Prehistoric Settlement in Southeast Wisconsin."

35. Barrett, "Ancient Aztalan."

36. Kristen Linnea Anderson, "The Aztalan Site Skeletal Inventory and Excavation History"; Katie Z. Rudolph, "A Taphonomic Analysis of Human Skeletal Material from Aztalan: Cannibalism, Hostility, and Mortuary Variability."

37. Goldstein and Freeman, "Aztalan."

38. Anderson, "The Aztalan Site Skeletal Inventory and Excavation History"; Rudolph, "A Taphonomic Analysis of Human Skeletal Material from Aztalan."

39. Rowe, "A Crematorium at Aztalan."

40. Richards and Jeske, "Location, Location, Location"; David F. Overstreet, "Cultural Dynamics of the Late Prehistoric Period."

41. Roland L. Rodell, "The Diamond Bluff Site Complex and Cahokia Influence in the Red Wing Locality"; Guy E. Gibbon and Clark A. Dobbs, "The Mississippian Presence in the Red Wing Area."

42. James B. Stoltman and George W. Christiansen III, "The Late Woodland Stage in the Driftless Area of the Upper Mississippi Valley."

43. Rodell, "The Diamond Bluff Site Complex and Cahokia Influence in the Red Wing Locality."

44. Samuel E. Munoz, Kristine E. Gruley, Ashton Massie, David A. Frye, Sissel Schroeder, and John W. Williams, "Cahokia's Emergence and Decline Coincided with Shifts of Flood Frequency on the Mississippi River."

Chapter 9. Burial Mound Construction and Use in Later Times

1. David F. Overstreet, "Oneota Prehistory and History."

2. For various views on the origins of the Oneota see James B. Stoltman, "A Reconsideration of the Cultural Processes Linking Cahokia to Its Northern Highlands during the Period A.D. 1000–1200"; Robert Hall, "Red Banks, Oneota, and the Winnebago: Views from a Distant Rock"; David F. Overstreet, "Cultural Dynamics of the Late Prehistoric Period"; and Robert F. Boszhardt, "Blind Dates and Blind Faith: The Timeless Story of the 'Emergent' Oneota McKern Phase."

3. James Stoltman, "The Appearance of the Mississippian Cultural Tradition in the Upper Mississippi Valley."

4. William Green, "Identity, Ideology, and Effigy Mound-Oneota Transformation."

5. Dale Henning, "Managing Oneota"; David F. Overstreet, "The Mero Complex and the Menominee Tribe: Prospects for a Territorial Ethnicity."

6. David Overstreet, *Oneota Tradition and Cultural History—New Data from the Old Spring Site (47WN350)*.

7. Jody O'Gorman, *The Tremaine Complex: Oneota Occupation in the La Crosse Locality, Wisconsin*; R. Eric Hollinger, "Residence Patterns and Oneota Social Dynamics."

8. Robert Jeske, ed., *Lake Koshkonong 2002/2003: Archaeological Investigations at Three Sites in Jefferson County, Wisconsin*; Seth Schneider, "Oneota Ceramic Production and Exchange: Social, Economic, and Political Interactions in Eastern Wisconsin between A.D. 1050–1400."

9. Robert A. Birmingham, "French Trade Goods from the Crabapple Point Site: A Possibility for a Historic Period Oneota Occupation on Lake Koshkonong."

10. Mark Bruhy, "The Zarling Lake Site (47 Fr-186): Oneota Presence in the Interior of Northern Wisconsin"; Mark E. Bruhy and Kathryn C. Egan-Bruhy, "Archibald Lake Mounds (47OC309): A Late Prehistoric Horticultural Village in

Wisconsin's Northern Highlands"; Overstreet, "The Mero Complex and the Menominee Tribe."

11. Michael M. Gregory, Jennifer R. Harvey, James A. Clark Jr., Lawrence J. Mier, and David F. Overstreet, "Phase I and Phase II Studies at Site 47 Mi 255, a Langford Tradition Occupation in Milwaukee County, Wisconsin"; Robert Jeske, "The Washington Irving Site: Langford Tradition Adaptation in Northern Illinois."

12. Kathleen M. Foley Winkler, "Oneota and Langford Mortuary Practices from Eastern Wisconsin and Northeast Illinois."

13. Reid A. Bryson and Robert U. Bryson, "The History of Woodland Climatic Environments: As Simulated with Archaeoclimatic Models."

14. Henning, "Managing Oneota."

15. David W. Benn, "Hawks, Serpents, and Birdmen: Emergence of the Oneota Mode of Production"; David W. Benn, "Developmental Oneota Culinary Assemblages and Stylistic Trends in Iowa"; Schneider, "Oneota Ceramic Production and Exchange."

16. Nancy O. Lurie, "Winnebago."

17. Victoria Dirst, "Reconsidering the Prehistory of Northeastern Wisconsin," 119; Overstreet, "Oneota Prehistory and History."

18. John A. Jeske, "The Grand River Mound Group and Camp Site"; Overstreet, "Oneota Prehistory and History." Enhanced knoll cemeteries are also documented for Oneota who lived in the Chicago area in James Brown, "Oneota Mortuary Contexts."

19. Paul Radin, *The Winnebago Tribe*, 237.

20. Overstreet, *Oneota Tradition and Cultural History*; see also Foley Winkler, "Oneota and Langford Mortuary Practices from Eastern Wisconsin and Northeast Illinois."

21. Hall, "Red Banks, Oneota, and the Winnebago," 51–52.

22. Robert Hall, *Archaeology of the Soul*, 155–168.

23. W. C. McKern, *The Clam River Focus*.

24. Leland Cooper, *Indian Mounds Park, Archaeological Site, Rice Lake, Wisconsin*.

25. Douglas A. Birk and Elden Johnson, "The Mdewakanton Dakota and Initial French Contact," 205.

26. Lynn M. Alex, *Iowa's Archaeological Past*.

27. William Green, "Examining Protohistoric Depopulation in the Upper Midwest."

28. Radin, *Winnebago Tribe*, 5–10.

29. Henning, "Managing Oneota."

30. James Warren Springer and Stanley R. Witkowski, "Siouan Linguistics and Oneota Archaeology."

31. Carol I. Mason, "Historic Identification and the Oneota."

32. Carol I. Mason, *Introduction to Wisconsin Indians: Prehistory to Statehood*.

33. The first documented European contact with the Ho-Chunk was in 1634, when Jean Nicolet visited a village in the western Great Lakes. Some historians and anthropologists think this meeting took place on the lower Door Peninsula, near an

area called Red Banks; the most prominent of these is the Ho-Chunk authority Nancy Lurie. See Nancy Oestreich Lurie and Patrick J. Jung, *The Nicolet Corrigenda: New France Revisited*. In a review of historic documents, Robert Hall suggested that the meeting occurred in the Chicago area and concluded that Ho-Chunk territory covered much of eastern Wisconsin and northern Illinois, as discussed in "Relating the Big Fish and the Big Stone: The Archaeological Identity and Habitat of the Winnebago in 1634." Recently, in "Where Nicolet and the Winnebagos First Met," Ronald J. Mason asserted that Nicolet met the Ho-Chunk on Lake Superior, but this has been challenged by Lurie and Jung in "Jean Nicolet (Again): Comment on Ronald J. Mason's 'Where Nicolet and Winnebagoes First Met.'" Whatever the case, the meeting with Nicolet probably preceded a decimating war with the Illinois.

34. John Blackhawk, "The Winnebago Indians and the Mounds."

35. Robert A. Birmingham and Lynne Goldstein, *Aztalan: Mysteries of an Ancient Indian Town*.

36. Richard C. Taylor, "Notes Respecting Certain Indian Mounds and Earthworks in the Form of Animal Effigies, Chiefly in Wisconsin Territory, U.S."; Stephen Taylor, "Description of Ancient Remains, Animal Mounds and Embankments, Principally in the Counties of Grant, Iowa and Richland, in Wisconsin Territory"; Increase Lapham, *Antiquities of Wisconsin, as Surveyed and Described*, 27, 30, 59.

37. Taylor, "Notes Respecting Certain Indian Mounds and Earthworks," 98.

38. Patty Lowe, *Indian Nations of Wisconsin: Histories of Endurance and Renewal*; Robert A. Birmingham, *Skunk Hill: A Native Ceremonial Community in Wisconsin*.

39. Lapham, *Antiquities of Wisconsin*, 59.

Chapter 10. Indian Mounds in the Modern World

1. 2015 Assembly Bill 620, introduced by Representatives Brooks, Gannon, Allen, Knodl, Swearingen, Vorpagel, and Sanfelippo; cosponsored by Senators Kopenga and Stroebel.

2. Douglas W. Owsley and Richard L. Jantz, eds., *Kennewick Man: The Scientific Investigation of an Ancient American Skeleton*; Morten Rasmussen et al., "Ancestry and Affiliations of Kennewick Man."

3. Robert A. Birmingham, "Charles E. Brown and the Mounds of Madison."

Bibliography

Alex, Lynn M. *Iowa's Archaeological Past*. Iowa City: University of Iowa Press, 2000.

Anderson, Kristen Linnea. "The Aztalan Site Skeletal Inventory and Excavation History." Master's thesis, University of Chicago, 1994.

Arzigian, Constance. "The Emergence of Horticultural Economies in Southwestern Wisconsin." In *Emergent Horticultural Economies of the Eastern Woodlands*, edited by William F. Keegan, 217–242. Occasional Paper no. 7. Carbondale: Southern Illinois University, Center for Archaeological Investigations, 1987.

Arzigian, Constance. "Fisher Mounds Site Complex (47VE825): 2001–2006 Investigations." *Wisconsin Archeologist* 96, no. 2 (2015): 119–213.

Atwater, Caleb. *Descriptions of the Antiquities Discovered in the State of Ohio and Other Western States*. Transactions and Collections of the American Antiquarian Society, vol. 1. Worcester, MA: American Antiquarian Society, 1820.

Baerreis, David A., Hiroshi Daifuku, and James E. Lundsted. "The Burial Complex of the Reigh Site, Winnebago County, Wisconsin." *Wisconsin Archeologist* 35, no. 1 (1954): 1–36.

Bakken, Charlotte T. "Preliminary Investigations at the Outlet Site." *Wisconsin Archeologist* 31, no. 2 (1950): 43–70.

Barrett, S. A. "Ancient Aztalan." *Bulletin of the Museum of the City of Milwaukee* 13 (1933): 1–602.

Barrett. S. A., and E. W Hawkes. "The Kratz Creek Mound Group." *Bulletin of the Public Museum of the City of Milwaukee* 3, no. 1 (1919): 1–138.

Barrett, S. A., and A. Skinner. "Certain Mounds and Village Sites of Shawano and Oconto Counties, Wisconsin." *Bulletin of the Public Museum of the City of Milwaukee* 10, no. 5 (1932): 401–552.

Barton, David A. "Skare Site Projectile Points." *Wisconsin Archeologist* 77, no. 1–2 (1996): 82.

Beaubien, Paul L. "Some Hopewellian Mounds at the Effigy Mound National Monument, Iowa." *Wisconsin Archeologist* 34, no. 2 (1953): 125–138.

Bibliography

Benn, David. "Developmental Oneota Culinary Assemblages and Stylistic Trends in Iowa." *Wisconsin Archeologist* 93, no. 1 (2012): 3–40.

Benn, David. "Hawks, Serpents, and Birdmen: Emergence of the Oneota Mode of Production." *Plains Anthropologist* 34, no. 125 (1989): 233–260.

Benn, David. "Some Trends and Traditions in Wisconsin Cultures of the Quad-State Region in the Upper Mississippi River Basin." *Wisconsin Archeologist* 60 (1979): 47–82.

Benn, David W. "The Woodland People and the Roots of Oneota." In *Oneota Archaeology: Past, Present, and Future*, edited by William Green, 91–140. Report no. 20. Iowa City: University of Iowa, Office of the State Archaeologist, 1995.

Benn, David, Arthur Bettis III, and R. Clark Mallam. "Cultural Transformations in the Keller and Bluff Top Mounds." *Plains Anthropologist Memoir* 27 (1993): 53–73.

Birk, Douglas A., and Elden Johnson. "The Mdewakanton Dakota and Initial French Contact." In *Calumet and Fleur-de-Lys: Archaeology of Indian and French Contact in the Midcontinent*, edited by John A. Walthall and Thomas E. Emerson, 203–240. Washington, DC: Smithsonian Institution Press, 1992.

Birmingham, Robert A. "Archaeological Investigation of a Proposed Dog Park and Disk Golf Course at Capital Springs Park, Dane County, Wisconsin." Report submitted to Dane County Parks, 2011.

Birmingham, Robert A. "An Archaeological Survey of Wisconsin Winnebago Land in Eagle Township, Richland County, Wisconsin." Report on file, Division of Historic Preservation, State Historical Society of Wisconsin, 1994.

Birmingham, Robert A. "Charles E. Brown and the Mounds of Madison." *Historic Madison: A Journal of the Four Lakes Region* 13 (1996): 17–29.

Birmingham, Robert A. "Charles E. Brown: Wisconsin Archaeologist." *Wisconsin Archeologist* 80, no. 1 (1999): 15–24. Special issue, "A Retrospective of Society Members' Contributions to the First 100 Volumes of *The Wisconsin Archeologist*," edited by David F. Overstreet.

Birmingham, Robert A. "French Trade Goods from the Crabapple Point Site: A Possibility for a Historic Period Oneota Occupation on Lake Koshkonong." Paper presented at the Midwest Archaeological Conference, Champaign, Illinois, 2014.

Birmingham, Robert. *Skunk Hill: A Native Ceremonial Community in Wisconsin*. Madison: Wisconsin Historical Society Press, 2015.

Birmingham, Robert A. *Spirits of Earth: The Effigy Mound Landscape of Madison and the Four Lakes*. Madison: University of Wisconsin Press, 2010.

Birmingham, Robert A., and Lynne Goldstein. *Aztalan: Mysteries of an Ancient Indian Town*. Madison: Wisconsin Historical Society Press, 2004.

Birmingham, Robert A., and Amy Rosebrough. "On the Meaning of Effigy Mounds." *Wisconsin Archeologist* 84, no. 1–2 (2003): 21–36.

Birmingham, Robert A., and Allen P. Van Dyke. "Chert and Chert Resources in the Lower Rock River Valley." *Wisconsin Archeologist* 62, no. 3 (1981): 347–360.

Blackhawk, John. "The Winnebago Indians and the Mounds." *Wisconsin Archeologist* 8, no. 3 (1928): 106–107.

Boszhardt, Robert F. "Angelo Punctuated: A Late Woodland Ceramic Type in Western Wisconsin." *Journal of the Iowa Archaeological Society* 43 (1996): 129–137.

Boszhardt, Robert F. "Blind Dates and Blind Faith: The Timeless Story of the 'Emergent' Oneota McKern Phase." *Wisconsin Archeologis*t 85, no. 1 (2004): 3–30.

Boszhardt, Robert F. "An Etched Pipe from Southeastern Minnesota." *Archaeology News* (Mississippi Valley Archaeology Center at UW–La Crosse) 24, no. 2 (June 2006): 1–2.

Boszhardt, Robert F. "The Lady in Red (Horn)." *Wisarch News* 15, no. 1 (2015): 10–13.

Boszhardt, Robert F. "Oneota Horizons: A La Crosse Perspective." *Wisconsin Archeologist* 79, no. 2 (1998): 196–226.

Bourne, Edward G. *Narratives of the Career of Hernando de Soto*. 2 vols. New York: Barnes, 1904.

Broihahn, John, and Amy Rosebrough. "Reconstructing Raisbeck: A Multi-Component Mound and Ritual Center in the Southern Driftless Area, Grant County, Wisconsin." State Archeology and Maritime Preservation Program Technical Report Series no. 14-0001. Wisconsin Historical Society, Madison, 2014.

Brown, Charles E. "The Arboretum: Notes and Reminiscences by Charles E. Brown." 1935, box 9. Charles E. Brown Papers, State Historical Society of Wisconsin, Madison.

Brown, Charles E. "Archaeological Items." *Wisconsin Archeologist*, o.s., 10, no. 3 (1911): 136–137.

Brown, Charles E. "The Intaglio Mounds of Wisconsin." *Wisconsin Archeologist*, o.s., 9, no. 1 (1910): 5–10.

Brown, Charles E. "Lake Wingra." *Wisconsin Archeologist*, o.s., 14, no. 3 (1915): 75–115.

Brown, Charles E. "The Preservation of the Man Mound." *Wisconsin Archeologist*, o.s., 7, no. 4 (1908): 140–154.

Brown, Charles E. "The Springs of Lake Wingra." *Wisconsin Magazine of History* 10, no. 3 (1927): 298–310.

Brown, Charles E. "Superstitions about Indian Mounds." 1931, box 4. Charles E. Brown Papers, State Historical Society of Wisconsin, Madison.

Brown, Charles E. "Water Spirit Legend, Told by Winnebago Indians." N.d., box 3. Charles E. Brown Papers, State Historical Society of Wisconsin, Madison.

Brown, Charles E. "The Winnebago as Builders of Wisconsin Earthworks." *Wisconsin Archeologist*, o.s., 10, no. 3 (1911): 124–129.

Brown, James. "Oneota Mortuary Contexts." Paper presented at the Midwest Archaeological Conference, Milwaukee, October 1993.

Bruhy, Mark E. "The Zarling Lake Site (47 Fr-186): Oneota Presence in the Interior of Northern Wisconsin." *Wisconsin Archeologist* 83, no. 2 (2002): 55–75.

Bruhy, Mark E., and Kathryn C. Egan-Bruhy. "Archibald Lake Mounds (47OC309): A Late Prehistoric Horticultural Village in Wisconsin's Northern Highlands." *Wisconsin Archeologist* 95, no. 1 (2014): 29–49.

Bryson, Reid A., and Robert U. Bryson. "The History of Woodland Climatic Environments: As Simulated with Archaeoclimatic Models." Paper of the University of Wisconsin Climatic Research Center, 2000.

Buikstra, Jane E., and Douglas K. Charles. "Centering the Ancestors: Cemeteries, Mounds and Landscapes of the Ancient North American Continent." In *Archaeologies of Landscape: Contemporary Perspectives*, edited by Wendy Asmore and A. Bernard Knapp, 219–228. Malden, MA: Blackwell, 1999.

Byers, A. Martin. *The Ohio Hopewell Episode: Paradigm Lost and Paradigm Gained.* Akron: University of Akron Press, 2004.

Canfield, William. "Survey Notebook." 1850s–1870s. Unpublished manuscript in the Charles E. Brown Papers, State Historical Society of Wisconsin, Madison.

Chastin, Matthew L., Alix C. Deymeir-Black, John E. Kelly, James A. Brown, and David C. Dunand. "Metallurgical Analysis of Copper Artifacts from Cahokia." *Journal of Archaeological Science* 38, no. 7 (2011): 1727–1736.

Christiansen, George W., III. *Archaeological Investigations along STH 60 between CTH W and STH 80 in Richwood and Eagle Townships in Richland County, Wisconsin*. Milwaukee: Great Lakes Archaeological Research Center, 2002.

Christiansen, George W., III. "Burial Mound and Earthwork Research Project." Office of the State Archaeologist, State Historical Society of Wisconsin, Madison, 1998.

Clauter, Judy A. "Ceramic Analysis from the Nitschke Mound Group (47DO27) and the Nitschke Garden Beds (47DO518) Sites." *Wisconsin Archeologist* 92, no. 2 (2011): 3–26.

Clifton, James A. "Potawatomi." In *Handbook of North American Indians*. Vol. 15, *Northeast*, edited by Bruce G. Trigger, 736–741. Washington, DC: Smithsonian Institution Press, 1978.

Cooper, Leland. *Indian Mounds Park, Archaeological Site, Rice Lake, Wisconsin*. Science Museum of the St. Paul Institute, Science Bulletin no. 6. St. Paul, MN: Science Museum of the St. Paul Institute, 1959.

Cooper, Leland. "The Red Cedar River Variant of the Wisconsin Hopewell Culture." *Bulletin of the Public Museum of the City of Milwaukee* 16, no. 2 (1932): 47–108.

Deák, Gloria. *Discovering America's Southeast: A Sixteenth Century View Based on the Mannerist Engravings of Theodore de Bry*. Birmingham, AL: Public Library Press, 1992.

Dewdney, Selwyn. *The Sacred Scrolls of the Southern Ojibway*. Glenbow-Alberta Institute, Calgary, Alberta. Toronto: University of Toronto Press, 1975.

Diaz-Grandos, Carol, James Duncan, and F. Kent Reilly. *Picture Cave: Unraveling the Mysteries of the Mississippian Cosmos.* Austin: University of Texas Press, 2015.

Dieterle, Richard. "The Gottschall Head." http://www.hotcakencyclopedia.com/ho.GottschallHead.html. Accessed May 15, 2017.

Dirst, Victoria. "Reconsidering the Prehistory of Northeastern Wisconsin." *Wisconsin Archeologist* 79, no. 1 (1998): 113–121. Special issue, "From the Northern Tier: Papers in Honor of Ronald J. Mason," edited by Charles E. Cleland and Robert A. Birmingham.

Dirst, Victoria. "Stockbridge Harbor: A Late Woodland Village on Lake Winnebago." Madison: Wisconsin Department of Natural Resources, State Historical Society of Wisconsin, 1995.

Dragoo, Don W., and Charles F. Wray. "Hopewell Figurine Rediscovered." *American Antiquity* 30 (1964): 195–199.

Duncan, David Ewing. *Hernando de Soto: A Savage Quest in the Americas*. New York: Crown, 1995.

Duncan, James R., and Carol Diaz-Granados. "Of Myths and Masks." *Midcontinental Journal of Archaeology* 25, no. 1 (2000): 1–26.

Emerson, Thomas E., K. Hedman, E. Hargrave, D. Cobb, and A. Thompson. "Paradigms Lost: Reconfiguring Cahokia's Mound 72 Beaded Burial." *American Antiquity* 81, no. 3 (2016): 405–425.

Emerson, Thomas E., Dale L. McElrath, and Andrew C. Fortier, eds. *Late Woodland Societies: Tradition and Transformation across the Mid-Continent*. Lincoln: University of Nebraska Press, 2000.

Fagan, Brian. *Ancient North America: Archaeology of a Continent*. New York: Thames and Hudson, 1995.

Finney, Fred A. "The Archaeological Legacy of Theodore H. Lewis: Letters, Papers, and Articles." *Wisconsin Archeologist* 87, no. 1–2 (2007). Special issue, edited by Fred A. Finney.

Finney, Fred A. "Intrasite and Regional Perspectives on the Fred Edwards Site and the Stirling Horizon in the Upper Mississippian Valley." *Wisconsin Archeologist* 94, no. 1–2 (2013): 3–248.

Foley Winkler, Kathleen M. "Oneota and Langford Mortuary Practices from Eastern Wisconsin and Northeast Illinois." PhD dissertation, Department of Anthropology, University of Wisconsin–Milwaukee, 2011.

Fowler, Melvin L., Jerome Rose, Barbara Vander Leest, and Steven R. Ahler. *The Mound 72 Area: Dedicated Space in Early Cahokia*. Reports of Investigations no. 54. Illinois State Museum Society, Springfield, 1999.

Freckmann, Kermit. "The Hagner Indian Mounds." *Wisconsin Archeologist* 23, no. 1 (1942): 1–16.

Freeman, Joan. "The Millville Site: A Middle Woodland Village in Grant County, Wisconsin." *Wisconsin Archeologist* 50, no. 2 (1969): 37–88.

Gerend, Alphonse. "Sheboygan County." *Wisconsin Archeologist* 19, no. 3 (1920): 121–192.

Gibbon, Guy E., and Clark A. Dobbs. "The Mississippian Presence in the Red Wing Area." In *New Perspectives on Cahokia: Views from the Periphery*, edited by James B. Stoltman, 281–306. Madison: Prehistory Press, 1991.

Gibson, Jon L. *Poverty Point: A Terminal Archaic Culture of the Lower Mississippi Valley*. Anthropological Study Series no. 7. Baton Rouge: Louisiana Archaeological Survey and Antiquities Commission, Department of Culture, Recreation and Tourism, 1996.

Goldstein, Lynne G., ed. *2013 Aztalan Excavations: Work on the Gravel Knoll and West of the Stockade*. East Lansing: Department of Anthropology Consortium for Archaeological Research, Michigan State University, 2015.

Goldstein, Lynne G. "Landscapes and Mortuary Practices: A Case for Regional Perspectives." In *Regional Approaches to Mortuary Analysis,* edited by Lane Anderson Beck, 101–120. New York: Plenum, 1995.

Goldstein, Lynne G., and Joan Freeman. "Aztalan: A Middle Mississippian Village." *Wisconsin Archeologist* 78, no. 1–2 (1997): 223–248. Special issue, "Wisconsin Archaeology," edited by Robert A. Birmingham, Carol I. Mason, and James B. Stoltman.

Goldstein, Lynne G., and Donald H. Gaff. "Recasting the Past: Examining Assumptions about Aztalan." *Wisconsin Archeologist* 83, no. 2 (2002): 98–110.

Goldstein, Lynne, Cynthia Klink, Ellen Ghere, Jeffrey Logsdon, Mary Imam, and Neil C. Tappen. "The Klug Island Site (47-Oz-67), Ozaukee County, Wisconsin: A Report on Test Excavations and Preliminary Analysis." In *The Southeastern Wisconsin Archaeology Program 1988–1989*, edited by Lynne Goldstein, 14–70. Milwaukee: University of Wisconsin–Milwaukee Report of Investigation #101, 1989.

Goldstein, Lynne G., and John D. Richards. "Ancient Aztalan: The Cultural and Ecological Context of a Late Prehistoric Site in the Midwest." In *Cahokia and the Hinterlands: Middle Mississippian Cultures of the Midwest*, edited by Thomas E. Emerson and R. Barry Lewis, 193–206. Urbana: University of Illinois Press, 1991.

Green, William. "Examining Protohistoric Depopulation in the Upper Midwest." *Wisconsin Archeologist* 74, no. 1–4 (1993): 290–393. Special issue, "Exploring the Oneota-Winnebago Direct Historical Connection," edited by David F. Overstreet.

Green, William. "Identity, Ideology, and Effigy Mound-Oneota Transformation." *Wisconsin Archeologist* 95, no. 2 (2014): 62–63.

Green, William. "Prehistoric Woodland Peoples in the Upper Mississippi Valley." In *Prehistoric Mound Builders of the Mississippi Valley*, edited by James B. Stoltman, 17–25. Davenport, IA: Putnam Museum, 1986.

Green, William, and Shirley Schermer. "The Turkey River Mound Group (13CT1)." In *Archaeological and Paleoenvironmental Studies in the Turkey River Valley, Northeastern Iowa*, edited by William Green, 131–198. Research Papers 13, no. 1. Iowa City: Iowa Office of the State Archaeologist, 1988.

Gregory, Michael M., Jennifer R. Harvey, James A. Clark Jr., Lawrence J. Mier, and David F. Overstreet. "Phase I and Phase II Studies at Site 47 Mi 255, a Langford Tradition Occupation in Milwaukee County, Wisconsin." Great Lakes Archaeological Research Center Report 99.038, Milwaukee, Wisconsin, 1999.

Hackenberger, Steven, He Ping, and Larry A. Johns. "Final Report of the Rock County Indian Mounds Project." Report on file, Division of Historic Preservation, State Historical Society of Wisconsin, 1993.

Hall, Robert. *The Archaeology of Carcajou Point*, 2 vols. Madison: University of Wisconsin Press, 1962.

Hall, Robert. *Archaeology of the Soul: North American Belief and Ritual*. Urbana: University of Illinois Press, 1997.

Hall, Robert. "Ghosts, Water Barriers, Corn, and Sacred Enclosures in the Eastern Woodlands." *American Antiquity* 41 (1976): 360–364.

Hall, Robert. "In Search of the Ideology of the Adena–Hopewell Climax." In *Hopewell Ideology: The Chillicothe Conference*, edited by D. W. Brose and N. Greber, 258–265. Kent, OH: Kent State University Press, 1979.

Hall, Robert. "Red Banks, Oneota, and the Winnebago: Views from a Distant Rock." *Wisconsin Archeologist* 74, no. 1–4 (1993): 10–79. Special issue, "Exploring the Oneota-Winnebago Direct Historical Connection," edited by David F. Overstreet.

Hall, Robert. "Relating the Big Fish and the Big Stone: The Archaeological Identity and Habitat of the Winnebago in 1634." In *Oneota Archaeology: Past, Present, and Future*, edited by William Green, 19–32. Report no. 20. Iowa City: University of Iowa, Office of the State Archaeologist, 1995.

Hansel, Ardith K., and David M. Mickelson. "A Reevaluation of the Timing and Causes of High Lake Phases in the Lake Michigan Basin." *Quaternary Research* 29, no. 2 (1988): 113–128.

Harris, Wendy G. "Upland Abandonment during the Middle Archaic Period: A View from Northeastern Illinois." *Wisconsin Archeologist* 83, no. 1 (2002): 3–18.

Henning, Dale. "Managing Oneota." *Wisconsin Archeologist* 79, no. 1 (1998): 122–130.

Henriksen, Harry C. "Utica Hopewell: A Study of Early Hopewellian Occupation in the Illinois River Valley." In *Middle Woodland Sites in Illinois*, edited by Elaine Bluhm Herold, 1–67. Urbana: Illinois Archaeological Survey, University of Illinois, 1965.

Henschel, Gary. "Henschel Mounds (47 Sb 29) as Possible Solstice Markers: A Progress Report." *Wisconsin Archeologist* 77, no. 1–2 (1996): 73–77.

Hickerson, Harold. "The Feast of the Dead among the Seventeenth Century Algonkians of the Upper Great Lakes." *American Anthropologist* 62 (1960): 81–107.

Hoffman, Walter. *The Menominee Indians*. Fourteenth Annual Report of the Bureau of American Ethnology, 1892–1893. Washington, DC: Smithsonian Institution, 1896.

Hollinger, R. Eric. "Residence Patterns and Oneota Social Dynamics." In *Oneota Archaeology: Past, Present, and Future*, edited by William Green, 141–174. Report no. 20. Iowa City: University of Iowa, Office of the State Archaeologist, 1995.

Hruska, Robert. "The Riverside Site: A Late Archaic Manifestation in Michigan." *Wisconsin Archeologist* 48, no. 3 (1967): 145–260.

Hudak, G. J. "Boulder Outlines in Southwestern Minnesota." *Plains Anthropologist* 17, no. 58 (1971): 345–346.

Hurley, William M. *An Analysis of Effigy Mound Complexes in Wisconsin*. Anthropological Papers no. 59. Ann Arbor: University of Michigan, Museum of Anthropology, 1975.

Hurley, William M. "The Late Woodland Stage: Effigy Mound Culture." *Wisconsin Archeologist* 67, no. 3–4 (1986): 283–301. Special issue, "Introduction to Wisconsin Archeology," edited by William Green, James B. Stoltman, and Alice B. Kehoe.

Hyer, Nathaniel. "Ruins of the Ancient City of Aztalan." *Milwaukee Advertiser*, February 25, 1837, n.p.

Iseminger, William. *Cahokia Mounds: America's First City.* Charleston, SC: History Press, 2010.

Jeske, John A. "The Grand River Mound Group and Camp Site." *Bulletin of the Public Museum of the City of Milwaukee* 3, no. 2 (1927): 139–214.

Jeske, Robert J. "Crescent Bay Hunt Club: Radiocarbon Dates and Research Summary." In *Program in Midwestern Archaeology (Southeastern Wisconsin Archaeology Program): 2000–2001*, edited by R. J. Jeske, 4–12. Archaeological Research Laboratory Report of Investigations no. 148. University of Wisconsin–Milwaukee, 2001.

Jeske, Robert J., ed. *Lake Koshkonong 2002/2003: Archaeological Investigations at Three Sites in Jefferson County, Wisconsin*. Archaeological Research Laboratory Report of Investigations No. 153. University of Wisconsin–Milwaukee, 2003.

Jeske, Robert J. "The Washington Irving Site: Langford Tradition Adaptation in Northern Illinois." In *Mounds, Modoc, and MesoAmerica: Papers in Honor of Melvin F. Fowler,* edited by Steven R. Ahler, 405–438. Illinois State Museum Scientific Papers. Springfield: Illinois State Museum, 2000.

Johnson, Eileen, David F. Overstreet, Daniel J. Joyce, and James A. Clark Jr. "The Mud Lake Mammoth and People in Southeastern Wisconsin." *Wisconsin Archeologist* 88, no. 1 (2007): 1–22.

Joyce, Daniel J. "Chronology and New Research on the Schaefer Mammoth (*Mammuthus primigenius*) Site, Kenosha County, Wisconsin, USA." *Quaternary International* 142–143 (2006): 44–57.

Kehoe, Alice. "The History of Wisconsin Archaeology." *Wisconsin Archeologist* 78, no. 1–2 (1997): 11–21. Special issue, "Wisconsin Archaeology," edited by Robert A. Birmingham, Carol I. Mason, and James B. Stoltman.

Kehoe, Thomas F., and Alice B. Kehoe. *Boulder Effigy Monuments in the Northern Plains. The Journal of American Folklore* 72, no. 284 (1959): 115–127.

Kelly, John Martin. "Delineating the Spatial and Temporal Boundaries of Late Woodland Collared Wares from Wisconsin and Illinois." Master's thesis, Department of Anthropology, University of Wisconsin–Milwaukee, 2002.

Kennedy, Roger G. *Hidden Cities: The Discovery and Loss of Ancient North American Civilization*. New York: Free Press, 1994.

Knox, James C. "Climatic Influence on Upper Mississippi Valley Floods." In *Flood Geomorphology*, edited by V. R. Baker, R. C. Kochel, and P. C. Patton, 279–300. New York: John Wiley and Sons, 1988.

Kuehn, Steven R. "The Crow Hollow Site: A Middle Woodland Archaic Campsite in Southwestern Wisconsin." *Wisconsin Archeologist* 88, no. 1 (2007): 23–50.

Lackey-Cornelison, Wendy. "Constructing Community and Cosmos: A BioArchaeological Analysis of Wisconsin Effigy Mound Mortuary Practices and Mound Construction." PhD dissertation, Department of Anthropology, Michigan State University, 2012.

Lapham, Increase. *Antiquities of Wisconsin, as Surveyed and Described*. Smithsonian Contributions to Knowledge. Washington, DC: Smithsonian Institution, 1855. Reprint, Madison: University of Wisconsin Press, 2001.

[Lapham, Increase A.] "Antiquities of Wisconsin." *Milwaukee Advertiser*, November 24, 1836.

Lapham, Increase. Papers. Wisconsin Historical Society, Madison.

Lapham, Increase A. *Wisconsin: Its Geography, Topography, History, Minerology: Together with Brief Sketches of Its Antiquities, Natural History, Soil, Productions, Population and Government*. Milwaukee: Hopkins, 1846.

Larsen, Curtis E. "Geoarchaeological Interpretation of Great Lakes Coastal Environments." In *Archaeological Sediments in Context,* edited by J. K. Stein and W. R. Farrand, 91–110. Orono: Center for the Study of Early Man, Institute for Quaternary Studies, University of Maine at Orono, 1985.

Le Page du Pratz, Antoine-Simon. *Histoire de Lousiane*. Paris: De Bure, 1758.

Lepper, Bradley T. "The Newark Earthworks: Monumental Geometry and Astronomy at a Hopewellian Pilgrimage Center." In *Hero, Hawk, and Open Hand: American Indian Art of the Ancient Midwest and South*, edited by Richard V. Townsend and Robert V. Sharp, 73–82. Chicago: Art Institute of Chicago; New Haven: Yale University Press, 2004.

Lepper, Bradley T., and Tod A. Frolking, "Alligator Mound: Geographical and Iconographical Interpretations of a Late Prehistoric Effigy Mound in Central Ohio." *Cambridge Archaeological Journal* 13, no. 2 (2003): 147–167.

Lewis, Theodore H. "Enclosures in Wisconsin." *American Antiquarian* 16 (1894): 357–361.

Lewis, Theodore H. "The 'Monumental' Tortoise Mounds of De-coo-dah." *American Journal of Archaeology and History of the Fine Arts* 2 (1886): 65–69.

Lewis, Theodore H. *The Northwestern Archaeological Survey: Fieldbooks and Related Volumes, 1880–1895*. St. Paul: Pioneer Press, 1898.

Loebel, Thomas J. "A Survey of Wisconsin Fluted Points." *Current Research in the Pleistocene* 24 (2007): 118–119.

Long, Stephen H. "Long Journal 1817—Down the Mississippi to Belle Fontaine, July 10 through August 15, 1817." In *The Northern Expeditions of Stephen H. Long: The Journals of 1817 and 1823 and Related Documents*, edited by Lucille M. Kane, June D. Holmquist, and Carolyn Gilman, 78–110. St. Paul: Minnesota Historical Society, 1978.

Lowe, Patty. *Indian Nations of Wisconsin: Histories of Endurance and Renewal.* Madison: Wisconsin Historical Society Press, 2001.

Lurie, Nancy O. "Winnebago." In *Handbook of North American Indians*. Vol. 15, *Northeast*, edited by Bruce G. Trigger, 690–707. Washington, DC: Smithsonian Institution Press, 1978.

Lurie, Nancy Oetreich, and Patrick J. Jung. "Nicolet (Again): Comment on Ronald J. Mason's 'Where Nicolet and the Winnebagoes First Met.'" *Wisconsin Archeologist* 95, no. 2 (2014): 303.

Lurie, Nancy Oestreich, and Patrick J. Jung. *The Nicolet Corrigenda: New France Revisited*. Long Grove, IL: Waveland Press, 2009.

Lynott, Mark J. *Hopewell Ceremonial Landscapes of Ohio: More Than Mounds and Geometric Earthworks.* Oxford, UK: Oxbow Books, 2014.

Mallam, Clark R. "Ideology from the Earth: Effigy Mounds in the Midwest." *Archaeology* 35, no. 4 (1982): 60–64.

Mallam, Clark R. *The Iowa Effigy Mound Manifestation: An Interpretative Model.* Iowa State Archaeologist Office Report no. 9. Iowa City: University of Iowa, Office of the State Archaeologist, 1979.

Mallam, Clark R. "The Mound Builders: An American Myth." *Journal of the Iowa Archaeological Society* 23 (1976): 145–175.

Martin, Susan. *Wonderful Power: The Story of Ancient Copper Working in the Lake Superior Basin.* Detroit: Wayne State University Press, 1999.

Mason, Carol I. "Archaeological Analogy and Ethnographic Example: A Case from the Winnebago." *Florida Journal of Anthropology Special Publication* 4 (1985): 95–104. Special issue, "Indians, Colonists, and Slaves: Essays in Memory of Charles H. Fairbanks," edited by Kenneth W. Johnson, Jonathan M. Leader, and Robert C. Wilson.

Mason, Carol I. "Historic Identification and the Oneota." In *Cultural Change and Continuity: Essays in Honor of James Bennet Griffin*, edited by Charles E. Cleland, 335–348. New York: Academic Press, 1976.

Mason, Carol I. *Introduction to Wisconsin Indians: Prehistory to Statehood*. Salem, WI: Sheffield, 1988.

Mason, Ronald J. *Inconstant Companions: Archaeology and North American Indian Oral Traditions.* Tuscaloosa: University of Alabama Press, 2006.

Mason, Ronald J. "Oneota and Winnebago Ethnogenesis: An Overview." *Wisconsin Archeologist* 74, no. 1–4 (1993): 400–421.

Mason, Ronald J. "Where Nicolet and the Winnebagos First Met." *Wisconsin Archeologist* 95, no. 1 (2014): 65–74.

Mason, Ronald J., and Carol Irwin. "An Eden-Scottsbluff Burial in Northeastern Wisconsin." *American Antiquity* 26 (1960): 43–57.

Maxwell, Moreau. "A Change in the Interpretation of Wisconsin's Prehistory." *Wisconsin Magazine of History* 33, no. 4 (1950): 427–443.

McGrath, Willis H. "The North Benton Mound in Ohio." *American Antiquity* 11, no. 1 (1945): 40–46.

McKern, W. C. *The Clam River Focus*. Milwaukee Public Museum Publications in Anthropology no. 9. Milwaukee: Milwaukee Public Museum, 1963.

McKern, W. C. "The Kletzien and Nitschke Mound Groups." *Bulletin of the Public Museum of the City of Milwaukee* 3, no. 4 (1930): 417–572.

McKern, W. C. "The Neale and McCaughry Mound Groups." *Bulletin of the Public Museum of the City of Milwaukee* 3, no. 3 (1928): 213–416.

McKern, W. C. "Preliminary Report on the Upper Mississippi Phase in Wisconsin." *Bulletin of the Public Museum of the City of Milwaukee* 16, no. 3 (1945): 109–235.

McKern, W. C. "A Wisconsin Variant of the Hopewell Culture." *Bulletin of the Public Museum of the City of Milwaukee* 10, no. 2 (1931): 185–328.

McKusick, Marshall. *The Davenport Conspiracy*. Iowa City: University of Iowa Press, 1970.

McKusick, Marshall. "A Disturbed Bear That Bears Watching and Other Remarks on an Iowa Effigy Mound Interpretive Model." *Wisconsin Archeologist* 61, no. 3 (1980): 352–358.

Mead, Barbara. "The Rehbein I Site (47-Ri-81)." *Wisconsin Archeologist* 60, no. 2 (1979): 91–182.

Meinholz, Norman, and Jennifer Kolb. *The Statz Site: A Late Woodland Community and Archaic Lithic Workshop in Dane County, Wisconsin*. Museum Archaeology Program, Archaeology Research Series no. 5. Madison: State Historical Society of Wisconsin, 1997.

Meinholz, Norman M., and Steven R. Kuehn. *The Deadman Slough Site: Late Paleo-indian/Early Archaic and Woodland Occupations along the Flambeau River, Price County, Wisconsin*. Museum Archaeology Program, Archaeology Research Series no. 4. Madison: State Historical Society of Wisconsin, 1996.

Milner, George R. "An Osteological Perspective on Prehistoric Warfare." In *Regional Approaches to Mortuary Analysis*, edited by Lane Anderson Beck, 221–238. New York: Plenum, 1995.

Mires, Peter, Jennifer L. Kolb, and Edgar S. Oerichbauer. "The Archaeological Resources of Northwestern Wisconsin: Region 1 Program, 1988–1989." Division of Historic Preservation, State Historical Society of Wisconsin, 1989.

Moffat, Charles R., and Robert F. Boszhardt. "Sand Country Prehistory: The Late Woodland Settlement of the Central River Drainage." *Wisconsin Archeologist* 88, no. 1 (2007): 51–77.

Moorehead, William King. "The Hopewell Group." *The Antiquarian* 1, no. 5 (1897): 236–243.

Munoz, Samuel E., Kristine E. Gruley, Ashton Massie, David A. Frye, Sissel Schroeder, and John W. Williams. "Cahokia's Emergence and Decline Coincided with Shifts of Flood Frequency on the Mississippi River." *Proceedings of the National Academy of Sciences of the United States of America* 113, no. 20 (2015): 6319–6324.

Newberg, Andrew, Eugene G. d'Aguili, and Vince Rause. *Why God Won't Go Away: Brain Science and the Biology of Belief.* New York: Ballantine Books, 2001.

O'Gorman, Jody. *The Tremaine Complex: Oneota Occupation in the La Crosse Locality, Wisconsin*. Museum Archaeology Program, Archaeology Research Series no. 3. Madison: State Historical Society of Wisconsin, 1994.

Ostberg, Neil J. "Additional Material from the Reigh Site, Winnebago County." *Wisconsin Archeologist* 37, no. 1 (1956): 28–31.

Overstreet, David F. "The Convent Knoll Site (47Wk327): A Red Ochre Cemetery in Waukesha, Wisconsin." *Wisconsin Archeologist* 6, no. 1 (1980): 34–90.

Overstreet, David F. "Cultural Dynamics of the Late Prehistoric Period." In *Mounds, Modoc and MesoAmerica: Papers in Honor of Melvin F. Fowler*, edited by Steven R. Ahler, 405–438. Illinois State Museum Scientific Papers. Springfield: Illinois State Museum, 2000.

Overstreet, David F. "The Mero Complex and the Menominee Tribe: Prospects for a Territorial Ethnicity." *Wisconsin Archeologist* 90, no. 1–2 (2009): 132–177.

Overstreet, David F. "Oneota Prehistory and History." *Wisconsin Archeologist* 78, no. 1–2 (1997): 250–297. Special issue, "Wisconsin Archaeology," edited by Robert A. Birmingham, Carol I. Mason, and James B. Stoltman.

Overstreet, David. *Oneota Tradition and Cultural History—New Data from the Old Spring Site (47WN350)*. Reports of Investigations no. 219. Great Lakes Archaeological Research Center, Milwaukee, Wisconsin, 1989.

Overstreet, David, Larry Doebert, Gary Henschell, Phil Sander, and David Wasion. "Two Red Ocher Mortuary Contexts from Southeastern Wisconsin: The Henschell Site (47 SB 29), Sheboygan County and the Barnes Creek Site (47 KN 41), Kenosha County." *Wisconsin Archeologist* 77, no. 1 (1996): 36–62.

Overstreet, David F., with Daniel J. Joyce, Ruth Blazina-Joyce, David Wasion, and Keith A. Sverdrup. *FY 1992 Historic Preservation Survey and Planning Grant: Early Holocene Megafaunal Exploitation, Kenosha County, Wisconsin*. Reports of Investigations no. 325. Great Lakes Archaeological Research Center, Milwaukee, Wisconsin, 1993.

Owsley, Douglas W., and Richard L. Janz, eds. *Kennewick Man: The Scientific Investigation of an Ancient American Skeleton*. College Station: Texas A&M University Press, 2014.

Pauketat, Timothy R., Robert F. Boszhardt, and Danielle M. Benden. "Trempealeau Entanglements: An Ancient Colony's Causes and Effects." *American Antiquity* 80, no. 2 (2015): 260–289.

Peet, Stephen D. "The Mound Builders." *American Antiquarian* 2, no. 3 (1880): 185–199.

Peet, Stephen D. *Prehistoric America*. Vol. 2. *Emblematic Mounds and Animal Effigies*. Chicago: American Antiquarian, 1890.

Penman, John T. "Late Woodland Sites in Southwestern Grant County, Wisconsin." *Journal of the Iowa Archaeological Society* 32 (1985): 1–36.

Penny, David W. "Continuities in Imagery and Symbolism in the Art of the Woodlands." In *Ancient Art of the American Woodland Indians*, edited by David S. Brose, James A. Brown, and David W. Penny, 147–198. Washington, DC: National Gallery of Art, 1985.

Philips, Ruth Bliss. "Dreams and Designs: Iconographic Problems in Great Lakes Twined Bags." In *Great Lakes Indian Art*, edited by David W. Penny, 52–68. Detroit: Wayne State University Press and the Detroit Institute of Arts, 1989.

Picard, Jennifer. "Northern Flint, Southern Roots: A Diachronic Analysis of Paleoethnobotanical Remains and Maize Race at the Aztalan Site (47-JE-0001)." Master's thesis, Department of Anthropology, University of Wisconsin–Milwaukee, 2013.

Pidgeon, William. *Traditions of De-coo-dah and Antiquarian Researches: Comprising Extensive Explorations, Surveys, and Excavations of the Wonderful and Mysterious Earthen Remains of the Mound-Builders in America; the Traditions of the Last Prophet of the Elk Nation Relative to Their Origin and Use; and the Evidences of an Ancient Population More Numerous Than the Present Aborigines.* New York: Thayer, Bridgman, and Fanning, 1853.

Pleger, Thomas C. "A Functional and Temporal Analysis of Copper Implements at the Chautuaqua Grounds Site (47-Mt-71): A Multicomponent Site at the Mouth of the Menominee River." *Wisconsin Archeologist* 73, no. 3–4 (1992): 160–176.

Pleger, Thomas C. "Old Copper and Red Ochre Social Complexity." *Midcontinental Journal of Archaeology* 25, no. 2 (2000): 169–190.

Pleger, Thomas C., and James Stoltman. "The Archaic Tradition in Wisconsin." In *Archaic Societies: Diversity and Complexity across the Midcontinent*, edited by Thomas Emerson, 697–723. Albany: SUNY Press, 2009.

Power, S. C. *Early Art of the Southeastern Indians: Feathered Serpents and Winged Beings*. Athens: University of Georgia Press, 2004.

Quilter, Jeffrey. "Introduction." In *A Pre-Columbian World*, edited by Jeffrey Quilter and Mary Miller, 7–19. Washington, DC: Dunbarton Oaks, 2006.

Radin, Paul. *The Road of Life and Death*. New York: Pantheon Books, 1945.

Radin, Paul. "Some Aspects of Winnebago Archaeology." *American Anthropologist* 13 (1911): 517–538.

Radin, Paul. *Winnebago Hero Cycles: A Study in Aboriginal Literature*. Baltimore: Waverly Press, 1948.

Radin, Paul. *Winnebago Myth Cycles: A Study in Aboriginal Myth Cycles*. Baltimore: Waverly Press, 1926.

Radin, Paul. *The Winnebago Tribe*. Lincoln: University of Nebraska Press, 1990. Originally published as the *Thirty-Seventh Annual Report of the Bureau of American Ethnography*, 1923.

Rajnovich, Grace. *Reading Rock Art: Interpreting the Indian Rock Paintings of the Canadian Shield.* Toronto: Natural Heritage/Natural History, 1994.

Rasmussen, Morten, Martin Sikora, Anders Albrechtsen, Thorfinn Sand Kornellis-seen, J. Victor Moreno-Mayar, G. David Poznik, Christoph P. E. Zollikofer, Marcia S. Ponce de Leon, Morten E. Allentoft, Ida Moltke, Hakon Jonsson, Cristina Valdiosera, Ripan S. Malhi, Ludovic Orlando, Carlos D. Bustamante, Thomas W. Stafford, David J. Meltzer, Rasmus Nielsen, Eske Willerslev. "Ancestry and Affiliations of Kennewick Man." *Nature* 523, no. 7561 (June 18, 2015), www.nature.com/nature/journal/v523/n7561/full/nature14625.

Reardon, Bill. "Oldest Carbon-14 Dated Copper Projectile Points from Wisconsin." *Wisconsin Archeologist* 95, no. 1 (2014): 86–87.

Richards, John D. "Ceramics and Culture at Aztalan: A Late Prehistoric Village in Southeastern Wisconsin." PhD dissertation, University of Wisconsin–Milwaukee, 1992.

Richards, John D. "Collars, Castellations, and Cahokia: A Regional Perspective on the Aztalan Ceramic Assemblage." *Wisconsin Archeologist* 84, no. 1–2 (2003): 139–153.

Richards, John D., and Robert Jeske. "Location, Location, Location: The Temporal and Cultural Context of Late Prehistoric Settlement in Southeast Wisconsin." *Wisconsin Archeologist* 83, no. 2 (2003): 139–153.

Riggs, Rodney E. "Human Skeletal Remains from the Poor Man's Farrah (47-Gt-365) and the Bade (47-Gt-365) Sites in Southwestern Wisconsin." *Journal of the Iowa Archaeological Society* 32 (1985): 37–74.

Ritzenthaler, Robert. "The Osceola Site: An 'Old Copper' Site Near Potosi, Wisconsin." *Wisconsin Archeologist* 38, no. 4 (1957): 186–203. Special issue, "The Old Copper Culture in Wisconsin," edited by Robert Ritzenthaler.

Ritzenthaler, Robert, and Warren Wittry. "The Oconto Site: Old Copper Manifestation." *Wisconsin Archeologist* 33, no. 4 (1952): 199–223.

Rodell, Roland. "The Diamond Bluff Site Complex and Cahokia Influence in the Red Wing Locality." In *New Perspectives on Cahokia: View from the Periphery*, edited by James B. Stoltman, 253–280. Madison: Prehistory Press, 1991.

Romain, William F. *LiDAR Assessment of Earthworks at Effigy Mound National Monument*. Newark: Ohio State University Newark Earthworks Center, 2013.

Rosebrough, Amy L. "Every Family a Nation: A Deconstruction and Reconstruction of the Effigy Mound 'Culture' of the Western Great Lakes of North America." PhD dissertation, Department of Anthropology, University of Wisconsin–Madison, 2010.

Rosebrough, Amy L. "Monuments and Mysteries: Social Geography of the Effigy Builders." *Wisconsin Archeologist* 95, no. 1 (2014): 5–28.

Rosebrough, Amy L. "National Historic Landmark Nomination for Greenfield Man Mound." Report on file, Division of Historic Preservation. Wisconsin Historical Society, Madison, 2015.

Rowe, Chandler W. "A Crematorium at Aztalan." *Wisconsin Archeologist* 39, no. 1 (1958): 102–110.

Rowe, Chandler W. *The Effigy Mound Culture of Wisconsin*. Milwaukee Public Museum Publications in Anthropology. Milwaukee: Milwaukee Public Museum, 1956.

Rudolph, Katie Z. "A Taphonomic Analysis of Human Skeletal Material from Aztalan: Cannibalism, Hostility, and Mortuary Variability." Master's thesis, University of Wisconsin–Milwaukee, 2009.

Rusch, Lynn A. "The Early and Late Woodland Occupations at the Bachman Site in East Central Wisconsin." Madison: State Historical Society of Wisconsin, 1988.

Ruth, Christine Ella. "Death, Decay and Reconstruction: An Osteological Analysis of Effigy Mound Material from Wisconsin." PhD dissertation, University of Wisconsin–Milwaukee, 1998.

Salkin, Philip. "The Lake Farms Phase: The Early Woodland Stage in Central Wisconsin as Seen from the Lake Farms Archaeological District." In *Early Woodland Archaeology,* edited by Ken Farnsworth and Thomas Emerson, 92–120. Kampsville Seminars in Archaeology. Kampsville, IL: Center for American Archaeology Research, 1986.

Salkin, Philip H. *Archaeological Mitigation Excavations at the Sticker Pond I Site (47DA424) in Middleton, Dane County. Wisconsin*. Reports of Investigations no. 353. Archaeological Consulting and Services, Verona, Wisconsin, 1987.

Salkin, Philip H. "The Horicon and Kekosgee Phases: Cultural Complexity in the Woodland Stage in Southwestern Wisconsin." In *Late Woodland Societies: Tradition and Transformation across the Continent*, edited by Thomas E. Emerson, Dale L. McElrath, and Andrew C. Fortier, 525–542. Lincoln: University of Nebraska Press, 2000.

Salzer, Robert J. "A Preliminary Report on the Gottschall Rockshelter (47Ia80)." *Wisconsin Archeologist* 68, no. 4 (1987): 419–472.

Salzer, Robert J. "The Wisconsin North Lakes Project: A Preliminary Report." In *Aspects of Upper Great Lakes Anthropology*, edited by Elden Johnson, 40–54. Minnesota Prehistoric Archaeology Series. St. Paul: Minnesota Historical Society, 1974.

Salzer, Robert J. "The Woodland Tradition: An Introduction." *Wisconsin Archeologist* 67, no. 3–4 (1986): 239–243. Special issue, "Introduction to Wisconsin Archeology," edited by William Green, James B. Stoltman, and Alice B. Kehoe.

Salzer, Robert J., and Larry A. Johns. *Final Report of the Dane County Indian Mounds Identification Project*. Report on file, Office of the State Archaeologist. Wisconsin Historical Society, Madison, 1992.

Salzer, Robert J., and G. Rajnovich. *The Gottschall Rockshelter: An Archaeological Mystery*. St. Paul, MN: Prairie Smoke Press, 2000.

Sampson, Kelvin W. "Conventionalized Figures on Woodland Ceramics." *Wisconsin Archeologist* 69, no. 3 (1988): 163–188.

Scherz, James P. *Eagle Mounds in Eagle Township (Richland County, Wisconsin)*. Report on file, Office of the State Archaeologist. Wisconsin Historical Society, Madison, 1993.

Scherz, James P. "Pertinent Aspects of Geometry, Astronomy, Distance, and Time." *Journal of the Ancient Earthworks Society* 3 (1991): M1–M52.

Schneider, Seth. "Oneota Ceramic Production and Exchange: Social, Economic, and Political Interactions in Eastern Wisconsin between A.D. 1050–1400." PhD dissertation, Department of Anthropology, University of Wisconsin–Milwaukee, 2015.

Schoolcraft, Henry Rowe. *The Indian Tribes of the United States*. Philadelphia: Lippincott, 1884.

Schroeder, Sissel. "Evidence for Paleoindians in Wisconsin and the Skare Site." *Plains Anthropologist* 52 (2007): 63–91.

Seeman, Erik R. *The Huron-Wendat Feast of the Dead: Indian-European Encounters in Early North America*. Baltimore: Johns Hopkins University Press, 2011.

Silverberg, Robert. *The Mound Builders of Ancient America*. New York: New York Graphic Society, 1976.

Skinner, Alanson. *Ethnology of the Ioway Indians*. Bulletin of the Public Museum of the City of Milwaukee. Milwaukee: Aetna Press, 1926.

Smith, Bruce D. "Introduction." In *Report on the Mound Explorations of the Bureau of Ethnology*, by Cyrus Thomas. Washington, DC: Smithsonian Institution Press, 1985.

Spindler, Louise S. "The Menominee." In *Handbook of North American Indians*. Vol. 15, *Northeast*, edited by Bruce G. Trigger, 708–724. Washington, DC: Smithsonian Institution Press, 1978.

Springer, James Warren, and Stanley R. Witkowski. "Siouan Linguistics and Oneota Archaeology." In *Oneota Studies*, edited by Guy Gibbon, 69–84. University of Minnesota Publications in Anthropology no. 1. Minneapolis: Department of Anthropology, University of Minnesota, 1982.

Squier, Ephraim G., and Edgar H. Davis. *Ancient Monuments of the Mississippi Valley*. Smithsonian Contributions to Knowledge, vol. 1. Washington, DC: Smithsonian Institution, 1848.

Stekel, Frank D., Larry A. Johns, and James P. Scherz. "Whitewater Effigy Mounds Park: The Maples Mound Group." *Wisconsin Archeologist* 72, no. 1–2 (1991): 118–126.

Sterling, William T. "A Visit to Aztalan in 1838." *Wisconsin Archeologist* 19, no. 1 (1920): 18–19.

Stevenson, Katherine P., Robert F. Boszhardt, Charles R. Moffat, Philip H. Salkin, Thomas C. Pleger, James L. Theler, and Constance M. Arizigian. "The Woodland Stage." *Wisconsin Archeologist* 78, no. 1–2 (1997): 140–201. Special issue, "Wisconsin Archaeology," edited by Robert A. Birmingham, Carol I. Mason, and James B. Stoltman.

Stevenson, Katherine P., Robert F. Boszhardt, Charles R. Moffat, Philip H. Salkin, Thomas C. Pleger, James L. Theler, and Constance M. Arzigian. "The Woodland Tradition." *Wisconsin Archeologist* 78, no. 1–2 (1997): 250–297. Special issue, "Wisconsin Archaeology," edited by Robert A. Birmingham, Carol I. Mason, and James B. Stoltman.

Steward, Julian H. *Theory of Cultural Change*. Urbana: University of Illinois Press, 1955.

Stoltman, James. "The Appearance of the Mississippian Cultural Tradition in the Upper Mississippi Valley." In *Prehistoric Mound Builders of the Mississippi Valley*, edited by James B. Stoltman, 26–34. Davenport, IA: Putnam Museum, 1986.

Stoltman, James B. "A Reconsideration of the Cultural Processes Linking Cahokia to Its Northern Highlands during the Period A.D. 1000–1200." In *Mounds, Modoc, and MesoAmerica: Papers in Honor of Melvin L. Fowler*, edited by Steve

Ahler, 439–454. Illinois State Museum Scientific Papers. Springfield: Illinois State Museum, 2000.

Stoltman, James B. "Tillmont (47CR460): A Stratified Prehistoric Site in the Upper Mississippi River Valley." Special issue, *Wisconsin Archeologist* 86, no. 2 (2005).

Stoltman, James B., Danielle M. Benden, and Robert F. Boszhardt. "New Evidence in the Upper Mississippi Valley for Pre-Mississippian Cultural Interaction with the American Bottom." *American Antiquity* 73, no. 2 (2008): 317–336.

Stoltman, James B., and George W. Christiansen III. "The Late Woodland Stage in the Driftless Area of the Upper Mississippi Valley." In *Late Woodland Societies: Tradition and Transformation across the Continent*, edited by Thomas E. Emerson, Dale L. McElrath, and Andrew C. Fortier, 497–524. Lincoln: University of Nebraska Press, 2000.

Stout, Arlow B. "Prehistoric Earthworks in Wisconsin." *Ohio Archaeological and Historical Quarterly* 20, no. 1 (1911): 1–30.

Stout, Arlow B. "The Winnebago and the Mounds." *Wisconsin Archeologist*, o.s., 9, no. 4 (1910–1911): 101–103.

Swanton, John R. *Indian Tribes of the Lower Mississippi Valley and Adjacent Coast of the Gulf of Mexico*. Bureau of American Ethnology, Bulletin no. 43. Washington, DC: Smithsonian Institution, 1911.

Taylor, Richard C. "Notes Respecting Certain Indian Mounds and Earthworks in the Form of Animal Effigies, Chiefly in Wisconsin Territory, U.S." *American Journal of Science and Art* 34 (1838): 88–104.

Taylor, Stephen. "Description of Ancient Remains, Animal Mounds and Embankments, Principally in the Counties of Grant, Iowa and Richland, in Wisconsin Territory." *American Journal of Science and Art* 44 (1843): 21–40.

Theler, James L. "The Early Woodland Component at the Mill Pond Site, Wisconsin." In *Early Woodland Archaeology*, edited by Ken Farnsworth and Thomas Emerson, 137–158. Kampsville Seminars in Archaeology. Kampsville, IL: Center for American Archaeology Research, 1986.

Theler, James L., and Robert E. Boszhardt. "Collapse of Critical Resources and Culture Change: A Model for the Woodland to Oneota Transformation in the Upper Midwest. "*American Antiquity* 71, no. 3 (2006): 433–472.

Theler, James L., and Robert E. Boszhardt. *Twelve Millennia: Archaeology of the Upper Mississippi Valley.* Iowa City: University of Iowa Press, 2003.

Thomas, Cyrus. *Report on the Mound Explorations of the Bureau of Ethnology*. Twelfth Annual Report of the Bureau of American Ethnology, 1890–1891. Washington, DC: Smithsonian Institution Press, 1985.

Trigger, Bruce. *The Children of Aataentsic: A History of the Huron People to 1660*. 2 vols. Montreal and Kingston: McGill-Queen's University Press, 1976.

Van Langen, Howard, and Thomas F. Kehoe. "Hilgen Spring Park Mounds." *Wisconsin Archeologist* 52, no. 1 (1971): 1–19.

Van Nest, Julieann, Douglas K. Charles, Jane Buikstra, and David L. Asch. "Sod Blocks in Illinois Hopewell Mounds." *American Antiquity* 66, no. 4 (2001): 633–650.

Warriner, Pliny. "Legend of the Winnebagos." *Wisconsin Historical Collections* 1 (1903): 86–93.

Wendt, Dan. *Late Woodland Site Distribution in Far Western Wisconsin*. Institute for Minnesota Archeology Report of Investigation no. 607, 2002.

West, George A. "The Indian Authorship of Wisconsin Antiquities." *Wisconsin Archeologist*, o.s., 6, no. 4 (1907): 167–256.

Whittaker, William E., and William Green. "Early and Middle Woodland Enclosures in Iowa." *North American Archaeologist* 31, no. 1 (2010): 27–57.

Willey, Gordon R., and Jeremy A. Sabloff. *A History of American Archaeology*. 3rd edition. San Francisco: Freeman, 1993.

Winkler, Marjorie Green. "Late Quaternary Climate, Fire, and Vegetation Dynamics." In *Sediment Records of Biomass Burning and Global Change*, edited by James S. Clark, Helene Cachier, Johann G. Goldammer, and Brina Stocks, 329–346. NATO ASI Series. Berlin Heidelberg: Springer-Verlag, 1997.

Winkler, M. G., A. M. Swain, and J. E. Kutzbach. "Middle Holocene Dry Period in the Northern Midwestern United States: Lake Levels and Pollen Stratigraphy." *Quaternary Research* 25 (1986): 235–250.

Witthoft, J. *Green Corn Ceremonialism in the Eastern Woodlands*. University of Michigan, Museum of Anthropology, Occasional Contributions no. 13. Ann Arbor: University of Michigan, Museum of Anthropology, 1949.

Wittry, Warren L. "Archaeological Studies of Four Wisconsin Rockshelters." *Wisconsin Archeologist* 40, no. 4 (1959): 137–267.

Wittry, Warren L. "The Kolterman Mound 18 Radiocarbon Date." *Wisconsin Archeologist* 37, no. 4 (1956): 133–134.

Wittry, Warren L., and Edgar G. Bruder. "Salvage Operations at the Kolterman Mound Group, Dodge County, Wisconsin." *Wisconsin Archeologist* 36, no. 1 (1955): 3–12.

Wittry, Warren L., and Robert E. Ritzenthaler. "The Old Copper Complex: An Archaic Manifestation in Wisconsin." *American Antiquity* 21 (1956): 244–254.

Young, Biloine Whiting, and Melvin L. Fowler. *Cahokia: The Great Native American Metropolis*. Urbana: University of Illinois Press, 2000.

Zamencnik, Angela M. "An Osteological Investigation of Lake Woodland Raisbeck Effigy Mound Group, Grant County, Wisconsin." Master's thesis, Department of Anthropology, University of Wisconsin–Milwaukee, 2009.

Zych, Thomas. "Aztalan's Northeast Mound: The Construction of Community." *Wisconsin Archeologist* 96, no. 2 (2015): 53–118.

Illustration Credits

Figure 1.1, based on a map by Amy Rosebrough

Figure 1.2, Wisconsin Historical Society, WHi [X3] 51039

Figure 1.3, from Lapham, *The Antiquities of Wisconsin*; reproduced with permission of the University of Wisconsin Press

Figure 1.4, LiDAR image produced by William F. Romain

Figure 1.5, LiDAR image produced by Geographic Techniques LLC from *Wisconsin-View* aerial and satellite imagery website

Figure 1.6, United States Department of Agriculture photograph, April 13, 1968; catalogue no. WQ 1 JJ 131, Department of Geography Map Library, University of Wisconsin–Madison

Figure 1.7 above, from Theodore H. Lewis, Northwestern Archaeological Survey, field notebook 23, Minnesota Historical Society

Figure 1.7 below, from Lapham, *The Antiquities of Wisconsin*; reproduced with permission of the University of Wisconsin Press

Figure 1.8, photo by Daniel Seurer

Figure 2.1, from Ephraim G. Squier and Edgar H. Davis, *Ancient Monuments of the Mississippi Valley*

Figure 2.2, from Richard C. Taylor, "Notes Respecting Certain Indian Mounds and Earthworks in the Form of Animal Effigies"

Figure 2.3, image of Lapham from Wisconsin Historical Society, WHi-2758; detail of map from Lapham, *The Antiquities of Wisconsin*; reproduced with permission of the University of Wisconsin Press

Figure 2.4, from William Pidgeon, *Traditions of De-coo-dah and Antiquarian Researches*

Figure 2.5, photograph of Lewis reproduced courtesy of the Goodhue County Historical Society, Red Wing, Minnesota; map from Theodore H. Lewis, Northwestern Archaeological Survey, field notebook 25, Minnesota Historical Society

Figure 3.1, from *Wisconsin Archeologist* 25, no. 2 (1944), reproduced with permission of Wisconsin Archeological Society

Figure 3.2, photograph used with permission of the Milwaukee Public Museum, neg. 406890
Figure 4.1, map by Robert Birmingham
Figure 4.2, photo by Robert Birmingham
Figure 4.3, photo by Robert Granflaten, Wisconsin Historical Society
Figure 4.4, images courtesy of the Milwaukee Public Museum
Figure 4.4 bottom right, from James, *A Narrative of the Captivity and Adventures of John Tanner during Thirty Years of Residence among the Indians*
Figure 4.5, map by Robert Birmingham
Figure 4.6, from Schoolcraft, *The Indian Tribes of the United States*
Figure 4.7, from Stevenson et al., "The Woodland Tradition"; used with permission of the Wisconsin Archeological Society
Figure 5.1, drawing by Clarence H. Webb, *Geoscience and Man* 17 (1982), used with permission of Louisiana State University, Baton Rouge
Figure 5.2, map by Robert Birmingham
Figure 5.3, drawing by Amy Rosebrough, after drawing in Gerend, "Sheboygan County"
Figure 5.4, from Squier and Davis, *Ancient Monuments of the Mississippi Valley*
Figure 5.5, from Stevenson et al., "The Woodland Stage"; used with permission of the Wisconsin Archeological Society
Figure 5.6, drawing by the University of Wisconsin–Madison Cartography Laboratory, after McKern, "A Wisconsin Variant of the Hopewell Culture"
Figure 5.7, photographs used with permission of the Milwaukee Public Museum
Figure 5.8 reproduced with permission of the Milwaukee Public Museum, neg. 70292
Figure 5.9 above, from Theodore H. Lewis, Northwestern Archaeological Survey, field notebook 20, Minnesota Historical Society
Figure 5.9 below, from Squier and Davis, *Ancient Monuments of the Mississippi Valley*
Figure 5.10 above, from McGrath, "The North Benton Mound in Ohio"; reproduced with permission of the Society for American Archaeology
Figure 5.10 below, from Moorehead, "The Hopewell Group"
Figure 5.11, from Squier and Davis, *Ancient Monuments of the Mississippi Valley*
Figure 5.12, from Boszhardt, "An Etched Pipe from Southeastern Minnesota"; reproduced with permission of the Mississippi River Archaeology Research Center, University of Wisconsin La Crosse
Figure 6.1, map by Robert Birmingham
Figure 6.2, LiDAR image produced by Geographic Techniques LLC from *Wisconsin-View* aerial and satellite imagery website
Figure 6.3, from Mead, "The Rehbain I Site (47-Ri-81)," reproduced with permission of the Wisconsin Archeological Society
Figure 7.1, reproduced courtesy of the Wisconsin Department of Natural Resources
Figure 7.2, map by Robert Birmingham
Figure 7.3 above, drawing by Phoebe Hefko, courtesy of the Office of the State Archaeologist
Figure 7.3 below, map adapted from Meinholz and Kolb, *The Statz Site*; reproduced

with permission of the Museum Archaeology Program of the Wisconsin Historical Society

Figure 7.4a, photo by Robert Granflaten, Wisconsin Historical Society

Figure 7.4b, from Salzer and Rajnovich, *The Gottschall Rockshelter*; used with permission of Robert Salzer

Figure 7.4c, reproduced with permission of Fred Finney

Figure 7.4d, reproduced with permission of the Milwaukee Public Museum, neg. 70129

Figure 7.4e, from Clauter, "Ceramic Analysis from the Nitschke Mound Group (47DO27) and the Nitschke Garden Beds (47DO518) Sites"; used with permission of the Wisconsin Archeological Society

Figure 7.4f, reproduced with permission of the Milwaukee Public Museum, neg. 70606

Figure 7.5a–b, drawing by Richard Dolan, after Sampson, "Conventionalized Figures on Woodland Ceramics"; used with permission of the Wisconsin Archeological Society

Figure 7.5c, drawing by Richard Dolan; used with permission of the Wisconsin Historical Society

Figure 7.6, Wisconsin Historical Society, WHi-34556

Figure 7.7, map by Amy Rosebrough

Figure 7.8, LiDAR image produced by Geographic Techniques LLC from *WisconsinView* aerial and satellite imagery website

Figure 7.9, LiDAR image produced by Geographic Techniques LLC from *WisconsinView* aerial and satellite imagery website

Figure 7.10, LiDAR image courtesy of William Romain

Figure 7.11, LiDAR image produced by Geographic Techniques LLC from *WisconsinView* aerial and satellite imagery website

Figure 7.12, drawings by Robert Birmingham

Figure 7.13, drawings by Robert Birmingham

Figure 7.14, LiDAR image produced by Geographic Techniques LLC from *WisconsinView* aerial and satellite imagery website; drawing based on inspections of surviving mounds and map in Theodore H. Lewis, Northwestern Archaeological Survey, field notebook 24, Minnesota Historical Society

Figure 7.15 above, map based on Theodore H. Lewis, Northwestern Archaeological Survey, field notebook 25, Minnesota Historical Society

Figure 7.15 below, LiDAR image produced by Geographic Techniques LLC from *WisconsinView* aerial and satellite imagery website

Figure 7.16, from Freckman, "The Hagner Indian Mounds," used with permission of the Wisconsin Archeological Society

Figure 7.17, map by Amy Rosebrough

Figure 7.18 above, from Lapham, *The Antiquities of Wisconsin*; reproduced with permission of the University of Wisconsin Press

Figure 7.18 below, Wisconsin Historical Society, image 123404, photo by John Broihahn

Figure 7.19, from Lapham, *The Antiquities of Wisconsin*; reproduced with permission of the University of Wisconsin Press
Figure 7.20a, Wisconsin Historical Society, image WHi [X3] 531102
Figure 7.20b–n, drawings by Robert Birmingham
Figure 7.21, drawings and map by Amelia Janes, Midwest Educational Graphics
Figure 7.22, Wisconsin Historical Society, image WHi [X3] 52437
Figure 7.23, from McKern, *The Clam River Focus*; used with permission of the Milwaukee Public Museum, negs. 414536 (above) and 414537 (below)
Figure 8.1 above, illustration by Lloyd Kenneth Townsend; courtesy of the Cahokia Mounds Historic Site
Figure 8.1 below, painting by William R. Iseminger; courtesy of the Cahokia Mounds Historic Site
Figure 8.2, map by Robert Birmingham
Figure 8.3 above, Wisconsin Historical Society, WHi [X3] 51038
Figure 8.3 below, photo courtesy of Robert Boszhardt
Figure 8.4, drawings by Mary Steinhauer from Salzer and Rajnovich, *The Gottschall Rockshelter*; photo from Salzer and Rajnovich, *The Gottschall Rockshelter*; both used with permission from Robert Salzer, Beloit College
Figure 8.5, map by Robert Birmingham
Figure 8.6 above, photograph by Dan Seurer
Figure 8.6 below, drawing from Rowe, "A Crematorium at Aztalan"
Figure 8.7 above, from Lapham, *The Antiquities of Wisconsin*; reproduced with permission of the University of Wisconsin Press
Figure 8.7 center, from Barrett, "Ancient Aztalan"
Figure 8.7 below, photo by Robert Birmingham
Figure 8.8, map by Clark Dobbs based on modern surveys and Theodore H. Lewis field notes
Figure 9.1, drawing by Nancy Hoffman, Museum Archeology Program; used with permission of the Wisconsin Historical Society
Figure 9.2, map by Amelia Janes and Robert Birmingham
Figure 9.3a, adapted from from Hall, *The Archaeology of Carcajou Point*, plate 23
Figure 9.3b, from Jeske, *The Grand River Mound Group and Campsite*, used with permission of the Milwaukee Public Museum
Figure 9.3c–e, drawings by Richard Dolan; used with permission of the Wisconsin Historical Society
Figure 9.3f, photograph from the collection of James Bussey from the Crabapple Point site on Lake Koshkonong
Figure 9.4, from Lapham, *The Antiquities of Wisconsin*; reproduced with permission of the University of Wisconsin Press
Figure 10.1, photo provided by Mary Lou Burczyk
Figure 10.2 above, photo by Mary Lou Burczyk
Figure 10.2 bottom left and right, photo by Robert Birmingham
Figure 10.3, photo by Jim Uhrinak

Index

Page numbers for illustrations and captions are in italics.

Adams site, *166*, 192
Adena Complex, 83–84, 86, 100, 138
agriculture (horticulture, cultivation, gardens, farming), 56, 87, 96, 103, 109, 110, 111, 115, 152, 153, 156, 161, 164–65, 167, 185–88, 193, 203, 219. *See also* beans; corn; gourds; squash; wild plants
Alabama, 184
Algonquian-speaking peoples, 135, 186, 197
alligator, 27
Alligator Mound (Ohio), 99–100, *99*
Allouez, Claude, 74
American Antiquarian Society, 6, 23
American Ethnological Society, 16, 20
Amherst Junction, 224
"Angelo Punctuated" pottery, 114. *See also* pottery
antiquarians, 19
Archaic tradition, 51, 67–87. *See also* Late Archaic stage/period; Middle Archaic stage/period
Armstrong site, 192
Ashland County, 156
astronomical observations, 85, 148, 150, 151
atlatl (spear thrower), 67, 102
Atwater, Caleb, 20
Avoca, 221
Avoca mound group, 221
Aztalan, 4, 12, *13*, 25, 39, 43–44, 47, 103, *105*, 108, *111*, *114*, 155, 165, *166*, 171–82, *172*, *174*, *177*, 184, 186–87, 198, 201, 221–22
Aztalan State Park. *See* Aztalan
Aztecs, 15, 19, 22, 44, 164

Bachman site, *82*, 88
Bade mound group, 55
Baraboo, 39, 43, 124, 139, 144, 209, 226–27; pipestone, 100; range, 144; River, 8, 144
Barrett, Samuel, 35, 43–44, 45, 172, 176, 178, 179, 180, 181
Barron County, 31, 96, 211
Bayfield County, 156
Beach site, 88
beans, 68, 187
bears, 74, 135, 137, 207; canine tooth artifacts, 32, 93, 95, 96; ceremonialism, 85–86, 137. *See also* clans, Ho-Chunk; clans, Menominee; effigy mounds, forms
Beloit, 28, 226
Beloit College Mounds, 226
Benden, Danielle, 167
Benn, David, 58, 88, 117
Bettis, Arthur, 58
birds, 59, 63, 66, 68, 80, 98, 99, 114, 115, 116, 136, 137. *See also* effigy mounds, forms; falcons; hawks; thunderbirds

Index

Bigelow mound group, 49
Birger figurine, 138
Birkmose Park, 226
Birmingham, Robert, xi, xii, 201, *207*
bison, 63, 116, 146, 187. *See also* buffalo
Blackhawk, John, 42, 197–98
Blackhawk Country Club Mounds, 213–14
Black Hawk War, 22
Black River, *11*
Black River Falls, 42, 197
Bloyer (Twin Lizard) mound group, *29*, *111*, *127*
Blue Mounds, 6
bone bundles. *See* burial customs; burial types
Boszhardt, Robert
bow and arrow, 102
Broihahn, John, 60, 61
Brown, Charles E., 34, 36–43, *42*, 45, 57, 135, 137, 138, 197, 202, 206, 213, 214, 215, 217, 218
Brown, Chip, xv
Brown County, 66
buffalo, 27, 90, 135, 137, 146, 187, 196, 197. *See also* clans, Ho-Chunk; effigy mounds, forms
Burczyk, Mary Lou, *207*
Bureau of Ethnology, 31, 32, 36, 37, 83
burial customs, 3, 31–32, 44, 74–81, *75*, 86–87, 89–90, *91*, 95–96, 125, 147–49, 158, 159–60, 178, 193, 196, 200, 220
Burial Sites Preservation Law, xi, 14, 56, 202–3
burial types: bone bundles, 44, 76, 86, 92, 105, 148, 157; cremation, 44, 76, 105, 148, 157; extended (in the flesh), 76, 86, 90, 92, 93, 105, 147; flexed, 44, 148, 157, 213; reburial, 61, 74, 75, 93
Burnett County, 205
Burnett County Historical Society, 54
Burrows Park, 214
Bussey, James, 191
Byers, Martin, 86

Cahokia, 12, 138, 150, 162–65, *163*, 166, 167, 168, 173, 175, 178, 179, 180, 182, 185, 190, 221, 228. *See also* Mississippian tradition/culture
Calumet Ceremony, 193
Calumet County Park, 211–12
Canada, 13, 28, 65, 67, 72, 147
Canfield, W. H., 144
cannibalism, 181
Carcajou Point site, *191*
Cassville, 124, 220
Cassville Bluffs Natural Area, 220
catlinite. *See* pipestone
Cedarburg, 89
ceremonial centers, 8, 49, 52, 86, 87, 94, 96, 112, 151, 152–54, 162, 164, 202, 206. *See also* mounds, function
cemeteries, 8, 44, 52, 55, 59, 69, 74–76, 78, 147, 152, 156, 189, 193, 202, 203
chain mounds. *See* compound (chain) mounds
charnel houses. *See* burial customs
Chautauqua Grounds site, *72*, 73, 77
Cherokee, 18, 161
Cherokee Marsh, 218
Chetek, 43
Cheyenne, 90, 159, 193
Chief Winneshiek. *See* Winneshiek, Chief
Chillicothe (Ohio), 20, *21*
Chippewa. *See* Ojibwe
Chippewa County, 212
Chippewa Falls, 212
Choctaw, 19, 161
Christiansen, George, 182
Cipra mound group, 213
Clam Lake mound, *111*, 158–59, *158*, 194
clams (mussels, shellfish), 46, 67, 87, 88, 105, 108, 112, 178
clans, 28, 36, 48, 57, 59, 82, 86, 87, 92, 94, 139, 155, 192; Ho-Chunk, 57, 59, 135, 137, 138, 147; Menominee, 70, 135, 137. *See also* moieties
climate, 67, 69, 70, 76, 111, 156, 189–90. *See also* Medieval Warm Climate; Neo-Boreal
collared pottery, *114*, 115, 122, 179. *See also* pottery
Columbia County, 212
compound (chain) mounds, *7*, 106–7, 220, 221, 224, 230
conical mounds, 3, 6, 7, 8, *10*, 15, 31, 35, 36, 39, 44, 81, 83, 84, 89, 91, 94, 100, 105, 106, 107, 118, 120, 121, 122,

125, 145, 147, 149, 151, 154, 155, 157, 158, 176, *177*, 178, 179, 182, 185, 192, 194, 201, 206, 211–30
Convent Knoll site, *64*, 78, 81, 83
Cooper, Leland, 194
Cooper mound site (Minnesota), 194
copper, 32, 47, 70–74, 76, 77, 83, 84, 86, 93, 95, 109, 149, 157, 180, 194, 196, 221. *See also* Old Copper Complex
corn (maize), 68, 87, 102–3, 108, 109, 110–11, 115, 152, 156, 161, 164, 167, 173, 175, 178, 186, 187, 198, 201, 215. *See also* agriculture; Green Corn ceremony
Crabapple Point site, *199*
Cranberry Creek Archaeological District and State Natural Area, 223
Cranberry Creek mound group, 3, *105*, *111*, 120–21, *121*, 223
Crawfish River, 22, 103, 165, 171, 179, 221
Crawford County, 213
Cree, 159
Creek (nation/tribe), 19, 161, 181
cremation. *See* burial customs; burial types
Crow Hollow site, 69
cultural ecology, 51–54
cultural resource management, 54–56
Cutler Park, 39, 43, 229
Cyrus Thomas mound group, 96, 220

Dakota (Santee) Sioux, 15, 48, 49, 186, 193, 197, 202
Dane County, 19, 23, *24*, 31, 55, *143*, 145, 207, 213–19
Dane County Parks Department, 55, 207
Daughters of the American Revolution, 223
Davenport (Iowa), 32
Davis, Edgar H., 20, 96–97, *99*
deer, 27, 50, 67, 68, 69, 88, 96, 110, 116, 137, 146, 156, 167, 171, 180, 187, 207. *See also* clans, Ho-Chunk; effigy mounds, forms
Deer, Ada, *207*
Delaware. *See* Leni-Lenape
De Soto, Hernando, 19, 161, 173
Devil's Lake, 100, 209
Devil's Lake State Park, *143*, *209*, 226–27
Diamond Bluff site, 3, 122, 155, *166*, 171, 182–83, *183*, 187, 192
Dick, Fred, 137
diffusionist theories, 13
disease, 13, 19, 53, 61, 195, 196, 197, 205
Division of Mound Exploration. *See* Bureau of Ethnology
DNA testing, 53, 205
Dodge County, 49, 153, 200, 219
Door Peninsula, 147, 188, 192, 246n33
Dorothy Carnes County Park/Rose Lake State Natural Area, 222
Douglas County, 15
Driftless Area, 62, 107, 132, 139
dualism, 36, 138, *142*
dugout canoes, 73
Dunn County, 220

eagle, 8, *9*, *10*, 27, 135, 136, 145, 153, 213. *See also* clans, Ho-Chunk; effigy mounds, forms
Eagle Township mound group, *24*, 132, *133*, *143*, 144–45, 169, 171, 225
Eagle Valley mound group, *105*, *106*
Early Woodland stage/period, 87–90, 115
Earth-Diver, 90
Earth-Maker, 36, 139, 141, 193. *See also* Native American cosmology
effigies, boulder/stone, 98–100, *98*, 144
Effigy Mound Ceremonial Complex, 61, 109–57
effigy mounds, xii, 3, 4, 5, 6, 7–10, 14, 20, 23–24, *25*, 30, 35–37, 41–42, 44, 45, 48–51, 52, 57–59, 60, 100, 109, 157, 192, 196, 198, 200, 207, 211–14, 216–19, 226–28; ceremonial landscapes, 7, 59, 102, 109, 122, 144, 201; dates, 48–51; distribution, *120*, 132, *134*, 139; views or perspectives, 7, 59, 108, 109, 119, 122, 126, 201, 220
effigy mounds, forms: aquatic/water mammals, 67, 122, 130; bears, 32, 100–101, 107, 121, *126*, 130, 132, 137, 139, 141, 143, 145, 207, 212, 213, 214, 216, 218, 219, 221, 223, 225, 226; birds, xii, 3, 15, 23, 37, 59, 80, 96–97, 107, 118, 121, 124, 125, 128–30, 132, *133*, 136, 144–45, 147, 154, 156, 170, 182, 192, 198, 209, 212–14, 216–20, 222–26, 228–30; bird-man, 136, *143*,

effigy mounds, forms (*continued*)
145, 147, 226; buffalo, 137; canines, 107, 130, 132, 137, 182, 214, 215, 218, 219, 224; crane, 138; crossed, 36, 141–43; deer, 137, 207, 216, 227; eagle, 8, *9*, *10*, 27, 136, 145, 153, 213; elk, 27, 137; fish, 139, 157; fork-tailed birds, *10*, 136, 138, 139, 145, 226; geese, 136, 138, 213, 214, 219; humans, 8, 39, 43, 102, 118, 124, 136, 143–47, 209, 227; "lizard," 22, 27, 29, 36, *127*, 130, 132, *133*, 137, 138, 141, 151, 228, 229; lower world, 105, 107, 130, 132, 137–39, 226; meanings, 56–60; pairs/twins, *133*, 141, *142*, 143; panther, 36, 130, 132, 137, 212, 214, 216, 227, 228; snakes, 8, 130, 138, 139; thunderbirds, 136, 143, 145, 153; turtles, 130, 132, 137, 222, 226; upper world, 59, 80, 85, 86, 88–89, 95, 105–6, 107, 116, 117, 130, 132, 134, 135, 136–45, *191*, 192, 199, 226; water spirit, 57, 107, 125, 130, 132, 137, 138, 139, *142*, 144, 147, 156, 182, 192, 210, 212, 214–16, 218, 219, 222, 227, 228, 229
Effigy Mounds National Monument (Iowa), *7*, *82*, 100, *105*, *111*, 106, *126*, 151, 230
effigy mound tradition, 48, 49. *See also* Effigy Mound Ceremonial Complex
elk, 27, 67, 104, 110, 146, 187. *See also* clans, Ho-Chunk; effigy mounds, forms
Elm Grove, 78
Elmside Park, 207, 214
enclosures, 10–11, 57, 83, 84, 86, 96–97, *97*, 119, 150, 152, 173, 229
equinoxes. *See* astronomical observations
ethnocentrism, 13

falcons, 58, 136, 170, 101, 192
Farwell's Point mound group, 216
Feast of the Dead, 74–75, 87, 149, 158
Finney, Fred, 171
fish, fishing, 67, 70, 72–73, 77, 88, 96, 108, 112, 157
Fish Lake, 229
Florida, 7, 79
Forest Hill Cemetery, 214–15
Fort Atkinson, 139, 141, 222, 223
Fort Atkinson Historical Society, 222
Four Lakes, 4, 36, 40, 109, 122, 129, 132, 145, 153, 213
fox, 107, 130, 214, 215, 218. *See also* effigy mounds, forms
Fox (nation/tribe), 32, 35, 37, 48, 107, 130, 137, *146*, 197, 198, 233n37
Fox River, *4*, 95, 123, 188, 230
Fred Edwards site, *166*, 171, 180

Gallatin, Albert, 16
Garman Nature Preserve, 222
Gasch mound group, *111*, *142*
General Atkinson mound group, 222
Geographic Techniques LLC, xv
Georgia, 12, 184
Gerend, Alphonse, 81
Glen Haven, *106*
glottochronology, 196
Goldstein, Lynne, 175, 180
Goodhue County (Minnesota), 182
Gottschall Rockshelter, 50, 58, *114*, 136, 168–71, *169*
gourds, 138
Governor Nelson State Park, 4, 215
Grand Medicine Society, 153. *See also* medicine societies
Grand Village site, *191*, 193
Grant County, 32, 55, 74, 171, 186, 220–21
Grant River, 171
Great Bear Mound, 230
Great Lakes, 74, 76, 115, 134, 190, 195, 196
Great Lakes Intertribal Council, 55, 107
Green Bay, 22, 66, 119, 147, 188, 192
Green Corn ceremony, 156, 164, 175, 178
Greenfield Man Mound. *See* Man Mound
Greenwood mound group, 176, 178
Ground Penetrating Radar, xiii
Gullickson's Glen, 144

Hall, Robert L., 52, 57–58, 59, 87, 90, 105, 119, 130, 132, 136, 137, 156, 170, 193, 247n33
Hancock, 229
Harper's Ferry "Great Group" (Iowa), 122
hawks, 58, 135, 136, 145, 165, *191*, 192. *See also* clans, Ho-Chunk
Heckewelder, John, 18

Heim Mound, 215
Henschel mound group, *64*, 81–82, *82*, 89, *111*, 151
High Cliff State Park, 4, 212
Highsmith, Hugh, 222
Hilgen Spring mound group, *82*, 89–90, 92
Hill, Alfred J., 29
Hixton, 66
Hixton Silicified Sandstone, 63, 66, 93, 95, 164, 167
hoaxes, 32
Ho-Chunk (Ho-Chunk-gara, Winnebago; nation/tribe), xiv, 14, 15, 22, 35–37, 41–42, 45–47, 48, 55, 57–58, 59, 90, 95, 116, 134–35, 136, 137, 138, 139, 141, *146*, 147, 150, 153, 155, 167, 169, 170, 186, 192, 193, 195–96, 197–98, 200, 202, 207, 209, 212, 214, 215, 217, 246–47n33
Hoffman, Walter, 35
Hopewell (Ceremonial Complex, Interaction Sphere, Culture), 10, 32, 83–101, 138, 164, 179, 221, 230; earthworks, 10, *21*, 32, 85–87, *85*, 96–97, 137; ceremonial centers, 86–87; mounds, 47, 86, 87, 92–93, 95, 98–99
hornstone, 69, 83, 84
Hudson, 226
Hudson mound group, 226
Hudson Park, 214
human being (man) mounds, 8, 39, 43, 102, 118, 124, 136, 143–47, 227. *See also* effigy mounds, forms
Hurley, William, 49–50, 56, 153
Huron (nation/tribe), 74–75, 87
Hyer, Nathaniel, 22

Ice Age, 62, 63, 69
Illinois, 8, 12, 31, 44, 47, *65*, 66, 84, 86, 91, 93, *94*, 95, 99, 103, 112, 115, *116*, 119, 136, 161, 162, 166, 171, 179, 180, 185, 188, 189, 228
Illinois River, 84, 92
Indian Mound Park (Chetek), 43
Indian Mound Park (McFarland), 215
Indian Mounds Park (Barron County), 211
Indian Mounds Park (Crawford County), 213. *See also* Cipra mound group
Indian Mounds Park (Juneau County), 224
intaglios, 44, 139, 223. *See also* panther intaglio
Inuit, 73
Iowa, 7, 8, 32, 52, 58, 82, 90, 85, 96, 100, 104, 106, 112, 119, 122, 171, 185, 192, 195, 230
Iowa County, 136, 169, 221
Ioway (nation/tribe), 47, 48, 136, 156, 169, 170, 186, 195, 197
Iron County, 156
Isle Royale, 170

Jackson County, 66
Jefferson, Thomas, 17
Jefferson County, 12, 22, 165, 221–23
Jefferson County Indian Mounds and Trail Park, 222
Johns, Larry, 55
Juneau County, 3, 223–24

Kansa (nation/tribe), 186
Kansas, 22, 200
Kennewick Man, 53–54, 204–5
Kenosha County, 63–64
Kenosha Public Museum, 73
keyhole structures, 112, *113*
Kickapoo, 197
Kickapoo River, 55, 69, 96, *97*, 107
Kingsley Bend mound group, *111*, 132–33
Kletzien mound group, 227
Klug site, *105*, 108, *111*
Kolterman mound group, 49, *111*, 126
Kratz Creek mound group, 44, 141, 148

Labrador, 79
La Crosse, 43, 55, 119, 188, 195
Lake Buffalo, 44
Lake Butte des Morts, 32
Lake Emily County Park, 224–25
Lake Kegonsa, 63
Lake Koshkonong, 36, 95, 181, 182, 187, 188, *191*, 192
Lake Mendota, 8–9, 40, 95, 124, 130–31, 136, 213–14
Lake Menomin, 220
Lake Michigan, 63, 69, 70, 76, 77, 108, 119, 138, 192, 195, 224

Lake Mills, 43, 171, 221
Lake Monona, 56, 95, 203, 207, 217, 220
Lake Park, 43, 224
Lake Side Park, 221
Lake Superior, 23, 69, 70, 84, 147, 156, 157, 197
Lake Tomahawk, 224
Lake Waubesa, 8, 63, 88, 153, 215
Lake Wingra, 41, 138, 218
Lake Winnebago, *142*, 188, 192, 211–12, 230
Lake Wissota State Park, 212
La Mere, Oliver, 36, 42, 138
Langford tradition, 188, 189
Lapham, Increase, xii, 6, *11*, 12, 14, 16, 22, 23, 25–26, *25*, 28, 39, 56, 139, *141*, 172, *177*, 198, *199*, 200, 212, 223, 229
La Pointe, 22
Late Archaic stage/period, 76, 88, 89, 96, 109, 122. *See also* Red Ochre Complex
Late Woodland stage/period, *51*, 96, 102–61, 167, 168, 169, 171, 175, 179, 181, 182, 184, 185, 186, 187, 189, 190, 195–96, 215–19, 221, 226, 229, 230. *See also* Effigy Mound Ceremonial Complex; effigy mounds
La Valle Man Mound, *143*, 144, 145, 146
Leni-Lenape (Delaware), 18
Lepper, Brad, xv
Lewis, Theodore H., 28, *29*, 30, 39, 96–97, *131*, 145, 153, 179, 220
Lewis, Tollef, 215
Lewis mound group, 215
Libby, Willard, 48
LiDAR (Light Detection and Ranging), xii, *7*, *9*, 61, *106*, *121*, *123*, *126*, *127*, *131*, 223
linear mounds, 7, 8, 10, 36, 44, 45–46, 81, 105, 107, 118, 120, 122, 124, 130, 139, *142*, 143, 144, 145, 147, 148. *See also* Effigy Mound Ceremonial Complex; Late Woodland stage/period
Lizard Mound County Park, *111*, 132–33, 228–29
Long, Stephen H., 4
longhouses, *55*, *187*
long-nosed god maskettes, 180. *See also* Aztalan
"Lost Race" myth, 12–21, 23, 26, 33, 35, 43, 85
Louisiana, 7, 79, *80*, 184
lower world, 59, 85, 86, 88, 89, 95, 105, 106, 107, 115, *116*, 117, 134, 135, 139. *See also* clans; effigy mounds, forms; moieties; Native American cosmology
Lurie, Nancy O., 247n33

Madeline Island, 147
Madison, 4, 6, 8, 14, 36, 38, 40, 41–42, 43, 55, *65*, 88, 109, 123, 124, 138, 145, 153, 207, 213–18
Madison Board of Commerce, 40
Madison cord-impressed pottery, 112, *114*, 115. *See also* pottery
Madison ware pottery, *114*, 115, 157. *See also* pottery
Mallam, R. Clark, 33, 52, 58, 119, 125, 130, 134
mammoth, 63, *64*, 66, 67
Man Mound (Baraboo), 39, *143*, 143–45, 147, 209, 227; County Park, 43, 124, 227
Maples mound group, *111*, 151, 228
marine artifacts, 69, 76, 83, 84, 178
Marquette (Iowa), 230
Marquette County, 44
Martin, Susan, 73
Mason, Carol I., *51*, 196
Mason, Ronald, 247n33
mastodon, 63, 66, 67
Mauston, 116
Max Andrae I and II mound group, 223. *See also* Cranberry Creek mound group
McFarland, 215
McKern, William C., 37–38, *46*, 48, 51, 158–59, 193, 194
Mdewakanton, 194. *See also* Dakota (Santee) Sioux
medicine men/people, 86, 115, *146*, 147
medicine societies, 58, 146, 147, 153
Medieval Warm Climate, 103, 190
megalithic sites, 150, 201
Menasha, 230
Mendota State Hospital (Mendota Mental Health Institute) mound group, 8, *111*, 124, 153, 216

Menominee: County, 156; River, 73, *77*
Menominee (nation/tribe), 15, 22, 35, 37, 44, 47, 48, 70, 73, 74, 117, 134, 135, 137, 186, 192, 197, 200, 206, *207*
Menomonie, 220
Mero Complex. *See* Diamond Bluff site
Mexico, 20, 23, 68, 86, 161, 172, 187
Miami (nation/tribe), 197
Michigan, 22, 70, 71, 77, 180, 185, 197; Upper Peninsula (northern), 70, *72*, 156, 157
Michigan State University, 173, 175
Middle Archaic stage/period, 109
Middle Mississippian culture. *See* Mississippian tradition/culture
Middleton, 215, 217
Middle Woodland stage/period, 84–86, 92–99, 160
Midewiwin, 147. *See also* medicine societies
Mid-Holocene Warm Climate (Hypsithermal), 69, 76, 104
Mill Pond site, 88
Millville site, 104, *105*, *111*
Milwaukee, 6, 22, 23, 38, 43, 139, 200, 224
Milwaukee County, 224
Milwaukee Public Museum (Public Museum of the City of Milwaukee), xv, 34, 35, 38, 43, 44, 45–46, 60, *64*, *71*, 89, 92, 96, 149, 158, 172, 180, 219, 227
Milwaukee River, 89, 138, 139, *140*, 229
Minnesota, 8, 28, 30, 34, 84, 95, 100, 115, 119, 157, 182, 185, 186, 192, 194, 197
Minnesota Historical Society, 30
Mishipeshu, Mishipizeu, *71*, 73–74
Mississippian tradition/culture, 12, 19, 46, 47, 51, 80, 103, 119, 122, 136, 138, 150, 155, 156, 161–84, 185, 186, 187, 190, *191*, 192, 193, 201, 221, 228
Mississippi River, 3, 6, *7*, *11*, 12, 15, 22, 27, 28, 31–32, 44, 46, 66, 74, *79*, 83, 85, 88, 92, 93, 95, 104, 106, 110, 122, 123, 155, 161, 162, 165, 166, 167, 182, 184, 188, 192, 195, 220, 224, 228, 230
Missouri, 28, 58, 162, 170, 185
Missouria (nation/tribe), 186
moieties, 86, 95, 105, 135, 192
Monona, 203, 206, *207*, *208*, 216, 217, 218
Monona Landmarks Commission, 206, *207*
mound builder myth, 12, 19–33
Mound Cemetery mounds (Racine), 43, 225
mounds: chronology, 43, *51*; dating, xii, 41, 48–51, 70, 73, 79, 88, 100, 103, 104, 107, 144, 154, 159, 182, 219, 220; distribution, *2*, 12, 36, 37, 39, 43, 52, 65, 119–20, 126, 132, 138, 144, 147; excavation, 9, 12, 14, 19, 32, 33, 44, 45–46, 47, 60–61, 69, 92, 96, 97, 98, 99, 101, 122, 148, 152, 153, 157, 158, 179, 194, 205, 213, 229, 230; function, 8, 49, 63, 78, 86, 147, 152, 164, 173, 174, 206; research history, 15–61; reuse in historic times, 198–200; preservation, xi, xii, 14, 34, 38–43, 54–56, 144, 202–3, 204, 208, 218; reconstruction, 55, 107, 173, 174, 224; symbolism, 57, 58, 135, 151, 155, 192. *See also* compound (chain) mounds; conical mounds; Early Woodland stage/period; effigy mounds; effigy mounds, forms; Late Archaic stage/period; Late Woodland stage/period; linear mounds; Middle Woodland stage/period; Mississippian tradition/culture; Oneota; platform (temple) mounds
Mount Horeb, *143*
Muscoda, 6, 8, 225
Myrick Park, 43

Natchez (nation/tribe), 19, 161, 162, 163
National Historic Preservation Act, xii, 54, 56, 202
National Register of Historic Places, 54
Native American cosmology, 36, 58–60, 80, 85, 88, 119, 130, 136, 147, 154, 201
Native American Graves and Repatriation Act (NAGPRA), 56, 61, 201
Nazca desert drawings and lines, 201
Nebraska, 22, 36, 37, 137, 138, 145, 185, 200
Necedah, 120, 223
Nelson Dewey State Park, 4, 220
Neo-Boreal (Little Ice Age), 184, 190
Newark Earthworks (Ohio), xv, *85*, 96–97. *See also* Hopewell

New Lisbon, 224
Nicholls Mound, *82*, 91–93, *91*
Nicolet, Jean, 195, 246–47n33
Nitschke mound group, *111*, *114*, 126–27, 148, 153, 219
Nitschke Mounds Park, 219
North Benton Hopewell mound (Ohio), 98
North Carolina, 84
Northern Highland American Legion State Forest, 224
Northern Michigan, 170
Northwestern Archaeological Survey, 28–29

Observatory Hill Mounds, 216
obsidian, 32, 69, 77, 86, 94
Oconto County, 139
Oconto site, *64*, 76
Ogechie ware pottery, 194. *See also* pottery
Ohio, 18, 20, *21*, 22, 26, 32, 47, 84–85, 96, *97*, *98*, 99, 100, 138, 150
Ohio River, 6, 10, 15, 18, 20, 57, 83, 84
Ojibwe (Chippewa), 15, 22, 35, 37, 48, 55, 56, 73, 117, 147, 194, 197, 200
Oklahoma, 184
Old Copper Complex, 47, 69–74, 76, 77, 78, 84, 109, 118
Old Copper Industry/Culture. *See* Old Copper Complex
Omaha (nation/tribe), 186
Oneida County, 224
Oneota, 47, 51, 103, 122, 136, 141, 155, 156, 161, 181, 182, 184, 185–96, *188*, *189*
oral tradition, 37, 41, 57–58, 60, 115, 196, 197–98, 202, 205
Osage (nation/tribe), 186
Osceola site, *64*, *72*, 74, 76
ossuary. *See* burial customs
Otoe (nation/tribe), 186
Ottawa (nation/tribe), 179, 197
Outlet Mound, *208*, 216
Outlet mound group, *82*, 94–96
oval mounds, 6, 122, 157–58, 174, 215, 216, 220, 224–26, 228

Paleo-Indian tradition, 51, 62–68, 73
panther intaglio (Fort Atkinson), 139, *140*, 223
Papal Edict of 1537, 17
Pauketat, Timothy, 167
Peet, Reverend Stephen, 18, 28
Perrot State Park, 4, 227–28
Pheasant Branch Conservancy Mounds, 217
Picnic Point mounds, 217
Pidgeon, William, 26–28, *28*
Pierce County, 3, 182
pipes (ceremonial), 25, 32, 86, 93, 94, 95, 149, 193. *See also* Calumet Ceremony
pipestone, 84, 94, 100, 193
pithouses, 112–13, 175, 187. *See also* keyhole structures
platform (temple) mounds, 10, *13*, 19, 44, 162, 167, *168*, 171, 173, 174, 179, 185, 221, 228. *See also* Aztalan; Mississippian tradition/culture; Trempealeau
Portage County, 224–25
Potawatomi, 15, 22, 37, 47, 48, 117, 197, 198, 199, 200, 206, *207*
pottery (ceramics), 25, 46–47, 49, 79, 80, 81, 83, 84, 86, 88, *89*, *94*, 104, 105, 107, 108, 112–19, 122, 149, 156, 157, 159, 166, 175, 179, 181, 182, 184, 185, 187, 188, 190–92, *191*, 193, 196, 219
Poverty Point (Louisiana), 79–80, *80*
Powell, John Wesley, 30, 31
Prairie du Chien, 4, 22, 27, 43, 92, 132, 200, 220
"princess" burial. *See* Aztalan
procession mound group, 221
pseudoscience, 27
Public Museum of the City of Milwaukee. *See* Milwaukee Public Museum

Quaas Creek Park, 229
Quackenbush, Bill, xv, *209*

Racine, 35, 43, 225
Racine County, 225
Radin, Paul, 36–38, 45–47, 57, 58, 134, 145, 147, 170, 195, 197
radiocarbon dating, xii, 41, 48–51, 70, 73, 79, 88, 100, 103, 104, 107, 144, 154, 159, 182, 219, 220
Raisbeck mound group, 3, 47, 60, 61, *111*, 122, *123*, 148, 155
Rajnovich, Grace, 170
Rave, John, 36

Red Banks, 147, 247n33
Red Cedar River, 220
Red Horn, 58, 170
red ochre, 76, 77, 78, 79, 81, 83, 159
Red Ochre Complex, 79–82, 86, 89–90
Red Wing Locality, 183–84
Rehbein I mound group, 55, *105*, *107*, *111*
Reigh site, *64*, *72*, 76
remote sensing. *See* Ground Penetrating Radar; LiDAR
Renier site, *64*, 66, 67
revitalization movements, 154
Rice Lake, 96, 194, 211, 220
Rice Lake mound group, 194, 211
Richards, John, 179, 180
Richland County, 55, *110*, 124, 136, *143*, 144, 153, 169, 225
Ridge mound group (Gasch mound group), *142*
Riverside Cemetery (Michigan), *64*, *72*, *77*
Rock County, 226
Rock River, 95, 119, 132, 139, 223
Rocky Mountains, 84
Romain, William, xv, 151
Rosebrough, Amy L., xxi, 60, 61, 130, 132
Rowe, Chandler, 23, 47–48

Sabloff, Jeremy A., 16
St. Croix County, 226
Salzer, Robert, 58, 136, 169–70
Samuel's Cave, 144
Sanders site, 49, *111*, 153
Santee Sioux. *See* Dakota (Santee) Sioux
Satterlee, John, 44
Sauk (nation/tribe), 35, 37, 48, 197, 198
Sauk County, *143*, 226–27
Sauk County Historical Society, 39, 227
scaffold burials. *See* burial customs
Schaeffer bird effigy, 225. *See also* Eagle Township mound group
Scherz, James, 8
Schwert mound group, *46*, 92
serpents, 138–39. *See also* Serpent Mound; snakes
Serpent Mound (Ohio), 99–100, *99*, 138
Shadewald, Frank, *110*, 225
Shadewald I and II mound groups, *110*, 225. *See also* Eagle Township mound group
Sheboygan, 81, 88, 227; County, 31, 81, 227; Marsh, 81–82, 151
Sheboygan Indian Mound County Park, 227
Shegonee, Art, 206, *207*
Sherwood, 212
Sentinel Hill mound group, 221
Silverberg, Robert, 16, 18–19, 27
Silver Mound, *64*, 66, 94, 164, 167
Siouan-speaking peoples, 22, 37, 47, 186, 197
Sioux. *See* Dakota (Santee) Sioux
Skare site, 63, *64*, 65–66
Skinner, Alanson, 35, 44–45, 170
Smith Park, 230
Smithsonian Institution, 6, 16, 20, 25, 27, 31–33, 92, 194, 211
snakes, 8, 90, 116, 130, 138, 139. *See also* clans, Ho-Chunk; effigy mounds, forms
Sny Magill mound group, 122
social status, 77, 81, 84, 87, 93, 94, 95, 149, 165, 178, 205
social structure, 23, 59, 76, 77, 86, 87, 95, 106, 156, 164, 195, 201. *See also* clans; moieties
Society of American Indians, 41
solstices. *See* astronomical observations
South America, 201
South Dakota, 185
Spanish *entrada*, 19
spear thrower. *See* atlatl
Spencer Lake mound, 159, 194
Springer, James, 196
springs, 59, 81, 89, 90, 125, 128, 213, 217, 219, 229
squash, 68, 87, 102, 104, 110, 187
Squier, Ephraim, 20, 96, *97*, *99*
State Archaeologist (Wisconsin), xi, xii, 39, 54, 60, *207*
State Historical Society of Wisconsin. *See* Wisconsin Historical Society
State Historic Preservation Office, xii, 54
Statz site, *111*, 112–13, 115, 152
Stevens Point, 49
Stockbridge, 211
Stoltman, James B., 51, 95, 182
Stout, Arlow B., 36, 40, 57, 137
sturgeon, 70, 73, 71, 139. *See also* clans, Menominee; effigy mounds, forms; fish, fishing

Taylor, Richard C., 6, 23, 35, 145, 198
temple mounds. *See* platform (temple) mounds
Ten Lost Tribes of Israel, 12, 17
tension zone, 119, 156
territorial markers, 78
Theler, James, 104, 167
Theresa, 200
Thomas, Cyrus, 31–33, 35, 83, 194, 221
thunderbirds, 57, 59, 80, 130, 135, 136, 137, 143, 145, 147, 153, 170, 210. *See also* clans, Ho-Chunk; effigy mounds, forms
Tillmont site, *82*, 95
tobacco, 199
Totem Mound Park, 226
trade, 67, 68–70, 72, 74, 76, 79, 84, 87, 93, 94, 96, 102, 109, 165, 171, 176, 180, 190, 194, 196, 198, 200
Trempealeau, 12, 91, 92, 94, 165, *166*, 167, *168*, 227–28; County, 46, 166, 192, 227–28; Mississippian colony, mounds, *11*, 167, 201, 228; Mountain, 167–68; River, 92
Turkey River, *64*, 83, *84*, 106; mound group, 83, *105*, 106
"Turkey Tail" (projectile point), *77*
Turtle River, 226
turtles, 58, 130, 132, 137, 169, 170, 222, 226. *See also* effigy mounds, forms
Twin Bluffs rock-art site, *117*

ulu, 73
underworld, 8, 73, 81, 90, 95, 99, 108, 115, 116, 117, 132, 138, 218, 229. *See also* Native American cosmology
University of Wisconsin Climatic Research Center, 104
University of Wisconsin–Madison, xiii, 40, 41, 95, 173, 216–17
University of Wisconsin–Milwaukee, 54, 173, 175, 179, 188, 219
Upper Iowa River, 186
Upper Mississippian culture. *See* Oneota
Upper Wakanda Park mound group, 49, 220
upper world, 59, 85, 86, 88–89, 95, 105–6, 107, 115, *116*, 117, 135, 136–45, 190, 192, 218, 226. *See also* clans, Ho-Chunk; clans, Menominee; Native American cosmology

Vernon County, 166
Vilas Park, 218
Vilas Park Circle, 218

Wakanda Park, 49, 220
Walworth County, 228
warfare, 18, 19, 27, 32–33, 61, 76, 78, 112
Washington County, 228–29
Washington State, 53, 204
Waterloo, 222
water spirit, 57, 59, 81, 88, 90, 99, 100–101, 107, 115–16, 121, 125, 130, 132, 135, 137, 138, 139, *142*, 143, 144, 147, 156, 182, 192, 210, 212, 214–16, 218, 219, 222, 227, 228, 229. *See also* clans, Ho-Chunk; effigy mounds, forms; Native American cosmology
Waukesha, 22, *25*, 39, 43, 118, *119*, *199*, 229
Waukesha County, 200, 229
Waunakee, 215
Waushara County, 229
West, George A., 35
West Bend, 138, 228–29
Westport, 218
Whistler Mounds Park, 229
White, Joseph, 41
Whitehorse, Harry, 207–8, *208*, 214
Whitewater, 228
Whitewater Effigy Mounds Preserve, 151, 228
Whitewing, Dalles, *207*
wild plants: gathering, 105, 111, 119; cultivation, 68, 105. *See also* wild rice
wild rice, 104, 111, 156, 187
Willy, Gordon R., 16
Winnebago, xiv, 198. *See also* Ho-Chunk
Winnebago County, 230
Winneshiek, Chief, 42
Wisconsin Archaeological Survey, 173
Wisconsin Archeological Society, xv, 34, 38–43, 137, 202, 206, 215, 217, 218, 227
Wisconsin Dells, 36, 42, 137, 212
Wisconsin Department of Natural Resources, 223

Wisconsin Department of Transportation, 212
Wisconsin Historical Society (State Historical Society of Wisconsin), xi, xii, xv, 4, 35, 36, 38, 39, 40, 54, 55, 60, 107, 112, 137, 153, 173, 197, 203, 213, 214, 218
Wisconsin Natural History Survey, 38
Wisconsin River, 6, 8, 29, 72, 92, 104, 107, 110, 120, 123, *127*, 132–33, 136, 144, 145, 153, 169, 198, 212–13, 220–21
Wisconsin State Archaeologist, xi, xii, 39, 54, 60, *207*
Wisconsin Statute 157.70, 202. *See also* Burial Sites Preservation Law
Witkowski, Stanley, 196
Wittry, Warren, 50, 51
Woodward Shores mound group, 130–31, *131*
Works Progress Administration, 214
world renewal rituals, 57, 59, 86, 87, 90, 125, 130, 135, 138, *142*, 151, 152, 154, 155, 156, 193
Wyalusing State Park, 4, 43, 220

Yahara Heights County Park, 218
Yahara Heights mound group, 218
Yahara River, 63, 112, 214, 216
Yellow River, 230
Yellow Thunder, 42
Yellow Thunder, Albert, *42*

Zych, Thomas, 175